REMEMBERING
THE
COVENANT
A COMMENTARY ON
THE BOOK OF MORMON

VOLUME 3

Denver C. Snuffer, Jr.

Published in the United States by Mill Creek Press.
Mill Creek Press is a registered trademark of Mill Creek Press, LLC.
www.millcreekpress.com

ISBN-10: 0-9891503-2-1
ISBN-13: 978-0-9891503-2-3

Printed in the United States of America on acid-free paper.

First Edition

Cover design by Mill Creek Press.

CONTENTS

VOLUME 3

2 NEPHI 32

2 Nephi 32:1–2

"And now, behold, my beloved brethren, I suppose that ye ponder somewhat in your hearts concerning that which ye should do after ye have entered in by the way. But, behold, why do ye ponder these things in your hearts? Do ye not remember that I said unto you that after ye had received the Holy Ghost ye could speak with the tongue of angels? And now, how could ye speak with the tongue of angels save it were by the Holy Ghost?"

It is the program of the Gospel that communication and understanding of God's will should be obtained through revelation. That revelation comes from contact with, and communication by, the Holy Ghost. The Holy Ghost is able to tell you "all things."[847]

You don't need another source once you are in contact with the Holy Ghost.

---

[847] Moses 6:61 "Therefore it is given to abide in you; the record of heaven; the Comforter; the peaceable things of immortal glory; the truth of all things; that which quickeneth all things, which maketh alive all things; that which knoweth all things, and hath all power according to wisdom, mercy, truth, justice, and judgment."
Moroni 10:4 "And when ye shall receive these things, I would exhort you that ye would ask God, the Eternal Father, in the name of Christ, if these things are not true; and if ye shall ask with a sincere heart, with real intent, having faith in Christ, he will manifest the truth of it unto you, by the power of the Holy Ghost."

It possesses the "record of heaven."[848]

Nephi is assuring us that we can come into possession of the fullness of truth by the means he has been explaining as the "doctrine of Christ." As a central, active part of that doctrine, the line of communication between you and God is opened. It is another reminder of counsel found in Deuteronomy:

"For this commandment which I command thee this day, it is not hidden from thee, neither is it far off. It is not in heaven, that thou shouldest say, Who shall go up for us to heaven, and bring it unto us, that we may hear it, and do it? Neither is it beyond the sea, that thou shouldest say, Who shall go over the sea for us, and bring it unto us, that we may hear it, and do it? But the word is very nigh unto thee, in thy mouth, and in thy heart, that thou mayest do it." (Deuteronomy 30:11–14)

Forget all the cultural assumptions and extras you hang onto. Leave them all behind and keep it simple:

You were a spirit before you were born.[849]

---

[848] Moses 6:61 "Therefore it is given to abide in you; the record of heaven; the Comforter; the peaceable things of immortal glory; the truth of all things; that which quickeneth all things, which maketh alive all things; that which knoweth all things, and hath all power according to wisdom, mercy, truth, justice, and judgment."

[849] Abraham 3:22–28 "Now the Lord had shown unto me, Abraham, the intelligences that were organized before the world was; and among all these there were many of the noble and great ones; And God saw these souls that they were good, and he stood in the midst of them, and he said: These I will make my rulers; for he stood among those that were spirits, and he saw that they were good; and he said unto me: Abraham, thou art one of them; thou wast chosen before thou wast born. And there stood one among them that was like unto God, and he said unto those who were with him: We will go down, for there is space there, and we will take of these materials, and we will make an earth whereon these may dwell; And we will prove them herewith, to see if they will do all things whatsoever the Lord their God shall command them; And they who keep their first estate shall be added upon; and they who keep not their first estate shall not have glory in the same kingdom with those who keep their first estate; and they who keep their second estate shall have glory added upon their heads for ever and ever. And the Lord said: Whom shall I send? And one answered like unto the Son of Man: Here am I, send me. And another answered and said: Here am I, send me. And the Lord said: I will send the first. And the second was angry, and kept not his first estate; and, at that day, many followed after him"

You were there when some were chosen to be "rulers," or in other words, teachers.[850]

You have within you a spirit that was in that group. You saw and participated in what went on, and have that somewhere still inside you. It is kept from you by the "veil of flesh" now covering your spirit.[851]

Somewhere within you lies the "record of heaven." Or more correctly, the Record of Heaven.[852]

If you gain access to it, it has the capacity to teach you the "truth of all things."[853]

Within it is such an abundance of truth that the things of God are not hidden from you, neither far off. It is not in heaven, so that you ask: who will go to heaven to bring it to us. It is not beyond the sea that you should ask who can go to bring it to us? But it is very close to you, in your own mouth, in your own heart, that you can do what is asked of you.[854]

Hence the saying of Christ that the Comforter will bring things to your remembrance.

---

[850] 2 Nephi 5:19 "And behold, the words of the Lord had been fulfilled unto my brethren, which he spake concerning them, that I should be their ruler and their teacher. Wherefore, I had been their ruler and their teacher, according to the commandments of the Lord, until the time they sought to take away my life."

[851] Hebrews 10:20 "By a new and living way, which he hath consecrated for us, through the veil, that is to say, his flesh;"

[852] Moses 6:61 "Therefore it is given to abide in you; the record of heaven; the Comforter; the peaceable things of immortal glory; the truth of all things; that which quickeneth all things, which maketh alive all things; that which knoweth all things, and hath all power according to wisdom, mercy, truth, justice, and judgment."

[853] Ibid.

[854] Deuteronomy 30:11–14 "For this commandment which I command thee this day, it *is* not hidden from thee, neither *is* it far off. It *is* not in heaven, that thou shouldest say, Who shall go up for us to heaven, and bring it unto us, that we may hear it, and do it? Neither *is* it beyond the sea, that thou shouldest say, Who shall go over the sea for us, and bring it unto us, that we may hear it, and do it? But the word *is* very nigh unto thee, in thy mouth, and in thy heart, that thou mayest do it."

Christ taught the kingdom of God is within you.

Why is it that the body is animated, with power of thought and communication, alive and vital while there is a spirit within it? But when the spirit departs, what then of the body? The power to live and breathe and move and do according to your will is gone at that point. But from whence came that power?[855] If it is God who is "lending you that power" then how closely are you connected to God? How immediate is His presence within you?

If you can gain access to God, will you need to go out, or will you instead need to go within?

Our minds are corrupted. I've spent time dealing with the corrosive influence of cultures from Babylon to today in _Nephi's Isaiah_. All that must be "ground to dust" and blown away.[856] That will occur within you. You are the battleground where the conflict is being fought. You are potentially the Temple of God.[857]

Awake and arise! Come to yourself and realize who you are. This "doctrine of Christ" will teach you all things you must know for life and salvation. But you ought not look to another to find what you already have. You must instead repent and return to God, who is your home.

---

[855] Mosiah 2:21 "I say unto you that if ye should serve him who has created you from the beginning, and is preserving you from day to day, by lending you breath, that ye may live and move and do according to your own will, and even supporting you from one moment to another—I say, if ye should serve him with all your whole souls yet ye would be unprofitable servants."

[856] Daniel 2:34–35 "Thou sawest till that a stone was cut out without hands, which smote the image upon his feet _that were_ of iron and clay, and brake them to pieces. Then was the iron, the clay, the brass, the silver, and the gold, broken to pieces together, and became like the chaff of the summer threshingfloors; and the wind carried them away, that no place was found for them: and the stone that smote the image became a great mountain, and filled the whole earth."

[857] 1 Corinthians 3:16 "Know ye not that ye are the temple of God, and _that_ the Spirit of God dwelleth in you?"

2 Nephi 32:3

"Angels speak by the power of the Holy Ghost; wherefore, they speak the words of Christ. Wherefore, I said unto you, feast upon the words of Christ; for behold, the words of Christ will tell you all things what ye should do."

Nephi makes these three things equal:

1. The power of the Holy Ghost to give words, which

2. Are the same as what angels would speak, which in turn

3. Are the same as the words of Christ.

Holy Ghost/words of angels/words of Christ. They are all the same as "the words of Christ" which will "tell you all things what ye should do."

If you will "feast upon the words of Christ" then you will know "all things what ye should do."

How do you unlock this power that potentially exists inside you? What tools have been given to us to receive access to this great inner record of truth?

Why are we given ordinances? If we will follow them and receive them, what do ordinances allow the Lord to open up for us?

You know if you are doing as you should. You cannot lie to yourself. You cannot deceive yourself about whether you will follow God with full purpose of heart, acting no deception, repenting of your sins, and with real intent.[858] If you do these things there is a law ir-

---

[858] 2 Nephi 31:13 "Wherefore, my beloved brethren, I know that if ye shall follow the Son, with full purpose of heart, acting no hypocrisy and no deception before God, but with real intent, repenting of your sins, witnessing unto the Father that ye are willing to take upon you the name of Christ, by baptism—yea, by following your Lord and your Savior down into the water, according to his word, behold, then shall ye receive the Holy Ghost; yea, then cometh the baptism of fire and of the Holy Ghost; and then can ye speak with the tongue of angels, and shout praises unto the Holy One of Israel."

revocably decreed which permits you to receive what is offered.[859]
You actually know if you have offered the correct sacrifice. (Lecture
6, in *Lectures on Faith* discussed here.) Just as you know when you are
unworthy before Him[860], you also know when your confidence before God grows naturally inside you and you follow the path to return to the light[861]. It is extraordinary and even miraculous, but it is
also absolutely natural.

The conditions were set before the foundation of the world and
all you must do to obtain these blessings is to follow the path. You
know if you are in the right way. You cannot lie to God, and as we
have seen in the discussion of the preceding verses, God is within
you.

Do you keep the commandments? Why? Are you doing so with
real intent, following the "doctrine of Christ" or just to be "seen of
men?"[862] When you do these things in secret, your Father (and you)

---

[859] D&C 130:20–21 "There is a law, irrevocably decreed in heaven before the foundations of this world, upon which all blessings are predicated— And when we obtain any
blessing from God, it is by obedience to that law upon which it is predicated."

[860] Mormon 9:4–5 "Behold, I say unto you that ye would be more miserable to dwell
with a holy and just God, under a consciousness of your filthiness before him, than ye
would to dwell with the damned souls in hell. For behold, when ye shall be brought to
see your nakedness before God, and also the glory of God, and the holiness of Jesus
Christ, it will kindle a flame of unquenchable fire upon you."

[861] D&C 121:45–46 "Let thy bowels also be full of charity towards all men, and to the
household of faith, and let virtue garnish thy thoughts unceasingly; then shall thy confidence wax strong in the presence of God; and the doctrine of the priesthood shall
distil upon thy soul as the dews from heaven. The Holy Ghost shall be thy constant
companion, and thy scepter an unchanging scepter of righteousness and truth; and thy
dominion shall be an everlasting dominion, and without compulsory means it shall
flow unto thee forever and ever."

[862] Matthew 6:1, 5 "Take heed that ye do not your alms before men, to be seen of
them: otherwise ye have no reward of your Father which is in heaven . . . And when
thou prayest, thou shalt not be as the hypocrites *are:* for they love to pray standing in
the synagogues and in the corners of the streets, that they may be seen of men. Verily I
say unto you, They have their reward."

know it and then come the rewards of having your heart right with God.[863]

At the end of the long search into all the universe to find God, you will discover the search leads you back to what was inside you all along. You came from Him, and He is with you. But to find Him you must return. The scriptures and teachings of Christ are filled with this journey and the battleground has always been within you. You need to remember. The Holy Ghost, the third member of the godhead, dwells inside you, provided you will receive it.

The laws irrevocably decreed are the very principles which permeate life itself. You are not separate from this "doctrine of Christ" but a living embodiment of it. If you live it, you will prove it. You are here to be proven.[864] What have you determined to prove with your life?

Nephi spoke in plainness to us. He could not find simpler language to describe this process. I have tried to be plain using other scriptures and language. But the great lesson can be reduced to this: Do what you have been taught. When you do it, the light will increase within you. That light is truth. It is intelligence, or light and truth, or the power of God.[865] All you must do to activate that light, gain that intelligence, and behold the glory of God is to keep His commandments.[866]

---

[863] Matthew 6:4, 6 "That thine alms may be in secret: and thy Father which seeth in secret himself shall reward thee openly. . . . But thou, when thou prayest, enter into thy closet, and when thou hast shut thy door, pray to thy Father which is in secret; and thy Father which seeth in secret shall reward thee openly."

[864] Abraham 3:25 "And we will prove them herewith, to see if they will do all things whatsoever the Lord their God shall command them;"

[865] D&C 93:36 "The glory of God is intelligence, or, in other words, light and truth."

[866] D&C 93:28 "He that keepeth his commandments receiveth truth and light, until he is glorified in truth and knoweth all things."

If you want to receive a "fullness" then the immediate door through which you pass is to keep the commandments.[867]

Most importantly, you must "follow the Son, with full purpose of heart, acting no hypocrisy and no deception before God, but with real intent, repenting of your sins, witnessing unto the Father that ye are willing to take upon you the name of Christ."[868] You alone will know if you have done this. Or rather, you and the Lord will know. When you are satisfied that there is no hypocrisy and no deception between you and God, that you have come to Him with real intent and repenting of your sins, witnessing through the ordinances (baptism and sacrament) that you will take upon you the name of Christ, then you qualify. If you do not, then you are not qualified.

I am completely satisfied that the people who gain such access, receive the blessings, or obtain a hope in Christ are ordinary people. They are not distinguished by their great intellect or powerful positions. They are typified only by the singleness of their heart and true devotion. There is not a whit of difference between what they believe and how they live. They do not excuse themselves from doing what they know to be right, even if it is painful, uncomfortable, or something they would never do on their own. They invariably do what the "words of Christ" bid them to do. No matter the price, they will follow Him; not a leader. Indeed, almost all of His servants are at odds with leadership. You know how completely He was at odds if you have read *Come, Let Us Adore Him*. To follow Him is to

---

[867] D&C 93:20 "For if you keep my commandments you shall receive of his fulness, and be glorified in me as I am in the Father; therefore, I say unto you, you shall receive grace for grace."

[868] 2 Nephi 31:13 "Wherefore, my beloved brethren, I know that if ye shall follow the Son, with full purpose of heart, acting no hypocrisy and no deception before God, but with real intent, repenting of your sins, witnessing unto the Father that ye are willing to take upon you the name of Christ, by baptism—yea, by following your Lord and your Savior down into the water, according to his word, behold, then shall ye receive the Holy Ghost; yea, then cometh the baptism of fire and of the Holy Ghost; and then can ye speak with the tongue of angels, and shout praises unto the Holy One of Israel."

have that same contention between you and the larger religious community of any age or dispensation. Stop trying to please men and start following Christ.

I do not know what more can be said than Nephi has been saying. Let's press on.

2 Nephi 32:4–5

"Wherefore, now after I have spoken these words, if ye cannot understand them it will be because ye ask not, neither do ye knock; wherefore, ye are not brought into the light, but must perish in the dark. For behold, again I say unto you that if ye will enter in by the way, and receive the Holy Ghost, it will show unto you all things what ye should do."

Comprehension of the "doctrine of Christ" is not based on command of a vocabulary or mastery of an argument. It is based on gathering light. Light is gathered by heed (obedience) and diligence alone.[869] By following the light you have received already, you grow in light.[870] This process leads to the "perfect day" where the light has chased away all darkness. This is how we, like Christ, can grow from grace to grace until we also receive a fullness.[871]

If you do not do this, then you may acquire a vocabulary with which to discuss the subject, but you will not have the light to comprehend it. Light can be shining all around you, but if you do not acquire light within yourself by your actions, you cannot compre-

---

[869] D&C 130:19 "And if a person gains more knowledge and intelligence in this life through his diligence and obedience than another, he will have so much the advantage in the world to come."

[870] D&C 50:24 "That which is of God is light; and he that receiveth light, and continueth in God, receiveth more light; and that light groweth brighter and brighter until the perfect day."

[871] D&C 93:20 "For if you keep my commandments you shall receive of his fulness, and be glorified in me as I am in the Father; therefore, I say unto you, you shall receive grace for grace."

hend the light. (See, e.g., D&C 6:21; D&C 10:58; D&C 34:2; D&C 39:2; D&C 45:7; and D&C 88:49.)

If it perplexes you, then ask God for understanding. He will tell you what to do. Follow His instruction. In this way you qualify to receive further light and knowledge by conversing with the Lord. He knows perfectly what you lack, and by the Holy Ghost within you will tell you what you must do.

If you will not humble yourself and ask for this to be made known to you, then you cannot be brought into the light. Then the only result will be to perish in the dark.

If you will follow the steps with the required real intent, acting no deception before God as you do, then you will receive the Holy Ghost. It will be unlocked to tell you what you lack and what you need to do. This inner light is a powerful source which can literally tell "you all things what ye should do."

It is in the doing that you find the learning. It is in the act of following Him that you learn to be like Him. Obedience is the means by which you gather light. The commandments are revelations of the inner person you ought to become. They are how you grow in the flesh to comprehend God in the Spirit. Your body is a veil that keeps you from Him. By subordinating the will of the flesh to the will of the Spirit, you gain light and truth.

Do it to understand it.

Once you understand you will be able to tell when someone speaks with the power of the Spirit words of eternal life, or if they are, as Nephi puts it: "perishing in the dark." There are many who claim to speak on the Lord's behalf who declare false, vain and foolish things. While they will be held to account for that, the point is not to condemn them. They may yet see the light, and repent and return. The point is that you must avoid being misled by those who would lead you astray. The few humble followers of Christ are warned that they will be taught the precepts of men and must use caution to avoid being misled.[872] We've discussed that already.

The proportions and the balances required to see things aright are too fine, too subtle and too difficult to put into words. They are harmony. Nephi's teachings are woven into one great whole. There are not isolated strains to be taken from the great whole and then given undeserved importance. They must fit together. You can only accomplish that when you see the whole by the light of the Holy Ghost within you.

Nephi is both pleading and warning in these two verses. He wants you to go to the source and be directed from there. To have the words of Christ available to you. To hear the words of angels as you draw near to the light. If you do not, then it is because you refuse to follow the steps he has described.

You must act to know. Without following through in your heart (which you cannot ever deceive) you can't draw near to the light. The discussion in *The Second Comforter* walks through line upon line that walk back into the light, and ultimately into Christ's presence. It is a modern manual to find Him.

2 Nephi 32:6

"Behold, this is the doctrine of Christ, and there will be no more doctrine given until after he shall manifest himself unto you in the flesh. And when he shall manifest himself unto you in the flesh, the things which he shall say unto you shall ye observe to do."

This is the totality of the matter: *the doctrine of Christ*.

Receive the Comforter and it will tell you what you must do.

---

[872] 2 Nephi 28:14 "They wear stiff necks and high heads; yea, and because of pride, and wickedness, and abominations, and whoredoms, they have all gone astray save it be a few, who are the humble followers of Christ; nevertheless, they are led, that in many instances they do err because they are taught by the precepts of men."

It will in turn lead you to the Second Comforter. He will then take you further still.

What does it mean that Christ "shall manifest Himself unto you in the flesh?" Is this speaking of the time when Christ appeared to the Nephites (3 Nephi 11:1–41, where He did declare doctrine)? Or is this speaking of Him appearing to each individual?[873] Is it both?

What does it mean that "the things which He shall say unto you shall ye observe to do?" What takes primacy—your culture, respected peers, leaders of society or government or church, or the Lord and His sayings? Why?

What does it mean that "no more doctrine" will be given until Christ "shall manifest Himself unto you in the flesh?" Was there more doctrine given to later Nephite prophets before Christ appeared in 3 Nephi? What about the very next writer-prophet of the Book of Mormon and his testimony of revelation from Christ?[874]

---

[873] John 14:23 "Jesus answered and said unto him, If a man love me, he will keep my words: and my Father will love him, and we will come unto him, and make our abode with him."
D&C 130:3 "John 14:23—The appearing of the Father and the Son, in that verse, is a personal appearance; and the idea that the Father and the Son dwell in a man's heart is an old sectarian notion, and is false."

[874] Jacob 1:4, 6 "And if there were preaching which was sacred, or revelation which was great, or prophesying, that I should engraven the heads of them upon these plates, and touch upon them as much as it were possible, for Christ's sake, and for the sake of our people. . . . And we also had many revelations, and the spirit of much prophecy; wherefore, we knew of Christ and his kingdom, which should come."
Jacob 4:6 "Wherefore, we search the prophets, and we have many revelations and the spirit of prophecy; and having all these witnesses we obtain a hope, and our faith becometh unshaken, insomuch that we truly can command in the name of Jesus and the very trees obey us, or the mountains, or the waves of the sea."
Jacob 7:5 "And he had hope to shake me from the faith, notwithstanding the many revelations and the many things which I had seen concerning these things; for I truly had seen angels, and they had ministered unto me. And also, I had heard the voice of the Lord speaking unto me in very word, from time to time; wherefore, I could not be shaken."

Was his ministry one that included the Lord "manifesting Himself unto [Jacob] in the flesh?"[875]

How and what is to be revealed? Although you may receive Christ "in the flesh," does it mean you may tell others all things you learn as a result? Or are you constrained and limited in what and how you measure to others? Who decides what is appropriate to include in your testimony, you or the Lord?[876]

If "what He shall say unto you shall ye observe to do," then what of criticism? What of those who will not accept your testimony? What if your testimony of Christ is dismissed as merely your "claims?" What if things done in meekness and humility are misconstrued and said instead to be done to get notice and popularity? Should you expect to be without criticism?

What does it mean that "the things which he shall say unto you shall ye observe to do?" Does it mean others will even understand why you do what you do? Does it mean it will be welcomed? Does it mean you will have some credential the world will recognize? Or will only those who hear the Master's voice respond?[877] If it is the Master's voice which should be heard, then how do you avoid introduc-

---

[875] 2 Nephi 11:3 "And my brother, Jacob, also has seen him as I have seen him; wherefore, I will send their words forth unto my children to prove unto them that my words are true. Wherefore, by the words of three, God hath said, I will establish my word. Nevertheless, God sendeth more witnesses, and he proveth all his words."

[876] Alma 12:9–10 "And now Alma began to expound these things unto him, saying: It is given unto many to know the mysteries of God; nevertheless they are laid under a strict command that they shall not impart only according to the portion of his word which he doth grant unto the children of men, according to the heed and diligence which they give unto him. And therefore, he that will harden his heart, the same receiveth the lesser portion of the word; and he that will not harden his heart, to him is given the greater portion of the word, until it is given unto him to know the mysteries of God until he know them in full."

[877] John 10:27 "My sheep hear my voice, and I know them, and they follow me:"

ing your own voice in His place? What if the words are a rebuke or warning? Should you hesitate?[878]

If you only have your testimony to offer, how likely is it to be persuasive in this world where rank, position, acclaim and popularity define influence? What if, as Bob Dylan penned: *"All I got is this red guitar, three chords and the truth."* What then? Is the truth resilient enough to endure in this hurricane of deceit and worldliness? It will, even if only with a few.

At your core, you love and respect Jesus Christ. When given the choice before your were born, you accepted and agreed to follow Him. That is why you are here. If you followed Him then, you ought to be willing to follow Him now. If you can find Him. I believe that anyone who can find the Master's words, no matter how unlikely a source by which they come, will follow them. The only means authorized to declare them is through persuasion, gentleness, meekness, love and pure knowledge.[879] As it turns out, that is enough. Those who have kept the Light of Christ shining within them will recognize His voice.[880]

---

[878] 3 Nephi 30:1–2 "Hearken, O ye Gentiles, and hear the words of Jesus Christ, the Son of the living God, which he hath commanded me that I should speak concerning you, for, behold he commandeth me that I should write, saying: Turn, all ye Gentiles, from your wicked ways; and repent of your evil doings, of your lyings and deceivings, and of your whoredoms, and of your secret abominations, and your idolatries, and of your murders, and your priestcrafts, and your envyings, and your strifes, and from all your wickedness and abominations, and come unto me, and be baptized in my name, that ye may receive a remission of your sins, and be filled with the Holy Ghost, that ye may be numbered with my people who are of the house of Israel."

[879] D&C 121:41 "No power or influence can or ought to be maintained by virtue of the priesthood, only by persuasion, by long-suffering, by gentleness and meekness, and by love unfeigned;"

[880] John 10:27 "My sheep hear my voice, and I know them, and they follow me:"

2 Nephi 32:7

"And now I, Nephi, cannot say more; the Spirit stoppeth mine utterance, and I am left to mourn because of the unbelief, and the wickedness, and the ignorance, and the stiffneckedness of men; for they will not search knowledge, nor understand great knowledge, when it is given unto them in plainness, even as plain as word can be."

Nephi has reached the limit of what he can say. He has alluded to the Second Comforter, or the appearance of Christ to you in the flesh, but then his message ends. He "cannot say more." But he has told you that when Christ appears to you that you should do what Christ tells you to do.

Then Nephi laments our unbelief, wickedness, ignorance and stiffneckedness. You have already been told that in the vocabulary of the Book of Mormon the word "unbelief" means that you do not understand correct doctrine. You accept false notions, or your understanding is so incomplete as to make it wrong.

What is "wicked" about not following the "doctrine of Christ" so that you can receive the tongue of an angel? What is wicked about not pressing forward in the light of the Holy Ghost to the point where you receive Christ in the flesh? Why would that failing be "wicked?"[881]

Why are we "ignorant?" Is it because of our lack of learning or sophistication, or instead because of it? Studied ignorance is the most indelible kind. It prevents someone from ever casting away unbelief. It enshrines unbelief.

These conditions are all culminated by "stiffneckedness." Meaning that we are not only in error, but we are decidedly committed to

---

[881] D&C 88:33 "For what doth it profit a man if a gift is bestowed upon him, and he receive not the gift? Behold, he rejoices not in that which is given unto him, neither rejoices in him who is the giver of the gift."

remaining so. We won't budge. Won't humble ourselves and ask the Lord to remove our scales of darkness. We just remain devoted disciples of unbelief, leading in turn to our wickedness, borne upon the shoulders of our ignorance. What a spectacle we are when seen in the light of the Holy Ghost—that is, through the eyes of a prophet like Nephi.

What is interesting is this comment comes at the very end of Nephi's ministry. It is an aged prophet carving his last message targeted to the last day audience of first gentiles, then secondarily the remnant, and finally the Jews. And to this latter-day audience beginning with us, Nephi is rebuking us. It must be because of his love for us. It must be motivated by the love of Christ, because it follows immediately after explaining to us the "doctrine of Christ." So whether it seems to be the case or not, this is a loving, kind, light-filled warning from someone who knows what we lack.

Soberly, however, this rebuke should be compared to the rebuke he leveled at Laman and Lemuel. He told them to stop debating the meaning of a revelation given to their father, and start asking God for answers. Compare Nephi's earlier warning and rebuke to his brothers with this verse addressed to us:

> "And they said: Behold, we cannot understand the words which our father hath spoken concerning the natural branches of the olive-tree, and also concerning the Gentiles. And I said unto them: **Have ye inquired of the Lord?** And they said unto me: We have not; for the Lord maketh no such thing known unto us. Behold, I said unto them: **How is it that ye do not keep the commandments of the Lord? How is it that ye will perish, because of the hardness of your hearts?** Do ye not remember the things which the Lord hath said?—If ye will not harden your hearts, and ask me in faith, believing that ye shall receive, with diligence in keeping my commandments, surely these things shall be made known unto you." (1 Nephi 15:7–11)

We read that and think ourselves better than Laman and Lemuel because we identify ourselves with Nephi. Nephi, on the other hand, sees our day, and identifies us with Laman and Lemuel. What a profound disconnect our arrogance causes between Nephi's meaning and our reading.

He is being as plain as words can be. And we are being as obstinate and obtuse as unbelief, wickedness, ignorance and stiffneckedness can cause. You can feel the irony.

2 Nephi 32:8

> "And now, my beloved brethren, I perceive that ye ponder still in your hearts; and it grieveth me that I must speak concerning this thing. For if ye would hearken unto the Spirit which teacheth a man to pray ye would know that ye must pray; for the evil spirit teacheth not a man to pray, but teacheth him that he must not pray."

Again we are called "beloved brethren" despite having just reminded us of our unbelief, wickedness, ignorance and stiffneckedness. His motive is our welfare. He doesn't care a whit about flattering us. He wants us saved.

Still you wonder if this can be true. Still you doubt and think it too much. Still you are left not knowing if the message comes from the Lord. But those doubts are because of your failure to pray. You just won't listen to the Spirit which teaches everyone they must pray. "For if ye would hearken unto the Spirit which teacheth a man to pray ye would know ye must pray."

Nephi knows this because he is a man of prayer. Nephi, as a man of prayer, is struck by the foolishness of deciding matters without prayer. To him it is amazingly obvious that prayer will rescue you from doubt. But Nephi knows why you won't pray to know the truth of things.

You want an authority to tell you.

You want the truth to become popular so it is easy to find.

You want certifications, scholarly support and widespread recognition of the truth.

You want someone whose position you respect to tell you what is true. And until they do, you feel confident you don't need to study it out and pray to know for yourself if it is true.

But Nephi catches you in the act and tells you this is because you are listening to "the evil spirit" which is the one who "teacheth not a man to pray, but teacheth him that he must not pray." So you are following the spirit. But it is an evil spirit you follow.

God's Spirit will always teach you to pray and to ask Him about the truth. And if you ask with a sincere heart, with real intent, He will manifest the truth unto you. He can tell you the truth of all things if you will ask and permit the Holy Ghost to respond.[882]

If the only way to find the truth is to search prayerfully for it before receiving a witness from the Holy Ghost that it is indeed true, what happens to you as a result? Do you gain a testimony of the process? Do you grow in light and truth by what you have experienced? Was this always meant to be direct between you and God? Is the method itself necessarily always to involve God?

Nephi is a prophet. And he's working to make others like him. That's the way it is, you see. Those who have something are eager to have others join them. They are not interested in praise or recognition. Instead they are interested in seeing other souls redeemed. Hence Nephi's blunt message and plain words. They are merciful indeed.

---

[882] Moroni 10:4–5 "And when ye shall receive these things, I would exhort you that ye would ask God, the Eternal Father, in the name of Christ, if these things are not true; and if ye shall ask with a sincere heart, with real intent, having faith in Christ, he will manifest the truth of it unto you, by the power of the Holy Ghost. And by the power of the Holy Ghost ye may know the truth of all things."

2 Nephi 32:9

"But behold, I say unto you that ye must pray always, and not faint; that ye must not perform any thing unto the Lord save in the first place ye shall pray unto the Father in the name of Christ, that he will consecrate thy performance unto thee, that thy performance may be for the welfare of thy soul."

Another significant reminder by a prophet of what is needed.

The great passage from Alma on prayer is an echo of Nephi.[883] Nephi said it first.

What is involved with "performing anything unto the Lord?" How much of what we do in our daily responsibilities ought to be performed "unto the Lord?"

Do not "perform any thing" for the Lord until you have "in the first place" prayed to consecrate your performance. Here Nephi teaches you how to live the law of consecration. You don't need others to join you. You don't need a city to live where all things are held in common. You only need your own pure intent, acting no hypocrisy, consecrating your performance to the Lord for the welfare of your soul.

If you "must not perform any thing unto the Lord" before praying and consecrating it "for the welfare of thy soul," then how should you proceed? How much thought should you take about the

---

[883] Alma 34:17–27 "Therefore may God grant unto you, my brethren, that ye may begin to exercise your faith unto repentance, that ye begin to call upon his holy name, that he would have mercy upon you; Yea, cry unto him for mercy; for he is mighty to save. Yea, humble yourselves, and continue in prayer unto him. Cry unto him when ye are in your fields, yea, over all your flocks. Cry unto him in your houses, yea, over all your household, both morning, mid-day, and evening. Yea, cry unto him against the power of your enemies. Yea, cry unto him against the devil, who is an enemy to all righteousness. Cry unto him over the crops of your fields, that ye may prosper in them. Cry over the flocks of your fields, that they may increase. But this is not all; ye must pour out your souls in your closets, and your secret places, and in your wilderness. Yea, and when you do not cry unto the Lord, let your hearts be full, drawn out in prayer unto him continually for your welfare, and also for the welfare of those who are around you."

Lord and your relationship with Him daily? How careful should you be about your words, thoughts and works?[884] It is again, a reminder that we should always remember Him, and keep His commandments which He has given us, that we may have His Spirit to be with us.[885]

What does it mean to "pray always, and not faint?" What does "praying" have to do with "fainting?" What does it mean to "faint?" Can you "faint" in your spiritual life? Is a physical "faint" merely an example of what happens to us in the spirit? If so, what must you do to avoid becoming "faint" in your prayers?

How many of your prayers have ended by your mind drifting away? No certain conclusion to the prayer, just a distracted mind becoming occupied by something other than the prayer being offered? Is that to "faint?"

What does "fainting" tell you about your vulnerability? What precautions do you need to take to be able to "pray always" and not be vulnerable to "fainting?"

Is the primary difference between the outcome of the lives of Nephi and Jacob on the one hand, and Laman and Lemuel on the other, how they regarded prayer?

What does having prayer as a priority say about an individual?

---

[884] Alma 12:14 "For our words will condemn us, yea, all our works will condemn us; we shall not be found spotless; and our thoughts will also condemn us; and in this awful state we shall not dare to look up to our God; and we would fain be glad if we could command the rocks and the mountains to fall upon us to hide us from his presence."

[885] D&C 20:77 "O God, the Eternal Father, we ask thee in the name of thy Son, Jesus Christ, to bless and sanctify this bread to the souls of all those who partake of it, that they may eat in remembrance of the body of thy Son, and witness unto thee, O God, the Eternal Father, that they are willing to take upon them the name of thy Son, and always remember him and keep his commandments which he has given them; that they may always have his Spirit to be with them. Amen."

2 NEPHI 33

2 Nephi 33:1–2

"And now I, Nephi, cannot write all the things which were taught among my people; neither am I mighty in writing, like unto speaking; for when a man speaketh by the power of the Holy Ghost the power of the Holy Ghost carrieth it unto the hearts of the children of men. But behold, there are many that harden their hearts against the Holy Spirit, that it hath no place in them; wherefore, they cast many things away which are written and esteem them as things of naught."

Nephi would like to teach us (his readers) all he taught those who lived with him and heard him speak. But he could not. Even the things he was able to etch in the metal record he left was incomplete when compared to the body of teachings he preached to his people.

There is also a significant difference between speaking and writing. When you speak there are many tools of speech—emphasis, movement, presence, and radiation of the Spirit to help the speaker measure the effect of the message on the audience. When Nephi taught by the power of the Holy Ghost, he was able to see how his audience was receiving it. He knew when it penetrated "unto the hearts of the children of men."

Writing was another matter. Particularly when it would be translated from one language to another before the gentiles would receive the words. The distance and language between Nephi and his audience is so great that Nephi came to the sad realization that a reader who is not already prepared to have the Spirit with them as they read will miss the power of the message.

In their presence Nephi could use the power of the Holy Ghost to affect the spirit of those who were listening. However, a reader separated by language and culture, and more than two millennia would have to have the Spirit first before being able to understand his message.

It was the recognition that many gentiles would read this record without possessing the Spirit that made Nephi acknowledge the gap between his spoken ministry and his written one. Those with "hard hearts" may be affected by his presence and preaching. Those with "hard hearts" who only have his written record, however, are going to "cast things away which are written and esteem them as things of naught." They won't recognize that they were from God, written by a prophet who knew God, and were the result of a commission to preach given by God. Instead they will think him "a thing of naught."

Nephi's message will mean far more to those who are prepared. For those who are not prepared, the message will be meaningless. Nothing. A thing of "naught" to be "cast away."

That is always the case. The Lord commissions someone with a message and the audience has a role in receiving the message. Powerful public ministries do not convince everyone. Even Nephi failed to convert Laman, Lemuel and the majority of those who were living together at the time of Lehi's death. Then, immediately upon Nephi's death, there were struggles in the society he helped found.

The process of salvation is always a work between God, His children, appropriately sent messages, and adversity and opposition. Nephi is reminding us how vital having the Spirit is to the success of understanding his written message. We should ask ourselves often if our hearts are open to receiving truth, no matter how it comes to us, and no matter how it may challenge our presumptions, pride and foolish traditions.

What a terrible thing it will be for some to realize they "esteemed as things of naught" the very words which might have saved them had they given heed.

2 Nephi 33:3

> "But I, Nephi, have written what I have written, and I esteem it as of great worth, and especially unto my people. For I pray continually for them by day, and mine eyes water my pillow by night, because of them; and I cry unto my God in faith, and I know that he will hear my cry."

Nephi's single-minded focus was life-long. Now, as he writes advanced in age, with a retrospective knowledge, and prophetic fore-knowledge of revelation, he confirms what he has written is "of great worth." When a prophet like Nephi appraises the work as "of great worth," it is important to realize that your disagreement with the assessment is a reflection on you, not him. It is a reflection of your own level of understanding rather than on the work itself.

Are Nephi's two books "of great worth" to you? Why? Can you articulate the reasons they have this "great worth" in everything you think and do in your daily life? How have they changed you? If there is nothing you can point to of value, then perhaps you have not yet found the "great worth" Nephi believed his writing to hold.

Why "especially unto [Nephi's] people?" Who are Nephi's "people?" Why would they be more valuable to them? Why would they have a special value to them, above the value to the gentiles?

When Nephi says he "prays continually for them," who is the group he identifies as "them?" Why does he pray for "them?"

Why does Nephi cry into his pillow at night because of "them?" Who are they and what did Nephi know would be the end of "them?"[886]

Nephi knew his cries to the Lord would not go unheard. He knew the Lord would keep a covenant made with Nephi concerning "them."[887] The remnant of Nephi's seed would not be utterly destroyed. Nevertheless, the future destruction would be near absolute, leaving only a remnant.

Despite this foreknowledge, Nephi nevertheless reports he made it a practice to nightly "cry unto my God in faith, and I know that he will hear my cry."

Nephi kept faith in the face of certain destruction of his descendants. Hope in the face of looming apostasy by his seed. Charity toward those who would reject the Lord.

He has ceased to be exclusively a prophet, and has risen to the role of intercessor and advocate for the unworthy. He has become covenantal father, and presiding Patriarch over a lineage whose redemption will come through his covenant with the Father. He has joined the ranks of the "fathers" toward whom hearts must turn in order to avoid cursing at the Lord's return.[888]

---

[886] 1 Nephi 12:19 "And while the angel spake these words, I beheld and saw that the seed of my brethren did contend against my seed, according to the word of the angel; and because of the pride of my seed, and the temptations of the devil, I beheld that the seed of my brethren did overpower the people of my seed."
1 Nephi 15:5 "And it came to pass that I was overcome because of my afflictions, for I considered that mine afflictions were great above all, because of the destruction of my people, for I had beheld their fall."

[887] 1 Nephi 13:30 "Nevertheless, thou beholdest that the Gentiles who have gone forth out of captivity, and have been lifted up by the power of God above all other nations, upon the face of the land which is choice above all other lands, which is the land that the Lord God hath covenanted with thy father that his seed should have for the land of their inheritance; wherefore, thou seest that the Lord God will not suffer that the Gentiles will utterly destroy the mixture of thy seed, which are among thy brethren."

[888] Malachi 4:6 "And he shall turn the heart of the fathers to the children, and the heart of the children to their fathers, lest I come and smite the earth with a curse."

The circle has closed and the eternal round is completed. Nephi has godly feelings and godly empathy for a doomed posterity. We behold at last the veil removed. We see such nobility of character, and greatness of soul that we are compelled to accept his role as teacher and ruler. He has taught righteousness all his days. Though his older brothers refused to acknowledge or accept him, we should not. His parting message suggests, however, that more of those who will read his record have the same spirit as Laman and Lemuel than will have the necessary spirit to recognize and "esteem of great worth" what he has provided to us.

It is almost too great to take in for the few who are the humble followers of Christ. However, they can avoid being led into error by recognizing in Nephi the teacher and ruler who was sent to deliver a message of salvation to a doomed people. For those who now live under the same prophetic doom,[889] Nephi represents a lifeline offered to those humble enough to accept his message. They will gladly recognize their plight, awake and arise and become people of prayer.

2 Nephi 33:4

"And I know that the Lord God will consecrate my prayers for the gain of my people. And the words which I have written in weakness will be made strong unto them; for it per-

---

[889] 3 Nephi 16:15 "But if they will not turn unto me, and hearken unto my voice, I will suffer them, yea, I will suffer my people, O house of Israel, that they shall go through among them, and shall tread them down, and they shall be as salt that hath lost its savor, which is thenceforth good for nothing but to be cast out, and to be trodden under foot of my people, O house of Israel."
3 Nephi 20:16 "Then shall ye, who are a remnant of the house of Jacob, go forth among them; and ye shall be in the midst of them who shall be many; and ye shall be among them as a lion among the beasts of the forest, and as a young lion among the flocks of sheep, who, if he goeth through both treadeth down and teareth in pieces, and none can deliver."
3 Nephi 21:12 "And my people who are a remnant of Jacob shall be among the Gentiles, yea, in the midst of them as a lion among the beasts of the forest, as a young lion among the flocks of sheep, who, if he go through both treadeth down and teareth in pieces, and none can deliver."

suadeth them to do good; it maketh known unto them of their fathers; and it speaketh of Jesus, and persuadeth them to believe in him, and to endure to the end, which is life eternal."

Nephi makes a practical application and provides us with an example of his teaching of "consecration." He knows the Lord God will "consecrate" his "prayers for the gain of [Nephi's] people." Notice that the benefit of that consecration is not for the welfare of Nephi's soul, but the welfare of others. Once again Nephi follows his teaching, and then elevates the purpose from "the welfare of [his own] soul" to the welfare of others.[890] His concerns are selfless, sacrificial and intercessory. He has become a man of charity and full of love for others. These whom he calls his "beloved brethren" and his "people" are, in fact, those who will destroy and supplant his own descendants. Although a "mixture" of his seed will be there, these people for whom he is consecrating his petitions to God are the Lamanite victors over his posterity. If you have read *Beloved Enos* you will see the elements of redemption playing out in Nephi's words similar to how they play out in Enos' words. Charity is the end result of this consecrated life.

Nephi's words were "written in weakness" but he knows the Lord God will make them "strong unto them." Who is "them?" How does the Lord God make "words strong" to someone? What power communicates the strength of Nephi's words?

What does Nephi mean by "it persuadeth them to do good?" Why is persuading to do good part of the way to recognize words from God?

---

[890] 2 Nephi 32:9 "But behold, I say unto you that ye must pray always, and not faint; that ye must not perform any thing unto the Lord save in the first place ye shall pray unto the Father in the name of Christ, that he will consecrate thy performance unto thee, that thy performance may be for the welfare of thy soul."

What does Nephi mean "it maketh known unto them of their fathers?" Which "fathers?" Does the reference to "their fathers" help you identify who "them" is referring to?

Why do words which will become strong always focus upon "Jesus, and persuade to believe in Him?" Can words which speak of something else, or other programs, initiatives, organizations and events ever "become strong?" Must the message focus upon Christ before it is possible for it to "become strong?"

Why must you "endure to the end, which is eternal life?" What end? We've asked that before, but not answered it. How long must the enduring last, if it is to result in "eternal life?" Will it be a great deal after this life before you have learned enough to be saved? Will you need to endure then, as now, for eternal life to be yours?

What else were you going to do after this life? Planning to play a harp and sit on a cloud somewhere with Captain Stormfield? Or were you planning to be engaged in a good cause, enduring to the end of all time and all eternity, worlds without end?

We encounter so much doctrine in Nephi's writing. It is almost impossible to understand this writer-prophet without some effort to learn the doctrine ourselves. Perhaps we de-emphasize doctrine at the peril of losing the very message Nephi wrote.

2 Nephi 33:5–6

"And it speaketh harshly against sin, according to the plainness of the truth; wherefore, no man will be angry at the words which I have written save he shall be of the spirit of the devil. I glory in plainness; I glory in truth; I glory in my Jesus, for he hath redeemed my soul from hell."

Nephi's writings "speaketh harshly against sin." This is because of "plainness of the truth." If you're going to speak plainly about sin, the words are necessarily harsh, because there's no other way to be plain about it. Warning against sin and pride is offensive.[891]

Those who become angry at the truth have "the spirit of the devil" in them. That is, they are under the devil's influence and deceived. Nephi understood this principle because of his older brothers' reactions.[892] So when someone becomes angry at the truth, they are in darkness.

Christ gave this as one of the signs of the deceived. They argue against the truth and become angry.[893]

Those who are Christ's, however, join with Nephi in glorying in plainness, even if it cuts or requires repentance. They appreciate the plain direction which allows them to follow in the true path. They appreciate truth, even when it condemns their acts and requires them to change. They glory in Christ, preferring Him to unbelief, traditions of men, and the arm of flesh.

Nephi knew Christ had redeemed his soul from hell, for He had declared it to Nephi. The reason Nephi understood the fullness of Christ's Gospel, could declare the doctrine of Christ, and was a prophet given a commission to teach was because he had been taught by the Lord.[894] The return to Christ's presence was not merely

---

[891] 2 Nephi 4:13 "And it came to pass that not many days after his death, Laman and Lemuel and the sons of Ishmael were angry with me because of the admonitions of the Lord."

[892] 1 Nephi 16:1–2 "And now it came to pass that after I, Nephi, had made an end of speaking to my brethren, behold they said unto me: Thou hast declared unto us hard things, more than we are able to bear. And it came to pass that I said unto them that I knew that I had spoken hard things against the wicked, according to the truth; and the righteous have I justified, and testified that they should be lifted up at the last day; wherefore, the guilty taketh the truth to be hard, for it cutteth them to the very center."

[893] 3 Nephi 11:29 "For verily, verily I say unto you, he that hath the spirit of contention is not of me, but is of the devil, who is the father of contention, and he stirreth up the hearts of men to contend with anger, one with another."

[894] 2 Nephi 11:2 "And now I, Nephi, write more of the words of Isaiah, for my soul delighteth in his words. For I will liken his words unto my people, and I will send them forth unto all my children, for he verily saw my Redeemer, even as I have seen him."

a spectacular event to write in a journal, or a bragging point to claim among others. Indeed, much of what Nephi obtained from the Lord was never recorded for us or Nephi's posterity. The return was to obtain light and truth, or intelligence, which is the glory of God. It was to be ministered to by the Perfect Teacher. This, in turn, made Nephi the great minister he became.

The Greatest Servant teaches servants to serve. They are not chosen to be idolized. They are not chosen so a band can strike up "Hail to the Chief" when they enter a room, as everyone rises in adoration and respect. Nor are they chosen to wear silk robes, with subservient sycophants kissing their ring in adoration, hoping for favors. They are chosen instead to serve, while being discarded, challenged, rejected and scorned. Yet in this they only follow their Master, who came not to be served, but to serve. Christ disparaged us gentiles because we submit to abuse and call our abusers our benefactors.[895]

We hardly understand the Gospel of Jesus Christ at all because we utterly reject its principles. We won't live them to know if they are true. Then in our ignorant darkness we judge the light.[896] All the while Nephi's words invite us to choose a different route, act with real intent, with full purpose of heart, repenting of our sins to find our way back into the light. Instead, we cling to the false traditions of our fathers, claiming for ourselves the prerogatives of God Himself,

---

[895] Luke 22:25–27 "And he said unto them, The kings of the Gentiles exercise lordship over them; and they that exercise authority upon them are called benefactors. But ye *shall* not *be* so: but he that is greatest among you, let him be as the younger; and he that is chief, as he that doth serve. For whether *is* greater, he that sitteth at meat, or he that serveth? *is* not he that sitteth at meat? but I am among you as he that serveth."

[896] D&C 58:30–33 "Who am I that made man, saith the Lord, that will hold him guiltless that obeys not my commandments? Who am I, saith the Lord, that have promised and have not fulfilled? I command and men obey not; I revoke and they receive not the blessing. Then they say in their hearts: This is not the work of the Lord, for his promises are not fulfilled. But wo unto such, for their reward lurketh beneath, and not from above."

believing we are better than others, and failing to see the burden of sin we carry in our blind ignorance.

Nephi may have gloried in plainness, but we glory in positive messages telling us we will be saved in our sins. Nephi may have gloried in Jesus, but we use His name to endorse our products and ratify our false teachings. Nephi may have urged the plainness of truth itself, but we market based on focus group tested and opinion polled results so our product line should get good market acceptance.

Nephi's way would work better, you know. The truth attracts those who seek truth. No matter how utterly it may fail in market testing, truth sells. Truth attracts. At least it attracts the Master's sheep, and we'll never be able to save any others anyway. So we should offer the truth to make a clarion call to those sheep. When we dilute it with the theories of marketing, the arm of flesh, salesmanship and branding, the sheep have no idea that there is any truth under the slick presentation. How can you hear the Master's voice in such a cacophony of Wall Street gibberish? Truth alone wins, prevails, succeeds against all opposition and will have its final vindication in the triumph of the Lamb!

I appreciate Nephi's plainness and preference for the truth. I think I may join him in that view. I suppose, however, it'll make some folks angry.

2 Nephi 33:7–9

"I have charity for my people, and great faith in Christ that I shall meet many souls spotless at his judgment-seat. I have charity for the Jew—I say Jew, because I mean them from whence I came. I also have charity for the Gentiles. But behold, for none of these can I hope except they shall be reconciled unto Christ, and enter into the narrow gate, and walk in the strait path which leads to life, and continue in the path until the end of the day of probation."

It is necessary to read all three verses to see what Nephi is saying. What distinctions does he make? Is his charity to his people unequivocal? Is his charity to the Jews unequivocal? Is his charity to the gentiles equivocal? Why?

Does the condition that appears in the final verse apply to the preceding group (gentiles) or to all three groups? How do the remarks made by Nephi in the prior verses we have looked at modify or explain which group the final limitation should be applied?

What has Nephi foreseen or said to suggest he has hope for his own people? What has he done to seek charity by his consecrated petitions for his own people? What has he said about the future inheritance of the covenant blessings for both his people and the Jews?

On the other hand, how little promise has he shown for the gentiles? How conditional are their latter-day rights? How much failure has been prophesied regarding the gentiles?

Since we've been discussing this for months, I am not going to repeat it. You can look to see the scope of Nephi's declarations for his people, for the Jews and for the gentiles. After you've done that, it becomes plain that Nephi has:

Charity for his people. Charity for the Jews, from whence he came.

Charity for the Gentiles, but he cannot hope for the gentiles except they shall be reconciled to Christ, enter into the narrow gate, walk in the strait path, and continue to do so until the end of the day of probation.

We are reminded again of the Savior's own prophecy of the failure of the gentiles.[897] We are reminded of the Lord's promise to take the fullness from us in 1841 if we did not complete the construction of the Nauvoo Temple within the allotted time given.[898] If we failed, we would be rejected. We did not complete the Nauvoo Temple in the three and a half years allotted after that revelation while Joseph was alive. Then Joseph was taken, much like Moses was taken.[899] What the Lord threatened we would lose permanently at the end of our appointment was the fullness of the priesthood, which He had already removed from us in 1841.[900] So the gentiles sit in a precarious position indeed.

You must answer for yourself the questions posed by Nephi's teaching:

- Have we been reconciled to Christ?

- Have we entered into the narrow gate?

- Do we walk in the strait path?

- If so, have we done so as a people until the end of our days of probation?

---

[897] 3 Nephi 16:10 "And thus commandeth the Father that I should say unto you: At that day when the Gentiles shall sin against my gospel, and shall reject the fulness of my gospel, and shall be lifted up in the pride of their hearts above all nations, and above all the people of the whole earth, and shall be filled with all manner of lyings, and of deceits, and of mischiefs, and all manner of hypocrisy, and murders, and priest-crafts, and whoredoms, and of secret abominations; and if they shall do all those things, and shall reject the fulness of my gospel, behold, saith the Father, I will bring the fulness of my gospel from among them."

[898] D&C 124:32 "But behold, at the end of this appointment your baptisms for your dead shall not be acceptable unto me; and if you do not these things at the end of the appointment ye shall be rejected as a church, with your dead, saith the Lord your God."

[899] D&C 84:25 "Therefore, he took Moses out of their midst, and the Holy Priesthood also;"

[900] D&C 124:28 "For there is not a place found on earth that he may come to and restore again that which was lost unto you, or which he hath taken away, even the fulness of the priesthood."

To be able to restore again that which we lost before 1841 would require someone truly mighty in Spirit. Fortunately, we have been promised that lifeline will be extended to us again at some point.[901] However even he will not be able to help a gentile who has not been diligent having their name written in the book of the law of God.

The mothers who minister to their children in patience and love will undoubtedly be among those whom the Lord will remember in that day. The first parable *The Busy Young Man* is about those little acts through which we find our Lord. *The Weathered Tree* is about the enduring power of a mother's love, and how like the Lord's own sacrifice, this often under-appreciated calling has been and continues to be.

Mothers oftentimes do not take time to study because they are too busy engaged in the *actual work* of charity, love, and service. Some may not be able to construct a scripture-based explanation or exposition, but they recognize truth by the light acquired within by their fidelity to the Lord's system of conferring light and truth.

I have been far more impressed with mothers in Zion than with the tattered remains of what is now called Zion by the gentiles. The pride and foolish traditions which claim authority while lamenting the lack of power are the expected results of the latter-day gentile stewardship according to Nephi.

The good news, and the thing we should rejoice over, is that Nephi does extend to us gentiles an opportunity to be saved. All we must do to join in the blessings is to:

- Be reconciled to Christ.

- Enter into the narrow gate.

---

[901] D&C 85:7 "And it shall come to pass that I, the Lord God, will send one mighty and strong, holding the scepter of power in his hand, clothed with light for a covering, whose mouth shall utter words, eternal words; while his bowels shall be a fountain of truth, to set in order the house of God, and to arrange by lot the inheritances of the saints whose names are found, and the names of their fathers, and of their children, enrolled in the book of the law of God;"

- Walk in the strait path.

- Endure to the end of our days of probation.

So we do have a choice. No matter what failings have occurred or things we lack.

It was Lifehouse who sang an anthem to yearning:

> Desperate for changing, starving for truth, . . . / Letting go of all I've held onto, I'm standing here until you make me move / I'm hanging by a moment here with you . . . / Forgetting all I'm lacking, Completely incomplete / I'll take your invitation, You take all of me . . .

I like that song. It is strangely applicable to the condition we find ourselves. But our yearning of course ought to be for the Redeemer who alone can save us.

2 Nephi 33:10

"And now, my beloved brethren, and also Jew, and all ye ends of the earth, hearken unto these words and believe in Christ; and if ye believe not in these words believe in Christ. And if ye shall believe in Christ ye will believe in these words, for they are the words of Christ, and he hath given them unto me; and they teach all men that they should do good."

After the conditional statement warning the gentiles of their need to be reconciled to Christ, Nephi speaks to his "beloved brethren" and the "Jews," but omits specific mention of the gentiles. Instead he refers to "all ye ends of the earth." This would include all those who are neither Jew, nor Israelite, nor gentile. This is a lot of people who are called "heathen" because they have little direct prophetic mention. Nephi, for example, only refers to them once in his writings.[902] In that single reference Nephi promises all, if they will repent and return to Christ, can be saved. All are invited. All can come. Everyone may learn of Christ, find Him and be saved.

There is a distinction between God's absolute willingness to accept all who will come to Him, on the one hand, and the prophetic foreknowledge of who would accept the invitation, on the other. The opportunity is open for all. There will be few who will accept.

Nephi's testimony is based on Christ and employs both Christ's doctrine and teachings. He assures us as readers that if we are willing to accept his writings we are, in fact, accepting the words of Christ. If you believe Christ, you will believe Nephi. For almost everything Nephi has written comes directly or indirectly from Christ. To believe in Nephi's words is to believe in Christ, and to believe in Christ is to accept Nephi's words.

Think about that for a moment. Nephi does not leave you wondering if the message will save you or not, whether he has some special inside information or not, or whether he has seen the Lord or not. He is direct and does not require you to guess. He has not adopted any equivocal or carefully studied words or phrases to tell you about Christ. He is blunt, even plain. His words offend those who are unwilling to surrender their sins and repent. He says what he has written "are the words of Christ." This means that before he taught, before he wrote, before he concluded his testimony, he consulted with and obtained approval from Christ.

There is nothing vague in Nephi's warnings, nor unclear in his message.

---

[902] 2 Nephi 26:33 "For none of these iniquities come of the Lord; for he doeth that which is good among the children of men; and he doeth nothing save it be plain unto the children of men; and he inviteth them all to come unto him and partake of his goodness; and he denieth none that come unto him, black and white, bond and free, male and female; and he remembereth the heathen; and all are alike unto God, both Jew and Gentile."

He openly invites the gentiles to repent. He does so repeatedly. He tells us that with the exception of only a few, we are condemned and will fail in our dispensation. As to those few, he warns us that we will be prone to err because of the things we are taught.[903] He offers us a clear, light filled body of teachings that will clarify for us the body of doctrine that will save us. However, we must take his warnings seriously and study them with care.

Imagine how much effort and thought went into preparing to carve into the metal plates. Imagine the amount of thought he employed before undertaking the final, permanent etchings to complete his ministry. His brother commented about how arduous the process was during his writing on the same plates.[904]

Nephi saw our day, and knew how difficult it would be for us. He wrote a message to be preserved and available no matter who would lead us, no matter what messages we would hear, no matter what confusion would develop. He gave us a message to announce the conditions of salvation over the heads of any foolish, vain or false teachings. They are a lifeline extended to the gentiles, as well as his beloved mixed blood descendants (the remnant), and the Jews.

Nephi knows his words will teach anyone who accepts them "to do good."

The gentile problem is not in reading his words, but in "believing in them." Gentile interpretation almost always involves unbelief. We do not let his words hold their "plain meaning" but want to construe them, read into them praise, and remove from them the blunt warn-

---

[903] 2 Nephi 28:14 "They wear stiff necks and high heads; yea, and because of pride, and wickedness, and abominations, and whoredoms, they have all gone astray save it be a few, who are the humble followers of Christ; nevertheless, they are led, that in many instances they do err because they are taught by the precepts of men."

[904] Jacob 4:1 "Now behold, it came to pass that I, Jacob, having ministered much unto my people in word, (and I cannot write but a little of my words, because of the difficulty of engraving our words upon plates) and we know that the things which we write upon plates must remain;"

ings given us. We want to make ourselves justified by the words that warn, condemn and challenge us to do more. Our unbelief separates us from Nephi's message even as we read his words.

It does no good to argue with him. It does no good to juxtapose his words of counsel and warning with other words of comfort and reassurance. He is alarmed by our condition and warns us to flee from error. We want to read into these words other ideas Nephi never intended.

When we began back with Alma Chapter 13, it was with the idea we would let the words speak for themselves. We were going to try and see what was being said apart from our own desires or hopes. We've been trying to let Nephi have his own words and meanings as we've been looking at his teachings, as well.

An inspired teacher will not offer their own words and pretend they come from Christ. They are not going to dare speak in the name of Christ if they offer only their suppositions, hopes, and understanding. They know, as Nephi, that to do so is to take the Lord's name in vain, and to preach for doctrines the commandments of men. It is often the case, however, that men will urge their own views hoping to make them more convincing, while using the name of Christ. Surely every such teacher will be held to account before Christ for every idle word spoken in His name without His authority or approval.

Nephi knew this doctrine. Nephi understood how weighty a matter it was to use the Lord's name in connection with teaching doctrine. Nephi writes in the full confidence that the Lord has approved his message, inspired his words, and will vindicate them to those who will believe them.

Personally, I would hardly dare to teach doctrine if I did not know what I say to be true. Nephi's example is perhaps more important in this respect than in any other. He is surely worthy to be called a "teacher and a ruler" by all of us.[905]

2 Nephi 33:11–12

> "And if they are not the words of Christ, judge ye—for Christ will show unto you, with power and great glory, that they are his words, at the last day; and you and I shall stand face to face before his bar; and ye shall know that I have been commanded of him to write these things, notwithstanding my weakness. And I pray the Father in the name of Christ that many of us, if not all, may be saved in his kingdom at that great and last day."

You judge. You decide. If you don't believe, Christ will vindicate Nephi's teachings, and you will learn just how wrong your judgment was. For Nephi will be at the judgment bar with Christ. You will stand "face to face" with Nephi as you stand before Christ. You will see, along with all those who abuse and treat true messengers as "things of naught," that you have rejected Christ when you rejected His words delivered by one authorized to speak in His name. Nephi invites you to judge his words with the confidence of knowing that he was given power to say all he said. And he had the Lord's confidence because he didn't say anything about what the Lord instructed him not to speak about.

You will one day know Nephi was "commanded of [Christ] to write these things." Nephi was commanded despite his "weakness." In this context "weakness" is a relative thing. Because Nephi had seen the Lord his perspective allowed him to measure himself

---

[905] 2 Nephi 5:19 "And behold, the words of the Lord had been fulfilled unto my brethren, which he spake concerning them, that I should be their ruler and their teacher. Wherefore, I had been their ruler and their teacher, according to the commandments of the Lord, until the time they sought to take away my life."

against perfection. It allowed him to assess the difference between the Lord as Teacher, and Nephi as servant.

The holiness, majesty and power of God were known to Nephi. He had already had the experience of seeing the absolute standard of holiness in Christ. For most people this will come at the last day, and will result in them understanding, for the first time, that they should have repented.[906] Nephi had already been able to reconcile himself to Christ. Therefore Nephi knew of his own "weakness" and of the power of redemption found through Christ.

Nephi's prayer was for the redemption of all. He hoped that "many of us, if not all, may be saved in his kingdom at that great and last day." Nephi knew he had been redeemed. Yet he identifies with all of us who read his words, and hoped all may be saved.

The measure of a prophet's ministry is in the salvation of others. Nephi does not celebrate his own redemption. He agonizes over the salvation of others. He labors for the redemption of "many . . . if not all" of the rest of mankind. This is the pattern. Redemption causes the redeemed to work for the salvation of others. Perhaps it might be better put that the reason someone obtains the kind of redemption Nephi obtained is because they are of a character to work for the redemption of others. There is no reason to withhold the promise of eternal life from them, because others will be redeemed as a result of their redemption. They will labor, preach, teach, intercede, seek, pray, and work tirelessly to bring others to the tree of life. They become a fellow-servant with Christ and labor alongside Him in the work of

---

[906] Mormon 9:3–5 "Then will ye longer deny the Christ, or can ye behold the Lamb of God? Do ye suppose that ye shall dwell with him under a consciousness of your guilt? Do ye suppose that ye could be happy to dwell with that holy Being, when your souls are racked with a consciousness of guilt that ye have ever abused his laws? Behold, I say unto you that ye would be more miserable to dwell with a holy and just God, under a consciousness of your filthiness before him, than ye would to dwell with the damned souls in hell. For behold, when ye shall be brought to see your nakedness before God, and also the glory of God, and the holiness of Jesus Christ, it will kindle a flame of unquenchable fire upon you."

redeeming others. This is one of the reasons for the parable of "The Busy Young Man" in *Ten Parables*.

Nephi is working directly toward redemption of others. There is no secondary or indirect route being taught. There is no attempt to get some kind of "activity" started, or to introduce a program to do anything apart from bringing you to repentance. He wants you to approach Christ directly through the power of the baptism of fire and the Holy Ghost, which will teach you all things you should do. He wants you to hear and speak with the tongues of angels. He does not want to entertain, distract, or emotionally move you. He wants you to come to Christ. Nephi only tells you the minimum about himself, giving only such information as may be relevant to his message concerning Christ. To the extent he is able, Nephi consistently draws your focus to the Lord.

There is great understanding of how a true friend of Christ lives, acts and thinks found in Nephi's writings. They are a urim and thummim into what you find in a man of God. Imitations will always exist. But the real thing is going to be far more like Nephi than Joel Osteen. More sleeves rolled up and fewer cuff-links.

I do hope we may all join Nephi and are saved in the kingdom at that last day. I hope we recognize how great Nephi's teachings are, and how they address our day with the message we need to hear and heed.

2 Nephi 33:13

"And now, my beloved brethren, all those who are of the house of Israel, and all ye ends of the earth, I speak unto you as the voice of one crying from the dust: Farewell until that great day shall come."

When Nephi paraphrased Isaiah 29 in 2 Nephi 27, he appropriated Isaiah's words to the coming forth of the Book of Mormon. He adapted them making a paraphrase rather than a quote. (I explain the reasons for this in *Nephi's Isaiah*.) Here he uses the Isaiah materials again to identify who he (Nephi) is: "the voice of one crying from the dust." The primary audience for his writings will be those who come to read the book in the last days; when mankind will be in possession of the record which has been printed and distributed to the masses.

Nephi's primary audience for his teachings are those who, like us, live in the last days after the Book of Mormon has come to light. Although Nephi's descendants would have access to these same records, their greatest work and worth would be in the last days. Hence Nephi identifying himself as a "voice of one crying from the dust."

There is also a secondary meaning. Because Nephi was mortal, he was made of the "dust of the ground."[907] He was a man testifying to the truthfulness, as a witness in mortality, of the great things which exist beyond the veil. He is one of us, and yet able to tell us of things to come. Therefore, his witness is given in mortal weakness, but with the power of God behind it. His own strength is dust. The power of Christ to redeem, however, is without limit.

Three distinct groups are addressed in the message: Nephi's descendants, called his "beloved brethren." They are "brethren" rather than "children" because they would descend primarily from his brother's seed who would overcome his. But there would be a mixture of his among them. So they were his "brethren."

The second are called "those who are of the house of Israel." These are the Jews, or others who keep their identity with Israel. Not the gentiles, who have been lost and must gain covenant status one by one, and thereafter live true to the covenant in order to be re-

---

907 Moses 3:7 "And I, the Lord God, formed man from the dust of the ground, and breathed into his nostrils the breath of life; and man became a living soul, the first flesh upon the earth, the first man also; nevertheless, all things were before created; but spiritually were they created and made according to my word."

deemed. "Those who are of the house of Israel" have been previously identified and discussed by Nephi in 2 Nephi 28.

The final group is "all ye ends of the earth." That is, the gentiles, heathen, and those who are not otherwise included even in prophetic mention. All mankind. All the ends of the earth may receive what is offered and attain to covenant status, if they repent, acting no deception, without hypocrisy, following Christ. And all are included in the broad sweep of Nephi's invitation to come to Christ.

His "farewell" is "until that great day shall come." That day is when you see the Lord in judgment with Nephi there beside Him. At that time you will be "face to face" with Nephi, accounting for your heed or neglect of his message. He just mentioned that in the prior verses. He now bids you good-by until that moment. So you should look forward to meeting Nephi at this point. Although you need to take his message seriously if you intend to enjoy the moment.

What other prophets have warned us that their message will confront us in the presence of Christ while he, the prophet-messenger, is there with us at the moment of judgment? Nephi is in a very small group of qualified messengers whose words should be taken with soberness and respect. He is a towering figure when measured by the correct standard. We seldom encounter such a man. When we do, we would be well advised to take counsel from him.

What more can he have said to alert us to the importance of his message?

2 Nephi 33:14

"And you that will not partake of the goodness of God, and respect the words of the Jews, and also my words, and the words which shall proceed forth out of the mouth of the Lamb of God, behold, I bid you an everlasting farewell, for these words shall condemn you at the last day."

From Nephi's perspective, if you deny his message, reject what is taught, and walk away from his teachings, then you "will not partake of the goodness of God." You have been offered fruit from the tree of life, and you're just unwilling to "partake of that goodness." It is ingratitude and foolishness.[908]

This word "partake" hearkens back to the tree in Lehi's and Nephi's dream. (Lehi's version is found in 1 Nephi 8.) People prefer to go join in a crowd inside a building. The building is a symbol of man's work. The "arm of flesh" is used to build such structures. No matter how "great" or "spacious" such work may be[909], it is nonetheless the product of human labor. In the dream, those who enter into the building do so to join the multitude in mocking and scorn of those who choose the tree instead.[910] In contrast to this, the tree bearing fruit is a product of nature—God's product. Man's labors do not produce trees. Without God, trees do not exist. Man cannot take credit for either the tree or its fruit. It is a gift given to him.

Now the gift must be obtained by coming to the tree. You cannot partake of its fruit while standing at a distance. You must go to the tree, take the fruit in your hand, and "partake of the goodness of God" before you are able to realize how "delicious" this goodness

---

[908] D&C 88:33 "For what doth it profit a man if a gift is bestowed upon him, and he receive not the gift? Behold, he rejoices not in that which is given unto him, neither rejoices in him who is the giver of the gift."

[909] 1 Nephi 8:31 "And he also saw other multitudes feeling their way towards that great and spacious building."

[910] 1 Nephi 8:33 "And great was the multitude that did enter into that strange building. And after they did enter into that building they did point the finger of scorn at me and those that were partaking of the fruit also; but we heeded them not."

truly is.[911] So Nephi's invitation to "partake of the goodness of God" is a reminder at the end of his record of the visions he received at the beginning of the record. Come, partake, be saved.

What would you need to do in order to "respect the words of the Jews, and also [Nephi's] words?" Why does he add "and the words which shall proceed forth out of the mouth of the Lamb of God?" Does this mean that if you have "respect" for Nephi's words and the Bible, you will receive other words? Words from "the mouth of the Lamb of God?" Does it suggest you will speak directly with Christ? That part of the fullness of this process is to once again speak to and hear from "the Lamb of God?" Will it result in Christ speaking to you in the flesh?[912]

Why will Nephi's words "condemn you at the last day?" Why does Nephi bid an "everlasting farewell" to those who won't "partake of the goodness of God?"

Is Nephi uncharitable? Are his words harsh, unkind or intemperate? Should he be praising us more and condemning us less? Is this a "hard thing" he has spoken to us?[913] If it is not harsh, unkind, or intemperate, then should this kind of warning be given by anyone who is concerned for the salvation of your soul? Why? If your messengers don't challenge you to repent, but instead use smooth words,

---

[911] 1 Nephi 8:10–12 "And it came to pass that I beheld a tree, whose fruit was desirable to make one happy. And it came to pass that I did go forth and partake of the fruit thereof; and I beheld that it was most sweet, above all that I ever before tasted. Yea, and I beheld that the fruit thereof was white, to exceed all the whiteness that I had ever seen. And as I partook of the fruit thereof it filled my soul with exceedingly great joy; wherefore, I began to be desirous that my family should partake of it also; for I knew that it was desirable above all other fruit."

[912] 2 Nephi 32:6 "Behold, this is the doctrine of Christ, and there will be no more doctrine given until after he shall manifest himself unto you in the flesh. And when he shall manifest himself unto you in the flesh, the things which he shall say unto you shall ye observe to do."

[913] 1 Nephi 16:2 "And it came to pass that I said unto them that I knew that I had spoken hard things against the wicked, according to the truth; and the righteous have I justified, and testified that they should be lifted up at the last day; wherefore, the guilty taketh the truth to be hard, for it cutteth them to the very center."

reassuring you in your present course, would their message conflict with Nephi's message? What would you make of such a conflict between their praise and reassurance, and Nephi's stark warnings?

2 Nephi 33:15

> "For what I seal on earth, shall be brought against you at the judgment bar; for thus hath the Lord commanded me, and I must obey. Amen."

Another reminder of Nephi's status. Not only does he preach the words of Christ, but he also has the authority and power to "seal on earth" his message. He obtained this directly from the Lord. He is a trusted servant, acting in the similitude of the Savior Himself. Holding the power to seal, he proceeds to do so. Those with eyes to see will realize this is an important punctuation mark on the the final statement he leaves for us in his message.

The power to seal and "the Lord commanded me, and I must obey" go hand in hand. One simply does not receive this kind of authority if they will begin to freelance. They are to use it only in the manner the Lord would use it. Although the power is theirs to use, they are governed by their character to use it only according to the Lord's command. Nephi, for example, received this acknowledgment when given the power to seal: "that all things shall be done unto thee according to thy word, for thou shalt not ask that which is contrary to my will."[914]

---

[914] Helaman 10:4–5 "Blessed art thou, Nephi, for those things which thou hast done; for I have beheld how thou hast with unwearyingness declared the word, which I have given unto thee, unto this people. And thou hast not feared them, and hast not sought thine own life, but hast sought my will, and to keep my commandments. And now, because thou hast done this with such unwearyingness, behold, I will bless thee forever; and I will make thee mighty in word and in deed, in faith and in works; yea, even that all things shall be done unto thee according to thy word, for thou shalt not ask that which is contrary to my will."

When Joseph Smith received this power it was given in connection with his calling and election made sure. It happened between 1829 and 1832, the exact date is unknown. It was reduced to writing in 1843 in D&C 132. It is my view that the revelation making mention of it was not a single event, but rather as many as five different revelations related to the same subject, all of which were dictated at the same time and included in Section 132. I've explained this earlier in a series of posts about Section 132. Go back and look here, here, here, here, here, and here if you don't remember it.

Joseph received this power, and this fullness between 1829 and 1832. However, by 1841 Joseph was no longer able to use it because it had been "taken from [the church]."[915] It would not affect Joseph individually, for his calling and election was made sure.[916] But if "taken," it would affect the church.

Nephi's power to "seal" his writings at the command of the Lord, and his own obedience, now make his words binding on all of us. They become covenantal. Hence the reference to remembering "the new covenant, even the Book of Mormon."[917] It is not merely interesting doctrine, nor even prophecy, but has reached covenantal status by virtue of the priestly seal placed upon it by Nephi. We ignore it at our peril. We define it as just a volume of scripture at our loss. It was intended to be studied and followed as the means to reassert a covenant between ourselves and God. By following its pre-

---

[915] D&C 124:28 "For there is not a place found on earth that he may come to and restore again that which was lost unto you, or which he hath taken away, even the fulness of the priesthood."

[916] D&C 132:49 "For I am the Lord thy God, and will be with thee even unto the end of the world, and through all eternity; for verily I seal upon you your exaltation, and prepare a throne for you in the kingdom of my Father, with Abraham your father."

[917] D&C 84:57 "And they shall remain under this condemnation until they repent and remember the new covenant, even the Book of Mormon and the former commandments which I have given them, not only to say, but to do according to that which I have written—"

cepts we can return to God's presence where we are endowed with light and truth, receive intelligence and understanding. Each of us is invited to make that return. Nephi lived it, and as a result was able to teach it. We should do the same. That is, live it to be able to understand and then teach it. *It is the doing that leads to the understanding.*

There is a great deal of what Nephi taught that we have not considered.

THE REMNANT

When I started, I doubted a blog was an appropriate venue to address a topic like the "remnant" of the Book of Mormon. This is still an experiment.

If you're new to this blog, you need to go back and start reading from the start. Then you'll have the foundation for understanding this topic as we move forward.

Undoubtedly there will be those who don't bother to read what has been written previously. They will make comments here about something that was thoroughly discussed in earlier posts. Just grin and bear it. For the most part, I will be ignoring it.

I've tried to remain focused even when there have been questions good enough to answer. But to start answering even very good questions is to hijack the topic and run afield. There have been occasional asides, but that's because of human weakness and the inability to resist temptation.

We are trying to fit our traditions about the remnant and their role into the framework of the Book of Mormon. From what we've seen so far, it should be clear that we, the Latter-day Saints, are identified as "gentiles" in the Book of Mormon. We are not ever identified as the "remnant." As a result, the prophecies about the "remnant" are not prophecies about us. They are primarily descendants of the Lamanites, but have some mixed blood of Nephi as well. They are grouped by the Lord into several different clans, and remain identified as "Nephites, and the Jacobites, and the Josephites, and the Zoramites . . . the Lamanites, and the Lemuelites, and the Ishmaelites." (D&C 3:17–18.) These are those who, though diminished in numbers, are still with us. They retain both a separate identity before the Lord and prophetic inheritance from previous covenants. They are not us and we are not them.

There are two great books which discuss two different views of where the Book of Mormon geography took place. One is by Sorenson, titled *An Ancient American Setting for the Book of Mormon*. The other is *Prophecies and Promises* by Meldrum and Porter. Sorenson says Central America, Porter and Meldrum say North America.

It is not necessary to resolve the question of Book of Mormon geography in order to have a discussion of this topic. The place could be either Central or North America. The result of the last genocidal wars was that the fighting spread into the Finger Lakes region of New York, with Moroni ultimately placing the plates in the Hill Cumorah, where Joseph Smith recovered them. Therefore, there were descendants of these people located in the North American area by the time the Book of Mormon record ends. Furthermore, during the time between 400 a.d., when the record ends, and the time of post-Revolutionary American in 1805, when Joseph Smith was born, there were many undocumented migrations of people we know nothing about other than what anthropology tells us, which is not much.

So when we get to Joseph Smith and his comments about the "descendants of the Book of Mormon" he is speaking at a time disconnected from the events in the Book of Mormon. I take Joseph's comments at face value, and presume them to be correct. When Joseph talks about the ancestors of the American Indians being the Book of Mormon people, I accept that.

Also, I think it is better to let the words of prophecy speak for themselves and not impose our own beliefs or traditions on them. We tend to see in the words meanings that are harmonious with our own preconceptions. It is better to abandon those preconceptions and see if the words give us any better or different explanation of what is to happen. That way we are not misinformed by the traditions of men, even if they come to us from very good men.

I do not judge what others believe, explain or teach. They are entitled to their beliefs. But each of us are entitled to believe and take at face value the words of prophecy in scripture, even if they collide with some other notions. I think it better to abandon the ideas which collide with scripture than it is to wrestle the scriptures to conform with the ideas. But you can do as you choose. I really do claim the privilege of worshiping Almighty God according to the dictates of my own conscience, and believe it my duty to allow all men the same privilege. I will let them worship how, where, or what they may. That's not a hollow statement for me. I believe in complete freedom of conscience for you and for me. We are accountable to God only for what we believe. Until the COB correlates that out of the Articles of Faith by editing instead of by conduct, I will continue to believe in, and practice the principle of freedom of belief. [That is why so many comments critical of me appear in this blog and why relatively few of those praising me are allowed through.]

So, with that brief introduction, we turn to the trail we've been on for some time. The remnant . . .

Part 2

The first statement about the existence of the Book of Mormon in our day was made by Moroni to Joseph Smith. Moroni stated, among other things: "he was a messenger sent from the presence of God to me, and that his name was Moroni; that God had a work for me to do; and that my name should be had for good and evil among all nations, kindreds, and tongues, or that it should be both good and evil spoken of among all people. He said there was a book deposited, written upon gold plates, giving an account of the former inhabitants of this continent, and the source from whence they sprang. He also said that the fulness of the everlasting Gospel was contained in it, as delivered by the Savior to the ancient inhabitants".[918] The "former inhabitants of this continent" would necessarily be North America.

The remnant came from people who frequently received a place called "this land" in the prophecies. For example: "we have obtained a land of promise, a land which is choice above all other lands; a land which the Lord God hath covenanted with me should be a land for the inheritance of my seed. Yea, the Lord hath covenanted this land unto me, and to my children forever, and also all those who should be led out of other countries by the hand of the Lord."[919] The relevant "land" is one which the ancestors of the remnant were promised would be choice above all other lands. A land of inheritance for the remnant. And one to which people would be "led out of other countries by the hand of the Lord" to later occupy. This is a refer-

---

[918] JS–H 1:33–34 "He called me by name, and said unto me that he was a messenger sent from the presence of God to me, and that his name was Moroni; that God had a work for me to do; and that my name should be had for good and evil among all nations, kindreds, and tongues, or that it should be both good and evil spoken of among all people. He said there was a book deposited, written upon gold plates, giving an account of the former inhabitants of this continent, and the source from whence they sprang. He also said that the fulness of the everlasting Gospel was contained in it, as delivered by the Savior to the ancient inhabitants;"

[919] 2 Nephi 1:5 "But, said he, notwithstanding our afflictions, we have obtained a land of promise, a land which is choice above all other lands; a land which the Lord God hath covenanted with me should be a land for the inheritance of my seed. Yea, the Lord hath covenanted this land unto me, and to my children forever, and also all those who should be led out of other countries by the hand of the Lord."

ence to Nephi's earlier vision wherein the unfolding history of the Americas were shown to him. That included the following:

There would be a man separated by "many waters" who would be wrought upon by the Spirit of God and make the journey across the "many waters" to the remnant "seed of my brethren, who were in the promised land."[920] This identifies Columbus, whose original landfall was in the West Indies of the Caribbean. However, the prophecy continues with greater details, increasingly focusing on a North American setting.

After the original discovery by the man wrought upon by the Spirit of God (Columbus), the same "Spirit of God . . . wrought upon other Gentiles" who also made the migration across the "many waters."[921] Again it is not unequivocal because migration included and still includes both North and South America.

When the gentile waves of immigration overtake the promised land, they are humbled, fleeing from captivity[922], and the power of God was upon them.[923] They were delivered by the power of God out of the hands of all other nations.[924] These gentile people are then "lifted up by the power of God above all other nations, upon the face of the land which is choice above all other lands, which is the land that the Lord God hath covenanted with thy father that his

---

[920] 1 Nephi 13:12 "And I looked and beheld a man among the Gentiles, who was separated from the seed of my brethren by the many waters; and I beheld the Spirit of God, that it came down and wrought upon the man; and he went forth upon the many waters, even unto the seed of my brethren, who were in the promised land."

[921] 1 Nephi 13:13 "And it came to pass that I beheld the Spirit of God, that it wrought upon other Gentiles; and they went forth out of captivity, upon the many waters."

[922] 1 Nephi 13:16 "And it came to pass that I, Nephi, beheld that the Gentiles who had gone forth out of captivity did humble themselves before the Lord; and the power of the Lord was with them."

[923] Ibid.

[924] 1 Nephi 13:19 "And I, Nephi, beheld that the Gentiles that had gone out of captivity were delivered by the power of God out of the hands of all other nations."

seed should have for the land of their inheritance."[925] That description seems to identify the United States, for there is no historic basis
for saying Canada, Mexico, Guatemala, Honduras, Cuba, Columbia
or Peru are or ever have been "lifted up by the power of God above
all other nations." The United States, however, as the world's single
recognized "superpower" has fit this description. If it is the area of
the United States being identified, then this is the "land that the Lord
God hath covenanted with thy father that his seed should have for
the land of their inheritance." Or, in other words, this is where one
should expect to find remains of the remnant who inherited and will
inherit again the land as their promise from the Lord.

The gentiles who inherited the area of the United States waged a
continuing campaign to dispossess the native people, succeeding in
causing them to dwindle, but not be utterly destroyed.[926] It is in the
United States, beginning in upper New York State that the gentiles
are given the chance to remove the "awful state of blindness"
through the restoration of the Gospel.[927] The coming forth of the

---

[925] 1 Nephi 13:30–31 "Nevertheless, thou beholdest that the Gentiles who have gone
forth out of captivity, and have been lifted up by the power of God above all other
nations, upon the face of the land which is choice above all other lands, which is the
land that the Lord God hath covenanted with thy father that his seed should have for
the land of their inheritance; wherefore, thou seest that the Lord God will not suffer
that the Gentiles will utterly destroy the mixture of thy seed, which are among thy
brethren. Neither will he suffer that the Gentiles shall destroy the seed of thy brethren."

[926]Ibid.

[927] 1 Nephi 32, 34 "Neither will the Lord God suffer that the Gentiles shall forever
remain in that awful state of blindness, which thou beholdest they are in, because of
the plain and most precious parts of the gospel of the Lamb which have been kept
back by that abominable church, whose formation thou hast seen. . . . And it came to
pass that the angel of the Lord spake unto me, saying: Behold, saith the Lamb of God,
after I have visited the remnant of the house of Israel—and this remnant of whom I
speak is the seed of thy father—wherefore, after I have visited them in judgment, and
smitten them by the hand of the Gentiles, and after the Gentiles do stumble exceedingly, because of the most plain and precious parts of the gospel of the Lamb which
have been kept back by that abominable church, which is the mother of harlots, saith
the Lamb—I will be merciful unto the Gentiles in that day, insomuch that I will bring
forth unto them, in mine own power, much of my gospel, which shall be plain and
precious, saith the Lamb."

Book of Mormon was a North American event, coming to the gentiles who are occupying the land covenanted to the fathers and upon which we would find the remnant.[928]

There is enough, therefore, in Nephi's prophecy to identify the area where the remnant would initially be found. That area is inside the United States. This is where the remnant would initially be swept away, smitten and afflicted by the gentiles. But they would not be utterly destroyed. A small fraction of them would be preserved, so the promises could be realized.[929]

So they were here. And some of them remain still. So, when we begin to identify who they are, the initial proof of their identity is found in Nephi's prophecy and our own history. I do not think it was intended to be particularly difficult to see what was prophesied or who was involved. But we need to pay some attention or we miss the information lying before us.

Joseph Smith also made statements identifying the former occupants of the area that is now the United States where the Book of Mormon people were situated. From his mother, Lucy Mack Smith, we have the following description of what Joseph told the family during the four years he was being educated by Moroni in the annual visits to the Hill Cumorah before obtaining possession of the plates: "During our evening conversations, Joseph would occasionally give

---

[928] 1 Nephi 13:35–36 "For, behold, saith the Lamb: I will manifest myself unto thy seed, that they shall write many things which I shall minister unto them, which shall be plain and precious; and after thy seed shall be destroyed, and dwindle in unbelief, and also the seed of thy brethren, behold, these things shall be hid up, to come forth unto the Gentiles, by the gift and power of the Lamb. And in them shall be written my gospel, saith the Lamb, and my rock and my salvation."

[929] 1 Nephi 13:30–31 "Nevertheless, thou beholdest that the Gentiles who have gone forth out of captivity, and have been lifted up by the power of God above all other nations, upon the face of the land which is choice above all other lands, which is the land that the Lord God hath covenanted with thy father that his seed should have for the land of their inheritance; wherefore, thou seest that the Lord God will not suffer that the Gentiles will utterly destroy the mixture of thy seed, which are among thy brethren. Neither will he suffer that the Gentiles shall destroy the seed of thy brethren."

us some of the most amusing recitals that could be imagined. He would describe the ancient inhabitants of this continent, their dress, mode of traveling, and the animals upon which they rode; their cities, their buildings, with every particular; their mode of warfare; and also their religious worship. This he would do with as much ease, seemingly, as if he had spent his whole life among them." The reference to "this continent" being a reference to North America.

There are other references by Joseph Smith, as well. In looking at this I am not trying to identify where Book of Mormon events occurred. Instead I am only interested in the subject of whether at the time of dispossession of the land, the people who were dispossessed were descendants who had promises extended to them in the Book of Mormon. It seems evident that is the case. It seems almost undeniable that the promised people who are yet to receive the benefit of an earlier covenant with Lehi and Nephi, Jacob and Enos, include those who were occupants of the area of the United States during the early years of American conquest.

Part 3

To understand our own history and prophecies, we have to look at the events taking place during the time of the revelations. The composition of people and geography were dynamic, and changing. They were anything but static. So when you look at events at a specific moment in time, you have to look at the composition of the land and people to understand what was occurring. If you miss it by a decade, you miss what was revealed.

From the beginning of the United States the Indians were a political problem in need of a solution for both State and Federal government. Various conflicts and battles resulted in temporary solutions. By the time we reach the end of the 1820's, a more general solution was needed. Andrew Jackson came to office with a plan to deal with the problem.

Andrew Jackson wanted the Indians removed from the eastern portion of the United States, from Maine to Florida and from the Atlantic to the Mississippi. He wanted them all relocated. Congress responded and passed the Indian Relocation Act of 1830, forcibly removing all Native Americans to the area owned by the United States and acquired from France in the Louisiana Purchase. The land used for the relocation was just beyond the western border of Missouri. In fact, the border town of Independence was located immediately adjacent to, and in the center of the relocated Indian tribes. You couldn't get any closer, and you couldn't be any more in the center than in Independence, Missouri.

Joseph Smith, expressing that "one of the most important points in the faith of the Church of the Latter-day Saints . . . is the gathering of Israel (of whom the Lamanites constitute a part)" seemed pleased that the American government was assisting in a gathering of the Lamanites, anticipating that it would facilitate their reception of the gospel. He even included in his history a positive statement expressing President Jackson's views on the Native Americans (*History of the Church* 2:357–60).

By 1831, after the relocation was well underway, the closest a white man could get to the Indians was Independence, Missouri. When you left Independence heading west, you would encounter the line dividing the land and establishing the territory the Federal Government exercised control over for the benefit of the tribes located there. It was for this reason the revelation given in 1831 refers to the "line running directly between Jew and Gentile."[930] The "Jew" being

---

[930] D&C 57:4 "Wherefore, it is wisdom that the land should be purchased by the saints, and also every tract lying westward, even unto the line running directly between Jew and Gentile;"

the American Indian tribes located across the border, and the "gentile" being the Americans, including the LDS missionaries at the time.

In 1830 the first missionary to the "Lamanites" was called. Oliver Cowdery was told, among other things, the following: "And now, behold, I say unto you that you shall go unto the Lamanites and preach my gospel unto them; and inasmuch as they receive thy teachings thou shalt cause my church to be established among them; and thou shalt have revelations, but write them not by way of commandment. And now, behold, I say unto you that it is not revealed, and no man knoweth where the city Zion shall be built, but it shall be given hereafter. Behold, I say unto you that it shall be on the borders by the Lamanites."[931]

Later the same month, Peter Whitmer was told to join Oliver in this first mission to the Lamanites. That revelation states: "Behold, I say unto you, Peter, that you shall take your journey with your brother Oliver; for the time has come that it is expedient in me that you shall open your mouth to declare my gospel; therefore, fear not, but give heed unto the words and advice of your brother, which he shall give you. And be you afflicted in all his afflictions, ever lifting up your heart unto me in prayer and faith, for his and your deliverance; for I have given unto him power to build up my church among

---

[931] D&C 28:8–9 "And now, behold, I say unto you that you shall go unto the Lamanites and preach my gospel unto them; and inasmuch as they receive thy teachings thou shalt cause my church to be established among them; and thou shalt have revelations, but write them not by way of commandment. And now, behold, I say unto you that it is not revealed, and no man knoweth where the city Zion shall be built, but it shall be given hereafter. Behold, I say unto you that it shall be on the borders by the Lamanites."

the Lamanites;"[932] Both Oliver and Peter Whitmer were assigned to find these Lamanites, preach the Gospel, and at some point a place where the city of Zion would be built would be revealed. So the Lamanite conversion and revealing of the city of Zion were to happen together. The remnant being required for Zion to be built.

You will recall we discussed earlier how the gentiles will only "assist" in building the city. The remnant will do most of the work.[933] (See 3 Nephi 21:23, discussed already.) So this mission was to locate the relevant group, and also locate the relevant spot where the remnant would construct the city of Zion.

In addition to Oliver and Peter, Parley Pratt and Ziba Peterson were called to serve this same mission. They went to Indians in New York, passed through Kirtland, and wound up in Independence at the end of the journey some time later. The Kirtland detour resulted in a large conversion, including Sidney Rigdon. Kirtland was the largest LDS congregation.

Well, the asides are interesting, but the point is that the search for Lamanites began in New York, and moved along until its end in a location center of the relocated tribes. It is immediately next to the boundary separating the Indians and whites, or in the language of revelation, "the Jews and gentiles."

By the following year, Joseph came to visit the area. With the large relocated group of Lamanite nations across the border, and Inde-

---

[932] D&C 30:5–6 "Behold, I say unto you, Peter, that you shall take your journey with your brother Oliver; for the time has come that it is expedient in me that you shall open your mouth to declare my gospel; therefore, fear not, but give heed unto the words and advice of your brother, which he shall give you. And be you afflicted in all his afflictions, ever lifting up your heart unto me in prayer and faith, for his and your deliverance; for I have given unto him power to build up my church among the Lamanites;"

[933] 3 Nephi 21:23 "And they shall assist my people, the remnant of Jacob, and also as many of the house of Israel as shall come, that they may build a city, which shall be called the New Jerusalem."

pendence the site from which all of them could be reached, Joseph received this revelation in July, 1831:

> "Hearken, O ye elders of my church, saith the Lord your God, who have assembled yourselves together, according to my commandments, in this land, which is the land of Missouri, which is the land which I have appointed and consecrated for the gathering of the saints. Wherefore, this is the land of promise, and the place for the city of Zion. And thus saith the Lord your God, if you will receive wisdom here is wisdom. Behold, the place which is now called Independence is the center place; and a spot for the temple is lying westward, upon a lot which is not far from the courthouse. Wherefore, it is wisdom that the land should be purchased by the saints, and also every tract lying westward, even unto the line running directly between Jew and Gentile; And also every tract bordering by the prairies, inasmuch as my disciples are enabled to buy lands. Behold, this is wisdom, that they may obtain it for an everlasting inheritance." (D&C 57:1–5)

At that moment in time we had everything in one convenient place. A land to build Zion, the remnant next door, central location, approval from God, and the permission to proceed with establishing a temple.

People, places, opportunities and events would all change between the early 1830's and the mid 1840's. Dramatically. And so we will follow a few of those events and the accompanying revelations which reflect the dynamic changes among both the Saints and the Lamanites.

Part 4

You should already be familiar with the history of the problems the Saints experienced in Missouri. Independence was hostile, and the Saints were driven away from Jackson County into surrounding areas. By 1833 the possibility of building in Independence was lost. A revelation assured the Saints that the place for Zion was not moved. The consoling revelation states:

> "Therefore, let your hearts be comforted concerning Zion; for all flesh is in mine hands; be still and know that I am God. Zion shall not be moved out of her place, notwithstanding her children are scattered. They that remain, and are pure in heart, shall return, and come to their inheritances, they and their children, with songs of everlasting joy, to build up the waste places of Zion—And all these things that the prophets might be fulfilled." (D&C 101:16–19)

Zion was intended to be built in the center of the last part of Lamanite land available in 1831. The fact that the gentiles were expelled does not mean the site for building Zion was automatically changed. The Lord reiterated Zion wasn't changed. The gentile children may be scattered, but the site would remain. More importantly, the Lamanite children were being scattered as well. The picture was changing on both sides of the line separating "Jew from gentile" in the years following the 1831 revelation.

By 1838 the conflict between Mormons and Missourians had escalated to the point that it was called the "Mormon War." The election battle at Gallatin on August 6, 1838 is at one end, and Joseph Smith's surrender at Far West in November, 1838 at the other.

Missouri was lost to the Saints. The natives voted to expel them, and Governor Lilburn Boggs signed the Extermination Order on October 27, 1838 requiring Mormons to be exterminated or driven from the State of Missouri; a curious piece of Americana that was not rescinded until some 137 years later on June 25, 1976 by Missouri Governor Christopher Bond.

The immediate aftermath of the Extermination Order was the battle at Haun's Mill, ultimately leading to the surrender in November by Joseph Smith. He was subsequently tried by a military tribunal and sentenced to death, but the death sentence was not carried out.

Joseph spent the winter of 1838–39 in the Liberty Jail, and in March 1839 wrote a letter from which we have taken three sections of the Doctrine and Covenants, Sections 121, 122 and 123. The possibility of building in Missouri was lost, at least for the time.

The Saints moved to Commerce, renamed it Nauvoo, and started a new city. This one was also identified not only as "Zion" but as the "cornerstone of Zion."[934] So, although "Zion" was not to be moved, by 1841 the "cornerstone of Zion" was now in Nauvoo. This is not a contradiction. Zion has never been moved. But the Lamanites were moving, the Saints were moving, and the opportunity to locate it in the places where it could have been constructed earlier were no longer relevant.

We read the words of Section 101 to mean that the location remains in Independence, Jackson County. It is possible, however, there is another meaning. That is, the location hasn't changed, although temporary opportunities existed earlier. It wasn't built earlier, and will be built, but when it is built, it will be at the place always prophesied for its construction. Zion was to be located on the top of the high mountains.[935] Jackson County has no mountains, no mountain range, no possibility of fulfilling the promised environs for establishing Zion.[936] Make the descriptions "spiritual" if you want, but

---

[934] D&C 124:2 "Your prayers are acceptable before me; and in answer to them I say unto you, that you are now called immediately to make a solemn proclamation of my gospel, and of this stake which I have planted to be a cornerstone of Zion, which shall be polished with the refinement which is after the similitude of a palace."

[935] Isaiah 40:9 "O Zion, that bringest good tidings, get thee up into the high mountain; O Jerusalem, that bringest good tidings, lift up thy voice with strength; lift *it* up, be not afraid; say unto the cities of Judah, Behold your God!"

[936] Isaiah 2:3 "And many people shall go and say, Come ye, and let us go up to the mountain of the Lord, to the house of the God of Jacob; and he will teach us of his ways, and we will walk in his paths: for out of Zion shall go forth the law, and the word of the Lord from Jerusalem."

a mountain setting is clearly required for the prophesied Zion.
(Psalms 133:3; Isaiah 52:7; Joel 3:17; Micah 4:2; 2 Nephi 12:3; D&C
49:25; among others.)

Zion was always intended to be built upon the mountain top.
(Isaiah 30:17.) Even a valley location in Salt Lake cannot answer to
the description given in prophecy. A valley floor is not the "top of
the mountain" upon which the beacon will be set. Zion has never
been moved. Nor will it. In the same revelation which confirms Zion
will not be moved, the Lord spoke of the Saints profaning the land
earlier identified as Zion.

> "For all those who will not endure chastening, but deny me,
> cannot be sanctified. Behold, I say unto you, there were jar-
> rings, and contentions, and envyings, and strifes, and lustful
> and covetous desires among them; therefore by these things
> they polluted their inheritances. They were slow to hearken
> unto the voice of the Lord their God; therefore, the Lord
> their God is slow to hearken unto their prayers, to answer
> them in the day of their trouble." (D&C 101:5–7.)

So the location identified for building Zion was lost. It was lost
because of the jarrings, contentions, envyings, strifes, lustful and
covetous desires. This caused the land to be "polluted" and rendered
it unfit for Zion. It is true, however, that in the same revelation making purchase of land in Jackson County was approved.[937] There is no
doubt a glorious future for Jackson County. But that will be by and
by. There is a gathering in the tops of the mountains which must
precede that. If there is not a gathering in the mountains first, then
ancient and modern prophecy will fail. There is to be a gathering

---

[937] D&C 101:70–71 "Which saith, or teacheth, to purchase all the lands with money,
which can be purchased for money, in the region round about the land which I have
appointed to be the land of Zion, for the beginning of the gathering of my saints; All
the land which can be purchased in Jackson county, and the counties round about, and
leave the residue in mine hand."

within the boundaries of the everlasting hills.[938] Zion will flourish upon the mountains.[939] There aren't any places in Missouri that qualify for this preliminary gathering.

If jarring and contending can pollute Zion, are we ready for it now? If envy and strife will make it unacceptable, how prepared are we to gather to Zion now? If lustful and covetous desires will make it unfit for an inheritance, are we above those weaknesses now? So, how soon ought we expect the establishment of Zion to get underway?

All of this is an aside to the subject of the remnant. But it is an important aside. The remnant will build the city of Zion. In 1830, when the earlier inhabitants were relocated to the area immediately adjacent to Jackson County, had the city been built it would have been there. It wasn't time. It also wasn't the place. So, although the future of that place may be glorious at some point, the city of Zion to be built by the remnant, would necessarily be built where the remnant is located. Their location, if it answers to the description of prophecy, would be mountainous, in the top of the mountains, and a suitable place for refuge during a time of upheaval. We'll follow the events of the 1840's with that in mind.

Part 5

Another principle that must be included in the mix of understanding the prophecies concerning the remnant is timing and patience.

When you speak of bloodlines and blessings, it is not possible to follow the details of interconnections across generations with any amount of accuracy. Even Joseph Smith, while certain of the remnant's existence and importance, was not certain of their identity.

---

[938] D&C 133:31–32 "And the boundaries of the everlasting hills shall tremble at their presence. And there shall they fall down and be crowned with glory, even in Zion, by the hands of the servants of the Lord, even the children of Ephraim."

[939] D&C 49:25 "Zion shall flourish upon the hills and rejoice upon the mountains, and shall be assembled together unto the place which I have appointed."

They needed to be found. Although some groups showed promise, they were not, and have not, been identified.

There were rumors of a people in the southwest, who made rugs, that may be the group.

There are those who are convinced the Hopi are the people. Hugh Nibley has spent time with the Hopi and written a great deal about them. He seemed satisfied they were likely the chosen remnant. He studied their year-end dance festivals and believed they contained elements of sacred narrative identifiable with the Gospel of Jesus Christ. I have LDS friends who have spent time among the Hopi who have the same view.

I do not believe it is necessary to identify who the remnant is. It is important to realize there is a prophetic destiny of a remnant, and to have a little humility about the limited gentile success which has been prophesied. But to go further than that is not always wise.

Everything in the Lord's plan is timed. You cannot change the timing. If, for example, you hurry to get where you think Zion will be established, and arrive before the burning and cleansing of that land, then you may have found the right spot, but you arrived at the wrong time. You will be killed, burned off the land as it is purged and prepared. The Lord alone controls timing. And timing is as important as any other portion of the Lord's plan.

Also, to identify the remnant beforehand is ill—advised. *They will be identified in the ordinary course of events.* They will fulfill their prophetic destiny. As it unfolds, it will be natural, appropriate and in accordance with the hand of God. There will be no need to force Zion.

Those who are the remnant may well be Hopi. Or, they may come from Hopi blood, if that is indeed the remnant bloodline. But during the time between the closing of the Book of Mormon history and the opening of American history, how many from that bloodline departed or were captured and carried away to another place. If only one left and migrated into Canada, later to intermarry and leave descendants, who have now intermarried and live in Alberta, Montana and Idaho, then they may have long ago lost any identity with the Hopi. But they may still be heirs according to the bloodline that is theirs.

How do we know the remnant does not now include businessmen in Mexico City, families in Peru, a physician in San Francisco, or a housewife in Florida, all of whom have the blood of the remnant within them, but they are without any knowledge of it? Nor can we know if there were intermarriages and migrations which make northern Mexico and Arizona filled with people who are the remnant, heirs of the promises, and destined to one day return to the faith of Christ. Who knows but what the in-migration of those regarded as "illegal aliens" currently inside the United States are not in possession of the blood that qualifies them as heirs of the promises.

They exist. They are known to the Lord. There may be great areas and people, as well as disbursed and assimilated individuals who are among those who are heirs. It is not important to "find" them in one sense, but critical that they be found in another. They will self-identify. That is, those in whom the promises will be fulfilled will act consistent with the promises. They will become known as they engage in the prophesied conduct. They will convert. They will become reunited through the Gospel of Jesus Christ. They will shake off the dust of history, arise and become glorious. They will blossom as a rose and build the New Jerusalem. We will not control that. It will be them awakening, not us attempting to assimilate them into our culture and society. The Indian Placement Program didn't work because it was not the means by which they are to be found. Pushing our culture on them will only create errors their return is intended to cure. And so the timing and means are critical for this to unfold in accordance with the Lord's plan.

If you were to know for certain exactly who was to fulfill the prophecies, and to visit with them today, you may be profoundly disappointed. Until the time is right, they won't be ready either. They will awaken on time. But until that time, you cannot rouse from slumber those who are not ready to awaken. That it WILL happen is certain. But the time is as important as any other component of the event.

Do the remnant people even know they are the Lord's and heirs of promises in the Book of Mormon? Probably not. They, the remnant, are to learn of these things from the gentiles.[940] Therefore it is unlikely they will know anything about it until the record of the Book of Mormon is delivered to them by the gentiles. So if they are to learn about these things from the gentiles, the first step will be educational. Gentiles need to become converted to the beliefs of the Book of Mormon, then bring these correct beliefs to the remnant. The remnant may have a glorious destiny, but not until after first the gentiles who believe in the words take them to the remnant and teach them.

Even if you knew the Hopi were the right people, that does not accomplish what the promises foretell. The remnant must be taught the truth. That will be taught by believing gentiles. We don't have many of those yet. So to deliver a copy of the Book of Mormon to a Hopi and expect that to result in spontaneous combustion producing light, truth and glory is at best a naive notion and at worst absolute foolishness. It won't happen that way. The right people must be brought the right message by a believing gentile, preaching the fullness of the Gospel to them. When that happens, Nephi's prophecy may begin to unfold. We lack qualified gentile ministers at present.

---

[940] 2 Nephi 30:3 "And now, I would prophesy somewhat more concerning the Jews and the Gentiles. For after the book of which I have spoken shall come forth, and be written unto the Gentiles, and sealed up again unto the Lord, there shall be many which shall believe the words which are written; and they shall carry them forth unto the remnant of our seed."

They labor under condemnation for not taking the Book of Mormon seriously or remembering the covenant made within it. So the first step is to convert a few gentiles.

Nevertheless, this is an important subject and worth taking time to understand. But with this, as with almost everything else in the Gospel, having it measured correctly and weighed in proportion is the only way to understand. So we proceed step by cautious step to try and dismantle false and corrupt notions, and to assemble the true ones. You must be patient to understand the Lord's plan. And therefore we proceed patiently in this subject, as well.

Patience is more than a virtue. It is critical to participating in the Lord's plan.

Part 6

A few additional statements by Joseph Smith and others add weight to the identity of the existing American Indian population at the time of the prophecies given to Joseph Smith.

When Joseph and Oliver went to seek answers about baptism on May 15, 1829, they explained the motivation for the inquiry. They report they were inspired "after writing the account given of the Savior's ministry to the remnant of the seed of Jacob, upon this continent." (*Messenger and Advocate* 1:15, October 1834.)

"The Book of Mormon is a record of the forefathers of our western Tribes of Indians," Smith wrote to N. C. Saxton, editor of a Rochester, New York, newspaper. "The land of America is a promised land unto them," where they would be instrumental in building a New Jerusalem." [Taken from Ronald Walker's paper: *Seeking the Remnant*; one of the first publications to take the role of the remnant found in the American Indians as a serious matter of study.]

On their mission to the Lamanites, Oliver and Parley were interviewed by newspapers as they went on their journey. *The Telegraph* published in Painesville, Ohio, on 16 and 30 November 1830, made the following mention about Oliver's interview: "He proclaims destruction upon the world in a few years. We understand that he is bound for the regions beyond the Mississippi, where he contemplates founding a 'City of Refuge' for his followers, and converting the Indians, under his prophetic authority." Cowdery also reportedly spoke of an about-to-rise Indian prophet, who would bring these events to pass.

Parley Pratt's autobiography discusses the Mission to the Lamanites. He describes how the missionaries didn't even hesitate in their mission after their tremendous success at Kirtland. They changed the entire center of gravity for the Church by the Kirtland conversions. But they retained their focus on the target of the remnant, whom they had been sent to teach. This was the first organized missionary effort after the organization of the church, and the target was the Lamanites. The priority and focus was remarkable, when you consider the abundance of potential white converts all around the tiny start-up church. It gives some indication of how important Joseph regarded the Lamanite remnant to be as an obligation for the restored church.

Winter did not slow their journey toward the western frontier and border with the relocated American Indian tribes. Here's a brief excerpt from Parley's writings:

> "We halted for a few days in Illinois, about twenty miles from St. Louis, on account of a dreadful storm of rain and snow, which lasted for a week or more, during which the slow fell in some places near three feet deep . . . In the beginning of 1831 we renewed our journey; and, passing through St. Louis and St. Charles, we traveled on foot for three hundred miles through vast prairies and through trackless wilds of snow— no beaten road; houses few and far between; and the bleak northwest wind always blowing in our faces with a keenness

which would almost take the skin off the face . . . We often ate our frozen bread and pork by the way, when the bread would be so frozen that we could not bite or penetrate any part of it but the outside crust.

"After much fatigue and some suffering we all arrived in Independence, in the county of Jackson, on the extreme western frontiers of Missouri, and the United States." (*Autobiography of Parley P. Pratt*, 40.)

Parley's account continues and explains how two of the missionaries took employment as tailors in Independence while the others crossed the boundary and "commenced a mission among the Lamanites, or Indians." (Ibid, 41.) They taught the Shawnees, then the Delaware, including the chief over ten tribes of Delaware. The sermon delivered to the gathering called by the chief, delivered by Oliver Cowdery, is set out on pp. 42–43 where it is clear Oliver understood the Delaware were descended from the Book of Mormon people. The chief replied:

"We feel truly thankful to our white friends who have come so far, and been at such pains to tell us good news, and specially this new news concerning the Book of our forefathers; it makes us glad in here—placing his hands on his own heart."

Although the Indian reaction was favorable, the Indian Agents were alarmed at the Mormon success. In particular they did not want the upstart religion to gain a foothold among the relocated Indians, and began to interfere with the missionary efforts.

Of interest to us, however, is Oliver's mention of the Rocky Mountains as the ultimate destination of the missionary effort, to be "with the Indians." (*The Telegraph*, Painesville, 18 January 1831, cited by Walker, above, on p. 9.) Walker writes:

"Smith gave a revelation requiring Sidney Gilbert to open a store in western Missouri that would allow 'clerks employed in his service' to go unto the Lamanites and 'thus the gospel may be preached unto them.' He also issued a confidential revelation that presaged the introduction of plural marriage. This latter statement promised that the elders would intermarry with the native women, making the red man's posterity 'white, delightsome, and just.'" (*Seeking the Remnant*, 10. Citations omitted.)

This early focus on the duty to find and preach to the remnant was not a passing concern. It was far more central to the early efforts than we realize as we review the events today. Today the view of the Lamanite remnant's role is, if anything, superficial. To the earliest converts, they were central. They would remain a focus of interest throughout not only Joseph's life, but also into the early part of the western migration. Indeed, the western movement of the church itself was related to locating the remnant.

Now there are a number of prophecies given in the Book of Mormon or Doctrine and Covenants which relate to why the remnant were a priority for Joseph Smith and the early church of this dispensation. The further we get from those times, however, the more we seem to forget the underlying reasons. We have become so successful as an organization, and prosper in every economic, political and social measure that it is hard to remember things. When Presidential candidates, the leader of the United States Senate, the Ambassador to China, business and educational leaders are members of the church, we do not relate as well to the promised cataclysms. Where once we may have welcomed destruction to end our persecutions, now we fear what we would lose. Our former poverty made us fear nothing in the destruction of the world, but now we have a great deal to lose and therefore we want to continue as we are. We have even redefined the term "remnant" to mean us, the Latter-day Saints, as if redefining it will remove the prophetic threat posed to the gentiles. (See *Children of the Covenant*, May, 1995 Ensign, the General Conference talk by Russell M. Nelson; in particular the interpretation given in footnote 15.) The careful distinctions between the remnant of the Book of Mormon on the one hand, and the gentiles on the other, has been forgotten, or altogether lost in our modern teachings. But that does not alter what Nephi or Christ meant in their prophecies that we still read in the Book of Mormon text.

We've worked to establish a basis for understanding the distinctions for several months now. With that foundation we will continue our search for understanding where we find ourselves in history, what group we are identified with and what we should expect in the coming calamities.

Onward, then . . .

Part 7

When Joseph had made a sufficient "offering" and "acknowledgments," the Lord gave another opportunity for the Saints to receive again what had been taken from them, that is the "fullness of the priesthood."[941]

To be permitted to undertake this, however, there would be a limited time appointed. After that appointment, the church would be rejected.[942] The time is not specified, but the work was to be under-

---

[941] D&C 124:1, 28 "Verily, thus saith the Lord unto you, my servant Joseph Smith, I am well pleased with your offering and acknowledgments, which you have made; for unto this end have I raised you up, that I might show forth my wisdom through the weak things of the earth. . . . For there is not a place found on earth that he may come to and restore again that which was lost unto you, or which he hath taken away, even the fulness of the priesthood."

[942] D&C 124:31–32 "But I command you, all ye my saints, to build a house unto me; and I grant unto you a sufficient time to build a house unto me; and during this time your baptisms shall be acceptable unto me. But behold, at the end of this appointment your baptisms for your dead shall not be acceptable unto me; and if you do not these things at the end of the appointment ye shall be rejected as a church, with your dead, saith the Lord your God."

taken by sending "swift messengers,"[943] and gathering all the Saints together with their gold, silver, antiquities, and precious things to construct this Temple.[944]

The Saints gathered to Nauvoo and by 1844 the population had swollen to 12,000. There were shops, brick homes, stores, and a Masonic Hall constructed in Nauvoo. There was a gunsmith shop, a university, library and wide streets. Unlike other frontier towns with adobe and log homes, Nauvoo boasted brick houses and affluence. This community was superior to anything else along the western boundary of the United States at the time.

When Joseph and Hyrum were killed on June 27, 1844, the Temple walls were not completed and no portion had been dedicated. After Joseph's death, the Saints rededicated themselves to finish the Temple. The exterior walls were completed in December, 1844 and the final sunstone put into place with some considerable difficulty.

On March 16, 1845 Brigham Young asked the Saints to rededicate themselves to building the Temple, promising them blessings if they would redouble their efforts to complete the building. On the following day 105 extra laborers showed up to help. (*History of the Church* 7:385–87.) It was not until 24 May 1845 that the capstone would be laid.

Joseph was dead for 18 months before the endowment was administered in the Nauvoo Temple on December 10th, 1845. Those

---

[943] D&C 124:26 "And send ye swift messengers, yea, chosen messengers, and say unto them: Come ye, with all your gold, and your silver, and your precious stones, and with all your antiquities; and with all who have knowledge of antiquities, that will come, may come, and bring the box-tree, and the fir-tree, and the pine-tree, together with all the precious trees of the earth;"

[944] D&C 124:26–27 "And send ye swift messengers, yea, chosen messengers, and say unto them: Come ye, with all your gold, and your silver, and your precious stones, and with all your antiquities; and with all who have knowledge of antiquities, that will come, may come, and bring the box-tree, and the fir-tree, and the pine-tree, together with all the precious trees of the earth; And with iron, with copper, and with brass, and with zinc, and with all your precious things of the earth; and build a house to my name, for the Most High to dwell therein."

who had been given some instruction regarding the Temple in Joseph's brick store, used what they had learned before Joseph's death to perform the ceremonies. A portion of the attic was temporarily dedicated for this work, even though the structure was incomplete. The final endowments were performed on February 7, 1846. On February 8, 1846 the Twelve prayed in the Temple to be able to finally complete and formally dedicate the Temple. The following day the Temple caught fire, damaging the area that had been used for the endowment requiring repairs to be made. A week later Brigham Young's party departed Nauvoo with the Temple still incomplete, but Nauvoo was a magnificent city that showed enormous culture, prosperity and success.

If you have visited Nauvoo since the beginning of the Church-sponsored Nauvoo Restoration, Inc. work, you know how amazing the city was when abandoned by the Saints. It was a tribute to labor, dedication, and perseverance. The Temple was incomplete and still under construction—not at all ready for dedication, but the city was a marvel. As the church leadership departed to the west, they left instruction to complete the Temple even though it would not be used.

Finally, on April 29, 1846 the Nauvoo Temple was complete enough to dedicate. The following day a private dedication service was conducted by Wilford Woodruff, Orson Hyde and about twenty others. The prayer was offered by Joseph Young, Brigham's brother. The next day a public dedication service was held with those attending charged $1.00 entrance fee to help pay those who had worked in completing the structure. In this dedication ceremony Elder Hyde offered the prayer and included the following: *"By the authority of the Holy Priesthood now we offer this building as a sanctuary to Thy Worthy Name. We ask Thee to take the guardianship into Thy hands . . . "*

The following Sunday Elder Hyde explained that the Temple needed to be completed for the church to be accepted by the Lord with our dead. He commented that the work had only been accomplished "by the skin of our teeth." (*Wilford Woodruff's Journal* 3:43.)

By September, 1846 a mob overran Nauvoo, and the caretakers gave the keys to the Temple doors to the mob. The mob was eventually shamed into returning the Temple to the caretakers and on October 20th the keys were returned to Brother Paine. The trustees of Nauvoo then tried to sell the Temple, but the best offer received was $100,000. A Missouri newspaper reported that the Temple was sold in June, 1847 to the Catholic Church for $75,000, but that the sale failed because of a defect in the title to the property.

On October 9, 1848 the Nauvoo Temple was destroyed by an arsonist.

In March, 1849 the French Icarians purchased the hollow shell of the destroyed Temple. On May 27, 1850 a storm blew down the north wall and made the structure so dangerous that it was further torn down to make it safe. Pieces of the blockwork were then sold and some of them were transported to be used in building projects outside the community, including to St. Louis. By 1865 the city removed what little remained. The site was then used for saloons, slaughter houses, hotels, grocery and drug stores, pool halls and private houses. ("The Nauvoo Temple", *The Instructor*, March 1965.)

From the time of Nauvoo until the present day, every President of The Church of Jesus Christ of Latter-day Saints either lived in Nauvoo between January 1841 and June 1844, or descended from those who lived there during the time. (Although some were called on missions and abandoned families who resided there for some of that time.)

Church history takes the view that Nauvoo was a triumph, and the Saints succeeded in accomplishing all that was required of them, and more. The stories of heroism, sacrifice and devotion that focus on the Nauvoo era are endless. Those families who trace their genealogy to ancestors in Nauvoo at that time defend the notion that the they are specially favored as families, and are among the noble and great chosen to lead others in mortality because of their great devotion and sacrifice.

The promise of a remnant holding authority and performing a central work in the establishment of Zion, as prophesied by the Book of Mormon and Doctrine and Covenants, would be a dramatic change in course for the church. This is something that will occur in any event. Indeed, coalitions, conspiracies and man's arm will be powerless to prevent it. Unlikely history is the stuff of scripture.

Prophecies will be fulfilled. Despite vanity and foolishness, error and unbelief, prophecies will be fulfilled.

Part 8

We've seen some of what the remnant is defined to mean. We've seen the definition in the Book of Mormon excludes gentiles. We've seen the converted gentiles comprising the Latter-day Saints are still defined as gentiles after conversion.

We've seen that the first formal mission called after the establishment of the church was sent to the Lamanites to find the remnant. We've seen how the mission went no further than the boundary where the Indian Nations were relocated by the US Government in 1830. What we haven't discussed is the interest Joseph Smith had in locating the remnant throughout his life.

When he was fleeing Nauvoo in late June, he intended to go to the Rocky Mountains. That was the location chosen precisely because it was where he hoped to find the remnant. He was talked into returning by those who claimed it was cowardly for him to flee. They used the Lord's analogy about the false shepherd who would flee when the flock was in danger.[945] He reportedly said "if my life is of no value to my friends, it is of no value to myself." He returned. With that, Joseph's attempt to locate and identify the remnant came to an end. However, before his final surrender, his intention was to go to the Rocky Mountains to locate the remnant.

The following entry appears on June 22, 1844 in *DHC* 6:547:

"About 9 p.m. Hyrum came out of the Mansion and gave his hand to Reynolds Cahoon, at the same time saying, 'A company of men are seeking to kill my brother Joseph, and the Lord has warned him to flee to the Rocky Mountains to save his life. Good-bye, Brother Cahoon, we shall see you again.' In a few minutes afterwards Joseph came from his family. His tears were flowing fast. He held a handkerchief to his face, and followed after Brother Hyrum without uttering a word."

In his final public address Joseph said, among other things:

"You will gather many people into the vastness of the Rocky Mountains as a center for the gathering of the people . . . you will yet be called upon to go forth and call upon the free men from Main to gather themselves together to the Rocky Mountains; and the Redmen from the West and all people from the North and from the South and from the East, and go to the West, to establish themselves in the strongholds of their gathering places, and there you will gather with the Redmen to their center from their scattered and dispersed situation, to become the strong arm of Jehovah, who will be a strong bulwark of protection from your foes." ("A Prophecy of Joseph the Seer" in *The Fate of the Persecutors of the Prophet Joseph Smith*, 154, 156.)

---

[945] John 10:11–13 "I am the good shepherd: the good shepherd giveth his life for the sheep. But he that is an hireling, and not the shepherd, whose own the sheep are not, seeth the wolf coming, and leaveth the sheep, and fleeth: and the wolf catcheth them, and scattereth the sheep. The hireling fleeth, because he is an hireling, and careth not for the sheep."

There is a well known quote that speaks volumes when considered as a whole:

> "I want to say to you before the Lord that you know no more concerning the destinies of this Church and Kingdom than a babe upon its mother's lap. You don't comprehend it. It is only a little handful of Priesthood you see here tonight, but this Church will fill North and South America—it will fill the world. It will fill the Rocky Mountains. There will be tens of thousands of Latter-day Saints who will be gathered in the Rocky Mountains, and there they will open the door for the establishing of the Gospel among the Lamanites . . . This people will go into the Rocky Mountains; they will there build temples to the Most High. They will raise up a posterity there, and the Latter-day Saints who dwell in these mountains will stand in the flesh until the coming of the Son of Man. The Son of Man will come to them while in the Rocky Mountains." *(Millennial Star,* Vol. 54 (1852), 605.)

We've seen how the primary effort to build the city of Zion will be the remnant's, and the gentiles will merely "assist" in the construction.

To see the remnant's role is more important than to understand their identity. Their identity will come. But their role is distinct and important. We are not them, and they have a destiny appointed them by covenant and promise. We cannot substitute ourselves for them. Nor can we fulfill the prophetic promises without them.

3 NEPHI 20

Christ had some specific teachings about the remnant we have not yet examined. We'll turn to that to add to our understanding of the remnant role:

3 Nephi 20:11

"Ye remember that I spake unto you, and said that when the words of Isaiah should be fulfilled—behold they are written, ye have them before you, therefore search them—"

Christ is speaking and will turn to the future destiny of the Nephites. By the time this statement was made, however, the Nephites were mingled with all other bloodlines. There were shortly to be no more "-ites" but only one people.[946]

The destiny of the future remnant will unfold in conformity with words spoken by Isaiah. They are adequate to foretell the future of the events involving the people on this, the American land. But we are supposed to "search them" to be able to get an understanding of what will unfold.

---

[946] 4 Nephi 1:17 "There were no robbers, nor murderers, neither were there Lamanites, nor any manner of -ites; but they were in one, the children of Christ, and heirs to the kingdom of God."

There is a plan. It was all foreseen. It will happen as the prophecies describe. However we need to trust the language and not impose other ideas upon the words.

3 Nephi 20:12

"And verily, verily, I say unto you, that when they shall be fulfilled then is the fulfilling of the covenant which the Father hath made unto his people, O house of Israel."

Isaiah's prophecies concerning the Israelite covenant will happen at the same time as the fulfillment of the covenants for the Nephite remnant. So things will develop simultaneously for all the chosen people. Not just locally, but globally.

Notice the reference to the "Father" and to "His people." Why is it the "Father's people" in this scripture? What significance is there to the covenant being fulfilled for the Father's people? Are they different from others? Can others have a covenant with Christ? Why is it the Father's people who will see the fulfillment of their covenants in this final, winding up of history?

How are "O house of Israel" and the "Father's people" related? Are they the same? Why or why not?

Why would all covenants come to a fulfillment at the same time? What is there of general historical development which requires all of these to be fulfilled simultaneously?

How would you prepare for the time when the fulfillment of all the covenants are to occur? Is there some kind of storage you should be assembling? What about things that put "oil" in a "lamp?" How would you go about getting that put together?

If the judgments of God will begin on His own house[947], then how do you prepare to avoid that judgment?

There is an upside to every prophecy, even in those predicting calamity. The upside consists in two things: First, avoiding the judgment by being prepared for it.[948] Second, recognizing it so as to not be alarmed or lose faith because of it.[949]

When you see the distresses which are to come, recognize them as signs given by the Lord and take comfort.[950]

Christ uses Isaiah as His source because Isaiah was inspired in what he wrote. We also have a record of his prophecy. Therefore, the Lord could speak in the first person and have us quote Him. However, He pays tribute to His own prophet by quoting the words of Isaiah. This is meekness indeed. Our Lord is not and never has been prideful. He is meek, and willing to let others have credit, share in triumph, and be treated as equals. How unlike Him are the gentile

---

[947] D&C 112:24–26 "Behold, vengeance cometh speedily upon the inhabitants of the earth, a day of wrath, a day of burning, a day of desolation, of weeping, of mourning, and of lamentation; and as a whirlwind it shall come upon all the face of the earth, saith the Lord. And upon my house shall it begin, and from my house shall it go forth, saith the Lord; First among those among you, saith the Lord, who have professed to know my name and have not known me, and have blasphemed against me in the midst of my house, saith the Lord."

[948] D&C 38:30 "I tell you these things because of your prayers; wherefore, treasure up wisdom in your bosoms, lest the wickedness of men reveal these things unto you by their wickedness, in a manner which shall speak in your ears with a voice louder than that which shall shake the earth; but if ye are prepared ye shall not fear."

[949] D&C 1:3 "And the rebellious shall be pierced with much sorrow; for their iniquities shall be spoken upon the housetops, and their secret acts shall be revealed. And the rebellious shall be pierced with much sorrow; for their iniquities shall be spoken upon the housetops, and their secret acts shall be revealed."

[950] Luke 21:8–13 "And he said, Take heed that ye be not deceived: for many shall come in my name, saying, I am *Christ;* and the time draweth near: go ye not therefore after them. But when ye shall hear of wars and commotions, be not terrified: for these things must first come to pass; but the end *is* not by and by. Then said he unto them, Nation shall rise against nation, and kingdom against kingdom: And great earthquakes shall be in divers places, and famines, and pestilences; and fearful sights and great signs shall there be from heaven. But before all these, they shall lay their hands on you, and persecute *you,* delivering *you* up to the synagogues, and into prisons, being brought before kings and rulers for my name's sake. And it shall turn to you for a testimony."

leaders who love to lord it over one another, holding each other as subservients. Christ, however, made Himself a servant of all.[951] He puts that same meekness on display again here, as he quotes from Isaiah. This shows the Lord's respect for Isaiah.

Interesting the things which become apparent the closer you look at our Lord. Interesting how much the Book of Mormon adds to the picture of our Lord. What a great volume of scripture we have been given.

3 Nephi 20:13

> "And then shall the remnants, which shall be scattered abroad upon the face of the earth, be gathered in from the east and from the west, and from the south and from the north; and they shall be brought to the knowledge of the Lord their God, who hath redeemed them."

Notice "remnants" is plural. This is Christ speaking, and the scope of the message is universal. It is not local. It includes local events, to be sure. But the time of this fulfillment will be global. All the "remnants" will be affected.

It will not matter if the particular "remnant" is anywhere "upon the face of the earth" they will be "gathered in."

Why would they necessarily be "gathered?" What is the purpose of "gathering?"

Why "gather" merely to then return them to their lands of inheritance?[952]

---

[951] Mark 10:42–44 "But Jesus called them *to him,* and saith unto them, Ye know that they which are accounted to rule over the Gentiles exercise lordship over them; and their great ones exercise authority upon them. But so shall it not be among you: but whosoever will be great among you, shall be your minister: And whosoever of you will be the chiefest, shall be servant of all"

[952] See discussion of 3 Nephi 21:27–28.

Which is more important, to gather physically or to gather "to the knowledge of the Lord their God?"

How could people gather "to the knowledge of the Lord their God?" What kind of "knowledge of the Lord God" will be involved? Do you get that knowledge by supporting men in their callings? Do men and their callings even matter? Can you grow in knowledge of God by following, even memorizing, a handbook; following, memorizing talks and inspirational literature? What does a person need to follow, to do, to abide by in order to gain "knowledge of the Lord their God?" What about those who testify to you about programs and personalities, but never preach about Christ and Him crucified?

Do true messengers speak about one another, or about their Lord? How can a man, any man, save you? Who alone has the capacity to redeem you? Is "knowledge of the Lord their God" related also to knowledge that He "hath redeemed them?" Can you "know" Christ and not acquire in the process of knowing Him the knowledge that He "hath redeemed" you?

Do you come to understand He has redeemed you by also coming to know Him?

Do Joseph's remarks about the Lord coming to visit with the remnant in the Rocky Mountains explain how both those coming from the four corners of the compass will gain "knowledge of the Lord their God" and also know He "hath redeemed them?"

Do you begin to see a pattern of consistent prophetic foreknowledge of the last days? Do Christ's words in this message of the Book of Mormon give any greater reason to believe in the promises?

If these promises are made by Him, should you expect it possible for you to go ahead and "gather in" to Him even before there are others willing to do so? Can this "gathering in" occur in your lifetime, for you? If God is no respecter of persons, then what would you need to do today to obtain the same blessings others will receive as they "gather in" in perhaps greater numbers in the future? Is it possible to do that? Are you willing to try?

It seems to me this doctrine is important in a macro sense in understanding prophetic promises and future gatherings. But it is perhaps more important in the micro sense, in that anything promised to anyone in any age is always available on the same principles to anyone willing to abide them at any time.[953] Do you really believe these teachings of our Lord? Then why not act on them?

I know these things are truly within the reach of almost all of you. The overwhelming majority of readers of this blog have lived better lives than I have You are almost all better qualified than I was. I believed these things, trusted the Lord, acted on His promises. As a result, I am among those who has been "gathered in" and I "know the Lord my God," having been "redeemed by Him." It is more than possible for you.

3 Nephi 20:14–15

"And the Father hath commanded me that I should give unto you this land, for your inheritance. And I say unto you, that if the Gentiles do not repent after the blessing which they shall receive, after they have scattered my people—"

Christ is speaking to a group of people and their descendants when making these remarks. The Father has commanded Christ to confirm to the Nephites they are given this land. "This land." So now the question of where Christ was while making these comments becomes important.

---

[953] D&C 130:20–21 "There is a law, irrevocably decreed in heaven before the foundations of this world, upon which all blessings are predicated—And when we obtain any blessing from God, it is by obedience to that law upon which it is predicated."

Where were they at the moment Christ spoke to them? That affects things, doesn't it? Was it Guatemala? Or the United States?

There are two ways of trying to determine the answer to this question. One would be to study the internal content of the Book of Mormon and try to reconstruct a location based on the clues there. This has been done with varying results. The two leading works on the two leading theories have been referred to in this post. There is another theory that the area was in the Gulf of Mexico. The land was completely reformed, broken up, and altered as a result of the upheavals of the 3 Nephi destruction, and the land no longer appears as it did once. It is now underwater. You can work and justify a number of locations based on the content of the Book of Mormon.

The other way is to take other sources that presumably knew, and accept what they said about the location. I've already quoted from both Moroni and Joseph Smith about the location. Both have placed the events in the area now known as the United States. Moroni's description of the Book of Mormon, and its people, was as follows:

"He said there was a book deposited, written upon gold plates, giving an account of the former inhabitants of this continent, and the source from whence they sprang." (JS–H 1:34.)

I presume Moroni knew, and that Joseph had no reason to misstate what he said. It would appear that the continent referred to by Christ using the words, "this land" was North America. And the promise from the Father, made by covenant, was with "the former inhabitants of this continent."

So the remnant was (at the moment Christ was speaking to this audience, and confirmed this covenant of the Father) located in North America. This does not mean they weren't mobile and subsequently moved about. This does not mean they did not disburse and occupy other portions of the North and South American land masses. This does not mean that other migrations of these people which scattered them elsewhere into the world have not occurred. Even if you confine everything to a North American venue for the entirety of the Book of Mormon account, there is still a gap between 400 a.d. when the narrative draws to a conclusion and the 1820's when the record comes to light again. Nothing closes that gap.

So if Moroni's comments to Joseph Smith can be trusted, then originally the people from whom the remnant came were people who lived on "this continent" at some time in history.

The gentiles are mentioned again here. They are reminded of the blessings they have received. They are reminded they were given the responsibility of scattering the remnant and disciplining them for the remnant's failings. But, once the gentiles are blessed, once they have scattered the remnant and destroyed most of them (leaving only a remnant of what was here before), then the gentiles are warned. They must repent. Without repentance the fate of the gentiles will be a similar holocaust of destruction, scattering and treading down; leaving only a remnant of the gentiles still upon the land.

So the roles will reverse. At first, the gentiles dominate and the remnant recedes, at last the remnant will dominate and the gentiles recede.

The remnant's role and the gentiles' pride are interconnected with one another. It is for this reason, if no other, the subject of the remnant is important to know something about.

So, we continue.

3 Nephi 20:16

> "Then shall ye, who are a remnant of the house of Jacob, go
> forth among them; and ye shall be in the midst of them who
> shall be many; and ye shall be among them as a lion among
> the beasts of the forest, and as a young lion among the flocks
> of sheep, who, if he goeth through both treadeth down and
> teareth in pieces, and none can deliver."

The descendants of Christ's audience remaining after the holocaust of gentile destruction (i.e., the "remnant of the house of Jacob") would be used by God to deliver judgment upon the gentiles.
First the descendants are to be reduced to a remnant by the gentiles,
but then the fortunes would be reversed. Initially the gentiles would
be the very embodiment of the "wrath of God" to "scatter" and
"smite" the descendants.[954] Following that, the gentiles are favored
of God and "prosper." This land becomes the temporary land of
inheritance for the gentiles, as well.[955]

But the gentiles would occupy the land on condition. They would
need to serve the God of the land, who is Jesus Christ.[956]

Ultimately, they will need to repent, or they will fill the measure of
their own cup of wrath by rejecting the fullness of the Gospel. The
gentiles would not continue in their humility, but would be offered
the fullness of the Gospel, reject it, then turn to their own pride,
even more proud of themselves than any comparable people upon

---

[954] 1 Nephi 13:14 "And it came to pass that I beheld many multitudes of the Gentiles
upon the land of promise; and I beheld the wrath of God, that it was upon the seed of
my brethren; and they were scattered before the Gentiles and were smitten."

[955] 1 Nephi 13:15 "And I beheld the Spirit of the Lord, that it was upon the Gentiles,
and they did prosper and obtain the land for their inheritance; and I beheld that they
were white, and exceedingly fair and beautiful, like unto my people before they were
slain."

[956] Ether 2:12 "Behold, this is a choice land, and whatsoever nation shall possess it shall
be free from bondage, and from captivity, and from all other nations under heaven, if
they will but serve the God of the land, who is Jesus Christ, who hath been manifested
by the things which we have written."

the earth. As Christ describes the latter-day gentiles, they will be full of mischief, lyings, deceits, hypocrisy and priestcrafts. Indeed, they will be full of all this and will also reject the fullness of the Gospel offered them by the Lord.[957]

When they do, Christ will "bring the fullness of my Gospel from among them."[958] Upon removing the fullness, and the gentiles being filled with their pride, priestcrafts, deceits and hypocrisy, the Lord will use the remnant who remain to return judgment upon the gentiles in the same manner the gentiles had earlier returned judgment upon the remnant.[959]

As Christ states above, using the words of Isaiah, "a remnant of the house of Jacob" will "go forth among them; and ye shall be in the midst of them who shall be many; and ye shall be among them as a lion among the beasts of the forest, and as a young lion among the flocks of sheep, who, if he goeth through both treadeth down and teareth in pieces, and none can deliver."

We've discussed the "beasts of the forest" and the "flocks of sheep" before. Both categories of gentiles will be swept away. None can deliver them from this coming judgment. The remnant will be the Lord's instrument of judgment upon the gentiles, and the gentile pride, priestcrafts, lyings, deceits will all come crashing down upon

---

[957] 3 Nephi 16:10 "And thus commandeth the Father that I should say unto you: At that day when the Gentiles shall sin against my gospel, and shall reject the fulness of my gospel, and shall be lifted up in the pride of their hearts above all nations, and above all the people of the whole earth, and shall be filled with all manner of lyings, and of deceits, and of mischiefs, and all manner of hypocrisy, and murders, and priestcrafts, and whoredoms, and of secret abominations; and if they shall do all those things, and shall reject the fulness of my gospel, behold, saith the Father, I will bring the fulness of my gospel from among them."

[958] Ibid.

[959] 3 Nephi 16:15 "But if they will not turn unto me, and hearken unto my voice, I will suffer them, yea, I will suffer my people, O house of Israel, that they shall go through among them, and shall tread them down, and they shall be as salt that hath lost its savor, which is thenceforth good for nothing but to be cast out, and to be trodden under foot of my people, O house of Israel."

them in judgment. Their idols will be trodden down and torn in pieces, for they are their own idols imagining in their own hearts themselves to be greater than any other people. Their image of themselves as high and lifted up will be brought down low, into the dust.[960] How like their master Mahon these gentiles have become. But then rejecting the fullness of the Gospel when it has been offered to a people always carries a heavy price.

The remnant will be doing the work of the Father in that day. For the judgment is the Lord's and not the remnant's. The remnant are only the means by which the judgment is delivered.

Cleansing precedes the blessing. And this blessed land will be Zion. But not while occupied by filthy people who idolize themselves, reject the fullness, support priestcrafts, lyings, deceit and hypocrisy calling it righteousness, truth and beauty. They cannot see their own condition, and will not trust the Lord to reveal it to them. They will say the Lord does not speak any more, and we have enough of the revelations of God.[961] They will say God has finished

---

[960] Compare Isaiah 14:12–17 "How art thou fallen from heaven, O Lucifer, son of the morning! *how* art thou cut down to the ground, which didst weaken the nations! For thou hast said in thine heart, I will ascend into heaven, I will exalt my throne above the stars of God: I will sit also upon the mount of the congregation, in the sides of the north: I will ascend above the heights of the clouds; I will be like the most High. Yet thou shalt be brought down to hell, to the sides of the pit. They that see thee shall narrowly look upon thee, *and* consider thee, *saying, Is* this the man that made the earth to tremble, that did shake kingdoms; *That* made the world as a wilderness, and destroyed the cities thereof; *that* opened not the house of his prisoners?"

[961] 2 Nephi 28:27–29 "Yea, wo be unto him that saith: We have received, and we need no more! And in fine, wo unto all those who tremble, and are angry because of the truth of God! For behold, he that is built upon the rock receiveth it with gladness; and he that is built upon a sandy foundation trembleth lest he shall fall. Wo be unto him that shall say: We have received the word of God, and we need no more of the word of God, for we have enough!"

His work of restoring truth, given His power to men, and now we must follow men to be saved.[962]

But the Lord will prove that He had more to say when the gentiles learn, too late, they trusted in the arm of flesh rather than in the Spirit which saves.[963] At that day, despite all the gentile petitions for relief from that God whose fullness they rejected, none will deliver.

The interplay between the gentiles and the remnant is a fascinating subject, with prophetic details given so as to allow us to appreciate the peril we find ourselves as gentiles in these last days. It is good we Latter-day Saints know we are safe and are part of a great, saved and favored community to be preserved against the coming judgments, isn't it? It is good we do not need to repent much if at all to be saved, because as we hear so very often: All is well. All is well.

"And he said, Go, and tell this people, Hear ye indeed, but understand not; and see ye indeed, but perceive not. Make the heart of this people fat, and make their ears heavy, and shut their eyes; lest they see with their eyes, and hear with their ears, and understand with their heart, and convert, and be healed."[964]

This is not about psychology. In fact using the tools of psychology to understand the invitation to come to Christ won't help.

Repentance is love. It is coming to Him. But coming to Him by learning of Him. It is not fear; though approaching God is indeed fearful. That fear in the approach arises from your own inner worthiness

---

[962] 2 Nephi 28:5 "And they deny the power of God, the Holy One of Israel; and they say unto the people: Hearken unto us, and hear ye our precept; for behold there is no God today, for the Lord and the Redeemer hath done his work, and he hath given his power unto men;"

[963] 2 Nephi 28:31 "Cursed is he that putteth his trust in man, or maketh flesh his arm, or shall hearken unto the precepts of men, save their precepts shall be given by the power of the Holy Ghost."

[964] Isaiah 6:9–10 "And he said, Go, and tell this people, Hear ye indeed, but understand not; and see ye indeed, but perceive not. Make the heart of this people fat, and make their ears heavy, and shut their eyes; lest they see with their eyes, and hear with their ears, and understand with their heart, and convert, and be healed."

before Him. It is unavoidable because none of us are worthy apart from Him. Therefore the dread of being before God will remain until He removes it by an act of His mercy.

The Lord and His prophets teach plainly what we all understood and all agreed upon before the world was begun. The plan we have is tried, true, and is the path by which all those who have ever ascended to heaven have made that ascent.

Focusing upon whether one's motivation is based upon fear or love is unhelpful. Focusing upon what the Lord says, and then what is meant by what the Lord says, is helpful. The inner man must change. The change is mandatory, and comes from knowing Him and learning of Him. But until the moment of relief is granted by Him, there will always be discomfort because of our fallen state and tendency to sin. This is why He is a "Comforter"—because He removes from us the discomfort we feel from sin. But we surely do feel (ALL of us feel) dread and fear because of what we lack as we approach the throne of grace. He "Comforts" us by freeing us from that terrible burden. But such freedom comes on His terms, based upon the eternal plan for removing sin, or it does not happen at all.

3 Nephi 20:17–19

"Thy hand shall be lifted up upon thine adversaries, and all thine enemies shall be cut off. And I will gather my people together as a man gathereth his sheaves into the floor. For I will make my people with whom the Father hath covenanted, yea, I will make thy horn iron, and I will make thy hoofs brass. And thou shalt beat in pieces many people; and I will consecrate their gain unto the Lord, and their substance unto the Lord of the whole earth. And behold, I am he who doeth it."

The remnant will be the instruments of Divine retribution against the gentiles. It will be the remnant's "hand" which "shall be lifted up upon thine adversaries." And it will be "all [the remnant's] enemies [which] shall be cut off." So, who will be the remnant's "adversaries?" Who will be their "enemies?"

The Lord promises to "gather my people together"——and the only ones He has called His people are the Nephite audience, never the gentiles.[965] The Lord's people to be gathered, the promised inheritors of the land, the chosen and covenant people are the remnant. This prophecy is about them. The gentiles are only included to the extent that a few of them will repent.[966]

The "sheaves into the floor" is a harvest image. It is an end-of-times view, because it involves harvest time. "Gathering the sheaves into the floor" is a reference to latter-day Zion, where a group is first "gathered" before the burning of the fields that always follows.

---

[965] 3 Nephi 16:8–9 "But wo, saith the Father, unto the unbelieving of the Gentiles—for notwithstanding they have come forth upon the face of this land, and have scattered my people who are of the house of Israel; and my people who are of the house of Israel have been cast out from among them, and have been trodden under feet by them; And because of the mercies of the Father unto the Gentiles, and also the judgments of the Father upon my people who are of the house of Israel, verily, verily, I say unto you, that after all this, and I have caused my people who are of the house of Israel to be smitten, and to be afflicted, and to be slain, and to be cast out from among them, and to become hated by them, and to become a hiss and a byword among them—"

3 Nephi 20:15, 27 "And I say unto you, that if the Gentiles do not repent after the blessing which they shall receive, after they have scattered my people— . . . And after that ye were blessed then fulfilleth the Father the covenant which he made with Abraham, saying: In thy seed shall all the kindreds of the earth be blessed—unto the pouring out of the Holy Ghost through me upon the Gentiles, which blessing upon the Gentiles shall make them mighty above all, unto the scattering of my people, O house of Israel."

3 Nephi 21:2 "And behold, this is the thing which I will give unto you for a sign—for verily I say unto you that when these things which I declare unto you, and which I shall declare unto you hereafter of myself, and by the power of the Holy Ghost which shall be given unto you of the Father, shall be made known unto the Gentiles that they may know concerning this people who are a remnant of the house of Jacob, and concerning this my people who shall be scattered by them;"

[966] 3 Nephi 16:13 "But if the Gentiles will repent and return unto me, saith the Father, behold they shall be numbered among my people, O house of Israel."

3 Nephi 21:6 "For thus it behooveth the Father that it should come forth from the Gentiles, that he may show forth his power unto the Gentiles, for this cause that the Gentiles, if they will not harden their hearts, that they may repent and come unto me and be baptized in my name and know of the true points of my doctrine, that they may be numbered among my people, O house of Israel;"

Again the Lord calls the remnant "my people" while clarifying that His people are those "with whom the Father hath covenanted." To covenant with the Father is to receive a Father. The Father does not covenant with strangers. His covenants are with His household. So this is the Family of God.

The "iron horn" and the "brass hoofs" are also symbolic images. What does a "horn" represent? In the context of judgment, does the "horn" hold additional meaning? Why is the horn said to be "iron?" What do the hoofs represent? In the context of judgment do the "hoofs" have additional meaning? Why are they "brass?" How stern and unrelenting will the judgment be? How complete will it become for the "people" to be "beat in pieces?" How terrible will the pouring out of judgment become?

Why would judgment be so severe upon a people who claim to be godly? Think about the introduction to Joseph Smith at the time the restoration of all things was offered.[967] Compare that to the statement made by the mortal Christ when the Pharisees were confronting Him about violating the rituals and practices of the religious hierarchy at the time.[968] Christ offered them the fullness of His Gospel and they rejected it. The judgment which followed was unlike anything that went before. Christ warned them it would be so.[969]

---

[967] JS–H 1:19 "I was answered that I must join none of them, for they were all wrong; and the Personage who addressed me said that all their creeds were an abomination in his sight; that those professors were all corrupt; that: 'they draw near to me with their lips, but their hearts are far from me, they teach for doctrines the commandments of men, having a form of godliness, but they deny the power thereof'."

[968] Mark 7:5–9 "Then the Pharisees and scribes asked him, Why walk not thy disciples according to the tradition of the elders, but eat bread with unwashen hands? He answered and said unto them, Well hath Esaias prophesied of you hypocrites, as it is written, This people honoureth me with *their* lips, but their heart is far from me. Howbeit in vain do they worship me, teaching *for* doctrines the commandments of men. For laying aside the commandment of God, ye hold the tradition of men, *as* the washing of pots and cups: and many other such like things ye do. And he said unto them, Full well ye reject the commandment of God, that ye may keep your own tradition."

[969] Matthew 24:21 "For then shall be great tribulation, such as was not since the beginning of the world to this time, no, nor ever shall be."

Nevertheless, they refused to accept the fullness offered them, continued on in their religious traditions, and were besieged by Roman legions and slain en masse. The account from Josephus is difficult and shocking to read. Mothers cannibalizing their infants to satiate their hunger pains. It is as if hell itself opened upon Jerusalem.

Rejection of the fullness of Christ's Gospel carries terrible consequences. We have seen it before. And, when it was rejected before, it was done in preference to traditions from men. The arm of flesh and a religion multiplied the commandments of men until every aspect of life was controlled by religion. How one dressed, what they ate, how they observed the Sabbath, what things were considered clean and unclean, how to appear in public in order to conform to the right look, vocabulary and conduct. These were very religious people. I've discussed them in *Come, Let Us Adore Him*. I assume you're familiar with that.

Thank goodness we are not like them. We have the fullness, don't we? We are safe and in the right path and none can molest us or make us afraid. For we are the chosen people.

Well those other people (not us) who rejected the fullness of the Gospel, those are the ones who will be broken into pieces. Then their "gain" and their "substance" will be consecrated to the Lord. So they will live the law of consecration after all! Only it will be postmortem. That is, once killed, the Lord can use their gain and substance to provide for His people.

Lest any forget the author and finisher of our faith, He speaks to us anew to remind us who is responsible for these deeds: "And behold, I am he who doeth it."

The Lord is, after all, the same yesterday, today and tomorrow. When He invites us in meekness to come to Him, we should realize that failure to come risks the judgments that have always been terrible to bear. Those Old Testament events we have a difficult time associating with Christ will become associated with Christ again. Just as His New Testament judgments were His and terrible to behold. He is the same. We should expect that when the time ends and we have not met our appointment, we actually do risk rejection and judgment.

3 Nephi 20:20

"And it shall come to pass, saith the Father, that the sword of my justice shall hang over them at that day; and except they repent it shall fall upon them, saith the Father, yea, even upon all the nations of the Gentiles."

Again the reminder is made to the gentiles. We who are associated with the gentiles[970] are numbered among "all the nations of the gentiles."

So this is Divine judgment, aimed at the gentiles who were offered, and then rejected the fullness of His Gospel. These are those who will be receiving the "sword of [His] justice." Even now, the "sword of [His] justice . . . hangs over us." For we are "at that day" now. So the sword "shall fall upon them, saith the Father" unless we "repent."

How does one repent when they have rejected the fullness? Would it have been easier to have accepted it when first offered? When did we neglect receiving it? If taken, how was it taken? How do we obtain it anew?

These seem to be important issues. They seem to involve the very subject of life and death, both mortally and eternally. Why, if so important, do we go about telling one another "odds are you're going to be exalted" when such alarms as these exist in Christ's own words

---

[970] D&C 109:60 "Now these words, O Lord, we have spoken before thee, concerning the revelations and commandments which thou hast given unto us, who are identified with the Gentiles."

in the Book of Mormon? What foolishness have we been given in place of the "plain words" of truth which Nephi and Christ Himself taught?

Do we get angry at the truth like Laman and Lemuel?[971] Do we take the truth to be a hard thing? Why do we get angry at the truth? Do we accept truth and welcome it, or think it is a terrible thing when we hear it?[972] Do those who are offended at the truth really have the spirit of the devil?[973]

The key for gentile survival is repentance. Time and time again the words "repent" or "repentance" are used to let the gentiles know there is an escape. But that escape does not come from receiving a hollow form of godliness without any power.[974] What is "priesthood" if there is no power in it?

Well the Book of Mormon continues to invite listening gentiles to repent. Over the heads of all responsible for failure, the Book of Mormon preaches repentance and truth. It preaches against priestcraft which teaches gentiles to worship man and rely upon the arm of flesh, the Book of Mormon invites gentiles to come and receive pure religion and knowledge of their Redeemer.

---

[971] 2 Nephi 1:26 "And ye have murmured because he hath been plain unto you. Ye say that he hath used sharpness; ye say that he hath been angry with you; but behold, his sharpness was the sharpness of the power of the word of God, which was in him; and that which ye call anger was the truth, according to that which is in God, which he could not restrain, manifesting boldly concerning your iniquities."

[972] 2 Nephi 28:28 "And in fine, wo unto all those who tremble, and are angry because of the truth of God! For behold, he that is built upon the rock receiveth it with gladness; and he that is built upon a sandy foundation trembleth lest he shall fall."

[973] 2 Nephi 33:5 "And it speaketh harshly against sin, according to the plainness of the truth; wherefore, no man will be angry at the words which I have written save he shall be of the spirit of the devil."

[974] JS–H 1:19 "I was answered that I must join none of them, for they were all wrong; and the Personage who addressed me said that all their creeds were an abomination in his sight; that those professors were all corrupt; that: 'they draw near to me with their lips, but their hearts are far from me, they teach for doctrines the commandments of men, having a form of godliness, but they deny the power thereof'."

The Book of Mormon is the cornerstone of our religion; the cornerstone of the religion of Jesus Christ. It is the most correct book. A man can get closer to God by abiding its precepts than any other book. We have had it warning and inviting us for 180 years and we still have not actually either learned its precepts nor begun to abide by them.

The times of the gentiles are drawing to a close. If there is to be any significant gentile repentance, it must happen soon or the sword of the Lord's justice, which hangs over us, will surely fall on us.

So this topic of remnant destiny and gentile destiny are intertwined. It is little wonder why Joseph found reason to send the first missionaries to find them; and sought to flee to the Rocky Mountains himself to find them the last week of his life. Our current proximity does not matter, however, if our hearts are far from the Lord's invitation to repent.

3 Nephi 20:21–22

"And it shall come to pass that I will establish my people, O house of Israel. And behold, this people will I establish in this land, unto the fulfilling of the covenant which I made with your father Jacob; and it shall be a New Jerusalem. And the powers of heaven shall be in the midst of this people; yea, even I will be in the midst of you."

The Lord will establish His people, including all of the "house of Israel." The plan is global. But when it comes to the Americas, His people are those in the audience at the moment He was speaking to "this people." And the land of promise for them is "this land." Meaning that wherever it was that Christ was speaking involved two things: The ancestors of the remnant, and the land of promise.

Now the statement gets interesting because Christ refers to a covenant He made personally with "your father Jacob." Which "Jacob" is this referring to? And, if the Old Testament father whose name was changed to Israel, then why refer to him by his earlier name ("Jacob") rather than by his new name ("Israel")? I've described the reasons for distinguishing between these two names for a single man in *Nephi's Isaiah*. It is relevant here and I'd remind you of that discussion.

In Jacob's final blessing to his sons, he blessed Joseph as one "separate from his brethren" to inherit a land "unto the utmost bound of the everlasting hills."[975] The covenant between Christ and Jacob affected this blessing given Joseph. It is in the "utmost bound of the everlasting hills" that Zion or the New Jerusalem is to be built. And it will be Jacob's posterity, the remnant visited by Christ, who will build it. Christ's visit to these people reaffirms the prior covenant, and reconfirms the Lord's intent to fulfill His covenant with Jacob. It is for Jacob's sake this is done. Covenants between the Lord and His sons are always fulfilled; for the Lord takes His word very seriously. His word cannot be broken.[976] But, as I have explained in *Beloved Enos*, these are the words of His covenants. It is not merely vain words spoken using His name as authority by those whom He did not authorize to speak such words.[977]

Since the statement involves global gathering of all the "house of Israel," it would appear this reference to "Jacob" is a reference to the global, overall covenant for the entire collection of remnants (plural)

---

[975] Genesis 49:26 "The blessings of thy father have prevailed above the blessings of my progenitors unto the utmost bound of the everlasting hills: they shall be on the head of Joseph, and on the crown of the head of him that was separate from his brethren."

[976] D&C 1:38 "What I the Lord have spoken, I have spoken, and I excuse not myself; and though the heavens and the earth pass away, my word shall not pass away, but shall all be fulfilled, whether by mine own voice or by the voice of my servants, it is the same."

[977] Matthew 7:22–23 "Many will say to me in that day, Lord, Lord, have we not prophesied in thy name? and in thy name have cast out devils? and in thy name done many wonderful works? And then will I profess unto them, I never knew you: depart from me, ye that work iniquity."

throughout the world, wherever they are scattered. However, the crowning portion of the covenant, the capstone which Jacob was given for his posterity in his covenant, was the promise of the New Jerusalem. When that New Jerusalem has come again, it will be "unto the fulfilling of the covenant which [Christ] made with your father Jacob."

Implicit in the return of a New Jerusalem is the redemption of a worthy assembly of Jacob's posterity. It is the culmination of history. It is the final redemption of a people among whom the Lord may take up His residency.

This New Jerusalem will involve "the powers of heaven" being "in the midst of this people." Also, the Lord "will be in the midst of you." For the Lord to take up His residence with people requires them to be saved, clean every whit, and to receive at last the "fullness of the Gospel of Jesus Christ." These are not pretenders who claim, but do not do. Even penitent harlots and publicans are preferred to the self-righteous who claim to be something they are not.[978]

Why are "the powers of heaven" mentioned first? Must the "powers of heaven" precede the Lord's presence? Is that why they are mentioned by the Lord first, and His dwelling among them is mentioned second? What does that suggest about the manner in which we proceed into the presence of the Lord? How do we experience the "powers of heaven?" What is that power? Is a "form of

---

[978] Matthew 21:28–32 "But what think ye? A *certain* man had two sons; and he came to the first, and said, Son, go work to day in my vineyard. He answered and said, I will not: but afterward he repented, and went. And he came to the second, and said likewise. And he answered and said, I *go*, sir: and went not. Whether of them twain did the will of *his* father? They say unto him, The first. Jesus saith unto them, Verily I say unto you, That the publicans and the harlots go into the kingdom of God before you. For John came unto you in the way of righteousness, and ye believed him not: but the publicans and the harlots believed him: and ye, when ye had seen *it*, repented not afterward, that ye might believe him."

godliness without any power" a sufficient substitute for the "powers of heaven?"[979]

Do the "powers of heaven" invariably precede and in turn lead to the Lord's presence? Why?

Reading these words you begin to see how our Lord is consistent and determined. His covenants matter. For the sake of those who have obtained a covenant with Him, He will always deliver what He promises. For those who break their covenants with Him, there is no promise. He has always been the same.[980]

Read again the words of condemnation given against us, which remain in effect still today:

> And the whole world lieth in sin, and groaneth under darkness and under the bondage of sin. And by this you may know they are under the bondage of sin, because they come not unto me. For whoso cometh not unto me is under the bondage of sin.

> And whoso receiveth not my voice is not acquainted with my voice, and is not of me. And by this you may know the righteous from the wicked, and that the whole world groaneth under sin and darkness even now.

> And your minds in times past have been darkened because of unbelief, and because you have treated lightly the things you

---

[979] JS–H 1:19 "I was answered that I must join none of them, for they were all wrong; and the Personage who addressed me said that all their creeds were an abomination in his sight; that those professors were all corrupt; that: 'they draw near to me with their lips, but their hearts are far from me, they teach for doctrines the commandments of men, having a form of godliness, but they deny the power thereof'."

[980] Leviticus 26:15–17 "And if ye shall despise my statutes, or if your soul abhor my judgments, so that ye will not do all my commandments, *but* that ye break my covenant: I also will do this unto you; I will even appoint over you terror, consumption, and the burning ague, that shall consume the eyes, and cause sorrow of heart: and ye shall sow your seed in vain, for your enemies shall eat it. And I will set my face against you, and ye shall be slain before your enemies: they that hate you shall reign over you; and ye shall flee when none pursueth you."

have received— Which vanity and unbelief have brought the whole church under condemnation. And this condemnation resteth upon the children of Zion, even all.

And they shall remain under this condemnation until they repent and remember the new covenant, even the Book of Mormon and the former commandments which I have given them, not only to say, but to do according to that which I have written— That they may bring forth fruit meet for their Father's kingdom; otherwise there remaineth a scourge and judgment to be poured out upon the children of Zion. (D&C 84:49–58.)

It is not that we haven't been warned. It is that we just will not allow the warnings to inform us. We prefer to pretend rather than to do. We certainly have a form of godliness, but we lament even in General Conference about the lack of power in that form.

3 Nephi 20:23

"Behold, I am he of whom Moses spake, saying: A prophet shall the Lord your God raise up unto you of your brethren, like unto me; him shall ye hear in all things whatsoever he shall say unto you. And it shall come to pass that every soul who will not hear that prophet shall be cut off from among the people."

If there were any doubt about who was meant in Deuteronomy 18:15–19[981], Christ clarifies it here. He, Christ, was always meant to

---

[981] Deuteronomy 18:15–19 "The Lord thy God will raise up unto thee a Prophet from the midst of thee, of thy brethren, like unto me; unto him ye shall hearken; According to all that thou desiredst of the Lord thy God in Horeb in the day of the assembly, saying, Let me not hear again the voice of the Lord my God, neither let me see this great fire any more, that I die not. And the Lord said unto me, They have well *spoken that* which they have spoken. I will raise them up a Prophet from among their brethren, like unto thee, and will put my words in his mouth; and he shall speak unto them all that I shall command him. And it shall come to pass, *that* whosoever will not hearken unto my words which he shall speak in my name, I will require *it* of him."

be the ultimate Law-Giver. He is the one who must be followed. He may send prophets, but it is Christ alone who is to be followed. Those who draw attention away from Him and turn attention to themselves will always lead astray. For the Lord alone can save. No man can.

We've been trying to make the matter clear for some time. Not merely in this blog, but by my writing and your reading the six books I've written before beginning this effort. The Lord alone is the one to whom each of us must look for hope and salvation. He is the one with whom you can covenant to receive salvation.

In the middle of this prophecy of remnant return and gentile holocaust, comes the reminder again of the Lord's primacy. Look to Him. Him alone. He is the one raised up to save mankind. He is the gentile hope.

The judgments the gentiles have merited by their refusal to accept the fullness of Christ's Gospel is not an impediment to you, if you will come to Him. It was always meant to be a singular event anyway. There is no collective salvation. Each person comes to Him one at a time. Even when He redeems a group, He visits with them individually.[982]

Those who will not "hear Him" will be "cut off from among the people." What does it mean to "hear Him?" How do you go about accomplishing that?

---

[982] 3 Nephi 11:13–17 "And it came to pass that the Lord spake unto them saying: Arise and come forth unto me, that ye may thrust your hands into my side, and also that ye may feel the prints of the nails in my hands and in my feet, that ye may know that I am the God of Israel, and the God of the whole earth, and have been slain for the sins of the world. And it came to pass that the multitude went forth, and thrust their hands into his side, and did feel the prints of the nails in his hands and in his feet; and this they did do, going forth one by one until they had all gone forth, and did see with their eyes and did feel with their hands, and did know of a surety and did bear record, that it was he, of whom it was written by the prophets, that should come. And when they had all gone forth and had witnessed for themselves, they did cry out with one accord, saying: Hosanna! Blessed be the name of the Most High God! And they did fall down at the feet of Jesus, and did worship him."

What does it mean to be "cut off from among the people?" What "people?" Why is being cut off from those people a curse? Where are you sent if you are not among the Lord's people? How do you go about rectifying that—joining in to be among those who "hear Him" and are part of His people?

Can you do it now? Do you have to wait till some distant future time or place? Why aren't you doing more about it now, then?

3 Nephi 20:24

> "Verily I say unto you, yea, and all the prophets from Samuel and those that follow after, as many as have spoken, have testified of me."

The Lord chose and established Israel. He would remain committed to them, although they went whoring after other gods.

Moses held the fullness of the priesthood. He conferred blessings upon others. Although Moses was taken from Israel, the blessings of the priesthood remained. Moses blessed Joshua, and Joshua held the blessings of the priesthood for so long as he lived. But the fullness of the priesthood, that portion which permitted a man to see God face to face, was taken with Moses.[983]

When Joshua died, both the priesthood that left with Moses, and the blessings from that priesthood were lost. What remained thereafter was a lesser form of priesthood called the Levitical or Aaronic

---

[983] D&C 84:20–25 "Therefore, in the ordinances thereof, the power of godliness is manifest. And without the ordinances thereof, and the authority of the priesthood, the power of godliness is not manifest unto men in the flesh; For without this no man can see the face of God, even the Father, and live. Now this Moses plainly taught to the children of Israel in the wilderness, and sought diligently to sanctify his people that they might behold the face of God; But they hardened their hearts and could not endure his presence; therefore, the Lord in his wrath, for his anger was kindled against them, swore that they should not enter into his rest while in the wilderness, which rest is the fulness of his glory. Therefore, he took Moses out of their midst, and the Holy Priesthood also;"

Priesthood. This continued to be ministered from Moses until Jesus Christ.

The prophets, however, were something different. They came through diverse families and from unexpected places. They were not part of the leading Levitical families and not even from that tribe on occasion. Their priesthood was not reckoned by what was then on the earth, but was given to them directly from heaven itself. Joseph Smith taught:

"All priesthood is Melchizedek, but there are different portions or degrees of it. That portion which brought Moses to speak with God face to face was taken away; but that which brought the ministry of angels remained. All the prophets had the Melchizedek Priesthood and were ordained by God himself" (*TPJS*, 180–81).

The men who held the higher form of priesthood, the fullness that made it possible for them to behold God face to face, were "all the prophets from Samuel and those that followed after." Having this form of priesthood they could behold God face to face and live.[984]

The power to see God face to face is not real if the man does not actually behold God face to face. It is powerless. It is theory. It is a notion and not a reality. This priesthood the revelation speaks about is not a theoretical idea, but an actual, real power which allows the person holding it to behold God and live. Therefore, when Christ states that "all the prophets from Samuel and those that followed after" had "testified of [Christ]" this is more than rhetoric. They became prophets by reason of the Lord having appeared and spoken to them; having testified of Himself to them. Therefore their status as prophets and their witness of Him were coequal. They sprang

---

[984] D&C 84:22–23 "For without this no man can see the face of God, even the Father, and live. Now this Moses plainly taught to the children of Israel in the wilderness, and sought diligently to sanctify his people that they might behold the face of God;"

from the very same thing—the same event. This, then, formed the basis for their service as the Lord's prophets. They knew Him. They could testify of what they knew, heard and saw, rather than what they believed to be true from what others had said. God had made Himself known to them.

Christ was confirming that these prophets had testified of Him because He was the one who had called them. He was the one who qualified them. He was the one whose witness and message they bore to others. The testimony of Jesus is the spirit of prophecy![985] Here He confirms again that those prophets sent by Him have testified they know Him. They do not testify of themselves, but of Him. They do not point to themselves, but they point to Him. They do not promise salvation through themselves, but invite others to come to Christ and be saved. They will understate rather than overstate their calling and standing before God.

3 Nephi 20:25–27

"And behold, ye are the children of the prophets; and ye are of the house of Israel; and ye are of the covenant which the Father made with your fathers, saying unto Abraham: And in thy seed shall all the kindreds of the earth be blessed. The Father having raised me up unto you first, and sent me to bless you in turning away every one of you from his iniquities; and this because ye are the children of the covenant—And after that ye were blessed then fulfilleth the Father the covenant which he made with Abraham, saying: In thy seed shall all the kindreds of the earth be blessed—unto the pouring out of the Holy Ghost through me upon the Gentiles, which blessing upon the Gentiles shall make them mighty above all, unto the scattering of my people, O house of Israel."

---

[985] Revelation 19:10 "And I fell at his feet to worship him. And he said unto me, See *thou do it* not: I am thy fellowservant, and of thy brethren that have the testimony of Jesus: worship God: for the testimony of Jesus is the spirit of prophecy."

These verses connect a single doctrine. That doctrine is at the heart of "turning of the hearts of the children to the fathers," which is the result of any restoration of the Gospel. The definition of "children of the prophets" is that one has accepted, believed, and followed the Lord's true messengers. They become children of Abraham and receive priestly authority sealing them into the family of God, joining the "fathers." From the time of Abraham until today, all who are redeemed have become a part of his household.

The phrase "turning the hearts of the children to the fathers" is a reference to the restoration of sealing authority, allowing a connection between man living on the earth, and the fathers (Abraham, Isaac and Jacob). In this dispensation, that restoration occurred when Joseph Smith was given the sealing authority and priesthood whereby he could ask and receive answers.[986] As discussed earlier, this was sometime between 1829 and 1833, though I think it was more likely the earlier date as I have explained. Coincident with receiving this authority, Joseph's calling and election was made sure.[987] I have explained this in *Beloved Enos*. This priesthood, having the hearts of the recipients turned to the fathers, and the promise of exaltation, are interconnected.

Abraham not only held this authority, but received the promise that all who received the Gospel after him would become his descendants. From the time of Abraham to the present, every saved

---

[986] D&C 132:45–47 "For I have conferred upon you the keys and power of the priesthood, wherein I restore all things, and make known unto you all things in due time. And verily, verily, I say unto you, that whatsoever you seal on earth shall be sealed in heaven; and whatsoever you bind on earth, in my name and by my word, saith the Lord, it shall be eternally bound in the heavens; and whosoever sins you remit on earth shall be remitted eternally in the heavens; and whosoever sins you retain on earth shall be retained in heaven. And again, verily I say, whomsoever you bless I will bless, and whomsoever you curse I will curse, saith the Lord; for I, the Lord, am thy God."

[987] D&C 132:49 "For I am the Lord thy God, and will be with thee even unto the end of the world, and through all eternity; for verily I seal upon you your exaltation, and prepare a throne for you in the kingdom of my Father, with Abraham your father."

soul has had their heart turned to him, become his son or daughter, and received that same priesthood.[988] When Joseph received this, he was not merely sealed up to eternal life, but he became part of the family of Abraham. If you remember the diagram of the celestial kingdom referred to earlier on this blog, you know Joseph became one of those who was grafted into the family tree, and would then in turn preside over others who were sealed up to eternal life thereafter.

The sealing authority used by Joseph in December, 1832, was to seal others up to eternal life.[989] This promise had been previously conferred upon Joseph in that portion of Section 132 referred to above. In fact, Joseph's use of that authority in December 1832 on behalf of others is evidence that the promise to him recorded in Section 132 was necessarily received earlier than December 1832. If it had not been received earlier, there would have been no need to make the statement in D&C 132:49 to Joseph, because of what is in Section 88. Why tell Joseph his calling and election was sure in 1843 if it had happened already in 1832? This is another reason you can know Section 132, although recorded in 1843, was in fact a revelation received by Joseph much earlier. It was reduced to writing in 1843 at Hyrum's request.

---

[988] Abraham 2:10–11 "And I will bless them through thy name; for as many as receive this Gospel shall be called after thy name, and shall be accounted thy seed, and shall rise up and bless thee, as their father; And I will bless them that bless thee, and curse them that curse thee; and in thee (that is, in thy Priesthood) and in thy seed (that is, thy Priesthood), for I give unto thee a promise that this right shall continue in thee, and in thy seed after thee (that is to say, the literal seed, or the seed of the body) shall all the families of the earth be blessed, even with the blessings of the Gospel, which are the blessings of salvation, even of life eternal."

[989] D&C 88:2–4 "Behold, this is pleasing unto your Lord, and the angels rejoice over you; the alms of your prayers have come up into the ears of the Lord of Sabaoth, and are recorded in the book of the names of the sanctified, even them of the celestial world. Wherefore, I now send upon you another Comforter, even upon you my friends, that it may abide in your hearts, even the Holy Spirit of promise; which other Comforter is the same that I promised unto my disciples, as is recorded in the testimony of John. This Comforter is the promise which I give unto you of eternal life, even the glory of the celestial kingdom;"

The reference to "turning the hearts of the fathers to the children" made by Elijah was not because Elijah conferred those keys upon Joseph in the Kirtland Temple[990], for they arrived years earlier than 1836. Elijah was confirming that the keys were now all returned so the hearts of the children could turn to the fathers, and in turn the father's hearts to the children.[991] And, so as to signify he was a true messenger, Elijah also showed a sign by his hand to Joseph whereby Joseph could recognize a true messenger.[992]

In Christ's statement to the Nephite audience, He confirmed that they were "the children of the prophets" because they followed the prophets' teachings. Therefore, because of their obedience they were "of the house of Israel" and had realized that status because "of the covenant which the Father made with your fathers." That covenant was given "unto Abraham" promising to Abraham: "And in thy seed shall all the kindreds of the earth be blessed." All those after the day of Abraham who received this priesthood and sealing would become the seed of Abraham. They become heirs of the promise, and children of Abraham. They are sealed up to eternal life and therefore their hearts have turned to the fathers.

Christ was sent to these Nephites because "The Father having raised me up unto you first, and sent me to bless you in turning away every one of you from his iniquities; and this because ye are the children of the covenant." Realizing the promises, and being visited by the Lord are also connected. When enough are ready to enter into

---

[990] D&C 110:16 "Therefore, the keys of this dispensation are committed into your hands; and by this ye may know that the great and dreadful day of the Lord is near, even at the doors."

[991] D&C 110:15 "To turn the hearts of the fathers to the children, and the children to the fathers, lest the whole earth be smitten with a curse—"

[992] D&C 2:1 "Behold, I will reveal unto you the Priesthood, by the hand of Elijah the prophet, before the coming of the great and dreadful day of the Lord."

this order, have their hearts turned to the fathers, receive the covenant, then the Lord will bring again Zion.

3 Nephi 20:27–28

". . . unto the pouring out of the Holy Ghost through me upon the Gentiles, which blessing upon the Gentiles shall make them mighty above all, unto the scattering of my people, O house of Israel. And they shall be a scourge unto the people of this land. Nevertheless, when they shall have received the fullness of my gospel, then if they shall harden their hearts against me I will return their iniquities upon their own heads, saith the Father."

The reason the gentiles received access to the Holy Ghost was to fulfill the purposes of the Father. The remnant would reject the Gospel, and as a result merit judgment. Judgment would come through the gentiles. For that to occur, the Holy Ghost needed to inspire gentile successes.

The Spirit would be responsible for such great gentile success that they will be made "mighty above all, unto the scattering of my people." That is, no other people will be able to prevail against the gentiles of North America while the Holy Ghost was with the gentiles. They will be a "scourge" upon the remnant as a result of the Father's judgments implemented by Christ, using the Holy Ghost.

The Spirit will entitle the gentiles to be offered the fullness. They will qualify by their acts and obedience. When you receive light and stay true to it, you are offered more light. The gentiles will accept and pursue more light, and will merit an opportunity to receive the fullness of the Gospel.

Gentiles did have the fullness of the Gospel, which requires the fullness of the priesthood that was offered while Joseph Smith was here. It was given sometime between 1829 and 1832, and removed before 1841.[993]

When the gentiles were offered the fullness, they displayed little interest in it. Joseph remarked:

> "I have tried for a number of years to get the minds of the Saints prepared to receive the things of God; but we frequently see some of them, after suffering all they have for the work of God, will fly to pieces like glass as soon as anything comes that is contrary to their traditions: they cannot stand the fire at all. How many will be able to abide a celestial law, and go through and receive their exaltation, I am unable to say, as many are called, but few are chosen." (*DHC* 6:184–185).[994]

When the Saints were given a final opportunity to receive the offered fullness extended to all, they needed to show their willingness to accept it by completing the Nauvoo Temple within a short time. They were given long enough to complete it, and if it was not completed in that appointed time, they would be rejected.[995] We have seen how the Saints proceeded to build Nauvoo and their own homes rather than the Nauvoo Temple from 1841 to June, 1844 when Joseph and Hyrum were killed. (See The Remnant Part VII.) When Joseph was taken, the Temple walls had not yet been completed to the second floor.

---

[993] D&C 132:45 "For I have conferred upon you the keys and power of the priesthood, wherein I restore all things, and make known unto you all things in due time."
D&C 124:28 "For there is not a place found on earth that he may come to and restore again that which was lost unto you, or which he hath taken away, even the fulness of the priesthood."

[994] See also D&C 121:40 "Hence many are called, but few are chosen."

[995] D&C 124:32 "But behold, at the end of this appointment your baptisms for your dead shall not be acceptable unto me; and if you do not these things at the end of the appointment ye shall be rejected as a church, with your dead, saith the Lord your God."

When the Twelve prayed in the Temple on February 8, 1846 that the Lord would bless the Saints to be able to complete the Temple, the Temple caught fire the next day.

Repairs and further work allowed a dedication to finally take place at the end of April, 1846, nearly two years after Joseph's death. The dedicatory prayer petitioned the Lord to "take guardianship into Thy hands," but by September the keys to the Temple doors were handed to a mob which had overrun Nauvoo. It was the position of Elder Hyde that the Saints performed as they were required "by the skin of our teeth," thereby escaping rejection by the Lord. (This was discussed in The Remnant Part VII.)

The prophecy of Christ, as commanded by the Father, foretells that if the gentiles do reject the fullness, then the Father will "return their iniquities upon their own heads." Meaning that the gentiles will, by reason of their rejection of what was offered them, merit condemnation for ingratitude.[996] They remain "filthy still" because that which would have cleansed them was not received in gratitude. It was rejected. When a people reject the Lord, the Lord, being governed by law, must reject them.

This is the reason the coming judgments are necessary. Where much is given (and we were offered everything) then much is expected.[997] When everything is rejected, then the punishment mer-

---

[996] D&C 88:33–35 "For what doth it profit a man if a gift is bestowed upon him, and he receive not the gift? Behold, he rejoices not in that which is given unto him, neither rejoices in him who is the giver of the gift. And again, verily I say unto you, that which is governed by law is also preserved by law and perfected and sanctified by the same. That which breaketh a law, and abideth not by law, but seeketh to become a law unto itself, and willeth to abide in sin, and altogether abideth in sin, cannot be sanctified by law, neither by mercy, justice, nor judgment. Therefore, they must remain filthy still."

[997] Luke 12:47–48 "And that servant, which knew his lord's will, and prepared not *himself*, neither did according to his will, shall be beaten with many *stripes*. But he that knew not, and did commit things worthy of stripes, shall be beaten with few *stripes*. For unto whomsoever much is given, of him shall be much required: and to whom men have committed much, of him they will ask the more."

ited reflects complete rejection of the Lord. You must keep this in mind as you read the judgments Christ prophesies upon the gentiles.

And remember also that no matter what the collective gentile conduct may be (or fail to be), the Lord approaches each of us individually. The Book of Mormon is intended as the final opportunity for gentile salvation. The church is under condemnation for failing to remember its contents and take them seriously.[998] That scourge needn't be applied to you, if you will "repent and remember the new covenant" offered to you. There is, for any gentile who will repent and take the covenants offered in the Book of Mormon, an opportunity to yet become associated with the remnant and an heir of the preservation and salvation offered to them.

As we survey the condition of the gentile church today, there seems to be less and less made of the Book of Mormon's contents. The Correlation Department's teachings are insubstantial and becoming even less so. However, you have the Book of Mormon in front of you. You don't need anyone to prepare a manual for you. You have the text itself.

I am hoping what I've written, particularly in *The Second Comforter*, will show you how the Book of Mormon teaches you the return to the fullness. *Nephi's Isaiah* informs you of the Book of Mormon's prophecies of our days and our failures. *Eighteen Verses* shows how Book of Mormon doctrinal teachings address every major dilemma of our day. *Beloved Enos* shows what the fullness will confer upon you. I believe whatever merit the Lord has conferred upon me arises

---

[998] D&C 84:54–58 "And your minds in times past have been darkened because of unbelief, and because you have treated lightly the things you have received— Which vanity and unbelief have brought the whole church under condemnation. And this condemnation resteth upon the children of Zion, even all. And they shall remain under this condemnation until they repent and remember the new covenant, even the Book of Mormon and the former commandments which I have given them, not only to say, but to do according to that which I have written— That they may bring forth fruit meet for their Father's kingdom; otherwise there remaineth a scourge and judgment to be poured out upon the children of Zion."

out of my serious study of the Book of Mormon. Though everyone may treat this covenant lightly, I have not. I would encourage you, therefore, to do the same, and prayerfully study the most correct volume of scripture we possess. It is a lifeline extended by the Lord to us. However, it cannot do you any good if you fail to act on its contents. Do the works, and you will know the doctrine. I suspect our universal failure to know doctrine today is because we do not live as we should. Understanding doctrine is tied to living it. The more you live it, the more you will comprehend it.[999] The less you live it, the more elusive it becomes to you. Until at last, you become like Deseret Book, incapable of offering anything other than romance novels, "inspirational" mush, and historical fiction, all with a veneer of Mormon vocabulary. Kitsch and superficiality, more distracting to the reader than edifying to their soul. Making one think there is some good being accomplished by participating, all the while forfeiting the days which might have been better spent.

---

[999] John 7:16–17 "Jesus answered them, and said, My doctrine is not mine, but his that sent me. If any man will do his will, he shall know of the doctrine, whether it be of God, or *whether* I speak of myself."

THE REMNANT CONTINUED

The interplay between the latter-day gentiles and the remnant has been illustrated repeatedly in the Book of Mormon prophecies. We have seen Nephi's prophecies of the event, and Christ's affirmation and expansion on the event.

Gentiles would be offered the fullness and would reject it. Then the gentiles would take the gospel to the remnant who would receive it. The remnant would then blossom with the gospel, ultimately establishing the New Jerusalem. When the New Jerusalem is built by the remnant, a few gentiles who had received the fullness would be able to "assist" in bringing again Zion.[1000]

We have at least a reasonable basis for fearing the gentiles rejected the fullness by not building the Temple in the "appointed time." In-

---

[1000] 3 Nephi 21:23–24 "And they shall assist my people, the remnant of Jacob, and also as many of the house of Israel as shall come, that they may build a city, which shall be called the New Jerusalem. And then shall they assist my people that they may be gathered in, who are scattered upon all the face of the land, in unto the New Jerusalem."

side this Temple, the fullness was to be revealed.[1001] Joseph Smith, who possessed the fullness, was taken 3 1/2 years after the revelation warning to act with speed in building the required Temple. When he died, the walls had not yet been completed to the second floor.

If we assume the worst, and the fullness was taken by the failure to complete the Temple in the permitted time, what then? Do the gentiles have no further use? Are the gentiles without a role in the latter-day events? That is hardly the case. The gentiles continue to occupy a central role in the latter-days, despite their failures.

The gentiles will bring the Gospel to the remnant.[1002] The gentiles will be commissioned to preach, teach, baptize, lay on hands for the gift of the Holy Ghost, carry the Book of Mormon forward throughout the world, and preserve truths which will enable others to be saved. The gentiles will shoulder a prophetic burden they alone will be able to bear off in the last days.

When Moses was taken, along with the higher priesthood he possessed, the Lord did not cease to recognize ancient Israel as His people. They were indeed His people, and the ones with whom He worked. He cared for, and watched over them, although we know in

---

[1001] D&C 124:28, 32 "For there is not a place found on earth that he may come to and restore again that which was lost unto you, or which he hath taken away, even the fulness of the priesthood. . . . But behold, at the end of this appointment your baptisms for your dead shall not be acceptable unto me; and if you do not these things at the end of the appointment ye shall be rejected as a church, with your dead, saith the Lord your God."

[1002] 1 Nephi 15:13–14 "And now, the thing which our father meaneth concerning the grafting in of the natural branches through the fulness of the Gentiles, is, that in the latter days, when our seed shall have dwindled in unbelief, yea, for the space of many years, and many generations after the Messiah shall be manifested in body unto the children of men, then shall the fulness of the gospel of the Messiah come unto the Gentiles, and from the Gentiles unto the remnant of our seed—And at that day shall the remnant of our seed know that they are of the house of Israel, and that they are the covenant people of the Lord; and then shall they know and come to the knowledge of their forefathers, and also to the knowledge of the gospel of their Redeemer, which was ministered unto their fathers by him; wherefore, they shall come to the knowledge of their Redeemer and the very points of his doctrine, that they may know how to come unto him and be saved."

hindsight they were a hard hearted and foolish people who rejected something far greater than what they kept. If we rejected a fullness by our own failures, that does not mean we are cut off. We are the Lord's people. We have a form of priesthood, and the right to organize and preach the Gospel throughout the world. We are being watched over. We are the means through which the Lord will bring to pass all of His latter-day plans.

You should also not worry that our collective limitations apply to individuals. That has never been the case. There have always been those who have risen up, shed their sins, repented and come to the Lord individually and been redeemed. That pattern appears throughout scriptures. The Book of Mormon is a product of one family, led by one man who repented in a generation scheduled for destruction. He led his family, preached the Gospel, had sons who accepted the invitation to receive from the fruit of the tree of life, and established a righteous branch of Israel. The Book of Mormon at its foundation is a testimony that the Lord is ever willing to receive any who will come to Him.

The gentiles are integral to the Lord's work. We should never fear that The Church of Jesus Christ of Latter-day Saints is meaningless, irrelevant or without God's watchful care. It is the means by which people are invited to come to Christ today.

In *Eighteen Verses* I describe the phenomena of building a new religion inside the original one established by revelation through Joseph Smith. This new, false religion is designed to interfere with the Gospel, enshrine worship or adoration of a priestly class instead of the worship of Christ. The Correlation Department's effort to correlate teaching has created a new ambition to correlate power and control over everything. Part of that involves the adoration of a person, or as I explained it in Catholic terms—the cult of personality. This is a tried and true pattern for compromising the Gospel and rendering it a means for controlling and dominating socially, politically, religiously, and ultimately dictatorially.

The way the adversary works is always the same. It is not to destroy the work of God by annihilation, but to co-opt it and make it his. Satan wants to supplant God as the god of this earth. Therefore, anytime God has a work underway, Satan is eager to rush in and become the one the Lord's work follows. The "arm of flesh" as opposed to the "Holy Ghost" is the difference between following in the single, strait, narrow path which alone will bring people back to God, and the altered and compromised path that will take you elsewhere.

I thought President Uchtdorf's analogy about the airplane being only one degree off would become 500 miles separated from its target at the equator was particularly apt. (*A Matter of a Few Degrees*, May, 2008 *Ensign*.) This is how men and institutions fail. How can mortal man be vulnerable to err, and committees of mortal men are not? It is an almost universal truth that committees multiply errors, not decrease them. And who of you have ever sustained the Correlation Department?

We are fools to believe that the same pattern of compromising the truth that resulted in the apostasy of the church established by Christ will not relentlessly press against the restoration of our day. I know there are quotes saying otherwise—that the church cannot be led astray—but I cannot believe them, try as I might. Joseph, Brigham, John Taylor, President George Cannon *all said the exact opposite*. Even when Wilford Woodruff was claiming he would "not lead the church astray" he did not mean what we have attributed to his words. He was saying, in effect: "Don't worry, the Manifesto is a lie. We're not really abandoning plural marriage." The Manifesto did NOT stop plural marriage and it was not a revelation. He referred to it as "beating the Devil at his own game." Meaning it was intended to mislead the public. It was a press release designed to stop the persecution of the church and the threatened legislation to dis-incorporate and confiscate the Temples. Criticism by the eastern press resulted in it becoming part of the Doctrine & Covenants. Plural marriages continued from then until after President Joseph F. Smith testified before the Senate in the seating of Senator Smoot in 1905. When the excommunications of the Apostles Taylor and Cowley in 1911 happened, it was not based on the Manifesto, but on the letter of President Joseph F. Smith actually ending the practice. The fundamentalist groups know this history and use it to persuade others that their current practices are justified. Their practices today are wrong, as I've discussed in *Beloved Enos*. But their use of history to trouble the unaware has been effective in many cases. [Now this is entirely a side issue and I'm not interested in pursuing it at this moment. I'm only mentioning it in the context of another thought.]

So ask yourself which is better:

1. Presume that no man can err who becomes a President of the LDS Church in direct contradiction to what Joseph Smith, Brigham Young, John Taylor and George Q. Cannon taught?

2. Presume that without the ratification of the Holy Ghost bearing testimony to you that a matter is true, no man can be trusted and your salvation is based on what God alone tells you to be true?

If you believe the first, your religion is new, post-Correlation and will damn you. I do not intend to disassociate with you, and will gladly let you practice your faith if you will permit me to practice mine. If you believe the second, you are a Latter-day Saint who accepts accountability for what you believe and will work out your salvation with fear and trembling before God. You believe as I do, that Joseph was the means through which the Lord initiated a work for the salvation of mankind, and that work continues today. You believe in revelation and in God's continuing hand with us still today. You accept such good things as come through The Church of Jesus Christ of Latter-day Saints, rejoice in them, pay tithing to them, and are blessed by what things the church continues to preserve and practice. However, you are not deluded into worship of men.

The gentiles include both. The gentiles will be instrumental to the Lord's work in the last days, whether they are Saints or Brethrenites. The remnant will come to the faith, receive the Gospel and become acquainted with their fathers through the Book of Mormon delivered by gentile hands.[1003] Without faithful gentile Saints, the work of the Father will not happen. Therefore, no matter the condition we find ourselves, we have an obligation to the Lord and the prophets who went before, to live as to bring these things to pass.

First, a slight detour because of comments or complaints. I am a member of The Church of Jesus Christ of Latter-day Saints. It is the only church I have ever joined. I owe to that church my knowledge of the truth. If you've read my original explanation of this blog, you would know that already. If you've read the books I've written, you'd know that already. I haven't changed my position. I'm still what I was all along—a faithful, active Latter-day Saint.

It is from the church I have received the ordinances of baptism and laying on of hands for the gift of the Holy Ghost.

It is from the church I have received the scriptures, other ordinances, and authority.

[1003] 2 Nephi 30:3–5 "And now, I would prophesy somewhat more concerning the Jews and the Gentiles. For after the book of which I have spoken shall come forth, and be written unto the Gentiles, and sealed up again unto the Lord, there shall be many which shall believe the words which are written; and they shall carry them forth unto the remnant of our seed. And then shall the remnant of our seed know concerning us, how that we came out from Jerusalem, and that they are descendants of the Jews. And the gospel of Jesus Christ shall be declared among them; wherefore, they shall be restored unto the knowledge of their fathers, and also to the knowledge of Jesus Christ, which was had among their fathers"

I pay tithing to the church, attend regular meetings with other members, and receive the Sacrament weekly. I raise my children to attend and be faithful to the church. I am grateful to the church for its programs for children.

I listen to General Conference, and attend a large gathering on the BYU campus with my sons every six months during the Priesthood Session of Conference. I drive my children by the conference center during conference to see the protesters and read their anti-Mormon signs. This reminds my children that, although we are in the majority here, we are not liked by the majority elsewhere.

I have no intention of ever leaving the church. I see no reason to ever do so. I know the church welcomes me and my family. I know they are grateful that I attend, pay tithing and support the programs as we are asked to do.

I mention that only to make certain that some of those who read here are not misled. I have no ambition to lead the church or any person other than my family. I am grateful others are called to do so. I pray for them and do not think I could do any better job than is being done. On the contrary, I think I would make things worse.

I love my fellow Latter-day Saints. Even those with whom I have deep disagreements over doctrine. I enjoy associating with people who can discuss some of the important issues facing us, even if we hold very different views of what the solutions should be. At the end of the day, in order for the church to survive, it needs to have a mechanism to bring debate to an end and make a decision. That mechanism is in place and I respect it. If it were to be altered, it would likely break the entire system. The system is essential for the church's survival.

I sustain President Monson and do not think anyone other than him has final decision-making authority in The Church of Jesus Christ of Latter-day Saints. Think about what it would mean if his decisions could be vetoed endlessly from his office down to the lay members. This would cease to be a meaningful organization.

We have tremendous problems facing the church at present. I think they are all due to the abandonment of a pattern originally restored, in favor of innovations recommended by social sciences. The Correlation Department has accelerated this metamorphosis of the church and now leads it. The possibility remains that the church will return to an earlier pattern, but that seems quite unlikely at this point. To paraphrase Deseret Book: "Doctrine doesn't sell now." Doctrine does not matter as it once did, and as a result, the gentiles are not even aware of the content of the scriptures, the messages addressed to **us**, the responsibilities which have been laid upon **us**, and the warnings about how **we** are proceeding. The prophetic pessimism of the Book of Mormon prophets is not found in the modern messages. In fact, the feel-good messages seem to be denounced by the Book of Mormon and foretold as a sign of **our own** erring.

As a single, private member of the church, the only tool available to me approved by scripture is persuasion. If what I write does not persuade, I own no office, hold no calling, and command no position from which to insist you trust, believe or accept what I write. Oddly, no priesthood position in the church, from the least to the greatest, is entitled to insist you trust, believe or accept what they say. (D&C 121:41.) I see very little demanding when it comes to actual presiding authorities. But I see a lot of that being urged vicariously, on behalf of presiding authorities, and in their names. It appears that between the Brethren who preside, and the common members, there is a disconnection wherein the Correlation Department has inserted themselves. Into that arena they have brought increasingly more intolerant and strict rule-making. I think there are talks every General Conference intended to work against that mischief. But, alas, the COB is a difficult beast to ride. It will take a grizzly bear to wrestle it into submission, I suspect.

In any event, the gentiles must fulfill their own destiny. Although there will be failings, limitations, foolishness and apostasy by the gentiles rejecting what is offered them, they will perform a great act. They will be the means of bringing back the remnant. There will be those who believe the Book of Mormon, teach correctly to the remnant about their own fathers, and assist in bringing about the New Jerusalem.

This interplay between gentile and remnant destinies is very real, and requires a work of the gentiles not yet completed.

I do not know how much further to pursue this topic. There are prophecies Joseph made about the Rocky Mountain gathering. There is the controversial "horse-shoe prophecy" about the travel of the Saints before the New Jerusalem would be founded. There is Joseph's finger on the map pointing where he suspected the New Jerusalem would be built. And the fellow who saw the pointing who speculated it was around where Snowflake, Arizona is presently located. However, the map had no borders, no states, and Snowflake didn't exist at the time. So a finger on a map could be hundreds of miles away from Snowflake. I'm not inclined to do much with that right now. I'm more inclined to take up some other stuff and leave the remnant alone for the time being.

As I said when this started, it was going to take a while. I'm thinking it might be better to change topics for a while and turn attention to some other things. The remnant will reappear in its own natural order as we move along in any direction we take. Their appearance is so widespread in latter-day prophecy that it is unavoidable. Many of you hadn't noticed it before. Now you have some background and ought to be able to pick up the matter on your own and see it for yourselves.

Text of the Supplemental Readings Mentioned

A Remarkable Prophecy By President John Taylor As Told by Edward Lunt, An Ordinance Worker in the Mesa Temple:

> He said that faithful Latter-day Saints would go to the south and would form a circle something like a horseshoe, before they return to Jackson County, Missouri. Said he, "Those only will be privileged to help build Jackson County who will be found willing and glad to obey the counsel and advice of the authorities who will be placed over them, and who will seek counsel that they may be guided and protected from dire want and distress."

> President Taylor also said that we will assist the Lamanites in building the New Jerusalem in Jackson county. He said that the vision to him appeared so terrible that he besought the Lord to close it up, but he saw that those who would keep the commandments and adhere to the authorities of the church would be the ones who would survive and not be destroyed. And that the lord would protect them as he did the children of Israel."

Journal of Mosiah Hancock:

Placing his [Joseph Smith's] finger on the map (I should think about where Snowflake, Arizona, is situated, or it could have been Mexico) he said, "The government will not receive you with the laws God designed that you should live, and those who are desirous to live the laws of God will have to go south. You will live to see men arise in power in the Church who will seek to put down your friends and the friends of our Lord and Savior, Jesus Christ. Many will be hoisted because of their money and the worldly learning which they seem to be in possession of; and many who are the true followers of our Lord and Savior will be cast down because of their poverty."

3 NEPHI 11

I have always wanted to do something with Christ's sermons to the Nephites. It seems to me that we've been running through prophecies and warnings which serve one purpose, and leaving another one neglected. Balance requires us to return to another important purpose of the Book of Mormon. Namely, testifying that Jesus is the Christ, the Savior and Redeemer of Israel and the whole world.

So for that part, we'll turn attention to Christ's Nephite sermons. I've already dealt with what I have termed the "Ceremony of Recognition" involved in Christ's initial appearance. That is covered in *The Second Comforter* and won't be repeated here. So I'm going to skip to these verses:

3 Nephi 11:18–20

"And it came to pass that he spake unto Nephi (for Nephi was among the multitude) and he commanded him that he should come forth. And Nephi arose and went forth, and bowed himself before the Lord and did kiss his feet. And the Lord commanded him that he should arise. And he arose and stood before him."

The Lord has appeared, is identified and recognized by those who were at the Bountiful Temple. (This is probably an open air temple much like what we find in the Parowan Gap. If you consider the entirety of the description, it is not likely a closed structure like we build.) And those who are there have engaged in an Hosanna shout.[1004] When the ceremony has ended and the place has become sanctified by His presence, and the body there recognizes and accepts Him as who and what He is, the stage has been set for a further ceremonial event.

Christ speaks to Nephi. He calls his name. Important stuff. Being called by name by the Son of God! Now we're seeing something really important. For those whose names are called by God are not merely being addressed. They are, the instant the Lord calls out their name, "called." That is, the Lord will never speak one's name to them unless He calls them to a work. So when we read that the Lord speaks to Nephi we know the Lord has both called Nephi's name and called the bearer of that name to do a work. Nephi knew it. The crowd knew it. All present would have understood that Nephi just became the chief prophet of those present.

Nephi is told to "come forth." It instantly puts us in mind of Lazarus being called forth from the tomb.[1005] Like Lazarus, who rose from the dead by the speaking of those words, Nephi now goes forth to a new life. Resurrected from his prior status and put into a minister's role by the Lord of all mankind.

Called, commanded to "come forth," and endowed immediately with the Lord's anointing voice, which bestows power and authority

---

[1004] 3 Nephi 11:17 "Hosanna! Blessed be the name of the Most High God! And they did fall down at the feet of Jesus, and did worship him."

[1005] John 11:43 "And when he thus had spoken, he cried with a loud voice, Lazarus, come forth."

upon a man[1006], Nephi arises from his kneeling position and steps forward.

Every knee remains bowed except Nephi's. For a brief moment, as he walks forward, he alone, of all those assembled in the crowd, is the one who stands in the presence of the Lord.[1007] Others kneel, Nephi stands. It is honor, glory and privilege being displayed in this ceremony. Christ as King and Lord calls, His chief servant rises while all others remain kneeling. We are getting informed about the Lord and His ways in detailed ceremony conveying vast information in passing movement. It is too wonderful for words.

Nephi knows what he must do. For the servant who has been called to stand above his peers must then descend below them. Pride is unthinkable when in the presence of such a meek and humble figure as our Lord. It is required that the balance be restored. Nephi, who has been made to rise, must on his own choose to descend and abase himself. Those who seek their own glory will fall, while those who seek to humble themselves will rise again. So Nephi does what any person filled with light and truth would do in these circumstances. He comes to the Lord, falls below all, and descends to kiss the Master's feet. He kneels again, bows to the ground. And in an ultimate sign of humility, he kisses His feet, which on any other being is the symbol of uncleanliness itself. Nephi can do nothing more to show his own submission to the Lord. He can do nothing further in ceremonial activity to say he is nothing and the Lord is everything. He can show no greater respect and gratitude. Here is a servant indeed. A chief servant to the Servant of servants! A Master and ser-

---

[1006] D&C 132:46 "And verily, verily, I say unto you, that whatsoever you seal on earth shall be sealed in heaven; and whatsoever you bind on earth, in my name and by my word, saith the Lord, it shall be eternally bound in the heavens; and whosoever sins you remit on earth shall be remitted eternally in the heavens; and whosoever sins you retain on earth shall be retained in heaven."

[1007] Luke 1:19 "And the angel answering said unto him, I am Gabriel, that stand in the presence of God; and am sent to speak unto thee, and to shew thee these glad tidings."

vant whose hearts are alike. Nephi is, above all else, showing to us all how we ought be.

The gentiles love those who rule over and exploit them.[1008] But Christ's true followers do not crave chief seats. They desire to serve. They will hold others up, even if it requires them to descend below to lift them. Nephi is not a gentile, nor one who would ever exercise unrighteous dominion over others.[1009]

The ceremony now requires the abased to respond to the Lord's command again. Nephi is commanded to "arise." It was not enough to "come forth" to the new life. Now, having been chosen, Nephi must also "arise." It is a terrible burden. How can man "arise?" How can a man assume his position alongside His Lord? How can one who feels more suited to kneel and kiss his Master's feet, rise up and look his Lord in the face? It is all too much. One hardly can bear the burden and difficulty to "arise" when it is the Lord's own countenance you must confront. Too much. Too difficult. Too heavy a burden to lay upon mere man. How does Nephi dare to respond to the command to "arise?"

Through the swirling anxiety following the command, Nephi doesn't have the strength to do so until the realization that "arising" is the Master's will. It is the Master's command. It can be done through faith in Him. For He gives no command without having prepared the means to accomplish it.[1010] It must be possible for Nephi to actually

---

[1008] Matthew 20:25 "But Jesus called them *unto him,* and said, Ye know that the princes of the Gentiles exercise dominion over them, and they that are great exercise authority upon them."

[1009] D&C 121:39 "We have learned by sad experience that it is the nature and disposition of almost all men, as soon as they get a little authority, as they suppose, they will immediately begin to exercise unrighteous dominion."

[1010] 1 Nephi 3:7 "And it came to pass that I, Nephi, said unto my father: I will go and do the things which the Lord hath commanded, for I know that the Lord giveth no commandments unto the children of men, save he shall prepare a way for them that they may accomplish the thing which he commandeth them."

arise. Though a lifetime's dread and remorse says to remain on your knees, it is the Master's will that you nonetheless arise. And so you begin the dreadful effort, and your trembling knees respond. To your own surprise you find it possible to arise and look into the face of Him who is compassion itself. There can be no pride in this, for rising is by His command, and not by your own will. You may want to join in Moses' chorus that "for this cause you know man is nothing!"[1011] But it isn't necessary to voice the thought. It is enough to understand the thought.

No man assumes this honor for himself. He must be called by God to stand in His presence.

And so Nephi arose, and stood before His Lord.

3 Nephi 11:22

"And again the Lord called others, and said unto them likewise; and he gave unto them power to baptize. And he said unto them: On this wise shall ye baptize; and there shall be no disputations among you."

Space was limited and the mechanics of writing was difficult for Mormon. Therefore, in his abridgment of the account, for all others "the Lord called," and the ceremony was repeated for each. In the process, He "said likewise" unto each of them. Every individual person was acknowledged by the Lord as having conferred upon each of them "power to baptize" by the Lord.

None of those who received this power had any doubt about their authority to act in this ordinance in the Lord's name. None of them lacked the "power" to baptize others. None of those who were present, and still kneeling during the ceremony, or who overheard the

---

[1011] Moses 1:10 "And it came to pass that it was for the space of many hours before Moses did again receive his natural strength like unto man; and he said unto himself: Now, for this cause I know that man is nothing, which thing I never had supposed."

Lord's words had any doubts about those who held a commission from Christ to baptize them. Finally, none of those present would have any doubts about the need to be baptized by this newly bestowed power.

Although every one of them had been baptized previously, it becomes apparent that once new power to baptize has been given by Christ, that power ought to be used. It is not given to be neglected. Nor can power endure through neglect. So when given, the power is to be used, and all who were present are candidates for baptism.

Then comes the instruction from Christ as to the manner for performing the ordinance. "On this wise shall ye baptize . . . " begins the instruction. If the Lord provides the power and then gives the instruction, can the ordinance be changed? What if someone else says they hold the keys, and we all accept the person does in fact hold the keys, can such a person change the manner of baptism? If there is a potential convert who is infirm, ill or elderly and is unable to be baptized in the prescribed manner, can the ordinance be changed in form to accommodate the need? That is exactly how the ordinance was changed after the New Testament times. A reasonable need, and accommodation for that need, resulted in an exception. Then the exception became the rule, and the original manner was forgotten.

If the Lord's instruction regarding the manner of baptism in this verse cannot be changed, even by one holding keys and authority to do so, then what about other ordinances? Can other ordinances be changed by one who holds keys if they choose to do them differently? Why not? What happens when the one in a recognized position to perform ordinances decides to make changes to the ordinances?

Assume for a moment the Lord instructs Nephi on how to perform baptism, but Nephi decides thereafter to make a change to it.

How would that reflect on Nephi? How would that reflect on the Lord? How would it reflect on the Lord's instruction? What about Joseph Smith's statement:

> "Ordinances instituted in the heavens before the foundation of the world, in the priesthood, for the salvation of men, are not to be altered or changed." (*TPJS*, 308)

If the Lord gave Nephi the "power" to baptize, does that carry with it the "power" to change it as well?

Well, the purpose behind the Lord giving instructions was that "there shall be no disputations among you." Does the instruction given by the Lord end as soon as we begin to see "disputations among" followers? Can an opinion poll that shows a majority of those who practice the ordinances don't relate to them anymore and want to see them altered, create a "disputation" that allows the instruction from the Lord to be altered?

As stupid as these questions may seem, there are people who are genuinely confused by them. So I ask them. You must decide if the Lord's instructions deserve respect and ought to be followed. Apparently men of good faith, honest hearts, and sincere desires can by reason of their status alone, contradict the Lord's instructions and people won't even blink. That's the beauty of the claim that Rome makes to having Peter's keys and the ability to seal on earth and in heaven. The Catholics can change anything and no one doubts they had the authority to do it. To allow the possibility that God would not support the Pope would be to entertain the unthinkable. So don't even hold that thought.

3 Nephi 11:23

"Verily I say unto you, that whoso repenteth of his sins through your words, and desireth to be baptized in my name, on this wise shall ye baptize them—Behold, ye shall go down and stand in the water, and in my name shall ye baptize them."

The candidate for baptism must first qualify themselves by "repent[ing] of his sins." That's an interesting *pre*-condition in the Lord's instruction. Until one has determined to abandon their sins, they are not fit for baptism. They first decide to lay things behind, move forward in following the Lord, determined to serve Him. This decision to make a change must come "through your words." Meaning that before someone can repent, they must first learn the conditions for repentance and following the Lord.

This is much like the instructions given by revelation to this dispensation about how baptism is to be performed. We were told, "All those who humble themselves before God, and desire to be baptized, and come forth with broken hearts and contrite spirits, and witness before the church that they have truly repented of all their sins, and are willing to take upon them the name of Jesus Christ, having a determination to serve him to the end, and truly manifest by their works that they have received of the Spirit of Christ unto the remission of their sins, shall be received by baptism into his church."[1012]

After having made the decision to be baptized with a broken heart and contrite spirit, confessing before the church that you have repented of your sins (or be willing to change and follow Christ),

---

[1012] D&C 20:37 "*And again, by way of commandment to the church concerning the manner of baptism*—All those who humble themselves before God, and desire to be baptized, and come forth with broken hearts and contrite spirits, and witness before the church that they have truly repented of all their sins, and are willing to take upon them the name of Jesus Christ, having a determination to serve him to the end, and truly manifest by their works that they have received of the Spirit of Christ unto the remission of their sins, shall be received by baptism into his church."

determined to endure to the end, a person receives from the Spirit of Christ a witness that changes their behavior. Their works show they are penitent. At this point a person is ready for baptism. Until then, they are not ready and the ordinance is not appropriate.

Now the instructions in Section 20 are more complete than the abbreviated statement in Christ's instructions to His Nephite disciples, but it is to the same effect. When this pattern is followed, people are converted and follow Christ. Their baptism matters and will change them. When these instructions are not followed, the ordinance is relatively meaningless and people drift off into inactivity. I believe today the numbers evidence that approximately 10% of those who are baptized are actually converted. The rest are just names and numbers used as membership statistics to be reported and proclaimed each April in a worldwide conference.

The Gospel of Christ is quite exact and it works whenever it is tried. It is tried today in about 10% of the cases of those who are baptized by our missionaries.

Perhaps the ordinance ought to be offered to more of our adults as they come to recognize that they may not have actually been prepared to receive the ordinance when given to them. No matter, there's always the Alma exception. (That's when in the course of baptizing someone else, you go ahead and take the covenant yourself.[1013]) Clearly Alma was baptizing Helam at the time, and added himself for good measure; he (Alma) feeling the need for the ordinance himself.

[1013] Mosiah 18:13–15 "And when he had said these words, the Spirit of the Lord was upon him, and he said: Helam, I baptize thee, having authority from the Almighty God, as a testimony that ye have entered into a covenant to serve him until you are dead as to the mortal body; and may the Spirit of the Lord be poured out upon you; and may he grant unto you eternal life, through the redemption of Christ, whom he has prepared from the foundation of the world. And after Alma had said these words, both Alma and Helam were buried in the water; and they arose and came forth out of the water rejoicing, being filled with the Spirit. And again, Alma took another, and went forth a second time into the water, and baptized him according to the first, only he did not bury himself again in the water."

He went ahead and was baptized again for good measure. This seems to be a precedent that would allow for others to do likewise—perhaps when performing a vicarious baptism for the dead. I leave the Alma exception for your own consideration, and will stop short of advocating such a thing. I just notice things and share what I notice. I'm not trying to convince anyone to do anything.

In Christ's instructions, and in Section 20, the heavy lifting of repentance precedes baptism. Then, after determining to change and follow Christ, leaving behind the foolish errors of the past, the person is fit to be baptized. At that point the baptism symbolizes the new life being undertaken. The presence of the Holy Ghost then ratifies the purging of the repentant, now baptized convert. But that comes next in Christ's teaching.

3 Nephi 11:24–25

> "And now behold, these are the words which ye shall say, calling them by name, saying: Having authority given me of Jesus Christ, I baptize you in the name of the Father, and of the Son, and of the Holy Ghost. Amen."

Christ prescribes the exact words to be used in the ordinance. However, the instruction we use today is slightly different in wording, but identical in meaning: Instead of: "Having authority given me of Jesus Christ" we say instead: "Having been commissioned of Jesus Christ."[1014]

After giving these disciples "power to baptize" Christ's instructions require them to say they have "authority" (in 3 Nephi) or today,

---

[1014] D&C 20:73 "The person who is called of God and has authority from Jesus Christ to baptize, shall go down into the water with the person who has presented himself or herself for baptism, and shall say, calling him or her by name: Having been commissioned of Jesus Christ, I baptize you in the name of the Father, and of the Son, and of the Holy Ghost. Amen."

hold a "commission"[1015] (in D&C 20). Is there a difference between "authority" to baptize and the "power" to baptize?

Why does the authorization come from Jesus Christ, but the ordinance get performed "in the name of the Father, and of the Son, and of the Holy Ghost?" The power to do the ordinance comes from the Son, but the ordinance is in the name of each member of the Godhead. Why?

Though they are one, the names show they occupy different roles and hold different responsibilities. (As to following and being sanctified by different laws and receiving different kingdoms.)[1016] We are in the fallen world where the primary means God communicates with man is through the Holy Ghost.[1017] When, however, a person rises up through the merits of Jesus Christ to receive Him as a minister, they are living in a Terrestrial law and inherit Terrestrial blessings.[1018] When He has finished His preparations with the person, and can bring them to the Father, the person is brought to a point where the

---

[1015] Ibid.

[1016] D&C 88:21–26 "And they who are not sanctified through the law which I have given unto you, even the law of Christ, must inherit another kingdom, even that of a terrestrial kingdom, or that of a telestial kingdom. For he who is not able to abide the law of a celestial kingdom cannot abide a celestial glory. And he who cannot abide the law of a terrestrial kingdom cannot abide a terrestrial glory. And he who cannot abide the law of a telestial kingdom cannot abide a telestial glory; therefore he is not meet for a kingdom of glory. Therefore he must abide a kingdom which is not a kingdom of glory. And again, verily I say unto you, the earth abideth the law of a celestial kingdom, for it filleth the measure of its creation, and transgresseth not the law—Wherefore, it shall be sanctified; yea, notwithstanding it shall die, it shall be quickened again, and shall abide the power by which it is quickened, and the righteous shall inherit it."

[1017] D&C 14:8 "And it shall come to pass, that if you shall ask the Father in my name, in faith believing, you shall receive the Holy Ghost, which giveth utterance, that you may stand as a witness of the things of which you shall both hear and see, and also that you may declare repentance unto this generation."

[1018] D&C 76:77 "These are they who receive of the presence of the Son, but not of the fulness of the Father."

Father can accept and acknowledge them as a son.[1019] They are then begotten of the Father.[1020] Through each of these steps, does baptism matter? Does one receive the companionship of the Holy Ghost without baptism? Do they come to Christ without baptism? Do they inherit what the Father has without baptism? Is baptism critical to the association with each member of the Godhead?

The point at which the person's journey is completed, and they may enter into the rest of the Lord is when the Lord declares by His own voice that the man's offering has been accepted and they are sealed up to eternal life. I've explained this on the blog as to Joseph Smith. I've explained it for Enos and others in *Beloved Enos*. The Gospel is the same now, as always before. Therefore, no matter how you will receive blessings of the Lord in the afterlife, it will be through the Gospel of Jesus Christ and by the ordinances instituted for claiming blessings. These were established as law to govern man's conduct here even before the world was.[1021]

Note also the person cannot receive the ordinance without also having their name stated. Why do you suppose it is necessary to first call out the name of the person before they receive an ordinance? Why would the Lord's instruction require a person to be "called"

[1019] D&C 76:54–59, 92 "They are they who are the church of the Firstborn. They are they into whose hands the Father has given all things—They are they who are priests and kings, who have received of his fulness, and of his glory; And are priests of the Most High, after the order of Melchizedek, which was after the order of Enoch, which was after the order of the Only Begotten Son. Wherefore, as it is written, they are gods, even the sons of God—Wherefore, all things are theirs, whether life or death, or things present, or things to come, all are theirs and they are Christ's, and Christ is God's. . . . And thus we saw the glory of the celestial, which excels in all things—where God, even the Father, reigns upon his throne forever and ever;"

[1020] Psalms 2:7 "I will declare the decree: the Lord hath said unto me, Thou *art* my Son; this day have I begotten thee."

[1021] D&C 130:20–21 "There is a law, irrevocably decreed in heaven before the foundations of this world, upon which all blessings are predicated—And when we obtain any blessing from God, it is by obedience to that law upon which it is predicated."

first? Though they are submitting to the ordinance voluntarily, why call their name?

Does it matter if the full legal name is used? We do that in the church, of course. But does it matter? If the Lord called Joseph by name at the time of the First Vision (and He did)[1022], what name do you suppose was called? Was it "Joseph Smith, Jr."? Or was it "Joseph"? Or was it that name used by his most intimate friend at the time?

Whenever a name is given by an angel in an appearance to parents, the name is always the first name, or the name their friends would call them.[1023] Similarly, when the Lord calls a man's name, He uses his first, given name.[1024] The Lord does not use formal names, but uses intimate names when addressing His servants.

We call the person to be baptized by name. Our practice is to use the full, legal name.

3 Nephi 11:26

"And then shall ye immerse them in the water, and come forth again out of the water."

The manner of baptism is clearly by immersion. To perform the ordinance, they must be put under the water and then "come forth again out of the water" to follow the instruction given by Christ.

[1022] JS–H 1:17 "It no sooner appeared than I found myself delivered from the enemy which held me bound. When the light rested upon me I saw two Personages, whose brightness and glory defy all description, standing above me in the air. One of them spake unto me, calling me by name and said, pointing to the other—*This is My Beloved Son. Hear Him!*"

[1023] Luke 1:13 "But the angel said unto him, Fear not, Zacharias: for thy prayer is heard; and thy wife Elisabeth shall bear thee a son, and thou shalt call his name John."
Luke 1:31 "And, behold, thou shalt conceive in thy womb, and bring forth a son, and shalt call his name JESUS."

[1024] 1 Samuel 3:4 "That the Lord called Samuel: and he answered, Here *am* I."
Exodus 3:4 "And when the Lord saw that he turned aside to see, God called unto him out of the midst of the bush, and said, Moses, Moses. And he said, Here *am* I."

The purpose of baptism is to follow Christ's example.[1025] It symbolizes the death of the old man of sin, and the resurrection into a new life in Christ.[1026] That symbol cannot be mirrored by sprinkling. It must involve immersion.

In immersion we are placed below the surface of the water, in the same way as the dead are buried below ground.

In immersion the breath of life is cut off while under the water, and restored anew when you "come forth again out of the water."

In the case of the officiator, they are the one who immerses and then brings the recipient up out of the water. Performing this ordinance puts the officiator in the role of the Lord who holds the keys of death[1027] and resurrection.[1028]

Those who are baptized, and those who officiate, enact, by symbol, some eternal truths regarding the plan of salvation. In the very moment the ordinance is performed there is a renewal in symbol of life, innocence, forgiveness and resurrection. The earth itself is blessed by such things as baptism and other ordinances. The earth

---

[1025] John 10:27 "My sheep hear my voice, and I know them, and they follow me:" John 14:15 "If ye love me, keep my commandments."

[1026] Romans 6:4 "Therefore we are buried with him by baptism into death: that like as Christ was raised up from the dead by the glory of the Father, even so we also should walk in newness of life."

[1027] Revelation 1:18 "*I am* he that liveth, and was dead; and, behold, I am alive for evermore, Amen; and have the keys of hell and of death."

[1028] 2 Nephi 2:8 "Wherefore, how great the importance to make these things known unto the inhabitants of the earth, that they may know that there is no flesh that can dwell in the presence of God, save it be through the merits, and mercy, and grace of the Holy Messiah, who layeth down his life according to the flesh, and taketh it again by the power of the Spirit, that he may bring to pass the resurrection of the dead, being the first that should rise."

itself is defiled when the ordinances are not kept exactly as prescribed.[1029]

The earth knows that God ordained the ordinances of heaven and earth.[1030] As regular and reliable as the movements of the sun and moon are, so too should the ordinances of the Lord be kept in their appointed ways.[1031]

The heavens and earth rejoice when the ordinances are kept. They symbolize eternal hope, man's acceptance of God's plan, and a presence of righteousness in a fallen world. Our own participation in ordinances are vital to our own renewal, and the renewal of all creation through redemption of each individual soul.

The baptism ordinance, like all those that follow after, is intended not merely to fulfill an initiation rite. It is intended to communicate light and truth into the mind of the individual who is performing and receiving the ordinance. It is meant to enlighten.

I have discussed previously the meaning of "come forth" used by Christ in restoring life to Lazarus[1032] and therefore won't repeat it again here. It is no accident the Lord employs the same meaning here as there. We are rising from the tomb of sin which imprisons us into the new life awaiting us in Christ.

[1029] Isaiah 24:5 "The earth also is defiled under the inhabitants thereof; because they have transgressed the laws, changed the ordinance, broken the everlasting covenant." Moses 7:28 "And it came to pass that the God of heaven looked upon the residue of the people, and he wept; and Enoch bore record of it, saying: How is it that the heavens weep, and shed forth their tears as the rain upon the mountains?"

[1030] Jeremiah 33:25 "Thus saith the Lord; If my covenant *be* not with day and night, *and if* I have not appointed the ordinances of heaven and earth;"

[1031] Jeremiah 31:35–36 "Thus saith the Lord, which giveth the sun for a light by day, *and* the ordinances of the moon and of the stars for a light by night, which divideth the sea when the waves thereof roar; The Lord of hosts *is* his name: If those ordinances depart from before me, saith the Lord, *then* the seed of Israel also shall cease from being a nation before me for ever."

[1032] John 11:43 "And when he thus had spoken, he cried with a loud voice, Lazarus, come forth."

The Lord is more than brilliant. He is filled with light and truth. The closer you draw to Him, the more light and truth you begin to receive from Him.

3 Nephi 11:27

"And after this manner shall ye baptize in my name; for behold, verily I say unto you, that the Father, and the Son, and the Holy Ghost are one; and I am in the Father, and the Father in me, and the Father and I are one."

The ordinance of baptism is to be done in the names of all three members of the Godhead. And, correspondingly, Christ wants us to understand the unity that exists between these three. They are "one" with each other.

The "oneness" of God the Father, His Son, and the Holy Ghost was discussed by Christ in His teachings of the New Testament. The Intercessory Prayer recorded in John 17, includes His expansion on the idea. There Christ taught:

"Neither pray I for these alone, but for them also which shall believe on me through their word; That they all may be one; as thou, Father, art in me, and I in thee, that they also may be one in us: that the world may believe that thou hast sent me. And the glory which thou gavest me I have given them; that they may be one, even as we are one: I in them, and thou in me, that they may be made perfect in one; and that the world may know that thou hast sent me, and hast loved them, as thou hast loved me. Father, I will that they also, whom thou hast given me, be with me where I am; that they may behold my glory, which thou hast given me: for thou lovedst me before the foundation of the world." (John 17:20–24)

This unity between the Father, Son and Holy Ghost is a point of doctrine raised by Christ in this teaching. It is important for us to understand that the message we receive from the Holy Ghost will be the same as the message we would receive from Christ. It is also important for us to rely on and have faith in Christ and the Holy Ghost so that we may trust them to bring us to the Father.

It is also a model for us to follow. We are supposed to drop our fears and worries, shed our ambitions and desires, and come together in unity until we are "one." The non-competitive, fully cooperative manner the Father, Son and Holy Ghost are "one" is the model of Zion itself. Divisions and strifes are unthinkable between the members of the Godhead. In contrast, among us they are unavoidable.

The ideal is always the standard. We push toward perfection. The Father lives in absolutes. Therefore we strive for the absolute, all the while struggling with our relative and incremental improvement. We are in the process of being "added upon."[1033] The Father, on the other hand, dwells where there is nothing but perfection.[1034] So for us the Mediator and the Savior establish the bridge between where we are forbidden to enter in sin, and the borrowed cleanliness which momentarily lets us enter in.

We are to become "one" with Them. It is a distant goal, to be accomplished after being "added upon" for a long time. Joseph taught in the King Follett Discourse: "Here, then, is eternal life—to know the only wise and true God; and you have got to learn how to be gods yourselves, and to be kings and priests to God, the same as all gods have done before you, namely, by going from one small degree to another, and from a small capacity to a great one; from grace to grace, from exaltation to exaltation, until you attain to the resurrection of the dead, and are able to dwell in everlasting burnings, and to sit in glory, as do those who sit enthroned in everlasting power . . .

[1033] Abraham 3:26 "And they who keep their first estate shall be added upon; and they who keep not their first estate shall not have glory in the same kingdom with those who keep their first estate; and they who keep their second estate shall have glory added upon their heads for ever and ever."

[1034] D&C 1:31 "For I the Lord cannot look upon sin with the least degree of allowance;"

When you climb up a ladder, you must begin at the bottom, and ascend step by step, until you arrive at the top; and so it is with the principles of the gospel—you must begin with the first, and go on until you learn all the principles of exaltation. But it will be a great while after you have passed through the veil before you will have learned them. It is not all to be comprehended in this world; it will be a great work to learn our salvation and exaltation even beyond the grave."

To become "one" will be to reach the end of a long journey. We can have promises of that end. We can receive covenants that will bring us there. But our arrival will "be a great while after [we] have passed through the veil" for "it is not all to be comprehended in this world." Moses was told that, also.[1035] We may be initiated, but to enter in will be "a great work to learn our salvation and exaltation even beyond the grave."

So the ideal of "one" with the Father, Son and Holy Ghost for us is distant, to be sought, to be kept before us, but not to be obtained until some time later. But to be "one" with each other is another matter. Being "one" is required of us for Zion to return. Zion is required for the Lord to dwell among us again. He is going to return to a Zion, no matter how few may be involved. He will come even if only two or three gather in His name.[1036] Zion may be small, but it will nonetheless be Zion before He can visit with her.

[1035] Moses 1:5 "Wherefore, no man can behold all my works, except he behold all my glory; and no man can behold all my glory, and afterwards remain in the flesh on the earth."

[1036] Matthew 18:20 "For where two or three are gathered together in my name, there am I in the midst of them."

3 Nephi 11:28–30

"And according as I have commanded you thus shall ye baptize. And there shall be no disputations among you, as there have hitherto been; neither shall there be disputations among you concerning the points of my doctrine, as there have hitherto been. For verily, verily I say unto you, he that hath the spirit of contention is not of me, but is of the devil, who is the father of contention, and he stirreth up the hearts of men to contend with anger, one with another. Behold, this is not my doctrine, to stir up the hearts of men with anger, one against another; but this is my doctrine, that such things should be done away."

The Lord's elaboration on "disputations" and "contentions" is important and consistent enough that all three verses should be considered together.

First, He clarifies that baptism must be done as He "commanded you." Deviations are not permitted and should not be asked for, or entertained. That is the thing about ordinances. When given, they are to be kept in exactly the manner they come from Him. When we change them we risk breaking the covenant between Him and ourselves.[1037]

The Book of Mormon is silent about the "disputations" which existed among them over baptism. However, when Christ says there has "hitherto been" disputes, we know they existed. It becomes apparent from later passages that one practice which caused some of the argument was the issue of baptizing infants. There were likely others, as well. The Lord wants that to end. Perform the ordinances as He sets them out, and stop arguing about the manner.

The reason arguments arise is because men stop gathering light by righteous behavior. When they lose light they cease to understand

---

[1037] Isaiah 24:5 "The earth also is defiled under the inhabitants thereof; because they have transgressed the laws, changed the ordinance, broken the everlasting covenant."

the truth. They stray from the correct practice of the ordinance because they are unable to understand its importance. They see no reason to continue the ordinance in one form when another seems to work just as well. The result is a change to the ordinance. It is ever the same. By the time the change is made, the ones making it are unaware of any importance associated with the ordinance they change. They discard what they view is meaningless. It would require a good deal more light and truth for them to understand the importance of what was given them. But that light and truth has passed away from them because of their conduct.

Into the darkness the devil enters with arguments over the ordinances: Why do it that way? It really doesn't mean anything. It is arcane and outdated. It doesn't really matter as long as you still have faith in Christ. [That particular lie is very effective because it allows the person to presume they have faith, when in fact they haven't the faith sufficient to obey Christ.] People will get more out of the changes if we make them. People will have greater peace of mind if we baptize their infants. We'll save more souls, because by baptizing them when they're infants we include everyone who would die before getting baptized. Our numbers will increase. We'll look more successful by getting more followers by adding their numbers into the group. What we change isn't important, anyway. If it were important, we would know that, and since it doesn't seem important to us, it must, in fact, not be important. Those who rebel at change are not really faithful. This shows inspiration; it's faith affirming. Change is proof that God is still leading us. . . . And other such arguments and persuasions from our adversary.

On the other hand, Christ is saying to keep the ordinances unchanged. And further, don't even begin to dispute them. They are off limits for argument, dispute and discussion. When you open the opportunity to dispute over the ordinances, you are allowing the devil an opportunity to influence the discussion and change the ordinances.

Disputes lead to contention, contention leads to anger, and anger is the devil's tool. So don't start down that road. Accept and understand the ordinances. If you are perplexed by them, then let those who understand speak, exhort, expound and teach concerning them. As they do, you will come into the unity of faith and become one. Perplexity cannot exist when there is light and truth. Light and truth comes from understanding the ordinances, not changing them. So do not begin the process through dispute. The purpose of discussion is not to dispute, which leads to contention, which leads to anger.

When the Gospel and its ordinances turn into something angry and contentious, then the Spirit has fled, and souls are lost. It is the devil's objective to prevent you from practicing the ordinances in the correct manner. But, more importantly, it is his objective to prevent you from becoming one. When he uses arguments over ordinances to cause disunity, he is playing with two tools at the same time. First, changing the ordinances brings about cursings, and second, encouraging contention and anger grieves the Spirit, and prevents the Saints from becoming one.

As a result, disputes or discussions over ordinances, which could lead to changing them, should not be entertained. As soon as the ordinances are open to dispute, reconsideration, alteration or to being changed, then you are opening the door to this whole process. It culminates in the souls of men being lost through apostasy. Once the ordinances are changed, the earth is cursed[1038] and Israel is scattered rather than gathered.[1039]

[1038] Ibid.

[1039] Jeremiah 31:36 "If those ordinances depart from before me, saith the Lord, *then* the seed of Israel also shall cease from being a nation before me for ever."

The devil knows this, even if men do not. Men are urged to take steps they presume have little effect, all the while being lied to by the enemy of their souls.

When men arrive at the point they are angry in their hearts with one another, they are not united by love as they are intended to be. These are the end results of the two paths. One leading to love and joy[1040], and the other to anger and wrath.[1041]

Disputes over ordinances are caused by the devil. Ordinances that preserve symbolic truths and have the power to save are turned into tools for the devil by disputations. It is a complete victory when discussions about changing ordinances are allowed to take place. Even good men are taken in by such disputes.

3 Nephi 11:31–32

"Behold, verily, verily, I say unto you, I will declare unto you my doctrine. And this is my doctrine, and it is the doctrine which the Father hath given unto me; and I bear record of the Father, and the Father beareth record of me, and the Holy Ghost beareth record of the Father and me; and I bear record that the Father commandeth all men, everywhere, to repent and believe in me."

When the Lord proclaims there is a "doctrine" belonging to Him, it is important to take note. As He begins His doctrinal statement, He first reminds us again of the unity between Himself, His Father and the Holy Ghost. This reminder of unity has followed the admo-

---

[1040] Helaman 5:44 "And Nephi and Lehi were in the midst of them; yea, they were encircled about; yea, they were as if in the midst of a flaming fire, yet it did harm them not, neither did it take hold upon the walls of the prison; and they were filled with that joy which is unspeakable and full of glory."

[1041] D&C 76:33 "For they are vessels of wrath, doomed to suffer the wrath of God, with the devil and his angels in eternity;"

nition to avoid contention and anger—things which prevent our becoming one with each other.

To understand His doctrine you must first know and understand that the doctrine originates with the Father. Christ has completely accepted and advocates the doctrine. Moreover He embodies it.

The Father's doctrine is that "all men, everywhere, [must] repent and believe in [Christ]." This is what the whole of creation hangs on: the atonement of the Son. It is through the Son's sacrifice that the Father's plan became operational. Now, to return to the Father all must do so in reliance upon the merits of the Son.[1042]

The Son preaches the doctrine of, and bears witness of the Father. The Father bears witness of the Son. The Holy Ghost bears record of the Father and Son.

When did the Father bear record of the Son? Did you notice that? The FATHER bears record of the Son! I'm not talking about Matthew or Luke's testimony that the Father bore record of the Son, because that is Matthew's and Luke's testimony. I'm not talking about Joseph Smith's record of the Father's testimony of the Son. I'm talking about the Father's testimony. When did you hear the Father bear record of the Son?

The Father *does* bear record of the Son. But you must go through the Son to get to the Father. When you do, acting in faith according to the conditions established for your salvation, then you will receive the Father's testimony or record of the Son for yourself. But implicit in this statement is the fact that access to the Father is possible by the means provided through the Son. That is a ratification of the fullness of the Gospel. It is an invitation to return to heaven and obtain from the Father a confirmation of your salvation.

[1042] John 3:16 "For God so loved the world, that he gave his only begotten Son, that whosoever believeth in him should not perish, but have everlasting life."

The Father's testimony is that our salvation comes through Christ. For us the Father has provided a Savior. If we repent, we can come back into the presence of God and enter into our salvation and exaltation. But it is through the means provided for us: A Savior, who is Christ the Lord.

We are commanded to:

1. Repent.

2. Believe in Christ.

To repent is to turn again to Him. To follow Him and leave behind your sinful ways. To abandon the world and worldliness and to choose to always remember Him, that you may have His spirit to be with you always.

To believe in Him is to accept, study, contemplate and ponder His teachings. It is not to just go along with a herd, but to rise up from your position and awaken from your slumber. It is to grow into knowledge about Him. Belief leads to faith and faith to knowledge. But the process is initiated by your belief (**correct understanding**) of His teachings.

The doctrine continues . . .

3 Nephi 11:33–34

"And whoso believeth in me, and is baptized, the same shall be saved; and they are they who shall inherit the kingdom of God. And whoso believeth not in me, and is not baptized, shall be damned."

Imagine the importance attached to the ordinance of baptism! It is an absolute minimum requirement. Upon the proper performance of this ordinance, hangs the difference between being "saved" and "inheriting the kingdom of God" on the one hand, and being "damned" on the other.

[As a complete aside: A few posts back there was a comment about what a burden it would be for "the church" and "the priesthood" if people seek re-baptism to renew commitments. It was made as we approached Christ's teachings on baptism. The comment was so immediate and so dark in tone and content it has caused me rethink the importance of this idea. Anytime an idea is confrontational and dark, I pause to consider why that is so. Here's what now occurs to me. What a terrible burden it would be to depart this life without the ordinance of baptism properly performed, by proper authority, in the proper manner, with repentance preceding the event. I would not want a dark and troubled soul to perform baptism for anyone, but a person filled with joy, hope and the Spirit, having a testimony in Christ like Nephi. These people would not find performing such an ordinance troubling.

If there is a hint of doubt held by any baptized member of the church, why would any right-thinking and charitable soul refuse them the right to be re-baptized? Now, I've suggested the Alma exception and how that might be accomplished in a time of reluctance and resistance to recommitment baptism. But it occurs to me upon further reflection that since the church doesn't recognize or record re-baptisms anyway, why would this concern the "heavy laden priesthood" which has no time for such things? Anyone holding authority, at any place where there is sufficient water to perform the rite, could accomplish it. Since the church doesn't record it, there is no need of witnesses. It could be done in private, at any time, or any place with sufficient water. It could be done by any person holding the office of Priest. It would be good practice for future missionaries if they were given the opportunity. I think the idea is one which ought to be acted upon with regularity, in private and without troubling the busy and overburdened church and priesthood. A close family member could take care of it, and I suspect all involved will soon recognize heaven's approval of the idea.]

Well, back to the subject at hand. Anciently the Jews practiced baptism in "living water." That is, in a naturally renewing body of water, like a river, lake or ocean. Living water was part of the symbol. We have fonts, and there is nothing wrong with that. But I have always cherished my baptism in the Atlantic Ocean.

Well, believing in Christ precedes baptism. In fact, belief in Christ causes baptism. The one results in the other. Without faith in Him, there is no need for baptism. This then makes the first step belief in Christ, and baptism the second step.

I've heard of those who obtain a testimony of Christ in adulthood, but who were baptized many years earlier at age 8. If belief in Christ is supposed to precede baptism, but in fact follows it, does that recommend repeating the ordinance? Does Christ's establishment of an order to these things, by the commandment of the Father, matter? If it matters, then why not try it? If tried and it "tastes good" then you have your answer. And if nothing changes, then you also have learned something, as well.

I was fortunate to be able to follow the proper sequence. I was 19 years old when I came to the church. I try to follow the proper sequence with my own children by teaching them before baptism and testifying of Christ to them in a way calculated to produce faith in Him. I would take no offense, however, if one of my children were to later want to be re-baptized as an affirmation of their continuing belief in Christ. I can't see why anyone would take offense.

What does it mean to "inherit the kingdom of God?" Would that be important to secure while alive? This work cannot be done after death, you know.[1043] However, if offered the opportunity now and a

---

[1043] D&C 138:33 "These were taught faith in God, repentance from sin, vicarious baptism for the remission of sins, the gift of the Holy Ghost by the laying on of hands," person declines it, they cannot afterwards receive it and inherit the "kingdom of God." They inherit another kingdom.[1044]

This is important enough a matter that I rather think the whole subject is worth careful consideration. Christ's teachings have been carefully preserved at great effort and come to us by way of revelation and direct inspiration from God. From a prophet to another prophet in composition, and through a prophet in translation. It holds a power for salvation in the kingdom of God. It is worth prayerful consideration. The outcome is the difference between the "kingdom of God" on the one hand and "damnation" on the other.

3 Nephi 11:35

> "Verily, verily, I say unto you, that this is my doctrine, and I bear record of it from the Father; and whoso believeth in me believeth in the Father also; and unto him will the Father bear record of me, for he will visit him with fire and with the Holy Ghost."

Belief in Christ necessarily means belief in the Father. To believe Christ is to accept His message of the Father's primacy and authority.

You see in these three members of the Godhead a full establishment of interconnected roles and responsibilities.

The Father ordains the plan. It is He who presides.

The Son implements the plan. It is He who makes the required sacrifice to save us.

The Holy Ghost activates the plan. It is the "fire" of the Holy Ghost which makes new, cleanses and perfects man's understanding.

These three are "one" and united. They provide mankind with the possibility for salvation and exaltation.

[1044] D&C 76:74 "Who received not the testimony of Jesus in the flesh, but afterwards received it."

Christ "bears record of it from the Father." This means that Christ is the Father's messenger announcing the Father's plan. What of the need for two witnesses?[1045] One of the criticisms of Christ's message was the absence of additional witnesses.[1046] Is Christ doing that same thing here with the Nephites? Does His announcement that He speaks for the Father constitute one, or two witnesses? The Father first bore witness of Christ.[1047] Now Christ bears witness of Him.

The Father's testimony always affirms the status of the Son as His Beloved, and of our need to "hear Him."[1048] The Father can, and does, acknowledge others as His.[1049] But, unlike the Son who has repeatedly visited this earth, walked upon it[1050], been handled by

---

[1045] Matthew 18:16 "But if he will not hear *thee, then* take with thee one or two more, that in the mouth of two or three witnesses every word may be established."

[1046] John 8:13–14 "The Pharisees therefore said unto him, Thou bearest record of thyself; thy record is not true. Jesus answered and said unto them, Though I bear record of myself, *yet* my record is true: for I know whence I came, and whither I go; but ye cannot tell whence I come, and whither I go."

[1047] 3 Nephi 11:6–7 "And behold, the third time they did understand the voice which they heard; and it said unto them: Behold my Beloved Son, in whom I am well pleased, in whom I have glorified my name—hear ye him."

[1048] Matthew 17:5 "While he yet spake, behold, a bright cloud overshadowed them: and behold a voice out of the cloud, which said, This is my beloved Son, in whom I am well pleased; hear ye him."
JS–H 1:17 "It no sooner appeared than I found myself delivered from the enemy which held me bound. When the light rested upon me I saw two Personages, whose brightness and glory defy all description, standing above me in the air. One of them spake unto me, calling me by name and said, pointing to the other—*This is My Beloved Son. Hear Him!*"
Matthew 3:17 "And lo a voice from heaven, saying, This is my beloved Son, in whom I am well pleased."

[1049] Psalms 2:7 "I will declare the decree: the Lord hath said unto me, Thou *art* my Son; this day have I begotten thee."

[1050] Luke 24:15–16 "And it came to pass, that, while they communed *together* and reasoned, Jesus himself drew near, and went with them. But their eyes were holden that they should not know him."

people[1051], and eaten here[1052], the Father does not come into contact with this earth in its fallen state.[1053] The only time the Father had contact with this earth was before the Fall, in the Paradisiacal setting of Eden—which was a Temple at the time.[1054] Whenever there has been contact with the Father thereafter, He has been at a distance from this earth.[1055]

[1051] Luke 24:36–39 "And as they thus spake, Jesus himself stood in the midst of them, and saith unto them, Peace *be* unto you. But they were terrified and affrighted, and supposed that they had seen a spirit. And he said unto them, Why are ye troubled? and why do thoughts arise in your hearts? Behold my hands and my feet, that it is I myself: handle me, and see; for a spirit hath not flesh and bones, as ye see me have."
3 Nephi 11:14–15 "Arise and come forth unto me, that ye may thrust your hands into my side, and also that ye may feel the prints of the nails in my hands and in my feet, that ye may know that I am the God of Israel, and the God of the whole earth, and have been slain for the sins of the world. And it came to pass that the multitude went forth, and thrust their hands into his side, and did feel the prints of the nails in his hands and in his feet; and this they did do, going forth one by one until they had all gone forth, and did see with their eyes and did feel with their hands, and did know of a surety and did bear record, that it was he, of whom it was written by the prophets, that should come."

[1052] John 21:13 "Jesus then cometh, and taketh bread, and giveth them, and fish likewise."

[1053] Matthew 17:5 "While he yet spake, behold, a bright cloud overshadowed them: and behold a voice out of the cloud, which said, This is my beloved Son, in whom I am well pleased; hear ye him."
JS–H 1:17 "It no sooner appeared than I found myself delivered from the enemy which held me bound. When the light rested upon me I saw two Personages, whose brightness and glory defy all description, standing above me in the air. One of them spake unto me, calling me by name and said, pointing to the other—*This is My Beloved Son. Hear Him!*"

[1054] Genesis 3:8 "And they heard the voice of the Lord God walking in the garden in the cool of the day: and Adam and his wife hid themselves from the presence of the Lord God amongst the trees of the garden."

[1055] Moses 7:24 "And there came generation upon generation; and Enoch was high and lifted up, even in the bosom of the Father, and of the Son of Man; and behold, the power of Satan was upon all the face of the earth."
1 Nephi 1:8 "And being thus overcome with the Spirit, he was carried away in a vision, even that he saw the heavens open, and he thought he saw God sitting upon his throne, surrounded with numberless concourses of angels in the attitude of singing and praising their God."
Alma 36:22 "Yea, methought I saw, even as our father Lehi saw, God sitting upon his throne, surrounded with numberless concourses of angels, in the attitude of singing and praising their God; yea, and my soul did long to be there."

There is a formality with the Father that does not exist with the Son. For example, the Son has eaten with mortal man while He was immortal, both before His ministry in the flesh[1056] and after.[1057] As our Redeemer, He is directly responsible for us and has contact with us to perform His redemptive service. The Father, on the other hand, is different in status, responsibility, glory, and dominion. The Son can appear to mortal man without showing His glory or requiring any alteration of the mortal who beholds Him.[1058] To behold the Father, to endure His presence, one must be transfigured.[1059] Mortal man cannot behold the Father's works while mortal, for if you comprehend them you cannot afterward remain mortal in the flesh.[1060]

The primary means to learn of Christ for mortal man is the Holy Ghost. It is this means which brings all things to your remembrance.[1061] Once the learning has culminated in preparation of

---

[1056] Exodus 24:9–11 "Then went up Moses, and Aaron, Nadab, and Abihu, and seventy of the elders of Israel: And they saw the God of Israel: and *there was* under his feet as it were a paved work of a sapphire stone, and as it were the body of heaven in *his* clearness. And upon the nobles of the children of Israel he laid not his hand: also they saw God, and did eat and drink."

[1057] Luke 24:41–43 "And while they yet believed not for joy, and wondered, he said unto them, Have ye here any meat? And they gave him a piece of a broiled fish, and of an honeycomb. And he took *it,* and did eat before them."

[1058] John 20:15–17 "Jesus saith unto her, Woman, why weepest thou? whom seekest thou? She, supposing him to be the gardener, saith unto him, Sir, if thou have borne him hence, tell me where thou hast laid him, and I will take him away. Jesus saith unto her, Mary. She turned herself, and saith unto him, Rabboni; which is to say, Master. Jesus saith unto her, Touch me not; for I am not yet ascended to my Father: but go to my brethren, and say unto them, I ascend unto my Father, and your Father; and *to* my God, and your God."

[1059] Moses 1:2 "And he saw God face to face, and he talked with him, and the glory of God was upon Moses; therefore Moses could endure his presence."

[1060] Moses 1:5 "Wherefore, no man can behold all my works, except he behold all my glory; and no man can behold all my glory, and afterwards remain in the flesh on the earth."

[1061] John 14:26 "But the Comforter, *which is* the Holy Ghost, whom the Father will send in my name, he shall teach you all things, and bring all things to your remembrance, whatsoever I have said unto you."

the individual, then the Savior has a continuing ministry.[1062] The Savior's ministry is to bring the person redemption.

When this process is complete, then it is the responsibility of those who have been redeemed to cry repentance to their neighbors.[1063] Indeed, the desire to bring others to receive redemption becomes their primary concern.[1064]

The process then produces those who bear testimony of the Son. If they are called of God, they will use scriptures to testify of Christ. This has always been the pattern ordained by God.[1065] They may understand the scriptures more clearly, because they have seen the same things as earlier prophets.[1066] But their testimonies will draw from the scriptures and the words of their brothers in Christ who went before as they testify of Him.

It is through such signs as these you know the Father and Son are one, and the Holy Ghost and the Son are one, and the messengers

---

[1062] John 14:21 "He that hath my commandments, and keepeth them, he it is that loveth me: and he that loveth me shall be loved of my Father, and I will love him, and will manifest myself to him."

[1063] D&C 88:74, 81 "And I give unto you, who are the first laborers in this last kingdom, a commandment that you assemble yourselves together, and organize yourselves, and prepare yourselves, and sanctify yourselves; yea, purify your hearts, and cleanse your hands and your feet before me, that I may make you clean; . . . Behold, I sent you out to testify and warn the people, and it becometh every man who hath been warned to warn his neighbor."

[1064] Mosiah 28:3 "Now they were desirous that salvation should be declared to every creature, for they could not bear that any human soul should perish; yea, even the very thoughts that any soul should endure endless torment did cause them to quake and tremble."

[1065] Jacob 7:10–11 "And I said unto him: Believest thou the scriptures? And he said, Yea. And I said unto him: Then ye do not understand them; for they truly testify of Christ. Behold, I say unto you that none of the prophets have written, nor prophesied, save they have spoken concerning this Christ."

[1066] JS–H 1:74 "Our minds being now enlightened, we began to have the scriptures laid open to our understandings, and the true meaning and intention of their more mysterious passages revealed unto us in a manner which we never could attain to previously, nor ever before had thought of. In the meantime we were forced to keep secret the circumstances of having received the Priesthood and our having been baptized, owing to a spirit of persecution which had already manifested itself in the neighborhood."

sent by them will testify of the Father, Son and Holy Ghost. These three are the ones in whom faith must be focused for salvation. Though the heavens may include hosts of others, saving faith must be focused in the Father, Son and Holy Ghost alone. Whenever attention and worship moves from the Father, Son and Holy Ghost, the result is invariably apostasy and false beliefs.[1067]

The doctrine of Christ is to be strictly followed. It alone delivers from destruction. All other paths lead to error, foolishness and the dark, where you will perish.[1068]

From following this process we obtain the necessary "fire and the Holy Ghost" which redeems, purges, purifies and changes us into a new creature in Christ.

I have said very little of my personal experiences because of how quickly people turn from following Christ to following men whenever attention is drawn to a man. Mankind is inclined toward idolatry. The church has become a great idol. I do not intend to supplant the Lord, nor to call attention to myself, nor to offer myself as an idol for others. *I cannot save anyone.* If not for Christ and His atonement, I would have only dread for my eternal state. The doctrine of Christ is

---

[1067] See Deuteronomy 16, 18, 19, and 19. Also 1 Corinthians 8:5–6 "For though there be that are called gods, whether in heaven or in earth, (as there be gods many, and lords many,) But to us *there is but* one God, the Father, of whom *are* all things, and we in him; and one Lord Jesus Christ, by whom *are* all things, and we by him."
2 Kings 17:13–16 "Yet the Lord testified against Israel, and against Judah, by all the prophets, *and by* all the seers, saying, Turn ye from your evil ways, and keep my commandments *and* my statutes, according to all the law which I commanded your fathers, and which I sent to you by my servants the prophets. Notwithstanding they would not hear, but hardened their necks, like to the neck of their fathers, that did not believe in the Lord their God. And they rejected his statutes, and his covenant that he made with their fathers, and his testimonies which he testified against them; and they followed vanity, and became vain, and went after the heathen that *were* round about them, *concerning* whom the Lord had charged them, that they should not do like them. And they left all the commandments of the Lord their God, and made them molten images, *even* two calves, and made a grove, and worshipped all the host of heaven, and served Baal."

[1068] Deuteronomy 8:19 "And it shall be, if thou do at all forget the Lord thy God, and walk after other gods, and serve them, and worship them, I testify against you this day that ye shall surely perish."

what the Father ordained as the means for salvation. Anyone who interferes with the process, or offers another means for salvation, cannot deliver.[1069] Whether it is an institution or an individual, no one other than Christ can save. Hence His title as Savior. For some reason mankind is so prone to error, so quick to leave the path, and so vulnerable to being deceived, that focus must remain on the Son, as empowered and sent by the Father, through the witness of the Holy Ghost, or we go astray. Joseph cautioned:

> "How much more dignified and noble are the thoughts of God, than the vain imaginations of the human heart! None but fools will trifle with the souls of men." (*TPJS*, 137)

3 Nephi 11:36

> "And thus will the Father bear record of me, and the Holy Ghost will bear record unto him of the Father and me; for the Father, and I, and the Holy Ghost are one."

The phrase: "And thus will the Father bear record of me" is referring to the Father visiting "him with fire and the Holy Ghost." This means that to the recipient of the baptism of fire and the Holy Ghost comes a witness to the person of the Father. When the baptism of fire and the Holy Ghost come to you, so does the Father's testimony of the Son.

You cannot receive this baptism and not have a testimony given to you by the Father of the Son.

In the Book of Mormon we read accounts of conversion experiences which include visitations of angels or opening of the heavens.[1070] These converts' experiences did not come after a lifetime

---

[1069] Mosiah 3:17 "And moreover, I say unto you, that there shall be no other name given nor any other way nor means whereby salvation can come unto the children of men, only in and through the name of Christ, the Lord Omnipotent."

[1070] See e.g., Mosiah 27:11–24; Alma 22:16–18, 23; Alma 19:12–19.

of study or reading a library of scholarly works. Indeed, in some cases the only information they had before the encounter came from the words of a missionary testifying to the truth.

Becoming converted is a question of sincerity, real intent, and asking God. It is not about the library you have read. Indeed, approaching it on purely intellectual terms has never produced a single convert. I've written a chapter on this in *Eighteen Verses*.

The problem is always obtaining a connection to the Father, Son and Holy Ghost. It is not a matter of scholarship. Joseph was anything but a scholar when he encountered God in the First Vision. He was young and ignorant. He read the Bible, believed in God's existence, and trusted the promise by James that if he were to ask God he would not be upbraided but would be answered.[1071] Therefore he decided to ask, with real intent, trusting in the promise.[1072]

Because he asked, he met God. Walking into the grove near his home that morning he was a foolish and ignorant boy. Walking back he was a prophet. Though it would be many years following that encounter before he appreciated how far he would have to go to gain knowledge of godliness and the mysteries of salvation. But all of his study and effort was informed by the scriptures and revelation. In my view, this is how it should be.

[1071] James 1:5–6 "If any of you lack wisdom, let him ask of God, that giveth to all *men* liberally, and upbraideth not; and it shall be given him. But let him ask in faith, nothing wavering. For he that wavereth is like a wave of the sea driven with the wind and tossed."

[1072] JS–H 1:12–13 "Never did any passage of scripture come with more power to the heart of man than this did at this time to mine. It seemed to enter with great force into every feeling of my heart. I reflected on it again and again, knowing that if any person needed wisdom from God, I did; for how to act I did not know, and unless I could get more wisdom than I then had, I would never know; for the teachers of religion of the different sects understood the same passages of scripture so differently as to destroy all confidence in settling the question by an appeal to the Bible. At length I came to the conclusion that I must either remain in darkness and confusion, or else I must do as James directs, that is, ask of God. I at length came to the determination to "ask of God," concluding that if he gave wisdom to them that lacked wisdom, and would give liberally, and not upbraid, I might venture."

Scriptures are an essential anchor of understanding. All truths should find a comfortable setting inside existing scripture. If a notion or teaching is jarringly contradictory of existing scripture, then there must be a very good reason or explanation before it should be accepted. It has been my experience that revelation does not contradict, but opens up meaning of the scriptures. This was Joseph's and Oliver's experience, as well.[1073]

When I study other materials, I do so to inform my reading and understanding of scripture, not to supplant it. I spend as much time with scripture study as I do with other writings. Although I could recite things using my own words, I find the language of scripture describes truths better than new wordings and therefore often use the language of scripture even if I do not show them in quotes. I also make frequent reference to scripture in this blog to show the reader that the scriptures are an existing library of material dealing with every part of Christ's Gospel. Since we have scripture made available to us at great effort from God and the prophets, it would be terribly ungrateful for us to fail to study what they have provided.

The "record" we already have of the Father's testimony of the Son, the Son's testimony of the Father, and the Holy Ghost's interaction with mankind is found in the scriptures. Although you may not see it fully without further revelation, it is nevertheless there. I have found the scriptures often open up further revelation. This is how Section 76, the First Vision, Section 138, Section 93, Section 132, and many other revelations have come to us. Search the meaning of scripture, and then ask God for what you do not see through your

---

[1073] JS–H 1:74 "Our minds being now enlightened, we began to have the scriptures laid open to our understandings, and the true meaning and intention of their more mysterious passages revealed unto us in a manner which we never could attain to previously, nor ever before had thought of. In the meantime we were forced to keep secret the circumstances of having received the Priesthood and our having been baptized, owing to a spirit of persecution which had already manifested itself in the neighborhood."

own effort. Appreciation for what has been given already produces further revelation.

The Father, Son and Holy Ghost are one. And the primary means for obtaining access to their "record" spoken of in this verse, is through the scriptures. Although I may try to shed additional light upon the meaning of scripture, I try to keep the scriptures an integral part of anything I write. (Excepting only the parables, where I felt free to let another tradition inform how and what I have written. And the proverbs, which I titled "Sayings" at the end of *The Second Comforter*, was another tradition as well.)

3 Nephi 11:37–38

> "And again I say unto you, ye must repent, and become as a little child, and be baptized in my name, or ye can in nowise receive these things. And again I say unto you, ye must repent, and be baptized in my name, and become as a little child, or ye can in nowise inherit the kingdom of God."

Repentance is not likely unless a person is willing to undergo a change to become more "childlike" in perspective and attitude. I've written a chapter on this in *The Second Comforter*. I used that as the basis for my comments at the recent Chiasmus Conference. It is more than just an analogy or good advice. It is a prerequisite. It is the only way you can "inherit the kingdom of God."

Children are open to change and willing to learn. They welcome new ideas for all ideas are new to them. The world is new to them. They feel their ignorance and are anxious to fill it with information and understanding. They know they are unable to cope with the world they live in unless they obtain more understanding than they have. So they relentlessly search to know more.

On the other hand, adults are generally closed. They believe they already know something, and therefore are unwilling to receive more.[1074]

Adults learn disciplines of study and then think the Gospel should be viewed by the tools of the scholar. To the economist, all of the Gospel appears to be financial. To the philosopher, all of the Gospel appears to be dialectic. To the lawyer it is a legal system. But the Gospel is separate from the understanding of men. It requires us to surrender our arrogance and foolishness and come as a child to learn anew everything about life and truth. This is why the Gospel always begins with creation, informs of the Fall, and preaches the Atonement.

We must "repent" because the foundation of accepting new truth begins with the realization that we're not getting anywhere by what we've already done. We need to abandon old ways and begin anew. Until we are open to the new truths offered through the Gospel, we can't even start the journey. We're headed in the wrong direction and don't even know it. First we need to realize our direction is wrong. Then stop going that way. When we turn to the new direction, we've begun repenting.[1075]

From repentance comes light and truth. At first, just turning to face the new direction is a great revelation. But you've not seen anything until you walk in that direction for a while. As you move toward the light and receive more, the world itself changes meaning and nothing you used to think important remains important.[1076]

[1074] 2 Nephi 28:29 "Wo be unto him that shall say: We have received the word of God, and we need no more of the word of God, for we have enough!"

[1075] 2 Corinthians 5:17 "Therefore if any man *be* in Christ, *he is* a new creature: old things are passed away; behold, all things are become new."

[1076] Isaiah 65:17 "For, behold, I create new heavens and a new earth: and the former shall not be remembered, nor come into mind."

Becoming as a little child, or repenting, must precede baptism if you are to be saved. Otherwise, you cannot "receive these things" or, in other words, you cannot accept the new truths and perspectives the Gospel will require you to know and accept. Unless these steps are taken you cannot "inherit the kingdom of God" because only such people will be able to enter.

Teachable. Open. Willing to receive more.

Able to endure difficulties as a result of the changes which come to them.

Patient.

Submissive to God.

And eager to learn more.[1077]

Not arrogant.

Not trying to fit the new truths into your existing framework of false notions.[1078]

Not resisting truth and arguing against it.[1079]

Not proud or boastful, secure in your own salvation.[1080]

[1077] Mosiah 3:19 "For the natural man is an enemy to God, and has been from the fall of Adam, and will be, forever and ever, unless he yields to the enticings of the Holy Spirit, and putteth off the natural man and becometh a saint through the atonement of Christ the Lord, and becometh as a child, submissive, meek, humble, patient, full of love, willing to submit to all things which the Lord seeth fit to inflict upon him, even as a child doth submit to his father."

[1078] Mark 2:22 "And no man putteth new wine into old bottles: else the new wine doth burst the bottles, and the wine is spilled, and the bottles will be marred: but new wine must be put into new bottles."

[1079] 1 Timothy 6:4–6 "He is proud, knowing nothing, but doting about questions and strifes of words, whereof cometh envy, strife, railings, evil surmisings, Perverse disputings of men of corrupt minds, and destitute of the truth, supposing that gain is godliness: from such withdraw thyself. But godliness with contentment is great gain."

[1080] Luke 18:11 "The Pharisee stood and prayed thus with himself, God, I thank thee, that I am not as other men *are*, extortioners, unjust, adulterers, or even as this publican."

Not holding a testimony that you will be saved while others around you will be lost because they do not believe as you do.[1081]

How few there will be who find it.[1082]

Most people are simply unwilling to repent. They have such truth as they are willing to receive already, and want nothing more.[1083]

Even Christ is unable to persuade them to accept His Gospel.

[1081] Alma 31:14–18 "Therefore, whosoever desired to worship must go forth and stand upon the top thereof, and stretch forth his hands towards heaven, and cry with a loud voice, saying: Holy, holy God; we believe that thou art God, and we believe that thou art holy, and that thou wast a spirit, and that thou art a spirit, and that thou wilt be a spirit forever. Holy God, we believe that thou hast separated us from our brethren; and we do not believe in the tradition of our brethren, which was handed down to them by the childishness of their fathers; but we believe that thou hast elected us to be thy holy children; and also thou hast made it known unto us that there shall be no Christ. But thou art the same yesterday, today, and forever; and thou hast elected us that we shall be saved, whilst all around us are elected to be cast by thy wrath down to hell; for the which holiness, O God, we thank thee; and we also thank thee that thou hast elected us, that we may not be led away after the foolish traditions of our brethren, which doth bind them down to a belief of Christ, which doth lead their hearts to wander far from thee, our God. And again we thank thee, O God, that we are a chosen and a holy people. Amen."

[1082] Matthew 7:14 "Because strait *is* the gate, and narrow *is* the way, which leadeth unto life, and few there be that find it."
3 Nephi 14:14 "Because strait is the gate, and narrow is the way, which leadeth unto life, and few there be that find it."
3 Nephi 27:33 "And it came to pass that when Jesus had ended these sayings he said unto his disciples: Enter ye in at the strait gate; for strait is the gate, and narrow is the way that leads to life, and few there be that find it; but wide is the gate, and broad the way which leads to death, and many there be that travel therein, until the night cometh, wherein no man can work."
D&C 132:22 "For strait is the gate, and narrow the way that leadeth unto the exaltation and continuation of the lives, and few there be that find it, because ye receive me not in the world neither do ye know me."

[1083] 2 Nephi 28:14–15 "They wear stiff necks and high heads; yea, and because of pride, and wickedness, and abominations, and whoredoms, they have all gone astray save it be a few, who are the humble followers of Christ; nevertheless, they are led, that in many instances they do err because they are taught by the precepts of men. O the wise, and the learned, and the rich, that are puffed up in the pride of their hearts, and all those who preach false doctrines, and all those who commit whoredoms, and pervert the right way of the Lord, wo, wo, wo be unto them, saith the Lord God Almighty, for they shall be thrust down to hell!"

3 Nephi 11:39

"Verily, verily, I say unto you, that this is my doctrine, and whoso buildeth upon this buildeth upon my rock, and the gates of hell shall not prevail against them."

This is the reason for this doctrine. It will allow those who accept and follow it to endure against all enemies. It will allow them to prevail.

Even the "gates of hell shall not prevail against them." Meaning that death and hell can have no claim upon them. They will not be taken captive either in this world[1084] or when they leave this world.[1085]

When we consider the Father is to bear record of the Son, and the Son bears record of the Father, and the Holy Ghost bears record of the Father and Son, then we realize this doctrine of Christ is designed to put us in contact with all three members of the Godhead. We are to join them. We are to be one with them.

There is no separating us from God when we have the record of each given to us.

It is interesting that the "rock" upon which we build is the Father, Son and Holy Ghost. There is abundant evidence of other "gods" and of "goddesses." It is beyond dispute that the "image of God"

[1084] Alma 12:11 "And they that will harden their hearts, to them is given the lesser portion of the word until they know nothing concerning his mysteries; and then they are taken captive by the devil, and led by his will down to destruction. Now this is what is meant by the chains of hell."

[1085] Alma 40:13 "And then shall it come to pass, that the spirits of the wicked, yea, who are evil—for behold, they have no part nor portion of the Spirit of the Lord; for behold, they chose evil works rather than good; therefore the spirit of the devil did enter into them, and take possession of their house—and these shall be cast out into outer darkness; there shall be weeping, and wailing, and gnashing of teeth, and this because of their own iniquity, being led captive by the will of the devil."

includes both "male and female."[1086] It is inescapable, therefore, that the God we worship includes a Father and a Mother. However, we are only to seek after the Father, Son and Holy Ghost as the "rock" upon which our salvation is to be built.

Oddly enough, mankind prefers a female deity over a male deity. Catholicism has reconciled this preference by the doctrine of Immaculate Conception and the cultic veneration of Mary. Pope John Paul II was an ardent believer in the Cult of Mary and made no secret of that veneration. It is almost beyond dispute that Mary's status is preferred over Christ's in the lives of the common Catholic.

In the Old Testament, the goddess Ashtoreth, (in her various iterations) was a leading figure in apostasies of ancient Israel. She was the female consort to Baal (who also had various spellings). The Egyptian counterpart being Hathor, whose image appears in figure 5 of Facsimile No. 2 in the Book of Abraham. The representation there being Egyptian—that is, emerging through the great cycle of life, afterlife and resurrection coming through the womb. An understanding of which Hugh Nibley was setting forth in *One Eternal Round*. This work was reduced in volume by half before publication. This resulted in problems with the published text. That, however, is another subject not relevant here.

Notwithstanding man's preference for the female god, for salvation we must anchor ourselves to the Father, Son and Holy Ghost. They are the "rock" upon which we must build to avoid the gates of hell, despite our knowledge of heaven, salvation and the necessary

---

[1086] Genesis 1:27 "So God created man in his *own* image, in the image of God created he him; male and female created he them."
Moses 2:27 "And I, God, created man in mine own image, in the image of mine Only Begotten created I him; male and female created I them."
Abraham 4:27 "So the Gods went down to organize man in their own image, in the image of the Gods to form they him, male and female to form they them."

unity of the sexes before salvation is obtained.[1087] It is through the union of the sexes that mortals imitate immortality, for all of us will die. Yet if joined together we will continue through the seed forever, as the gods.[1088]

There is also the continuing trouble about polygamy which so often afflicted the discussions on this blog before comments were discontinued. Those who preach on the subject often speak out of the coarseness of ambition and insecurity (for those always go together), and without understanding how a marriage must work to warrant preservation beyond this life.

Ask yourself what kind of a relationship would be godlike? What association between a man and a woman would be something the heavens would want to preserve and continue? Is an ambitious man who looks upon a woman as someone to rule over worthy of heavenly preservation? Is such a man worthy of one wife, let alone several?

Wouldn't you expect the relationship between a man and woman worthy of eternal preservation to evidence such things as equality, respect, kindness, joyful and voluntary interchange of thoughts, and to be grounded in love? Wouldn't you expect such a marriage to be part of heaven, though the parties live as mortals on the earth? Why would you expect a form of marriage, having as its chief output, unhappy but frequently pregnant women, having an absentee husband to be godlike?

[1087] 1 Corinthians 11:11 "Nevertheless neither is the man without the woman, neither the woman without the man, in the Lord."

[1088] D&C 132:20–22 "Then shall they be gods, because they have no end; therefore shall they be from everlasting to everlasting, because they continue; then shall they be above all, because all things are subject unto them. Then shall they be gods, because they have all power, and the angels are subject unto them. Verily, verily, I say unto you, except ye abide my law ye cannot attain to this glory. For strait is the gate, and narrow the way that leadeth unto the exaltation and continuation of the lives, and few there be that find it, because ye receive me not in the world neither do ye know me."

Have you read the tenth parable in *Ten Parables*? If you have and still think you need a "brood" of women to become godlike, then you haven't understood the tenth parable.

Foolishness never was enlightenment. Ambition is unbecoming in a candidate for exaltation. We will keep going into Christ's sermons to the Nephites and, as we do, you will find He emphasizes how to become like Him through service and abasing yourself. By sacrifice and devotion to the best interests of others. Not by compulsion, dominion and ruling over others.

If you want to prevail against the gates of hell, then Christ's simple doctrines need to become yours. They need to be how you live and what you do. They are the only rock upon which you can build and have something which will endure the buffetings of hell itself.

If a man hasn't made a single woman happy, why would he be trusted to have more wives? Why would he want them? What does such a man think the purpose of marriage to be? Gratification? Industrial baby-production? What's the reason? If happiness is the end of our design by God, then wouldn't you need to find someone who can live in peace and happiness with another person as their husband as the first step? If that is true, then why isn't that challenge enough in a marriage between one man and one woman? Until that has been conquered, why should misery be multiplied by adding additional spouses into a failed interpersonal relationship?

Too many people are advocating too many alternatives which distract from the simplicity of what is really needed. There aren't enough marriages worthy of preservation. Make yours one of them. That is a very good work and challenge enough for all of us at present.

3 Nephi 11:40

"And whoso shall declare more or less than this, and establish it for my doctrine, the same cometh of evil, and is not built upon my rock; but he buildeth upon a sandy foundation, and the gates of hell stand open to receive such when the floods come and the winds beat upon them."

Here is Christ's explanation of why we must focus on these doctrines to be saved. I've heard more words of caution about speaking "more" than I've ever heard cautioning about "less." Both are a problem. It is more fashionable today to speak less about Christ's doctrine, or to circumscribe it into so narrow a meaning as to render it powerless in effect.

First, as to "more." When we "declare more" we are getting ahead of the process. We aren't to worship the "hosts of heaven," nor a heavenly mother. Despite all we may know about Her, that knowledge won't save. Other personages or ministers cannot save either. Gabriel will not. Enoch will not. Michael will not. Only the Son will save; and the Father will bear testimony of Him. Interesting stories about individual spiritual encounters or experiences will not save. They are evidence that heaven is still attending to us, but the details are for the individual. The experiences that will save have already been recorded in scripture for our general instruction. Outside of scripture those individual experiences are only useful to the extent they shed light upon scriptural accounts. If a person can help you understand Daniel's visionary encounters by what they have been shown, then their personal experiences are not as important as the light they may shed upon Daniel's prophecy. Similarly what I've written is helpful only to understand scripture, and not otherwise. Even the account of Gethsemane is anchored in scripture and useful only to the extent it sheds light upon what has been given to us in the New Testament Gospels, Nephi's prophecy, Alma's testimony and D&C 19. I do think my account goes further to explain what occurred than any other writing which has come to my attention. Nevertheless the scriptures are needed as the primary tool for understanding our Lord's atonement. So the definition of "more" would include such things that supplant scripture or suggest anything is more important than the Father, Son and Holy Ghost; but things as may shed additional light on the meaning of scripture.

Interestingly enough, when we "declare less" we are also condemned. It works both ways. It's a two-edged sword. Not "more nor less" is permitted. We sometimes greet preaching "less" with applause, because we want less. But that is no better than missing the mark while preaching "more." Perhaps it is worse, because it represents a rejection of truth. It is active suppression of what needs to be proclaimed.

All of us must be concerned about declaring less. Deleting or omitting is as serious a matter as adding. Either will allow the gates of hell to prevail.

When you adopt creedal Historic Christianity and amalgamate the Father, Son and Holy Ghost into a single cosmic siamese-triplet construct, you are declaring them as less. The disembodiment of God the Father was a lie to supplant and replace Him by another disembodied pretender claiming to be the god of this world.

Christ's teaching here is preliminary to the Sermon that follows. In the coming Sermon we will read a better preserved version of the Sermon on the Mount from Jerusalem, called here the Sermon at Bountiful. But this explanation of doctrine is given by Christ first. The foundation of doctrine of the oneness of the Father, Son and Holy Ghost, the conferral of power to baptize, and manner of baptism come before the great Sermon. First we receive the instruction to avoid disputes. These disputes lead to contention that lays the foundation for anger between men. This doctrine is so foundational that Christ covers it before any other teaching. Therefore, you should realize its importance.

We will be captured by hell if we do not understand and follow these teachings. Though they are Christ's very first instructions, we almost never discuss them. You may want to re-read these verses again, and realize their fundamental importance.

Christ is saying it is "evil" to do more or less with His doctrine. It surely is, for ignoring, altering, omitting or enlarging leads to evil.

3 Nephi 11:41

"Therefore, go forth unto this people, and declare the words which I have spoken, unto the ends of the earth."

This is the charge given by Christ to the twelve whom He had called and given power to baptize. It was overheard by those who had been witnessing these events. But the charge is to the twelve.

The obligation to declare the doctrine of Christ, preach repentance, baptize with authority and make known the Father, Son and Holy Ghost is imposed upon the twelve. This burden, therefore, rests on them and is theirs to bear off "unto this people." They are to warn everybody of these obligations. Not just those who were there.

The extent of the duty runs "unto the ends of the earth." From where they were at the time Christ was preaching, to the entire North and South American continents and all those who may be living there at the time were the assigned mission field to whom the doctrine of Christ was to be declared.

The break between this portion of Christ's teachings and what would follow is interesting to consider. The remainder of His teachings will form the primary message foundational to Christianity. It is the new, higher law which replaces the earlier Law of Moses. Yet this portion, declared by Christ as His "doctrine" is the part to be taken first and declared everywhere. Why?

A fair conclusion to reach is that before you consider the new, higher law you must first:

- Repent
- Be Baptized
- Receive the Holy Ghost
- Have a correct understanding of God the Father, God the Son, and the Holy Ghost

These things precede His replacement of the older, lower law with His new, higher law. It is reasonable to conclude you will not comprehend His follow-on teachings if you have not first repented, been baptized, received the Holy Ghost, and understand the God-head. Or, even more to the point: You will never be able to LIVE His new, higher law unless these steps are taken first. Until then you may aspire, but you will not be able to live them. They address the heart, rather than just conduct. They go to the deepest convictions inside you, what motivates you, and the reasons for your conduct. Your conduct will follow these precepts when you have been changed. For the required change, the tools discussed first must be acquired.

He will return to the themes of this opening statement, declaring nothing more or less than what He has taught should be given as His.[1089]

So we turn from this introductory, first statement of His doctrine to His great foundational Sermon at Bountiful in which the higher law is first given in one, complete statement of what we are to become. It is not merely direction to us. It is also a revelation of what kind of person Christ was. He explains it Himself . . .

[1089] 3 Nephi 18:12–13 "And I give unto you a commandment that ye shall do these things. And if ye shall always do these things blessed are ye, for ye are built upon my rock. But whoso among you shall do more or less than these are not built upon my rock, but are built upon a sandy foundation; and when the rain descends, and the floods come, and the winds blow, and beat upon them, they shall fall, and the gates of hell are ready open to receive them."

3 NEPHI 12

3 Nephi 12:1

"And it came to pass that when Jesus had spoken these words unto Nephi, and to those who had been called, (now the number of them who had been called, and received power and authority to baptize, was twelve) and behold, he stretched forth his hand unto the multitude, and cried unto them, saying: Blessed are ye if ye shall give heed unto the words of these twelve whom I have chosen from among you to minister unto you, and to be your servants; and unto them I have given power that they may baptize you with water; and after that ye are baptized with water, behold, I will baptize you with fire and with the Holy Ghost; therefore blessed are ye if ye shall believe in me and be baptized, after that ye have seen me and know that I am."

Nephi and the other twelve heard and recorded the words we've been reviewing in Chapter 11. But here Christ makes certain all others who were present also knew the same doctrine. Notice the following:

"He stretched forth His hand." What does that mean? Why is it noted in the record? Why would the fact that He stretched forth His hand be significant enough to etch into metal plates?

Why does it say Christ "cried unto them?" How loud would He need to make His voice before it would be considered "crying" out to the audience? This suggests that what was covered in Chapter 11 was not loud enough for all those present to hear. But what follows He wants everyone to hear.

The Sermon at Bountiful begins with a new beatitude. "Blessed are ye if ye shall give heed unto the words of these twelve whom I have chosen from among you to minister unto you." A commenter recently suggested this means that any person ever called to any council of twelve is entitled to the same kind of status. Is that correct? Does membership in a group entitle someone to respect? Would receiving power directly from Christ entitle a person to respect? What if someone were to receive power from Christ, but not be included in some presiding group? For example, John the Baptist received power from an angel to overthrow the kingdom of the Jews at eight days old. He was never among a presiding group.[1090] Paul was given power directly from heaven, calling himself "born out of due time" because he became a witness after Christ's resurrection and was not among the leadership when first visited.[1091] Which does this apply to: those called to preside, or those called directly by the Lord (as the scriptures testify is sometimes the case)? Or does it only apply to the twelve disciples the Lord was referring to standing before the crowd on that day? Is limiting it to that narrow an application appropriate? Is expanding it to include anyone ever called to preside too broad an application? How are you to decide that question?

[1090] D&C 84:28 "For he was baptized while he was yet in his childhood, and was ordained by the angel of God at the time he was eight days old unto this power, to overthrow the kingdom of the Jews, and to make straight the way of the Lord before the face of his people, to prepare them for the coming of the Lord, in whose hand is given all power."

[1091] 1 Corinthians 15:8–10 "And last of all he was seen of me also, as of one born out of due time. For I am the least of the apostles, that am not meet to be called an apostle, because I persecuted the church of God. But by the grace of God I am what I am: and his grace which *was bestowed* upon me was not in vain; but I laboured more abundantly than they all: yet not I, but the grace of God which was with me."

Is it appropriate for Christ to couple "minister to you" with "and to be your servants?" Can a "servant" exercise authority over you as the gentiles do?[1092] Why not?

When Christ says these people have "power to baptize you" and then promises that He, Christ, "will baptize you with fire and with the Holy Ghost" does this promise mean that Christ will send the Holy Ghost if you are baptized by one having power from Him? Always? If it hasn't happened, does that mean the one who baptized you did not have this "power?" Why or why not? What is the relationship between the power to baptize, and the promise of the Holy Ghost? What role does your own repentance have to play? Christ has previously given the order of things, and included repentance first.

What does the statement mean: "blessed are ye if ye shall believe in me and be baptized, after that ye have seen me and know that I am." How likely would it be for you to "believe in [Christ] after that ye have seen [Him]?" Do you suspect any of those who were present would not believe in Him? Why?

Would you expect those present to believe in Him after seeing Him descend from heaven, hear the voice of the Father testify of Him, see His wounds, witness Him healing all their sick, and beholding angels minister in tongues of fire to their young children? Would you be able to do so? What about reading the record of the events in the Book of Mormon; is that enough to testify of Him? Can you ask in prayer if these things about Christ are true and get a testimony of them for yourself? Have you done so? Have you acquired belief in Him as a result of praying to know if they are true? Can you then believe in Him? Are you "blessed" for it? Do you "know that He is?"

[1092] Luke 22:25–26 "And he said unto them, The kings of the Gentiles exercise lordship over them; and they that exercise authority upon them are called benefactors. But ye *shall* not *be* so: but he that is greatest among you, let him be as the younger; and he that is chief, as he that doth serve."

What more do you need to do in order to "know that He is?" Why haven't you done that yet?

3 Nephi 12:2

> "And again, more blessed are they who shall believe in your words because that ye shall testify that ye have seen me, and that ye know that I am. Yea, blessed are they who shall believe in your words, and come down into the depths of humility and be baptized, for they shall be visited with fire and with the Holy Ghost, and shall receive a remission of their sins."

Some people are given knowledge.[1093] This would include the Prophet Joseph Smith. Others believe on their words and trust in Christ through what they have learned from witnesses of Him.[1094] This would include President Thomas S. Monson, who in last General Conference testified he has no question about the testimonies of those who have seen Him. As President Monson testified: "I have read—and I believe—the testimonies of those who experienced the grief of Christ's Crucifixion and the joy of His Resurrection. I have read—and I believe—the testimonies of those in the New World who were visited by the same risen Lord. I believe the testimony of one who, in this dispensation, spoke with the Father and the Son in a grove now called sacred and who gave his life, sealing that testimony with his blood. Declared he: 'And now, after the many testimonies which have been given of him, this is the testimony, last of all, which we give of him: That he lives! For we saw him, even on the right hand of God; and we heard the voice bearing record that he is the Only Begotten of the Father.' The darkness of death can always be

---

[1093] D&C 46:13 "To some it is given by the Holy Ghost to know that Jesus Christ is the Son of God, and that he was crucified for the sins of the world."

[1094] D&C 46:14 "To others it is given to believe on their words, that they also might have eternal life if they continue faithful."

dispelled by the light of revealed truth. 'I am the resurrection, and the life,' spoke the Master. 'Peace I leave with you, my peace I give unto you.' Over the years I have heard and read testimonies too numerous to count, shared with me by individuals who testify of the reality of the Resurrection and who have received, in their hours of greatest need, the peace and comfort promised by the Savior." (He is Risen!, Sunday Morning Session, April 2010 Session; footnotes omitted.)

Why would someone be "more blessed" because they "believe in the words" of those who have "seen Christ" than those who have seen Him? What is it about believing on the words of those who *have seen* which is "more blessed" than the ones who see Him?

Notice once again the connection between having seen the Lord and "ye know that I am." Notice the use of "I am" in the statement of the Lord about Himself.

Now note too how the "believing in the words" is not enough, because He adds action to the belief. That is, those who "believe in your words" are required then to "come down into the depths of humility and be baptized" for the "blessing" to have any effect. It is not enough for someone to be moved to believe when they hear a witness of Christ, they must also respond to His invitation to be baptized. Before being baptized they need also to "come down into the depths of humility." The intention and inner meaning are everything. But the outward act confirms the inner change which takes place.

Action is married to belief and intent. Both are necessary.

When it is done in faith, sincerity, complying with the steps the Lord has prescribed, He promises to visit the obedient "with fire and with the Holy Ghost." This is how a person will know they have received "a remission of their sins."

The instructions of the Lord are intended to change lives. Change is repentance. And repentance leads to redemption. He expects our behavior to mirror our beliefs, because if behavior does not model our professed beliefs then we are hypocrites—not converts.

This is why commandments are given to us. They tell us how we can continue to receive and renew a continuing conversion to Christ's way of life. Commandments are not a burden to bear but a roadmap to follow. They are not a measuring stick to judge and then abuse others. It is a light for us to follow.

These explanations by Christ are beyond the question of "faith verses works" because Christ is telling us we act from our heart in faith, receive ordinances because of our faith, then have our hearts filled again. We proceed from grace to grace. This is how Christ received the fullness, and the only way we may receive the fullness.[1095]

The task of knowing God always begins by trusting on the words of those who have seen Him. But it should never end there. Everyone is invited to lay aside their sins, call upon God in faith, obey His commandments, listen to the voice of inspiration and do as you are

---

[1095] D&C 93:12–14, 19–29 "And I, John, saw that he received not of the fulness at the first, but received grace for grace; And he received not of the fulness at first, but continued from grace to grace, until he received a fulness; And thus he was called the Son of God, because he received not of the fulness at the first. . . . I give unto you these sayings that you may understand and know how to worship, and know what you worship, that you may come unto the Father in my name, and in due time receive of his fulness. For if you keep my commandments you shall receive of his fulness, and be glorified in me as I am in the Father; therefore, I say unto you, you shall receive grace for grace. And now, verily I say unto you, I was in the beginning with the Father, and am the Firstborn; And all those who are begotten through me are partakers of the glory of the same, and are the church of the Firstborn. Ye were also in the beginning with the Father; that which is Spirit, even the Spirit of truth; And truth is knowledge of things as they are, and as they were, and as they are to come; And whatsoever is more or less than this is the spirit of that wicked one who was a liar from the beginning. The Spirit of truth is of God. I am the Spirit of truth, and John bore record of me, saying: He received a fulness of truth, yea, even of all truth; And no man receiveth a fulness unless he keepeth his commandments. He that keepeth his commandments receiveth truth and light, until he is glorified in truth and knoweth all things. Man was also in the beginning with God. Intelligence, or the light of truth, was not created or made, neither indeed can be."

told, thereby coming to see Him face-to-face.[1096] This is the reason for the book *The Second Comforter*. It is a manual for how any person can come back into the presence of the Lord and join those witnesses who can testify they have seen Him.

He lives. And He is the same, yesterday, today and forever.

3 Nephi 12:3

"Yea, blessed are the poor in spirit who come unto me, for theirs is the kingdom of heaven."

The blessing referred to for those who are "poor in spirit" comes as a result of "coming unto" Christ. Any who come to Christ will receive "the kingdom of heaven." However, to obtain it, you must "come unto [Christ]."

Christ is approachable. But the approach is determined by the Gospel. The earlier "doctrine of Christ" taught in Chapter 11 tells you how to "come unto Christ."

Belief on His teachings, then repentance and baptism are all essential prerequisites to coming to Him.

What does it mean to be "poor in spirit?" Does that make you more open to Him? Have you ever had a season in which you felt "poor in spirit?" Were you more open to Him as a result?

Before I converted, though I did not consider myself a candidate to convert, I also felt a hollowness in life. There was something missing. The void inside us was meant to be there. Filling it was always the responsibility of the Gospel. We were all meant to feel "poor in spirit" until we find truth. Then, upon finding truth, we were meant to "come unto Christ" so the void may be filled. Coming to Christ is

---

[1096] D&C 93:1 "Verily, thus saith the Lord: It shall come to pass that every soul who forsaketh his sins and cometh unto me, and calleth on my name, and obeyeth my voice, and keepeth my commandments, shall see my face and know that I am;"

the return to life and light. It is the journey back to that light from where we originated.

Converting was more of a homecoming than anything else. The Gospel rings true and His sheep hear His voice [1097] because these are things we long ago accepted and decided to follow.[1098] Each of us needs to be converted. Even if you were raised in the church, you still need to convert. The steps Christ is outlining are the ones each of us are expected to follow. Whether you do so as an adult, or did so earlier in life, we are all required to "come unto Christ" and be converted.

We are not meant to remain "poor in spirit" but to "come to Christ" and move beyond that. Moving beyond it we find ourselves joyfully informed that "ours is the kingdom of heaven." We cannot claim it for ourselves. But Christ can claim it for us. This is how our poverty of spirit is to be cured. The Lord juxtaposes poverty with the riches of heaven itself. The contrast is designed to make us think, and to make us grateful. We were always intended to have joy. Above all else, Christ is a Deliverer from sorrow.[1099]

3 Nephi 12:4

"And again, blessed are all they that mourn, for they shall be comforted."

This is unconditional. "All" are included. "All they that mourn" will be blessed.

Between sessions of conference Saturday I attended a friend's funeral. Mourning because of death is the first cause we associate

---

[1097] John 10:27 "My sheep hear my voice, and I know them, and they follow me:"

[1098] See Abraham 3.

[1099] Revelation 7:17 "For the Lamb which is in the midst of the throne shall feed them, and shall lead them unto living fountains of waters: and God shall wipe away all tears from their eyes."

with this promise. Over death, however, He has gained the victory. It was His mission and ministry to bring about victory over death. "And he will take upon him death, that he may loose the bands of death."[1100] This done now, though death continues to claim all of us. We know we will have part in His victory. Comfort from that victory will come to us all.

Death is not the only cause of mourning, however. We all experience afflictions, troubles, temptations, and pains while mortal. He has gained the victory over all of these also: "And he shall go forth, suffering pains and afflictions and temptations of every kind; and this that the word might be fulfilled which saith he will take upon him the pains and the sicknesses of his people. And he will take upon him death, that he may loose the bands of death which bind his people; and he will take upon him their infirmities, that his bowels may be filled with mercy, according to the flesh, that he may know according to the flesh how to succor his people according to their infirmities. Now the Spirit knoweth all things; nevertheless the Son of God suffereth according to the flesh that he might take upon him the sins of his people, that he might blot out their transgressions according to the power of his deliverance; and now behold, this is the testimony which is in me."[1101]

[1100] Alma 7:12 "And he will take upon him death, that he may loose the bands of death which bind his people; and he will take upon him their infirmities, that his bowels may be filled with mercy, according to the flesh, that he may know according to the flesh how to succor his people according to their infirmities."

[1101] Alma 7:11–13 "And he shall go forth, suffering pains and afflictions and temptations of every kind; and this that the word might be fulfilled which saith he will take upon him the pains and the sicknesses of his people. And he will take upon him death, that he may loose the bands of death which bind his people; and he will take upon him their infirmities, that his bowels may be filled with mercy, according to the flesh, that he may know according to the flesh how to succor his people according to their infirmities. Now the Spirit knoweth all things; nevertheless the Son of God suffereth according to the flesh that he might take upon him the sins of his people, that he might blot out their transgressions according to the power of his deliverance; and now behold, this is the testimony which is in me."

Do you mourn because of afflictions? Temptations? Pains? Sickness? Infirmities? The troubles of the flesh? Sins and transgressions? It does not matter the cause of your mourning, Christ has suffered all these things so that He may understand the troubles of the flesh and, by understanding them to overcome them all. By overcoming them all, He then in turn can share the victory.

Your failures are not going to be reason to punish you. If you repent, they will be lessons from which to learn. The guilt will be removed, you will be comforted, and the lessons will remain. Your mortal trials will confer upon you the taste of the fruit of the tree of knowledge of good and evil.[1102] You will have learned from what you suffer the difference between the two, and have the benefit of Christ's atonement to remove all guilt.[1103]

All will be comforted from every offense they have ever suffered. All that remains will be the choices you have made.[1104] The offenses you suffered at the hands of others will be made up to you. All infirmities you have been plagued with while mortal will be

---

[1102] Genesis 3:17–19 "And unto Adam he said, Because thou hast hearkened unto the voice of thy wife, and hast eaten of the tree, of which I commanded thee, saying, Thou shalt not eat of it: cursed *is* the ground for thy sake; in sorrow shalt thou eat *of* it all the days of thy life; Thorns also and thistles shall it bring forth to thee; and thou shalt eat the herb of the field; In the sweat of thy face shalt thou eat bread, till thou return unto the ground; for out of it wast thou taken: for dust thou *art,* and unto dust shalt thou return."

[1103] 2 Nephi 2:26 "And the Messiah cometh in the fulness of time, that he may redeem the children of men from the fall. And because that they are redeemed from the fall they have become free forever, knowing good from evil; to act for themselves and not to be acted upon, save it be by the punishment of the law at the great and last day, according to the commandments which God hath given."

[1104] Moroni 7:16–17 "For behold, the Spirit of Christ is given to every man, that he may know good from evil; wherefore, I show unto you the way to judge; for every thing which inviteth to do good, and to persuade to believe in Christ, is sent forth by the power and gift of Christ; wherefore ye may know with a perfect knowledge it is of God. But whatsoever thing persuadeth men to do evil, and believe not in Christ, and deny him, and serve not God, then ye may know with a perfect knowledge it is of the devil; for after this manner doth the devil work, for he persuadeth no man to do good, no, not one; neither do his angels; neither do they who subject themselves unto him."

removed.[1105] Only your choices will remain as either a continuing blessing or continuing affliction. But that is your choice.[1106]

Earth's valuable lessons will remain with you, and inform you eternally with knowledge of good and evil. In this you will have become like God.[1107] But the experiences you suffer, which are the means of learning good from evil, will all be removed. You will no longer "mourn" for anything. You will, however, remain accountable for your choices.

This is the perfectly balanced experience. Through it we learn and gain experience[1108] but we are only burdened by what we voluntarily

---

[1105] Alma 40:23 "The soul shall be restored to the body, and the body to the soul; yea, and every limb and joint shall be restored to its body; yea, even a hair of the head shall not be lost; but all things shall be restored to their proper and perfect frame."

[1106] Alma 41:13–14 "O, my son, this is not the case; but the meaning of the word restoration is to bring back again evil for evil, or carnal for carnal, or devilish for devilish—good for that which is good; righteous for that which is righteous; just for that which is just; merciful for that which is merciful. Therefore, my son, see that you are merciful unto your brethren; deal justly, judge righteously, and do good continually; and if ye do all these things then shall ye receive your reward; yea, ye shall have mercy restored unto you again; ye shall have justice restored unto you again; ye shall have a righteous judgment restored unto you again; and ye shall have good rewarded unto you again."

Moroni 7:18–19 "And now, my brethren, seeing that ye know the light by which ye may judge, which light is the light of Christ, see that ye do not judge wrongfully; for with that same judgment which ye judge ye shall also be judged. Wherefore, I beseech of you, brethren, that ye should search diligently in the light of Christ that ye may know good from evil; and if ye will lay hold upon every good thing, and condemn it not, ye certainly will be a child of Christ."

[1107] Genesis 3:22 "And the Lord God said, Behold, the man is become as one of us, to know good and evil: and now, lest he put forth his hand, and take also of the tree of life, and eat, and live for ever:"

[1108] See Abraham 3.

impose upon ourselves through our choices.[1109] The promised "comfort" against our mourning will be complete if we have chosen to follow Christ, and incomplete if we have chosen to reject Him. Because He can only remove all the burdens of nature and mortality imposed as a condition of life here, He cannot remove those voluntarily assumed by wrong choice while living here.[1110]

The balance between necessary experience and accountability is maintained. Through Christ are all things made possible.

3 Nephi 12:5

"And blessed are the meek, for they shall inherit the earth."

This earth abides by a Celestial Law.[1111] Therefore, it is destined to become a Celestial Kingdom because it will be sanctified by a Ce-

---

[1109] 1 Nephi 15:32–33 "And it came to pass that I said unto them that it was a representation of things both temporal and spiritual; for the day should come that they must be judged of their works, yea, even the works which were done by the temporal body in their days of probation. Wherefore, if they should die in their wickedness they must be cast off also, as to the things which are spiritual, which are pertaining to righteousness; wherefore, they must be brought to stand before God, to be judged of their works; and if their works have been filthiness they must needs be filthy; and if they be filthy it must needs be that they cannot dwell in the kingdom of God; if so, the kingdom of God must be filthy also."

[1110] Mosiah 16:8–13 "But there is a resurrection, therefore the grave hath no victory, and the sting of death is swallowed up in Christ. He is the light and the life of the world; yea, a light that is endless, that can never be darkened; yea, and also a life which is endless, that there can be no more death. Even this mortal shall put on immortality, and this corruption shall put on incorruption, and shall be brought to stand before the bar of God, to be judged of him according to their works whether they be good or whether they be evil—If they be good, to the resurrection of endless life and happiness; and if they be evil, to the resurrection of endless damnation, being delivered up to the devil, who hath subjected them, which is damnation—Having gone according to their own carnal wills and desires; having never called upon the Lord while the arms of mercy were extended towards them; for the arms of mercy were extended towards them, and they would not; they being warned of their iniquities and yet they would not depart from them; and they were commanded to repent and yet they would not repent. And now, ought ye not to tremble and repent of your sins, and remember that only in and through Christ ye can be saved?"

[1111] D&C 88:25 "And again, verily I say unto you, the earth abideth the law of a celestial kingdom, for it filleth the measure of its creation, and transgresseth not the law—"

lestial Law.[1112] The destiny of the earth is glory.[1113] Therefore, to "inherit the earth" is to inherit a Celestial Glory.

Since this is so, you need to understand the definition of "meekness." Elder Hales made these remarks about "meekness" in General Conference: "To be meek, as defined in Webster's dictionary, is 'manifesting patience and longsuffering: enduring injury without resentment.' Meekness is not weakness. It is a badge of Christian courage." (*Christian Courage: The Price of Discipleship*, October 2008 General Conference, Elder Robert D. Hales.)

I've given another explanation in *Beloved Enos*. There I explained it is necessary to be meek first before being trusted with great power. The power to seal on earth and in heaven is something which cannot be handled apart from meekness. Without meekness a man cannot be trusted with such a power. When Enos used the power, he did so meekly. He asked rather than pronounced. He petitioned rather than decreed. Though the Lord would hearken to his words, he refrained from acting.

This is because the proper way to use such authority is only and strictly in conformity with the Lord's will. The reason Nephi received the authority was because he was meek. The account of the conferral is also the account of his qualification:

[1112] D&C 88:25–29 "And again, verily I say unto you, the earth abideth the law of a celestial kingdom, for it filleth the measure of its creation, and transgresseth not the law—Wherefore, it shall be sanctified; yea, notwithstanding it shall die, it shall be quickened again, and shall abide the power by which it is quickened, and the righteous shall inherit it. For notwithstanding they die, they also shall rise again, a spiritual body. They who are of a celestial spirit shall receive the same body which was a natural body; even ye shall receive your bodies, and your glory shall be that glory by which your bodies are quickened. Ye who are quickened by a portion of the celestial glory shall then receive of the same, even a fulness."

[1113] D&C 84:101 "The earth hath travailed and brought forth her strength;
And truth is established in her bowels;
And the heavens have smiled upon her;
And she is clothed with the glory of her God;
For he stands in the midst of his people."

"Blessed art thou, Nephi, for those things which thou hast done; for I have beheld how thou hast with unwearyingness declared the word, which I have given unto thee, unto this people. And **thou hast not feared them, and hast not sought thine own life, but hast sought my will, and to keep my commandments**. And now, because thou hast done this with such unwearyingness, behold, I will bless thee forever; and I will make thee mighty in word and in deed, in faith and in works; yea, even that **all things shall be done unto thee according to thy word, for thou shalt not ask that which is contrary to my will**. Behold, thou art Nephi, and I am God. Behold, I declare it unto thee in the presence of mine angels, that ye shall have power over this people, and shall smite the earth with famine, and with pestilence, and destruction, according to the wickedness of this people. Behold, **I give unto you power, that whatsoever ye shall seal on earth shall be sealed in heaven; and whatsoever ye shall loose on earth shall be loosed in heaven**; and thus shall ye have power among this people. And thus, if ye shall say unto this temple it shall be rent in twain, it shall be done. And if ye shall say unto this mountain, Be thou cast down and become smooth, it shall be done. And behold, if ye shall say that God shall smite this people, it shall come to pass.**And now behold, I command you, that ye shall go and declare unto this people, that thus saith the Lord God, who is the Almighty: Except ye repent ye shall be smitten, even unto destruction**." (Helaman 10:4–11.)

This is meekness. First, Nephi had conducted his life meekly. He did not fear others. He was not afraid to lose his standing, even his life. He kept God's commandments to him above all else. He possessed an iron will, his face like flint, unwilling to waiver from what the Lord would have him say and do. He could not be tempted to betray the Lord's will. Therefore, the Lord knew by the way Nephi lived his life that he would "not ask that which is contrary to [the Lord's] will." Never.

Therefore, when the Lord had tried him and determined he was willing to serve Him at all costs, he qualifies to receive trust from God. That trust allows the Lord to confer upon the man great power. (See also *TPJS*, 150:

> "After a person has faith in Christ, repents of his sins, is baptized for the remission of his sins, and receives the Holy Ghost (by the laying on of hands), which is the first Comforter, then let him continue to humble himself before God, hungering and thirsting after righteousness and living by every word of God. The Lord will soon say unto him, 'Son, thou shalt be exalted.' When the Lord has thoroughly proved him and finds that the man is determined to serve him at all hazards, then the man will find his calling and election made sure.")

Meekness is required to qualify for great power. And you know a man is meek when, having great power, he uses it strictly in conformity with the Lord's will; never varying from the Lord's command, and never pursuing his own agenda. This kind of meekness is men is a rare thing. Nephi, after receiving that power, was instructed that he was to deliver the Lord's message: "thus saith the Lord God, who is Almighty: Except ye repent ye shall be smitten, even unto destruction." It is the Lord's judgment. It is a meek man who delivers it. But such judgments only come after the Lord has a meek soul upon whom He can place this trust. For He has covenanted to always first employ such a servant before imposing judgments upon mankind.[1114]

Therefore, when the Lord teaches the "meek shall inherit the earth" it is a statement which includes exaltation for the meek. It is one of the Lord's deepest teachings, and most profound descriptions of those who will be exalted and why.

[1114] Amos 3:7 "Surely the Lord God will do nothing, but he revealeth his secret unto his servants the prophets."

3 Nephi 12:6

"And blessed are all they who do hunger and thirst after righteousness, for they shall be filled with the Holy Ghost."

This is not about hunger or poverty. This is about fasting and
seeking after righteousness.

You qualify for this blessing by hungering "after righteousness."
You qualify by thirsting "after righteousness." In other words, you
receive the Holy Ghost in proportion to the hunger and thirst you
display to receiving it.

Fasting is a promised means for increasing the Holy Ghost in
your life. We read this about Alma when he served as High Priest
over the church:

"And this is not all. Do ye not suppose that I know of these
things myself? Behold, I testify unto you that I do know that
these things whereof I have spoken are true. And how do ye
suppose that I know of their surety? Behold, I say unto
you **they are made known unto me by the Holy Spirit of
God. Behold, I have fasted and prayed many days that I
might know these things of myself.** And now I do know
of myself that they are true; for the Lord God hath made
them manifest unto me by his Holy Spirit; and this is the spirit
of revelation which is in me. And moreover, I say unto you
that it has thus been revealed unto me, that the words which
have been spoken by our fathers are true, even so according
to the spirit of prophecy which is in me, which is also by the
manifestation of the Spirit of God." (Alma 5:45–47.)

Fasting and praying opens the Spirit. It allows you to know a matter through the power of the Holy Ghost. Again, we read this about
the Sons of Mosiah who were completing their service as
missionaries:

" . . . Alma did rejoice exceedingly to see his brethren; and what added more to his joy, they were still his brethren in the Lord; yea, and they had waxed strong in the knowledge of the truth; for they were men of a sound understanding and they had searched the scriptures diligently, that they might know the word of God. But this is not all; **they had given themselves to much prayer, and fasting; therefore they had the spirit of prophecy, and the spirit of revelation, and when they taught, they taught with power and authority of God.**" (Alma 17:2–3)

They not only searched the scriptures, but they also spent time praying and fasting, that they might show God their earnest commitment to know the truth. The result was the "spirit of prophecy, and the spirit of revelation." Or, in other words, they were filled with the Holy Ghost.

The Lord speaks in simple formulas. They work; when tried in sincerity, acting no hypocrisy, with real intent, they work. Halfhearted efforts are not so effective. But when a soul, any soul, hungers and thirsts after righteousness, they are filled with the Holy Ghost.

This sometimes presents a problem for those who have medical conditions which prevent them from fasting. In *The Second Comforter,* I've suggested there are other ways to subordinate the desires of the flesh as a way to "hunger and thirst" while keeping medical needs satisfied. Reducing calories, or doing without some other thing as a form of "fasting" can be substituted. The decision would be between you and the Lord, but there are always ways provided for meeting what the Lord asks, including fasting by those who are medically unable.[1115]

[1115] 1 Nephi 3:7 "And it came to pass that I, Nephi, said unto my father: I will go and do the things which the Lord hath commanded, for I know that the Lord giveth no commandments unto the children of men, save he shall prepare a way for them that they may accomplish the thing which he commandeth them."

This sermon is a blue-print of the Lord's new charter for mankind. It is the new, higher way of living. It is intended to result in a new spiritual life for those willing to live it. Therefore you should not dismiss "hunger and thirst for righteousness" as something trivial. If you are among those who does not believe the Lord speaks with them, take these invitations from the Lord seriously. They are designed to reconnect you with God. They have the power to accomplish it.

Also, in the case of the Sons of Mosiah, there was actual "power" which came through this means. These missionaries could teach "with power and authority of God" because of their fasting, prayer and study of scripture.

3 Nephi 12:7

"And blessed are the merciful, for they shall obtain mercy."

The standard applied to us is the standard we apply to others. This is repeatedly set out in scripture:

Alma teaching his son Corianton recorded:

"Therefore, my son, see that you are merciful unto your brethren; deal justly, judge righteously, and do good continually; and if ye do all these things then shall ye receive your reward; yea, ye shall have mercy restored unto you again; ye shall have justice restored unto you again; ye shall have a righteous judgment restored unto you again; and ye shall have good rewarded unto you again. For that which ye do send out shall return unto you again, and be restored; therefore, the word restoration more fully condemneth the sinner, and justifieth him not at all." (Alma 41:14–15)

Moroni's final discussion about the Gospel included these words:

"And now, my brethren, seeing that ye know the light by which ye may judge, which light is the light of Christ, see that ye do not judge wrongfully; for with that same judgment which ye judge ye shall also be judged." (Moroni 7:18.)

Peter asked a practical question about the extent of forgiving others. He wanted a mathematical limit to be set. The Lord, however, raised the limit beyond an ability to reasonably count:

"Then came Peter to him, and said, Lord, how oft shall my brother sin against me, and I forgive him? till seven times? Jesus saith unto him, I say not unto thee, Until seven times: but, Until seventy times seven." (Matthew 18:21–22.)

There are others. I'd commend the chapter on the Atonement in *Come, Let Us Adore Him* for a more complete explanation of this doctrine.

If you want mercy from the Lord, you must give it to your fellow man. If you do not show mercy to your fellow man, the Lord cannot provide it to you. There is a law which binds the Lord to the same standard you set for yourself. It is an irrevocable law. Therefore, the Lord teaches us to show mercy so that we might merit mercy. We are the final beneficiaries of all the mercy we show to others.

It really is true that "what you send out shall return unto you again," to quote Alma. This is called "karma" in another faith. It is a true principle. Perhaps it operates within an larger time frame than just this life, but it operates, nonetheless. Alma knew the truth and was teaching it to his son.

It was Laban's judgment of Nephi and his brothers that got him killed. I've discussed this in *The Second Comforter*. It was his decision that a robber was worthy of death[1116] which sealed his fate. For

---

[1116] 1 Nephi 3:13 "And behold, it came to pass that Laban was angry, and thrust him out from his presence; and he would not that he should have the records. Wherefore, he said unto him: Behold thou art a robber, and I will slay thee."

when he became a robber[1117], then the Lord was free to show him the same judgment he had rendered.[1118] Sometimes what you send out returns to you again in this life

3 Nephi 12:8

"And blessed are all the pure in heart, for they shall see God."

This is a remarkable promise. Would you like to see God? Then first purify your heart.

Notice this is not just ritual purity, which had been the focus of the Law of Moses. Christ is replacing earlier ritual based purity with internal purity.

He speaks about the heart, rather than the hands and feet. Christ is speaking about beholding God, unlike the retreat Israel took from the offered opportunity at Sinai.[1119] He is returning to the time of Moses, when a higher way might have been chosen.

Purity of the heart is a borrowed benefit from the Savior. Man cannot become clean before God without the necessary offering of a

---

[1117] 1 Nephi 3:25 "And it came to pass that when Laban saw our property, and that it was exceedingly great, he did lust after it, insomuch that he thrust us out, and sent his servants to slay us, that he might obtain our property."

[1118] 1 Nephi 4:11 "And the Spirit said unto me again: Behold the Lord hath delivered him into thy hands. Yea, and I also knew that he had sought to take away mine own life; yea, and he would not hearken unto the commandments of the Lord; and he also had taken away our property."

[1119] D&C 84:22–25 "For without this no man can see the face of God, even the Father, and live. Now this Moses plainly taught to the children of Israel in the wilderness, and sought diligently to sanctify his people that they might behold the face of God; But they hardened their hearts and could not endure his presence; therefore, the Lord in his wrath, for his anger was kindled against them, swore that they should not enter into his rest while in the wilderness, which rest is the fulness of his glory. Therefore, he took Moses out of their midst, and the Holy Priesthood also;"

sacrifice. The Law of Moses taught this, but Christ would actually bring it to pass.[1120]

Christ's atonement cleanses us.[1121]

When we repent we turn to Christ and listen to and follow Him. Until then, we are not even facing the right direction in life.

Some reminders of how the heart may be purified:

- Let virtue constantly prevail in your thoughts.[1122]

- Pray to the Father with a devoted heart.[1123]

- Repent and call upon God with a contrite spirit, asking the atonement to be applied to your sins.[1124]

- Fast and pray often, that you may become humble.[1125]

[1120] Alma 34:36 "And this I know, because the Lord hath said he dwelleth not in unholy temples, but in the hearts of the righteous doth he dwell; yea, and he has also said that the righteous shall sit down in his kingdom, to go no more out; but their garments should be made white through the blood of the Lamb."

[1121] Alma 13:11 "Therefore they were called after this holy order, and were sanctified, and their garments were washed white through the blood of the Lamb."
Ether 13:10 "And then cometh the New Jerusalem; and blessed are they who dwell therein, for it is they whose garments are white through the blood of the Lamb; and they are they who are numbered among the remnant of the seed of Joseph, who were of the house of Israel."

[1122] D&C 121:45 "Let thy bowels also be full of charity towards all men, and to the household of faith, and let virtue garnish thy thoughts unceasingly; then shall thy confidence wax strong in the presence of God; and the doctrine of the priesthood shall distil upon thy soul as the dews from heaven."

[1123] Moroni 7:48 "Wherefore, my beloved brethren, pray unto the Father with all the energy of heart, that ye may be filled with this love, which he hath bestowed upon all who are true followers of his Son, Jesus Christ; that ye may become the sons of God; that when he shall appear we shall be like him, for we shall see him as he is; that we may have this hope; that we may be purified even as he is pure. Amen."

[1124] Mosiah 4:2 "And they had viewed themselves in their own carnal state, even less than the dust of the earth. And they all cried aloud with one voice, saying: O have mercy, and apply the atoning blood of Christ that we may receive forgiveness of our sins, and our hearts may be purified; for we believe in Jesus Christ, the Son of God, who created heaven and earth, and all things; who shall come down among the children of men."

[1125] Helaman 3:35 "Nevertheless they did fast and pray oft, and did wax stronger and stronger in their humility, and firmer and firmer in the faith of Christ, unto the filling their souls with joy and consolation, yea, even to the purifying and the sanctification of their hearts, which sanctification cometh because of their yielding their hearts unto God."

- Follow what light you have to receive more light, until you
  have the "perfect day" in which you are a vessel of light.[1126]

It is also interesting that what must be "pure" is the "heart."
There are so many other things one might measure. But what the
Lord looks upon to determine purity is the "heart."

I've said that there is almost nothing about us that can become
perfect in this life. The only thing that can approach perfection, however, is our intent. We can mean to follow God at all times. Even if
the dilemmas of life make it impossible to actually do so, we can still
intend to follow Him. We may not even know if what we are doing
pleases Him, or how to resolve conflicting interests or commandments. We may even be making a mistake, but if our intent is right,
our hearts may be pure.

This is also one of the reasons we cannot judge another. They
may be weak, foolish and error prone, but if they intend to be doing
the right then God alone can measure their heart and decide whether
they are approved. It would take a God to know if the person's life,
training, understanding and intent are pure before Him. I suspect
there are those we look upon as deluded and even evil but the Lord
views them with compassion and understanding. He may find their
hearts to be perfect even before the heart of the proud who claim
they have and follow the truth. Though a person may misunderstand
a great deal, still if they have love for their fellow man, relieve suffer-

---

[1126] D&C 50:24 "That which is of God is light; and he that receiveth light, and continueth in God, receiveth more light; and that light groweth brighter and brighter until
the perfect day."
D&C 93:28 "He that keepeth his commandments receiveth truth and light, until he is
glorified in truth and knoweth all things."

ing where they can, give patience to the foolish and water to the thirsty, they may be perfect before God.[1127]

There are so many illusions here. Some who are regarded as high and lifted up by God, temperate in their conduct, studying how they are seen by others before acting; are in fact wretched, miserable, poor and naked.[1128] I say with authority that there are some regarded as the very chiefest of the righteous among the Latter-day Saints who are before God wretched, miserable, poor and naked. They cannot survive even a glance from His all seeing eye. Yet they pretend they share in His vision, when they do not.

How few hearts are pure before God. How rare a thing it is to contemplate such a person. How few we produce in this restoration of the Gospel. We remain as a people too low, too mean, too vulgar,

---

[1127] Luke 18:9–14 "And he spake this parable unto certain which trusted in themselves that they were righteous, and despised others: Two men went up into the temple to pray; the one a Pharisee, and the other a publican. The Pharisee stood and prayed thus with himself, God, I thank thee, that I am not as other men *are*, extortioners, unjust, adulterers, or even as this publican. I fast twice in the week, I give tithes of all that I possess. And the publican, standing afar off, would not lift up so much as *his* eyes unto heaven, but smote upon his breast, saying, God be merciful to me a sinner. I tell you, this man went down to his house justified *rather* than the other: for every one that exalteth himself shall be abased; and he that humbleth himself shall be exalted."

[1128] Revelation 3:14–17 "And unto the angel of the church of the Laodiceans write; These things saith the Amen, the faithful and true witness, the beginning of the creation of God; I know thy works, that thou art neither cold nor hot: I would thou wert cold or hot. So then because thou art lukewarm, and neither cold nor hot, I will spue thee out of my mouth. Because thou sayest, I am rich, and increased with goods, and have need of nothing; and knowest not that thou art wretched, and miserable, and poor, and blind, and naked:"

too condescending to be called of God. No wonder we stumble and fall backward and many are taken in snares.[1129]

3 Nephi 12:9

"And blessed are all the peacemakers, for they shall be called the children of God."

More often than not those who are "peacemakers" will be abused. They will at least have to endure aggression and give a soft word in return.[1130] There will be no end to the peace which comes from Christ because there was no end to the suffering He was willing to endure.[1131]

When we hearken to the Lord's commandments we have peace like a river flowing.[1132] This is because the "Lord shall fight for you, and ye shall hold your peace." (Exodus 14:14.) The Lord will fight Zion's battles.[1133]

[1129] Isaiah 8:11–17 "For the Lord spake thus to me with a strong hand, and instructed me that I should not walk in the way of this people, saying, Say ye not, A confederacy, to all *them to* whom this people shall say, A confederacy; neither fear ye their fear, nor be afraid. Sanctify the Lord of hosts himself; and *let* him *be* your fear, and *let* him *be* your dread. And he shall be for a sanctuary; but for a stone of stumbling and for a rock of offence to both the houses of Israel, for a gin and for a snare to the inhabitants of Jerusalem. And many among them shall stumble, and fall, and be broken, and be snared, and be taken. Bind up the testimony, seal the law among my disciples. And I will wait upon the Lord, that hideth his face from the house of Jacob, and I will look for him."

[1130] Proverbs 15:1 "A Soft answer turneth away wrath: but grievous words stir up anger."

[1131] Isaiah 9:7 "Of the increase of *his* government and peace *there shall be* no end, upon the throne of David, and upon his kingdom, to order it, and to establish it with judgment and with justice from henceforth even for ever. The zeal of the Lord of hosts will perform this."

[1132] Isaiah 48:18 "O that thou hadst hearkened to my commandments! then had thy peace been as a river, and thy righteousness as the waves of the sea:"

[1133] D&C 105:14 "For behold, I do not require at their hands to fight the battles of Zion; for, as I said in a former commandment, even so will I fulfil—I will fight your battles."

When a man is right before God, even his enemies are at peace with him.[1134] At least until his time comes and his mission is completed.[1135]

When the Lord was taken with violence and crucified, He was at peace.[1136] He purchased peace through what He suffered. He alone can share that with all.[1137]

Through Him, the "peacemakers" have found this peace. This is why they have become His "children" for He has begotten them.[1138]

In a world of violence and abuse, it is peace we seek. But that peace comes only to the children of God and only because they know they are the children of God. At their rebirth, they are at rest from the cares of this dreary world, and informed by a better promise of things to come.[1139]

[1134] Proverbs 16:7 "When a man's ways please the Lord, he maketh even his enemies to be at peace with him."

[1135] D&C 122:9 "Therefore, hold on thy way, and the priesthood shall remain with thee; for their bounds are set, they cannot pass. Thy days are known, and thy years shall not be numbered less; therefore, fear not what man can do, for God shall be with you forever and ever."
John 19:10–11 "Then saith Pilate unto him, Speakest thou not unto me? knowest thou not that I have power to crucify thee, and have power to release thee? Jesus answered, Thou couldest have no power at all against me, except it were given thee from above: therefore he that delivered me unto thee hath the greater sin."

[1136] Luke 23:24 "And Pilate gave sentence that it should be as they required."

[1137] Isaiah 53:5 "But he *was* wounded for our transgressions, *he was* bruised for our iniquities: the chastisement of our peace *was* upon him; and with his stripes we are healed."

[1138] Mosiah 27:25 "And the Lord said unto me: Marvel not that all mankind, yea, men and women, all nations, kindreds, tongues and people, must be born again; yea, born of God, changed from their carnal and fallen state, to a state of righteousness, being redeemed of God, becoming his sons and daughters;"

[1139] See discussion on Alma 13:29.
Alma 13:29 "Having faith on the Lord; having a hope that ye shall receive eternal life; having the love of God always in your hearts, that ye may be lifted up at the last day and enter into his rest."
Moroni 7:3 "Wherefore, I would speak unto you that are of the church, that are the peaceable followers of Christ, and that have obtained a sufficient hope by which ye can enter into the rest of the Lord, from this time henceforth until ye shall rest with him in heaven."

Those who bring peace bring hope to this world. This world is filled with tribulation, but the Lord has overcome this world.[1140] Many have experienced this peace, become children of God, and then been persecuted, hated, reviled and killed.[1141]

Peace is a gift from Christ, and His peace is for this world and for the world to come.[1142]

But the promise of triumph is hereafter, when the world can no longer make any claim upon a child of God.[1143]

[1140] John 16:33 "These things I have spoken unto you, that in me ye might have peace. In the world ye shall have tribulation: but be of good cheer; I have overcome the world."

[1141] Hebrews 11:33–35 "Who through faith subdued kingdoms, wrought righteousness, obtained promises, stopped the mouths of lions, Quenched the violence of fire, escaped the edge of the sword, out of weakness were made strong, waxed valiant in fight, turned to flight the armies of the aliens. Women received their dead raised to life again: and others were tortured, not accepting deliverance; that they might obtain a better resurrection:"

[1142] John 14:27 "Peace I leave with you, my peace I give unto you: not as the world giveth, give I unto you. Let not your heart be troubled, neither let it be afraid."

[1143] D&C 122:4 "And although their influence shall cast thee into trouble, and into bars and walls, thou shalt be had in honor; and but for a small moment and thy voice shall be more terrible in the midst of thine enemies than the fierce lion, because of thy righteousness; and thy God shall stand by thee forever and ever."
D&C 135:6–7 "Hyrum Smith was forty-four years old in February, 1844, and Joseph Smith was thirty-eight in December, 1843; and henceforward their names will be classed among the martyrs of religion; and the reader in every nation will be reminded that the Book of Mormon, and this book of Doctrine and Covenants of the church, cost the best blood of the nineteenth century to bring them forth for the salvation of a ruined world; and that if the fire can scathe a green tree for the glory of God, how easy it will burn up the dry trees to purify the vineyard of corruption. They lived for glory; they died for glory; and glory is their eternal reward. From age to age shall their names go down to posterity as gems for the sanctified. They were innocent of any crime, as they had often been proved before, and were only confined in jail by the conspiracy of traitors and wicked men; and their *innocent blood* on the floor of Carthage jail is a broad seal affixed to "Mormonism" that cannot be rejected by any court on earth, and their *innocent blood* on the escutcheon of the State of Illinois, with the broken faith of the State as pledged by the governor, is a witness to the truth of the everlasting gospel that all the world cannot impeach; and their *innocent blood* on the banner of liberty, and on the *magna charta* of the United States, is an ambassador for the religion of Jesus Christ, that will touch the hearts of honest men among all nations; and their *innocent blood,* with the innocent blood of all the martyrs under the altar that John saw, will cry unto the Lord of Hosts till he avenges that blood on the earth. Amen."

Though a man may declare peace, the world will not be at peace until the Lord slays the wicked.[1144] Peace, as all other sacred things in our day, must be internal. We live in a day of overwhelming ignorance, foolishness and wickedness. It is not possible to obtain peace except on the terms which allow it. If you live those, you will have peace. But the world will not live them with you.

Patrick Henry put the problem of peace in this world into immortal words: "Gentlemen may cry, Peace, Peace——but there is no peace. The war is actually begun! The next gale that sweeps from the north will bring to our ears the clash of resounding arms! Our brethren are already in the field! Why stand we here idle? What is it that gentlemen wish? What would they have? Is life so dear, or peace so sweet, as to be purchased at the price of chains and slavery? Forbid it, Almighty God! I know not what course others may take; but as for me, give me liberty or give me death!"

The war remains today, but now it is against all righteousness. We wrestle not against flesh and blood, but against spiritual wickedness in high places.[1145] Elder Packer cannot even preach a sermon to a congregation of Saints belonging to a church over which he holds office without the anger and vilification of the homosexual community and others being aroused.

[1144] Revelation 19:11–16 "And I saw heaven opened, and behold a white horse; and he that sat upon him *was* called Faithful and True, and in righteousness he doth judge and make war. His eyes *were* as a flame of fire, and on his head *were* many crowns; and he had a name written, that no man knew, but he himself. And he *was* clothed with a vesture dipped in blood: and his name is called The Word of God. And the armies *which were* in heaven followed him upon white horses, clothed in fine linen, white and clean. And out of his mouth goeth a sharp sword, that with it he should smite the nations: and he shall rule them with a rod of iron: and he treadeth the winepress of the fierceness and wrath of Almighty God. And he hath on *his* vesture and on his thigh a name written, KING OF KINGS, AND LORD OF LORDS."

[1145] Ephesians 6:12 "For we wrestle not against flesh and blood, but against principalities, against powers, against the rulers of the darkness of this world, against spiritual wickedness in high *places.*"

If you are to find peace, and to become a peacemaker here, then it is through the Gospel of Jesus Christ. The world will not know peace again until He returns. To be a child of God and know peace is, in our day, to cry repentance and to bring others to Christ.

3 Nephi 12:10

"And blessed are all they who are persecuted for my name's sake, for theirs is the kingdom of heaven."

It is not just persecution, but persecution "for [His] name's sake" that makes you blessed. When you are doing what you should for His name's sake, you are likely to provoke persecution. He will later explain this is almost inevitable. It won't be because you are provoking it by your obnoxious behavior. It is because people will question your sincerity and commitment. The world expects hypocrites. They regard everyone with suspicion. And, let's face it, most charlatans adopt religion as one of their cloaks. We'll get to that a little further into this sermon from the Lord.

The kind of persecution which produces the "kingdom of heaven" is, of course, martyrdom. Originally the word "martyr" meant witness, but so many of the early Christian witnesses were killed that it came to have the modern meaning, that is one who dies for their faith.

Martyrs were seen in John's vision below the altar of God.[1146] This of course means they were holy because of their sacrifice. The heavenly altar being a symbol of them having shed their blood as wit-

---

[1146] Revelation 6:9 "And when he had opened the fifth seal, I saw under the altar the souls of them that were slain for the word of God, and for the testimony which they held:"

nesses. Joseph Smith and Hyrum joined those who qualified for such a witness.[1147]

Zenos, author of the Olive Tree allegory,[1148] prophet of the three days of darkness upon the isles of the sea, witness of the Lord's burial in a sepulcher[1149] seven centuries before His birth, was slain for his testimony.[1150]

Stephen was killed for his testimony but clearly inherited the kingdom of heaven.[1151]

There are many others, including Able, Isaiah, Peter, Paul and Abinadi.

[1147] D&C 135:7 "They were innocent of any crime, as they had often been proved before, and were only confined in jail by the conspiracy of traitors and wicked men; and their *innocent blood* on the floor of Carthage jail is a broad seal affixed to "Mormonism" that cannot be rejected by any court on earth, and their *innocent blood* on the escutcheon of the State of Illinois, with the broken faith of the State as pledged by the governor, is a witness to the truth of the everlasting gospel that all the world cannot impeach; and their *innocent blood* on the banner of liberty, and on the *magna charta* of the United States, is an ambassador for the religion of Jesus Christ, that will touch the hearts of honest men among all nations; and their *innocent blood,* with the innocent blood of all the martyrs under the altar that John saw, will cry unto the Lord of Hosts till he avenges that blood on the earth. Amen."

[1148] Jacob 5:1 "Behold, my brethren, do ye not remember to have read the words of the prophet Zenos, which he spake unto the house of Israel, saying:"

[1149] And the God of our fathers, who were led out of Egypt, out of bondage, and also were preserved in the wilderness by him, yea, the God of Abraham, and of Isaac, and the God of Jacob, yieldeth himself, according to the words of the angel, as a man, into the hands of wicked men, to be lifted up, according to the words of Zenock, and to be crucified, according to the words of Neum, and to be buried in a sepulchre, according to the words of Zenos, which he spake concerning the three days of darkness, which should be a sign given of his death unto those who should inhabit the isles of the sea, more especially given unto those who are of the house of Israel.

[1150] Helaman 8:19 "And now I would that ye should know, that even since the days of Abraham there have been many prophets that have testified these things; yea, behold, the prophet Zenos did testify boldly; for the which he was slain."

[1151] Acts 7:55–59 "But he, being full of the Holy Ghost, looked up stedfastly into heaven, and saw the glory of God, and Jesus standing on the right hand of God, And said, Behold, I see the heavens opened, and the Son of man standing on the right hand of God. Then they cried out with a loud voice, and stopped their ears, and ran upon him with one accord, And cast *him* out of the city, and stoned *him:* and the witnesses laid down their clothes at a young man's feet, whose name was Saul. And they stoned Stephen, calling upon *God,* and saying, Lord Jesus, receive my spirit."

Blessed are those who are willing to endure persecution for His name's sake. For they are those who are willing develop faith which cannot be obtained in any other way. It is through the sacrifice of all things that faith necessary for salvation is developed. Read again the post on Lecture 6 of the Lectures on Faith on April 21, 2010.

Beginning with faith to follow Him, then enduring persecution as a result, to offering the sacrifice necessary to develop faith, then inheriting the kingdom of heaven, the Gospel of Christ is one great whole.

Sometimes we bring persecution upon ourselves because we are unwise. The Lord will address that. We are to take offenses, but not give them. When we unwisely give offenses and cause persecution, that is not for His name's sake. There is a balance between wisdom and righteousness.

As an aside on the subject of persecution I wanted to add this:

I've thought about Elder Packer's talk and the homosexual community's reaction to it. Elder Packer was right, and he was addressing a community of believers who look to him for teachings like the ones given in that talk. Nobody ought to take offense at that. If you can prevent Elder Packer's teaching in that setting, then you can invade and stop talk in any setting on any subject.

However, nothing in that talk would encourage or justify invading the privacy and causing the shame visited upon the Rutgers University student who committed suicide. The invasion of his privacy was cruel, the act of publicizing it was a calculated act of terrible insult. His grief, despair, and subsequent suicide are the fault of those who invaded his privacy and exposed his weakness. It was wrong. Elder Packer's talk was to benefit a community of believers, not to persecute an audience of unbelievers.

I have friends I ride Harley's with who have absolutely no interest in Mormonism. One of my dear friends hates my church, thinks it barbaric and unenlightened. But that does not stop our mutual friendship nor define the areas about which we find common ground. Another person's differing views are only offensive when they demand I accede to them. If they will suspend judgment against me because of my faith, I am willing to suspend judgment against them because of theirs. This ought to define the boundaries of conduct, not militant demands for conceding the argument on questions of faith and belief. I can believe that my friend's lifestyle is corrupt and even immoral. But so long as he does not expect me to join him, I am pleased to be a friend, share what we have in common, and leave our differences for polite disagreement.

There are some sins I simply do not understand. But if my friendship may help someone to understand my faith, then I would sooner be friends with someone of another faith than one of my own. I do not expect many people to accept what I believe. In fact, I think there are very few fellow Latter-day Saints who believe or understand the Gospel as I do. If I were to limit my friends to those with whom I have everything in common, then my wife and children alone would be my friends.

Elder Packer should have the right to speak and preach the truth as he understands it. Those who would censor him are wrong.

If he is mistaken, then point out his error in a kindly way and seek to reclaim him. But condemning, protesting and attacking only shows intolerance and coercion which all of us have a responsibility to resist and condemn. It is wrong when the homosexual community does it, and it is wrong when the church does it. Win the argument with persuasion and strong reasoning. Yelling, condemning and protesting only attempts to silence thought, not to provoke it into correct understanding.

Now I'm off topic . . .

3 Nephi 12:11–12

"And blessed are ye when men shall revile you and persecute, and shall say all manner of evil against you falsely, for my sake; For ye shall have great joy and be exceedingly glad, for great shall be your reward in heaven; for so persecuted they the prophets who were before you."

If your actions are misjudged, that is only norMalachi There have been charlatans using religion to cloak their evil deeds from the beginning of time. They are so widespread, so often exposed for what they really are, that humanity has a legitimate skepticism about those who come in the name of the Lord.

From Jimmy Swaggart's prostitutes to Ted Haggard's homosexual encounters, the evangelical world has been rocked by the sexual misconduct of ministers. Catholic priesthood sexual abuse has been so widespread that there is a whole legal industry devoted to bringing and defending claims from victims of that abuse. The LDS Church has quietly settled a number of claims on both coasts and adjusted how membership records are documented and what precautions are taken when calling a man to teach in Primary because of sexual misconduct and associated legal claims.

The Burt Lancaster film *Elmer Gantry* was based on the Sinclair Lewis novel and illustrated the life and deeds of a false prophet. Indeed, the term "prophet" is rarely used in modern vernacular outside of LDS circles unless coupled with the term "false." "False prophet" is expected. What is unexpected is the contrary.

So when first reactions are taken, it will always be to sneer, to jeer, to mock and to suspect those who come in the name of the Lord. They are right to do that. Everyone OUGHT to question motives. Everyone OUGHT to think you're a fraud. They should expect you are like all those others in whom society trusted. No one wants to follow Jim Jones to their death, drinking strychnine laced Kool-Aid in another mass-suicide. That has happened too often already. Indeed, the fruits of such false prophets have been so devastating, so evil, so wrong in spirit and result that only a fool would be eager to trust you even should you have a pure heart and a true message.

The first reaction should be skepticism which will result in an attempt to measure your sincerity. Until you've been tested by the world, there is no reason for the world to believe anything you have to say. They will revile you, thinking you just another fraud. They will persecute you as if a charlatan, though you are His disciple. They will say all manner of evil against you falsely, all the while thinking they are only giving you what you deserve.

This is how the world decides if you are following Him. They have seen and heard no end of those who have claimed to follow Him, and you are no different in their eyes. That is, until you have actually followed Him; borne their criticism, returned good for evil, and shown how devoted you are in fact, as Christ will address in coming verses. When you have proven your devotion, then some few will soften their hearts. Others will remain unwilling to admit the truth, even when it is apparent you are His.

This is the way in which Christ lived His life. These teachings are an explanation of Him. And, in turn, it is also an explanation of the lives of any who follow Him. To follow Him, and to learn of His ways always requires experiencing some of what He experienced. While He assumed a full measure of these teachings, we are required to experience some of what He did only to allow us to understand Him. But these teachings are meant to be lived. They are meant to be applied and tested. If you test them, you will discover Him through them.

You will also come to know and understand the prophets who went before. This is a timeless brotherhood. Some of them invariably also come to succor their fellow Saint. This is always the same when the fullness of the Gospel of Jesus Christ is lived on the earth.

3 Nephi 12:13

"Verily, verily, I say unto you, I give unto you to be the salt of the earth; but if the salt shall lose its savor wherewith shall the earth be salted? The salt shall be thenceforth good for nothing, but to be cast out and to be trodden under foot of men."

Salt is a preservative, but in this case it is for the culinary benefit. It produces "savor." That is, the taste of the whole is affected by the presence of a little.

You don't need much to preserve the whole. Abraham's negotiation to preserve Sodom demonstrated that only a little of the "salt" is required for an entire population to receive the Lord's blessings.[1152]

[1152] Genesis 18:17–33 "And the Lord said, Shall I hide from Abraham that thing which I do; Seeing that Abraham shall surely become a great and mighty nation, and all the nations of the earth shall be blessed in him? For I know him, that he will command his children and his household after him, and they shall keep the way of the Lord, to do justice and judgment; that the Lord may bring upon Abraham that which he hath spoken of him. And the Lord said, Because the cry of Sodom and Gomorrah is great, and because their sin is very grievous; I will go down now, and see whether they have done altogether according to the cry of it, which is come unto me; and if not, I will know. And the men turned their faces from thence, and went toward Sodom: but Abraham stood yet before the Lord. And Abraham drew near, and said, Wilt thou also destroy the righteous with the wicked? Peradventure there be fifty righteous within the city: wilt thou also destroy and not spare the place for the fifty righteous that *are* therein? That be far from thee to do after this manner, to slay the righteous with the wicked: and that the righteous should be as the wicked, that be far from thee: Shall not the Judge of all the earth do right? And the Lord said, If I find in Sodom fifty righteous within the city, then I will spare all the place for their sakes. And Abraham answered and said, Behold now, I have taken upon me to speak unto the Lord, which *am but* dust and ashes: Peradventure there shall lack five of the fifty righteous: wilt thou destroy all the city for *lack of* five? And he said, If I find there forty and five, I will not destroy *it*. And he spake unto him yet again, and said, Peradventure there shall be forty found there. And he said, I will not do *it* for forty's sake. And he said *unto him*, Oh let not the Lord be angry, and I will speak: Peradventure there shall thirty be found there. And he said, I will not do *it,* if I find thirty there. And he said, Behold now, I have taken upon me to speak unto the Lord: Peradventure there shall be twenty found there. And he said, I will not destroy *it* for twenty's sake. And he said, Oh let not the Lord be angry, and I will speak yet but this once: Peradventure ten shall be found there. And he said, I will not destroy *it* for ten's sake. And the Lord went his way, as soon as he had left communing with Abraham: and Abraham returned unto his place."

Progress is enough in our day.[1153] As long as the wheat is still growing, it is enough.

How can salt "lose its savor" except through contamination or impurities? When that is lost, the salt cannot preserve. There is no remaining savor. Then the salt is nothing more than common dirt, to be cast aside and trodden under foot.

This is the gentile predicament in the last days. They will, of course, lose their savor. They will reject the fullness offered to them.[1154] When they do, they will be torn apart and trodden under foot.[1155]

Notice it is the Lord who "gives unto you to be the salt of the earth." This condition is a gift from God. Through repentance, or turning to Him, you can receive this. Without repentance you cannot become the salt.

There are no private lives. Every life counts. Your private devotions are more important than your public notice. The salt which preserves may be unknown, likely is unknown, to most people. But if you are the salt, then your private life of devotion to the Lord is saving the lives of many others. The angels want to begin the harvest.

[1153] Luke 13:30 "And, behold, there are last which shall be first, and there are first which shall be last."

[1154] 3 Nephi 16:10 "And thus commandeth the Father that I should say unto you: At that day when the Gentiles shall sin against my gospel, and shall reject the fulness of my gospel, and shall be lifted up in the pride of their hearts above all nations, and above all the people of the whole earth, and shall be filled with all manner of lyings, and of deceits, and of mischiefs, and all manner of hypocrisy, and murders, and priest-crafts, and whoredoms, and of secret abominations; and if they shall do all those things, and shall reject the fulness of my gospel, behold, saith the Father, I will bring the fulness of my gospel from among them."

[1155] 3 Nephi 20:16 "Then shall ye, who are a remnant of the house of Jacob, go forth among them; and ye shall be in the midst of them who shall be many; and ye shall be among them as a lion among the beasts of the forest, and as a young lion among the flocks of sheep, who, if he goeth through both treadeth down and teareth in pieces, and none can deliver."
3 Nephi 21:12 "And my people who are a remnant of Jacob shall be among the Gentiles, yea, in the midst of them as a lion among the beasts of the forest, as a young lion among the flocks of sheep, who, if he go through both treadeth down and teareth in pieces, and none can deliver."

They are impatient to begin reaping and cutting down the wicked now.[1156] There is only time given because of a few who deserve more time to grow in faith before the harvest begins.[1157] Your growth is all that is keeping the harvest from beginning now. Therefore, how you proceed has consequences far beyond your own life.

When wheat is ripe it will be protected. When tares are ripe they will be burned. But the tender plants worthy of preservation are the only ones allowed more time.[1158] I advocate for them and realize how tenuous a position humanity itself is in at present. But you are the ones in the balance and for whom time is granted. How much longer no one knows, but your sins are not private. Your repentance is critical to all of creation. Do not think your life is your own. All of us have a share in your good works.

Do not think the Savior's words are without cosmic significance. I define "cosmic" to include the cosmos or organized creation here. Even the earth itself longs to be freed from the burden of sin upon her face.[1159] It is the Lord alone who has granted you time to repent. This current state of the creation we live is affected by the promise held in those who are repenting. As soon as that hope ends, and no further repentance is to occur, then the harvest will begin. Therefore, becoming salt has never been so important as it now is.

[1156] D&C 86:5 "Behold, verily I say unto you, the angels are crying unto the Lord day and night, who are ready and waiting to be sent forth to reap down the fields;"

[1157] D&C 86:6–7 "But the Lord saith unto them, pluck not up the tares while the blade is yet tender (for verily your faith is weak), lest you destroy the wheat also. Therefore, let the wheat and the tares grow together until the harvest is fully ripe; then ye shall first gather out the wheat from among the tares, and after the gathering of the wheat, behold and lo, the tares are bound in bundles, and the field remaineth to be burned."

[1158] D&C 86:4 "But behold, in the last days, even now while the Lord is beginning to bring forth the word, and the blade is springing up and is yet tender—"

[1159] Moses 7:48 "And it came to pass that Enoch looked upon the earth; and he heard a voice from the bowels thereof, saying: Wo, wo is me, the mother of men; I am pained, I am weary, because of the wickedness of my children. When shall I rest, and be cleansed from the filthiness which is gone forth out of me? When will my Creator sanctify me, that I may rest, and righteousness for a season abide upon my face?"

3 Nephi 12:14–16

"Verily, verily, I say unto you, I give unto you to be the light of this people. A city that is set on a hill cannot be hid. Behold, do men light a candle and put it under a bushel? Nay, but on a candlestick, and it giveth light to all that are in the house; Therefore let your light so shine before this people, that they may see your good works and glorify your Father who is in heaven."

Here, again, is a reference to Zion. Zion will be that city upon a hill which cannot be hidden. It will tower over the landscape, elevated both physically and spiritually. It will be the mountain of the Lord in the top of the mountains.[1160] He will dwell there.[1161] I've already addressed this and won't repeat it again here.

What is the "light" which you are to be to "this people?" Who are "this people?" What is to be a "light of this people?"

If you have light, how is it to be shared? Within The Church of Jesus Christ of Latter-day Saints the obligation to preach, teach, exhort and expound is imposed upon everyone having the office of Priest and above.[1162] Members of both sexes were commanded in

---

[1160] Isaiah 2:2–3 "And it shall come to pass in the last days, *that* the mountain of the Lord's house shall be established in the top of the mountains, and shall be exalted above the hills; and all nations shall flow unto it. And many people shall go and say, Come ye, and let us go up to the mountain of the Lord, to the house of the God of Jacob; and he will teach us of his ways, and we will walk in his paths: for out of Zion shall go forth the law, and the word of the Lord from Jerusalem."

[1161] 2 Nephi 14:5 "And the Lord will create upon every dwelling-place of mount Zion, and upon her assemblies, a cloud and smoke by day and the shining of a flaming fire by night; for upon all the glory of Zion shall be a defence."
D&C 76:66 "These are they who are come unto Mount Zion, and unto the city of the living God, the heavenly place, the holiest of all."
D&C 84:2 "Yea, the word of the Lord concerning his church, established in the last days for the restoration of his people, as he has spoken by the mouth of his prophets, and for the gathering of his saints to stand upon Mount Zion, which shall be the city of New Jerusalem."

[1162] D&C 20:46 "The priest's duty is to preach, teach, expound, exhort, and baptize, and administer the sacrament,"

1832 to teach one another the doctrines of the Gospel.[1163] If you have light and refuse to share it with others, are you putting a candle under a bushel?

How do you let the light you have shine through "good works?" That is how it is supposed to be shown. Christ's teaching explains that people are to see your "good works" as the means for your light to shine. How would that be accomplished?

Most interesting of all is that upon seeing your good works, the glory is to be given "your Father who is in heaven." How would your works reflect on Him rather than on yourself? What would you need to do in order for those benefited by your efforts to turn their thanks to God, rather than to you?

If you were interested in your good works reflecting credit to "your Father who is in heaven" how many monuments would you want built to your memory? How many buildings would you want named after you? How many statutes would you want carved of your likeness and put on display for men to admire?

The light should point to the Lord, who can save. It is nevertheless the case that some have become subjects of adoration or veneration despite their inability to save anyone. Those who are distracted from following the Lord become Telestial and continue to suffer the deaths of false religion.[1164] These are no better than the liars, adulterers and whoremongers.[1165] They became these vessels of God's

---

[1163] D&C 88:77 "And I give unto you a commandment that you shall teach one another the doctrine of the kingdom."

[1164] D&C 76:99–101 "For these are they who are of Paul, and of Apollos, and of Cephas. These are they who say they are some of one and some of another—some of Christ and some of John, and some of Moses, and some of Elias, and some of Esaias, and some of Isaiah, and some of Enoch; But received not the gospel, neither the testimony of Jesus, neither the prophets, neither the everlasting covenant."

[1165] D&C 76:103–104 "These are they who are liars, and sorcerers, and adulterers, and whoremongers, and whosoever loves and makes a lie. These are they who suffer the wrath of God on earth."

wrath because they worshiped men, rather than God. If, therefore, prophets such as Moses, Elias, John, Peter and Enoch have such followers despite preaching that salvation is in Christ alone, then how much worse is it for a man to intentionally cultivate adoration for himself? How much worse is it to deliberately invite this error?

What steps should you take to make certain there are no thunderous celebrations broadcast on television on your birthdays? How quick would you be to reaffirm you are nothing and no-one, and salvation is through Christ and not a man? How clear would you be about your own weakness, foolishness and inability to save another? How often would you point to the Lord who alone can save?

It is not enough to be religious. Hell will be filled with the religious. It is not enough to proclaim you have light if you do not live according to its principles. The sermon we are looking at now is the Lord's careful formulation of the principles which will save. He delivered it often during His mortal ministry. When He was resurrected and ministered to lost sheep, including the Nephites, He delivered the same address to them all.

Above all other sources of information about the path back to God, this is the greatest message of all. Within it are the very steps that are required for life and salvation, spoken by the author of salvation.

3 Nephi 12:17–18

"Think not that I am come to destroy the law or the prophets. I am not come to destroy but to fulfil; For verily I say unto you, one jot nor one tittle hath not passed away from the law, but in me it hath all been fulfilled."

The Lord sends ministers with a commission to transition from one dispensation of the Gospel to another. From Adam until Enoch there was an order, but with Enoch that order changed. Wickedness and rebellion required a new approach, and Enoch was commissioned to bring it about.[1166] Mankind was in such a state of rebellion that their time was to end. Enoch gathered together people upon a high mountain where he established a city which would survive the destruction by becoming Zion.[1167]

Soon after Enoch was called, the Lord called another, giving him also a dispensation of the Gospel. He, however, was to remain on the earth.[1168] With him a new covenant was made.[1169]

Both Enoch and Noah were contemporaries, but each had been given a dispensation of the Gospel. The covenant with Enoch did not disannul the covenant with Adam. Nor did the covenant with Noah contradict the covenant with Enoch.

[1166] Moses 6:32–34 "And the Lord said unto Enoch: Go forth and do as I have commanded thee, and no man shall pierce thee. Open thy mouth, and it shall be filled, and I will give thee utterance, for all flesh is in my hands, and I will do as seemeth me good. Say unto this people: Choose ye this day, to serve the Lord God who made you. Behold my Spirit is upon you, wherefore all thy words will I justify; and the mountains shall flee before you, and the rivers shall turn from their course; and thou shalt abide in me, and I in you; therefore walk with me."

[1167] Moses 7:17–21 "The fear of the Lord was upon all nations, so great was the glory of the Lord, which was upon his people. And the Lord blessed the land, and they were blessed upon the mountains, and upon the high places, and did flourish. And the Lord called his people Zion, because they were of one heart and one mind, and dwelt in righteousness; and there was no poor among them. And Enoch continued his preaching in righteousness unto the people of God. And it came to pass in his days, that he built a city that was called the City of Holiness, even Zion. And it came to pass that Enoch talked with the Lord; and he said unto the Lord: Surely Zion shall dwell in safety forever. But the Lord said unto Enoch: Zion have I blessed, but the residue of the people have I cursed. And it came to pass that the Lord showed unto Enoch all the inhabitants of the earth; and he beheld, and lo, Zion, in process of time, was taken up into heaven. And the Lord said unto Enoch: Behold mine abode forever."

[1168] Moses 7:42–43 "And Enoch also saw Noah, and his family; that the posterity of all the sons of Noah should be saved with a temporal salvation; Wherefore Enoch saw that Noah built an ark; and that the Lord smiled upon it, and held it in his own hand; but upon the residue of the wicked the floods came and swallowed them up."
Genesis 6:12–14 "And God looked upon the earth, and, behold, it was corrupt; for all flesh had corrupted his way upon the earth. And God said unto Noah, The end of all flesh is come before me; for the earth is filled with violence through them; and, behold, I will destroy them with the earth. Make thee an ark of gopher wood; rooms shalt thou make in the ark, and shalt pitch it within and without with pitch."

[1169] Genesis 9:8–9 "And God spake unto Noah, and to his sons with him, saying, And I, behold, I establish my covenant with you, and with your seed after you;"

Abraham also received a dispensation of the Gospel.[1170] Moses also.[1171]

Christ also received a dispensation of the Gospel in the same manner as all those who went before.[1172]

Christ fulfilled all the law. Not merely the Law of Moses, which indeed pointed to Him,[1173] but also every part of the Gospel from Adam to Christ's earthly ministry.[1174] All have testified of Him and He has completed His ministry in strict conformity with all that was foreshadowed, all that was prophesied, all that was anticipated of Him. Just how completely He did this is not possible to understand with the current state of our scriptures. But He did fulfill all righteousness, complete every assignment, accomplish every task and live in conformity with every prophesy concerning Him.

Not one matter respecting Him was left undone. From His hair to His feet, all that was foreshadowed or prophesied was done by

---

[1170] Abraham 2.

[1171] Moses 1:3–4 "And God spake unto Moses, saying: Behold, I am the Lord God Almighty, and Endless is my name; for I am without beginning of days or end of years; and is not this endless? And, behold, thou art my son; wherefore look, and I will show thee the workmanship of mine hands; but not all, for my works are without end, and also my words, for they never cease."

[1172] Matthew 4:11 "Then the devil leaveth him, and, behold, angels came and ministered unto him."
Matthew 17:1–3 "And after six days Jesus taketh Peter, James, and John his brother, and bringeth them up into an high mountain apart, And was transfigured before them: and his face did shine as the sun, and his raiment was white as the light. And, behold, there appeared unto them Moses and Elias talking with him."

[1173] Galatians 3:24 "Wherefore the law was our schoolmaster *to bring us* unto Christ, that we might be justified by faith."

[1174] Jacob 4:4 "For, for this intent have we written these things, that they may know that we knew of Christ, and we had a hope of his glory many hundred years before his coming; and not only we ourselves had a hope of his glory, but also all the holy prophets which were before us."
Jacob 7:11 "And I said unto him: Then ye do not understand them; for they truly testify of Christ. Behold, I say unto you that none of the prophets have written, nor prophesied, save they have spoken concerning this Christ."

Him. He turned not His face from those who spit at Him.[1175] He let Himself be shorn as a sheep and kept silent as it was done.[1176]

He inherited Kingship, but deferred His reign to another time.[1177]

He fulfilled, but did not destroy. In this He was like those whom He sent before to complete and open anew. In one hinge point of history a dispensation closes and another opens. Enoch and Noah, Abraham and Moses were all commissioned to open and close. For the Lord, however, He divided the spoil. He sent John to close,[1178] leaving it to Himself to open.[1179] Mankind cannot measure humility or meekness, but in Christ was a fullness of both.

Men in their insecurity and vanity want honors, awards, recognition and fame. The Lord has hidden from us most of what He did, most of what He is. He is content to confine the record of His doings to the minimum necessary for our understanding so we may have faith in Him. But the extent of His doings mankind has yet

---

[1175] Isaiah 50:6 "I gave my back to the smiters, and my cheeks to them that plucked off the hair: I hid not my face from shame and spitting."
Matthew 26:57 "And they that had laid hold on Jesus led *him* away to Caiaphas the high priest, where the scribes and the elders were assembled."

[1176] Isaiah 53:7 "He was oppressed, and he was afflicted, yet he opened not his mouth: he is brought as a lamb to the slaughter, and as a sheep before her shearers is dumb, so he openeth not his mouth."

[1177] John 18:36 "Jesus answered, My kingdom is not of this world: if my kingdom were of this world, then would my servants fight, that I should not be delivered to the Jews: but now is my kingdom not from hence."

[1178] D&C 84:27–28 "Which gospel is the gospel of repentance and of baptism, and the remission of sins, and the law of carnal commandments, which the Lord in his wrath caused to continue with the house of Aaron among the children of Israel until John, whom God raised up, being filled with the Holy Ghost from his mother's womb. For he was baptized while he was yet in his childhood, and was ordained by the angel of God at the time he was eight days old unto this power, to overthrow the kingdom of the Jews, and to make straight the way of the Lord before the face of his people, to prepare them for the coming of the Lord, in whose hand is given all power."

[1179] John 8:12 "Then spake Jesus again unto them, saying, I am the light of the world: he that followeth me shall not walk in darkness, but shall have the light of life."

to find out.[1180] This is more than a tribute to Him. He has understated His accomplishments. He has hidden His glory from us. He has made less of Himself, that we may not be unable to identify with Him. He is meeker and more humble than mankind understands.

He can be trusted with all power because He will never abuse it.[1181] He will use it to serve others.[1182]

In Christ was all fulfilled. In Him is all fulfilled. In Him dwells the fullness of the Godhead bodily.[1183] He is the light who came to His own, but we will not receive Him.[1184]

He was, He is, and He has risen. Above all others and all else, He has risen. And because of this He has made it possible for others also to rise. Everything He has done was in fulfillment of the law, pointing for us the way. Now it is only left for us to follow, trusting in Him.

3 Nephi 12:19

"And behold, I have given you the law and the commandments of my Father, that ye shall believe in me, and that ye shall repent of your sins, and come unto me with a broken heart and a contrite spirit. Behold, ye have the commandments before you, and the law is fulfilled."

[1180] D&C 76:2 "Great is his wisdom, marvelous are his ways, and the extent of his doings none can find out."

[1181] Matthew 28:18 "And Jesus came and spake unto them, saying, All power is given unto me in heaven and in earth."

[1182] Luke 22:27 "For whether *is* greater, he that sitteth at meat, or he that serveth? *is* not he that sitteth at meat? but I am among you as he that serveth."

[1183] Col. 2:9 "For in him dwelleth all the fulness of the Godhead bodily."

[1184] John 1:10–11 "He was in the world, and the world was made by him, and the world knew him not. He came unto his own, and his own received him not."

This hearkens back to the doctrine of Christ given preliminarily to the audience. Repent. Be baptized. Receive the Holy Ghost. These commandments are the foundation upon which all else is to be built.

To all that He explained before, He has added, "repent of your sins, and come unto me with a broken heart and a contrite spirit." Repenting will be accompanied by a broken heart and contrite spirit. When you turn to Him and see clearly for the first time how dark your ways have been, it should break your heart. You should realize how desperately you stand in need of His grace to cover you, lift you, and heal you. You can then appreciate the great gulf between you and Him.[1185]

If you had to bear your sins into His presence it would make you burn with regret and fear.[1186] Your own heart must break.

When you behold how little you have to offer Him, your spirit becomes contrite. He offers everything. And we can contribute nothing but our cooperation. And we still reluctantly give that, or if we give a little of our own cooperation we think we have given something significant. We have not. Indeed, we cannot.[1187] He honors us

---

[1185] Moses 1:10 "And it came to pass that it was for the space of many hours before Moses did again receive his natural strength like unto man; and he said unto himself: Now, for this cause I know that man is nothing, which thing I never had supposed."

[1186] Mormon 9:3–5 "Then will ye longer deny the Christ, or can ye behold the Lamb of God? Do ye suppose that ye shall dwell with him under a consciousness of your guilt? Do ye suppose that ye could be happy to dwell with that holy Being, when your souls are racked with a consciousness of guilt that ye have ever abused his laws? Behold, I say unto you that ye would be more miserable to dwell with a holy and just God, under a consciousness of your filthiness before him, than ye would to dwell with the damned souls in hell. For behold, when ye shall be brought to see your nakedness before God, and also the glory of God, and the holiness of Jesus Christ, it will kindle a flame of unquenchable fire upon you."

[1187] Mosiah 2:20–21 "I say unto you, my brethren, that if you should render all the thanks and praise which your whole soul has power to possess, to that God who has created you, and has kept and preserved you, and has caused that ye should rejoice, and has granted that ye should live in peace one with another—I say unto you that if ye should serve him who has created you from the beginning, and is preserving you from day to day, by lending you breath, that ye may live and move and do according to your own will, and even supporting you from one moment to another—I say, if ye should serve him with all your whole souls yet ye would be unprofitable servants."

if He permits us to assist. We should proceed with alacrity when given the chance to serve.

How patiently He has proceeded with teaching us all. We have the law, we have the commandments. Still we hesitate. Still He invites and reminds us: Repent. Come to Him. Do what was commanded. The law is fulfilled, and He is its fulfillment. Look to Him and be saved.

The heart that will not break does not understand the predicament we live in. The proud spirit is foolish and blind. Our perilous state is such that we can forfeit all that we have ever been by refusing Christ's invitation to repent and turn again to Him.

But we still hesitate. We still hold back.

He really can save you. He has that power. He holds those keys. Even death and hell are conquered by Him.[1188] But His victory cannot become ours unless we repent and turn again to Him.

Think of those you have lost to the grave. All those living will likewise be lost unless we come to Christ. We have hope only in Him.

It seems too simple a thing to achieve so great a result. It has always been like that.[1189] Look to Him and be saved. Keep His commandments. Repent. He can and will lead you from wherever you find yourself at present back into the light. It really does not matter what foolish traps you have surrounding you. So soon as you turn to

---

[1188] Mosiah 15:7–9 "Yea, even so he shall be led, crucified, and slain, the flesh becoming subject even unto death, the will of the Son being swallowed up in the will of the Father. And thus God breaketh the bands of death, having gained the victory over death; giving the Son power to make intercession for the children of men—Having ascended into heaven, having the bowels of mercy; being filled with compassion towards the children of men; standing betwixt them and justice; having broken the bands of death, taken upon himself their iniquity and their transgressions, having redeemed them, and satisfied the demands of justice."

[1189] 1 Nephi 17:41 "And he did straiten them in the wilderness with his rod; for they hardened their hearts, even as ye have; and the Lord straitened them because of their iniquity. He sent fiery flying serpents among them; and after they were bitten he prepared a way that they might be healed; and the labor which they had to perform was to look; and because of the simpleness of the way, or the easiness of it, there were many who perished."

face Him, He will direct you back safely. Repent and keep His commandments and they will bring you to Him.

3 Nephi 12:20

"Therefore come unto me and be ye saved; for verily I say unto you, that except ye shall keep my commandments, which I have commanded you at this time, ye shall in no case enter into the kingdom of heaven."

There goes the argument that all you need do to be saved is "confess Jesus." It doesn't work that way. You must keep His commandments. If you don't, then "ye shall in no case enter into the kingdom of heaven." It is not possible to "come unto [Him]" and "be saved" without also keeping His commandments. It is the only true measure of coming to Him. "Except ye shall keep [His] commandments . . . ye can in no case enter into the kingdom of heaven." Entry is barred unless you follow Him. If He needed baptism to enter, then clearly we do as well.[1190]

There is no space between faith in Christ and behavior evidencing that faith. There is no dichotomy between "grace" and "works" because it is by our conduct we merit grace. Christ received grace by

---

[1190] 2 Nephi 31:5 "And now, if the Lamb of God, he being holy, should have need to be baptized by water, to fulfil all righteousness, O then, how much more need have we, being unholy, to be baptized, yea, even by water!"

the things He did.[1191] The manner by which we receive grace is through keeping His commandments.[1192]

Grace, or power to move closer to God, is also an increase of light. Light grows only as you move closer to it. But you have choice, and must elect to move closer to the light.[1193] The great proof text for salvation by confession of faith alone is Romans 10:9:

"That if thou shalt confess with thy mouth the Lord Jesus, and shalt believe in thine heart that God hath raised him from the dead, thou shalt be saved."

This is offered as if Paul had priority over Christ, if the two conflict. However, Paul does not conflict, for in the same letter he teaches:

"Know ye not, that to whom ye yield yourselves servants to obey, his servants ye are to whom ye obey; whether of sin unto death, or of obedience unto righteousness? But God be thanked, that ye were the servants of sin, but ye have obeyed from the heart that form of doctrine which was delivered you." (Romans 6:16–17)

[1191] D&C 93:11–14 "And I, John, bear record that I beheld his glory, as the glory of the Only Begotten of the Father, full of grace and truth, even the Spirit of truth, which came and dwelt in the flesh, and dwelt among us. And I, John, saw that he received not of the fulness at the first, but received grace for grace; And he received not of the fulness at first, but continued from grace to grace, until he received a fulness; And thus he was called the Son of God, because he received not of the fulness at the first."

[1192] D&C 93:19–20 "I give unto you these sayings that you may understand and know how to worship, and know what you worship, that you may come unto the Father in my name, and in due time receive of his fulness. For if you keep my commandments you shall receive of his fulness, and be glorified in me as I am in the Father; therefore, I say unto you, you shall receive grace for grace."

[1193] D&C 93:27–28 "And no man receiveth a fulness unless he keepeth his commandments. He that keepeth his commandments receiveth truth and light, until he is glorified in truth and knoweth all things."
D&C 50:23–25 "And that which doth not edify is not of God, and is darkness. That which is of God is light; and he that receiveth light, and continueth in God, receiveth more light; and that light groweth brighter and brighter until the perfect day. And again, verily I say unto you, and I say it that you may know the truth, that you may chase darkness from among you;"

Righteousness comes by obedience. Obedience requires action. Without conforming conduct to the Lord's commandments, it is impossible to enter into the kingdom of heaven. Paul understood this, and lived his life accordingly. Who worked more than Paul to spread the Gospel? If his life was filled with works from the time of his conversion to the time of his martyrdom, then does not his example prove the necessity of obedience to the Lord's commandments? How then are his words twisted to mean confession alone, without obedience, can save? Even if someone were mistaken and in good faith sincerely believed Paul to justify salvation by confession alone, how did Paul become greater than Christ?

The Lord's instructions are clear and obedience to His and the Father's commandments are a threshold requirement for salvation. Without obedience to them you cannot enter the kingdom of heaven.

Grace is a gift, but the gift must be received. Only those willing to "receive" it, merit grace.[1194] It is "received" in the way the Lord ordained and in no other way.[1195]

Only the deceived or the wicked would contradict the Lord's teaching that "except ye keep [His] commandments" then "ye cannot enter into the kingdom of heaven." Yet there are those who both make this claim in the various Protestant denominations, and are trying to advance this position into the LDS faith, as well. We would be better served by forgetting how to make ourselves seem more

---

[1194] D&C 88:32–35 "And they who remain shall also be quickened; nevertheless, they shall return again to their own place, to enjoy that which they are willing to receive, because they were not willing to enjoy that which they might have received. For what doth it profit a man if a gift is bestowed upon him, and he receive not the gift? Behold, he rejoices not in that which is given unto him, neither rejoices in him who is the giver of the gift. And again, verily I say unto you, that which is governed by law is also preserved by law and perfected and sanctified by the same. That which breaketh a law, and abideth not by law, but seeketh to become a law unto itself, and willeth to abide in sin, and altogether abideth in sin, cannot be sanctified by law, neither by mercy, justice, nor judgment. Therefore, they must remain filthy still."

[1195] D&C 130:21 "And when we obtain any blessing from God, it is by obedience to that law upon which it is predicated."

Protestant, and instead accepting and teaching what Christ established as the sole basis for entering the kingdom of heaven.

3 Nephi 12:21–22

> "Ye have heard that it hath been said by them of old time, and it is also written before you, that thou shalt not kill, and whosoever shall kill shall be in danger of the judgment of God; But I say unto you, that whosoever is angry with his brother shall be in danger of his judgment. And whosoever shall say to his brother, Raca, shall be in danger of the council; and whosoever shall say, Thou fool, shall be in danger of hell fire."

Christ is elevating the Law of Moses by raising the expectation for human conduct. He moves from mere outward conduct into the inner soul of the man. You are not doing as you should if all you do is refrain from killing. Instead, you need to remove anger.

The prior obligation ("said by them of old") focused only on your conduct, now it is your motivation.

You can judge another based on conduct. They either do or do not do something. The conduct is observable, and therefore capable of being judged. Now, however, Christ moves the battleground inside a person. It is now in the heart. On such terrain as that, man is incapable of knowing, and therefore, of judging.

With anything involving truth and rules of conduct, there are always some reasons to depart from the rule. Christ departed from this rule. So we must consider the departures to understand the rule.

First, however, we need to know and understand the rule. The "judgment" which you are "in danger of" by being angry with your brother is not your brother's anger, but God's. The judgment of God is provoked by those who are angry with their brother.

We are not to be angry with our brother because that is the beginning of a whole sequence of events, the culmination of which may be killing. Before killing, however, there are other troubles and offenses along the way. Anger leads to abuse. It leads to discourtesy, dishonesty, and cheating. It justifies miserable conduct because you think it right to give offenses to another. It corrodes relationships and makes society sick.

If you can prevent this at the heart, you can heal society. Refrain from letting offenses turn into anger. Deal with them inside, showing forgiveness and compassion. He will stress this further in subsequent verses.

The terms "Raca" and "fool" are derisive names. Christ is saying that applying derisive names to others is wrong, even damning. He is not preventing you from identifying foolishness. He often spoke of fools and foolishness.[1196] He would even use the term "foolish" in this same sermon.[1197] So it is not at all inappropriate to use the term "fool" or "foolish" when discussing foolishness. What is wrong it to regard your fellow man with derision and use terms of derision to describe them.

[1196] Matthew 23:17 "*Ye* fools and blind: for whether is greater, the gold, or the temple that sanctifieth the gold? . . . *Ye* fools and blind: for whether *is* greater, the gift, or the altar that sanctifieth the gift?"

Matthew 25:2–8 "And five of them were wise, and five *were* foolish. They that *were* foolish took their lamps, and took no oil with them: But the wise took oil in their vessels with their lamPsalms While the bridegroom tarried, they all slumbered and slept. And at midnight there was a cry made, Behold, the bridegroom cometh; go ye out to meet him. Then all those virgins arose, and trimmed their lamPsalms And the foolish said unto the wise, Give us of your oil; for our lamps are gone out."

Luke 12:20 "But God said unto him, *Thou* fool, this night thy soul shall be required of thee: then whose shall those things be, which thou hast provided?"

Luke 24:25 (after His resurrection): "Then he said unto them, O fools, and slow of heart to believe all that the prophets have spoken:"

2 Nephi 29:4, 6 "But thus saith the Lord God: O fools, they shall have a Bible; and it shall proceed forth from the Jews, mine ancient covenant people. And what thank they the Jews for the Bible which they receive from them? Yea, what do the Gentiles mean? Do they remember the travails, and the labors, and the pains of the Jews, and their diligence unto me, in bringing forth salvation unto the Gentiles? . . . Thou fool, that shall say: A Bible, we have got a Bible, and we need no more Bible. Have ye obtained a Bible save it were by the Jews?"

[1197] 3 Nephi 14:26 "And every one that heareth these sayings of mine and doeth them not shall be likened unto a foolish man, who built his house upon the sand—"

Even with this rue of conduct, however, Christ applied a derisive term to King Herod. He called him "that fox."[1198] This was a term of derision, but appropriately applied to a wicked king meriting derision. He was corrupt, evil and vile. Therefore, with respect to Herod, Christ's example allows for terms of derision to be appropriately applied to those who merit them. Christ was able to weigh the heart. For Him to make that conclusion was a matter of Divine prerogative. I suppose that we are equally entitled to apply such terms of judgment and condemnation, including terms of derision, if we obtain them by inspiration from the Lord. That is, if the Lord inspires such a term of derision to be used, then it would be appropriate despite this verse. For whatever we do, even if sharpness is involved, is appropriate when moved upon by the Holy Ghost.[1199] So, also, even killing another can be done when the Lord is the one deciding life and death.[1200]

The tendency is to always think the exceptions allow your anger. I would suspect the best approach is to do as Nephi did. That is, insist upon following the one standard of conduct and always refrain. Always. Then, if the Lord is going to have it otherwise, leave it to the

---

[1198] Luke 13:31–32 "The same day there came certain of the Pharisees, saying unto him, Get thee out, and depart hence: for Herod will kill thee. And he said unto them, Go ye, and tell that fox, Behold, I cast out devils, and I do cures to day and to morrow, and the third *day* I shall be perfected."

[1199] D&C 121:43 "Reproving betimes with sharpness, when moved upon by the Holy Ghost; and then showing forth afterwards an increase of love toward him whom thou hast reproved, lest he esteem thee to be his enemy;"

[1200] 1 Nephi 4:10–13 "And it came to pass that I was constrained by the Spirit that I should kill Laban; but I said in my heart: Never at any time have I shed the blood of man. And I shrunk and would that I might not slay him. And the Spirit said unto me again: Behold the Lord hath delivered him into thy hands. Yea, and I also knew that he had sought to take away mine own life; yea, and he would not hearken unto the commandments of the Lord; and he also had taken away our property. And it came to pass that the Spirit said unto me again: Slay him, for the Lord hath delivered him into thy hands; Behold the Lord slayeth the wicked to bring forth his righteous purposes. It is better that one man should perish than that a nation should dwindle and perish in unbelief."

Lord to make that insistence so dramatic, so undeniable, so compelling, that you know it is the Lord's judgment and not your own. Removing anger from the heart is a difficult enough challenge to last the rest of your life. To start thinking any passing offense justifies an exception because it may be "inspired" is the way of a fool. Do as Christ bids you to do in this sermon. If He wants a different approach, you ought to require that to be made absolutely clear by Him before you depart from this standard.

Remember how often great souls have interceded for their fellow man. I've written about that so often in my books I won't repeat it again. However, intercession for your fellow man, including those who give offense to you, is one of the hallmarks of the saved soul. This is who Abraham was, and why he became a friend of God. I've hesitated to even discuss the exceptions to the rule because everyone wants the exceptions to apply to them. No one wants to comply with the rule. The higher way is, however, found in following the rule. It should be an absolute sacrifice, and a painful one at that, for the exception to be applied in your life. If an inspired condemnation is required at your hand and by your voice, then immediately afterwards you should make intercession with the Lord for those condemned. That is the way of those who know the Lord. Those who have been forgiven much—including those who have been forgiven everything—always love much in return.[1201]

3 Nephi 12:23–24

"Therefore, if ye shall come unto me, or shall desire to come unto me, and rememberest that thy brother hath aught against thee— Go thy way unto thy brother, and first be reconciled to thy brother, and then come unto me with full purpose of heart, and I will receive you."

[1201] Luke 7:47 "Wherefore I say unto thee, Her sins, which are many, are forgiven; for she loved much: but to whom little is forgiven, *the same* loveth little."

Notice the offense is taken by the brother, not by you. It is presumed that you haven't taken offense against him. If he, however, 'hath aught against thee"—meaning that if you have done anything to cause him an offense, you have steps to take.

Notice that your relationship with the Lord comes second, *after* you have made amends with any you have offended.

You can't bring "full purpose of heart" when there is a lingering offense you have not attempted to cure. This kind of mental distraction alters you.

If you realize you've offended someone it likely means you know your conduct has been uncharitable. You did something wrong. You hurt another.

Inventory of your conduct is something to be done before approaching the Lord. If you have offended someone you need to take the steps to free your conscience from it. Only then can you bring "full purpose of heart" in approaching God.

When the heart is right, then the Lord can "receive you." When the heart is not right, you cannot be received.

He's said this before, of course. His doctrine in the preceding chapter required repentance before baptism precisely so you could be right in the heart before the ordinance takes place.[1202]

Other Book of Mormon writers said the same thing as well:

"For behold, God hath said a man being evil cannot do that which is good; for if he offereth a gift, or prayeth unto God, except he shall do it with real intent it profiteth him nothing. . . . And likewise also is it counted evil unto a man, if he shall pray and not with real intent of heart; yea, and it profiteth him nothing, for God receiveth none such." (Moroni 7:6, 9.)

[1202] 3 Nephi 11:23 "Verily I say unto you, that whoso repenteth of his sins through your words, and desireth to be baptized in my name, on this wise shall ye baptize them—Behold, ye shall go down and stand in the water, and in my name shall ye baptize them."

"Wherefore, my beloved brethren, I know that if ye shall follow the Son, with full purpose of heart, acting no hypocrisy and no deception before God, but with real intent, repenting of your sins, witnessing unto the Father that ye are willing to take upon you the name of Christ, by baptism—yea, by following your Lord and your Savior down into the water, according to his word, behold, then shall ye receive the Holy Ghost; yea, then cometh the baptism of fire and of the Holy Ghost; and then can ye speak with the tongue of angels, and shout praises unto the Holy One of Israel." (2 Nephi 31:13)

"But as oft as they repented and sought forgiveness, with real intent, they were forgiven." (Moroni 6:8.)

You bring your whole heart to Him. That He can receive. That He can work with. Less than that, it is not possible for Him to offer you anything. You will invariably reject what He offers. Acting as the hypocrite will neither fool you or Him. Hence Nephi's counsel in 2 Nephi 31:13 quoted above, and discussed previously in this blog.

3 Nephi 12:25–26

"Agree with thine adversary quickly while thou art in the way with him, lest at any time he shall get thee, and thou shalt be cast into prison. Verily, verily, I say unto thee, thou shalt by no means come out thence until thou hast paid the uttermost senine. And while ye are in prison can ye pay even one senine? Verily, verily, I say unto you, Nay."

This notion of agreeing with your adversaries is difficult for most people. It requires you to submit to what is sometimes unjust demands. He is saying to submit anyway. Do not rebel against the adversaries in life, but accommodate them.

Give to the unjust what they demand, so that they may see your good works and understand there is a higher way. Without your example, they cannot understand.

Retaliation continues the cycles. Someone eventually needs to lay down their just claim for retribution and simply take the injury without returning anything in return. This was what Christ did. He took everyone's injuries and returned only forgiveness.

Now He asks for His followers to do some of the same. The failure to tolerate injustice can spiral into continuing the conflict, until there is prison. The prison to fear is not one made by men. But if you are cast into that prison then you cannot come out until you have paid the highest price.[1203] It is better to repent because this payment made even God, the greatest of all, to tremble with pain and shrink from the burden.[1204]

[1203] D&C 76:84–85, 105, 106 "These are they who are thrust down to hell. These are they who shall not be redeemed from the devil until the last resurrection, until the Lord, even Christ the Lamb, shall have finished his work. These are they who suffer the vengeance of eternal fire. These are they who are cast down to hell and suffer the wrath of Almighty God, until the fulness of times, when Christ shall have subdued all enemies under his feet, and shall have perfected his work;"

[1204] D&C 19:15–18 "Therefore I command you to repent—repent, lest I smite you by the rod of my mouth, and by my wrath, and by my anger, and your sufferings be sore—how sore you know not, how exquisite you know not, yea, how hard to bear you know not. For behold, I, God, have suffered these things for all, that they might not suffer if they would repent; But if they would not repent they must suffer even as I; Which suffering caused myself, even God, the greatest of all, to tremble because of pain, and to bleed at every pore, and to suffer both body and spirit—and would that I might not drink the bitter cup, and shrink—"

It is not possible to pay the price while in prison. The price must be paid by a person while in the flesh.[1205] Any who are consigned to prison dwell in darkness, awaiting deliverance from Him whom they rejected while in the flesh.[1206] They become dependent upon others working to pay the debt on their behalf.[1207]

The sermon delivered by Christ is the foundation of how man ought to relate to fellow-man. It is the pattern on which it becomes possible to dwell in peace with one another. It is the groundwork for Zion.

We need to look at this sermon as the guideline for changing our internal lives, so we may become a fit and proper resident with others who are Saints. Even Saints will give inadvertent offenses. Even Saints will disappoint one another from time to time. To become "one" in the sense required for redeeming a people and restoring them again to Zion is beyond any person's reach if they cannot internalize this sermon.

The purpose of this sermon is not to equip you to judge others. It has no use for that. It is designed to change you. You need to become something different, something higher, something more holy.

[1205] Luke 16:22–26 "And it came to pass, that the beggar died, and was carried by the angels into Abraham's bosom: the rich man also died, and was buried; And in hell he lift up his eyes, being in torments, and seeth Abraham afar off, and Lazarus in his bosom. And he cried and said, Father Abraham, have mercy on me, and send Lazarus, that he may dip the tip of his finger in water, and cool my tongue; for I am tormented in this flame. But Abraham said, Son, remember that thou in thy lifetime receivedst thy good things, and likewise Lazarus evil things: but now he is comforted, and thou art tormented. And beside all this, between us and you there is a great gulf fixed: so that they which would pass from hence to you cannot; neither can they pass to us, that *would come* from thence."

[1206] D&C 138:20–22 "But unto the wicked he did not go, and among the ungodly and the unrepentant who had defiled themselves while in the flesh, his voice was not raised; Neither did the rebellious who rejected the testimonies and the warnings of the ancient prophets behold his presence, nor look upon his face. Where these were, darkness reigned, but among the righteous there was peace;"

[1207] D&C 138:33 "These were taught faith in God, repentance from sin, vicarious baptism for the remission of sins, the gift of the Holy Ghost by the laying on of hands,"

That will require you to reexamine your heart, your motivations, and your thoughts. It will require you to take offenses and deliberately lay them down without retaliation. When you do, you become someone who can live in peace with others. Living in peace with others is the rudimentary beginning of Zion. It will not culminate in a City set on the hilltop until there is a population worthy of dwelling in the high places, in peace, without poor among them.[1208]

Christ's sermon is not merely a description of what kind of person He is. It is a description of what kind of person will qualify to live with Him.[1209]

3 Nephi 12:27–29

"Behold, it is written by them of old time, that thou shalt not commit adultery; But I say unto you, that whosoever looketh on a woman, to lust after her, hath committed adultery already in his heart. Behold, I give unto you a commandment, that ye suffer none of these things to enter into your heart;"

Here it is again—the heart. It is the intent and not just the act. It is not enough that you stop short of doing the thing commanded in the Law of Moses. Christ is attacking the root cause, the internal trouble which causes the mistakes.

The Law of Moses is not being replaced with a new era of easy grace triggered by confession for salvation. The Head of the new Dispensation, Christ, is instead providing a much higher standard for mankind to adopt in place of carnal commandments.

[1208] Moses 7:17–18 "The fear of the Lord was upon all nations, so great was the glory of the Lord, which was upon his people. And the Lord blessed the land, and they were blessed upon the mountains, and upon the high places, and did flourish. And the Lord called his people Zion, because they were of one heart and one mind, and dwelt in righteousness; and there was no poor among them."

[1209] Luke 9:23 "And he said to *them* all, If any *man* will come after me, let him deny himself, and take up his cross daily, and follow me."

You must raise your thoughts to a higher level. Sexual appetites and passions must be kept within the bounds the Lord has prescribed. For this new, higher standard, it is not enough to just refrain from immoral acts, but you must purge thoughts. Neither lust of a woman, nor any of "these things" should "enter into your heart." This uniform standard applies to all: male and female, married or single, without regard to who or what causes your lusts. It is universal.

The raging controversy going on at present over President Packer's last General Conference address entirely misses the point. Whether your sexual attraction is male or female, it is to be confined in thought and deed to the bounds prescribed by the Lord, and the Lord has rather clearly identified the bounds in this sermon.

The heart is where sin begins. So it is the heart which Christ would have us cleanse. All else will follow.

No one knows how formidable an obstacle this is until they have confronted it themselves. Nor can a person who confronts this challenge succeed at the first attempt. C.S. Lewis made such a profound observation on this subject it is worth quoting here:

> "No man knows how bad he is till he has tried very hard to be good. A silly idea is current that good people do not know what temptation means. This is an obvious lie. Only those who try to resist temptation know how strong it is. After all, you find out the strength of the German army by fighting against it, not by giving in. You find out the strength of a wind by trying to walk against it, not by lying down. A man who gives in to temptation after five minutes simply does not know what it would have been like an hour later. That is why bad people, in one sense, know very little about badness. They have lived a sheltered life by always giving in. We never find out the strength of the evil impulse inside us until we try to fight it: and Christ, because he was the only man who never yielded to temptation, is also the only man who knows to the

full what temptation means—the only complete realist." (CS Lewis, *Mere Christianity*, Chapter 11.)

Those who would rather settle into a comfortable enjoyment of their sins find discomfort in being reminded they are wrong. So when President Packer reminds them of this, it is painful, and they want him to retract his words. It would be better to consider them, for whether he retracts them or not, it will not change the underlying problem of sin. Only by confronting and overcoming sins within us will we ever become people who will be preserved in the coming harvest.

Imagine, if you can, the idea of impurity being a compound which exists within you. A compound that could be identified by the Lord and burned away. Think of it like the fuller's soap or the refiner's fire, where impurity is removed and something pure and clean is left behind.[1210] To survive that burning purge there must be so little to burn away that the injury from the burn will not threaten life. It is a useful way to examine what is inside you. And a useful way to reconsider your thoughts.

This leads to the final question: What is the difference between the mind and the "heart?" This commandment addresses the "heart" in you. What is the "heart?"

3 Nephi 12:30

"For it is better that ye should deny yourselves of these things, wherein ye will take up your cross, than that ye should be cast into hell."

[1210] Malachi 3:2–3 "But who may abide the day of his coming? and who shall stand when he appeareth? for he *is* like a refiner's fire, and like fullers' soap: And he shall sit *as* a refiner and purifier of silver: and he shall purify the sons of Levi, and purge them as gold and silver, that they may offer unto the Lord an offering in righteousness."

Each person's cross is individual. Carrying "your cross" is not the same as carrying mine. Therefore, when you "deny yourself of these things" what you surrender and what you take up will be "your cross" and never mine.

It is odd how we are able to spot from a distance the weaknesses of others. We have highly acute sensitivities about others' flaws. But we rarely appreciate the crosses they bear.

How hard a burden a man carries when he disciplines himself to rise daily, and work to sacrifice for his family, is not at all the same across the economic scale. Nor, for that matter, is the daily service carried on by mothers who have deprived themselves of other pursuits to raise sometimes ungrateful children.

But "hell" is where we are cast when we are pained by the regrets of having lived without discipline, having lived selfishly.[1211] We will stand "naked" before God. All of what we want hidden will be before us, revealed and exposed to view.

The "hell" of it all will be our regret, for we are our own tormentor. The torment of a disappointed mind will be like fire and brimstone to the regretful (*TPJS*, 357).

Christ is advising us in a kindly way how to prevent that moment of fear, regret and torment. He is telling us how to escape it. These teachings are not a threat addressed at us, but a caution about the future moment when these teachings apply to us all.

It is as if the Lord wants us to know clearly beforehand what we are going to wish we had done instead. Now, in mortality, while we can still change how things will turn out, He is telling us how to accomplish that. In an understatement, He advises: "it is better to deny

---

[1211] Mormon 9:4–5 "Behold, I say unto you that ye would be more miserable to dwell with a holy and just God, under a consciousness of your filthiness before him, than ye would to dwell with the damned souls in hell. For behold, when ye shall be brought to see your nakedness before God, and also the glory of God, and the holiness of Jesus Christ, it will kindle a flame of unquenchable fire upon you."

yourself" than it will be to indulge. You may find it a "cross" as you do, but if you deny yourself now it will let you escape "hell" in the future. It is kindly advice, without a threat. It is a warning about the road you have taken, and guidance on how you can avoid the collision that is coming.

Whatever the "cross" is you take up in your daily effort to live inside the bounds prescribed by the Lord, it will be worth it. By heeding His counsel, you will become someone better and avoid becoming devilish.

The temptations each of us face are unique to the individual. What is universal, however, is the limit placed upon temptations. They are never too great to resist. There is always an escape provided by the Lord.[1212] Nor are you given any commandment you cannot obey.[1213] However, that is not to say temptation is easily overcome. Weakness is our lot.[1214]

What then are you to make of your cross? If you've tried to deny yourself and failed, does it mean you are hopeless? Is the persistent failure to lift the cross you have been called to bear proof that you are just unable to merit salvation? Does the relentless return to temptation mean you are lost? Are you necessarily doomed because you have not found the escape promised by Paul's writing to the Corinthians?

[1212] 1 Corinthians 10:13 "There hath no temptation taken you but such as is common to man: but God *is* faithful, who will not suffer you to be tempted above that ye are able; but will with the temptation also make a way to escape, that ye may be able to bear *it.*"

[1213] 1 Nephi 3:7 "And it came to pass that I, Nephi, said unto my father: I will go and do the things which the Lord hath commanded, for I know that the Lord giveth no commandments unto the children of men, save he shall prepare a way for them that they may accomplish the thing which he commandeth them."

[1214] Ether 12:27 "And if men come unto me I will show unto them their weakness. I give unto men weakness that they may be humble; and my grace is sufficient for all men that humble themselves before me; for if they humble themselves before me, and have faith in me, then will I make weak things become strong unto them."

Life is filled with cycles. When we battle and fail one day, then join the battle again, but fail again; then another, and another and another, what is the use? What do we make of such persistent failure, such continuing weakness? Is the lesson that we are lost? Or is it that we are weak? Weaker than we had ever imagined. Weaker than you could ever suppose man to be.[1215] Is this evidence that you are doomed? Or is it merely a patient God proving to your utter satisfaction that you are indeed in need of saving grace to rescue you from where you find yourself? Is this the moment when, while filling your belly with husks along with the swine you've descended to accompany, you wake up?[1216] If you will finally surrender your pride, come forward with a broken heart and real intent, returning to your Father, He will joyfully receive you still.[1217] There is joy in heaven over you when you awaken.

Weakness is nothing, for all are weak. It is a gift, given to break your heart. Your broken heart will qualify you for His company.

[1215] Moses 1:10 "And it came to pass that it was for the space of many hours before Moses did again receive his natural strength like unto man; and he said unto himself: Now, for this cause I know that man is nothing, which thing I never had supposed."

[1216] Luke 15:11–17 "And he said, A certain man had two sons: And the younger of them said to *his* father, Father, give me the portion of goods that falleth *to me*. And he divided unto them *his* living. And not many days after the younger son gathered all together, and took his journey into a far country, and there wasted his substance with riotous living. And when he had spent all, there arose a mighty famine in that land; and he began to be in want. And he went and joined himself to a citizen of that country; and he sent him into his fields to feed swine. And he would fain have filled his belly with the husks that the swine did eat: and no man gave unto him. And when he came to himself, he said, How many hired servants of my father's have bread enough and to spare, and I perish with hunger!"

[1217] Luke 15:18–24 "I will arise and go to my father, and will say unto him, Father, I have sinned against heaven, and before thee, And am no more worthy to be called thy son: make me as one of thy hired servants. And he arose, and came to his father. But when he was yet a great way off, his father saw him, and had compassion, and ran, and fell on his neck, and kissed him. And the son said unto him, Father, I have sinned against heaven, and in thy sight, and am no more worthy to be called thy son. But the father said to his servants, Bring forth the best robe, and put *it* on him; and put a ring on his hand, and shoes on *his* feet: And bring hither the fatted calf, and kill *it*; and let us eat, and be merry: For this my son was dead, and is alive again; he was lost, and is found. And they began to be merry."

Whether a leper, an adulteress, a tax collector or a blind man, He can heal it all. But what He cannot do, and you must alone bring to Him, is that broken heart required for salvation.

William Ernest Henley wrote *Invictus*:

> Out of the night that covers me,
> Black as the Pit from pole to pole,
> I thank whatever gods may be
> For my unconquerable soul.
>
> In the fell clutch of circumstance
> I have not winced nor cried aloud.
> Under the bludgeonings of chance
> My head is bloody, but unbowed.
>
> Beyond this place of wrath and tears
> Looms but the Horror of the shade,
> And yet the menace of the years
> Finds, and shall find, me unafraid.
>
> It matters not how strait the gate,
> How charged with punishments the scroll.
> I am the master of my fate:
> I am the captain of my soul.

Orson F. Whitney penned the response in *The Soul's Captain*:

> Art thou in truth? Then what of him
> Who bought thee with his blood?
> Who plunged into devouring seas
> And snatched thee from the flood?
>
> Who bore for all our fallen race
> What none but him could bear—
> The God who died that man might live,
> And endless glory share?
>
> Of what avail thy vaunted strength,

Apart from his vast might?

Pray that his Light may pierce the gloom,

That thou mayest see aright.

Men are as bubbles on the wave,

As leaves upon the tree.

Thou, captain of thy soul, forsooth

Who gave that place to thee?

Free will is thine—free agency

To wield for right or wrong;

But thou must answer unto him

To whom all souls belong.

Bend to the dust that head "unbowed,"

Small part of Life's great whole!

And see in him, and him alone,

The Captain of thy soul.

We choose. We live with our choices. It is better to deny ourselves and take up our individual crosses.

3 Nephi 12:31–32

"It hath been written, that whosoever shall put away his wife, let him give her a writing of divorcement. Verily, verily, I say unto you, that whosoever shall put away his wife, saving for the cause of fornication, causeth her to commit adultery; and whoso shall marry her who is divorced committeth adultery."

First and foremost, this is a verse dealing with male conduct. The verse is masculine in orientation and word usage, and deals with a male's prerogative under the law that existed then. So applying this new, higher law, beyond that is not warranted, as will be more clearly seen in the discussion below.

The ease with which a divorce could be granted made the serious nature of the act unappreciated. Today it is still unappreciated. Divorce rates among Latter-day Saints have risen to practically mirror the population at large. We follow all the surrounding social trends, but are a little slower in getting there. We are not "peculiar" any longer. We are just slower.

Christ was re-enshrining the significance of marriage. It should not be easy to end a marriage. But, then again, perhaps the kind of marriage Christ is speaking of is one of a higher order and rarely exists here.

Although there are reasons for every marriage to be treated as sacred and worth preserving, it was always intended for there to be a higher purpose in marriage. It was intended to be an eternal union, inside of which sacred acts mirroring heaven itself take place. Bringing into this world new life by the loving union of two partners is a mirror of heaven. Such things are, or ought to be, most sacred.

But a higher kind of union, where love is the prevailing rule, is not often established here. More often than not, the marriages of this world are corrupted, just as society itself is corrupted.

I hardly dare offer a different view of these verses, because people think they know what they're reading in them. I'm not sure we have ever seen what Christ is actually speaking about. Though caution would suggest otherwise, I'm going to go ahead with offering a different view.

First, this is always interpreted to be discussing things which are coarse or material, but it comes immediately following a discussion about the inner or spiritual self. This suggests our normal reading of this language may be incorrect. When the focus of Christ's new and higher law is the inner man, then to read this as applying to outward behavior (fornication/adultery) may miss the point.

Second, notice the contrast between the only justified reason for terminating the marriage (fornication) and the subsequent results (adultery). Two different words are used, suggesting two different meanings are present.

I've consulted with John Hall about the New Testament language in the Matthew account of this sermon, where "**porneia**" is the typical rendering. There the meaning of the first word which we render "fornication" could be a variety of things including: prostitution, sexual permissiveness or merely a sexual act. But, if the word was "**poneria**" then it could, by broad measure, mean bad acts (with no sexual connotation at all).

There is a possibility that the correct way to read this could be rendered in this way: "Whoever puts away his wife for any reason other than the lack of marital intimacy . . . " That would mean the only justified reason to end the marriage is that the marriage has ended within the heart. There is no longer any love in the relation. It has died. It is no longer worthy of preservation, and therefore, the death of the heart justifies the death of the relation.

However, the focus is on the woman's heart. That is, if the woman still retains marital intimacy for the husband, he cannot be justified in putting her away. He is obligated to retain as his wife the woman who loves him. If he puts away such a wife, then he causes her to commit adultery.

This, then, raises the issue of the meaning of adultery. We tend to view it as a physical act involving sexual union with another. But adultery also holds the connotation of unfaithfulness, as in Israel becoming unfaithful and playing the part of an adulteress, worshiping other gods.[1218] When forced away by the man she loves, a woman

---

[1218] Jeremiah 3:8 "And I saw, when for all the causes whereby backsliding Israel committed adultery I had put her away, and given her a bill of divorce; yet her treacherous sister Judah feared not, but went and played the harlot also."

is then "adulterated" by the act of the man. He is accountable for the treachery involved in dissolving the marriage which the woman wanted, and forcing her into the relation with either no one, or with another man. Either one is "adulterating" the marriage which she had with him. He is accountable for that uncharitable, unkind, and unjustified treatment of the woman.

On the other hand, when she has lost affection for him, and the union has become hollow and without love, then the marriage is dead and continuation of the relation is a farce. It is not a marriage. In fact, it is a pretense and an abomination unworthy of preservation. It will not endure. It is not eternal and not possible to preserve beyond the grave.

No union that has not been sealed by the Holy Spirit of Promise will endure beyond the grave.[1219] The reason for sealing such a marriage by the promise of the Spirit is because it replicates the kind of holy union found in heaven. It is like unto the unions between gods and goddesses. It is worthy of preservation because it is eternal. It is enduring. It is worth preserving into all eternity. It is sealed because the gods recognize on the earth a mirror of what is found in heaven

---

[1219] References include, among others, D&C 132:7, 18 "And verily I say unto you, that the conditions of this law are these: All covenants, contracts, bonds, obligations, oaths, vows, performances, connections, associations, or expectations, that are not made and entered into and sealed by the Holy Spirit of promise, of him who is anointed, both as well for time and for all eternity, and that too most holy, by revelation and commandment through the medium of mine anointed, whom I have appointed on the earth to hold this power (and I have appointed unto my servant Joseph to hold this power in the last days, and there is never but one on the earth at a time on whom this power and the keys of this priesthood are conferred), are of no efficacy, virtue, or force in and after the resurrection from the dead; for all contracts that are not made unto this end have an end when men are dead. . . . And again, verily I say unto you, if a man marry a wife, and make a covenant with her for time and for all eternity, if that covenant is not by me or by my word, which is my law, and is not sealed by the Holy Spirit of promise, through him whom I have anointed and appointed unto this power, then it is not valid neither of force when they are out of the world, because they are not joined by me, saith the Lord, neither by my word; when they are out of the world it cannot be received there, because the angels and the gods are appointed there, by whom they cannot pass; they cannot, therefore, inherit my glory; for my house is a house of order, saith the Lord God."

itself. Therefore heaven ratifies and approves the relationship. They do not create such relations in heaven, but instead recognize them here, and approve them for eternal duration. Without such a relationship, the parties are worthy of continuation as angels, but not as spouses, as Christ would put it elsewhere.[1220]

It is true enough that the restored Gospel allows everyone the opportunity to come to the Temple and receive ordinances which hold the promise of an eternal union. But those are relationships where the parties are on probation. They are given as an opportunity to work out your salvation before God. They are given so that if you are true and faithful, the time may come when you are called up and chosen by the Holy Spirit of Promise to be kings and queens, priests and priestesses, whereas now you are only given opportunity to prove yourself worthy to become such.

There are many unhappy Latter-day Saint marriages which exist in name only. The notorious high record use of anti-depressants by women in Utah is driven in large part by unhappy marriages they believe ought to be preserved because of a misunderstanding of these verses. Yet the underlying reality that the union causes suffering rather than rejoicing cannot be escaped. So they alter their natural reaction to the unhappy union by altering the brain with chemicals. Such a marriage cannot endure into eternity. Though the woman may sacrifice herself to preserve her heart's desire to be a faithful, married mother, her unworthy marriage is not what will endure. It cannot be sealed by the Holy Spirit of Promise, though she may be otherwise qualified.

[1220] Matthew 22:30 "For in the resurrection they neither marry, nor are given in marriage, but are as the angels of God in heaven."
D&C 132:17 "For these angels did not abide my law; therefore, they cannot be enlarged, but remain separately and singly, without exaltation, in their saved condition, to all eternity; and from henceforth are not gods, but are angels of God forever and ever."

Now, to be clear, I do not advocate divorce, particularly where minor children are involved. But I do advocate a higher view of the marital union where the prevailing reason for the union is love. This should be the whole preparation for marriage. Before contracting the union, the parties should look for that spouse with whom they can find heaven on earth. Unhappy marriages might all be saved if the parties would repent. The higher ideal is not impossible for any union to seek and find. That is the right of every party here, if they will but seek after it. If however, after every effort has been made to both find, and cultivate such a union, it proves to be an impossibility, then the parties ought to use the precious time allotted to them in mortality to find a union which will be worthy of continuation. Not at the expense of their children, who are entitled to have both parents raise them. The Holy Spirit of Promise was intended to be shed upon many marriages, rather than a comparative few. Happiness was the design of our creation. When we avoid it by our misconduct and foolishness, we do not please heaven. Nor does gritting our teeth, putting up with miserable relationships, and enduring an unholy union please heaven or merit some eternal reward.

These words of Christ are speaking of a higher way to conduct our lives. To read into them exclusively outward behavior, when the whole import of the sermon addresses the inner-man, is out of context. I think we hardly understand the Lord's meaning. But, then again, perhaps it is best if we do not understand His full meaning until we are ready to see for ourselves what great things the Lord has in store for those who love Him.[1221] Perhaps it is best that man is not capable of making them known.

Now, as to the woman, there is another standard. He does not articulate it here, but can be found throughout scripture. A woman's love of and fidelity to her husband is more often than not a product of her nature. It takes quite a fool to turn a wife's natural affection for him into distrust and bitterness. But there are churlish men, as we know from scripture. Sometimes they marry an Abigail.[1222]

[1221] D&C 76:114–117 "But great and marvelous are the works of the Lord, and the mysteries of his kingdom which he showed unto us, which surpass all understanding in glory, and in might, and in dominion; Which he commanded us we should not write while we were yet in the Spirit, and are not lawful for man to utter; Neither is man capable to make them known, for they are only to be seen and understood by the power of the Holy Spirit, which God bestows on those who love him, and purify themselves before him; To whom he grants this privilege of seeing and knowing for themselves;"

[1222] 1 Samuel 25:3 "Now the name of the man *was* Nabal; and the name of his wife Abigail: and *she was* a woman of good understanding, and of a beautiful countenance: but the man *was* churlish and evil in his doings; and he *was* of the house of Caleb."

3 Nephi 12:33–37

"And again it is written, thou shalt not forswear thyself, but shalt perform unto the Lord thine oaths; But verily, verily, I say unto you, swear not at all; neither by heaven, for it is God's throne; Nor by the earth, for it is his footstool; Neither shalt thou swear by thy head, because thou canst not make one hair black or white; But let your communication be Yea, yea; Nay, nay; for whatsoever cometh of more than these is evil."

This revokes the oath making of the earlier Dispensation. When an oath was taken it was to be performed without fail.[1223] It was binding. Ancient Israel relied on vows to govern their conduct.[1224] Oaths were relied on because they bound your conduct before God.

Christ is putting an end to the practice. No further vow-making was to take place. In its place say "yea" or say "nay," but nothing further to bind your soul before God.

Swearing by men who possess nothing is foolish and prideful. Particularly when they swear by heaven, because it is not theirs to promise. Nor should they swear by the earth, because it is not theirs

---

[1223] Numbers 30:2 "If a man vow a vow unto the Lord, or swear an oath to bind his soul with a bond; he shall not break his word, he shall do according to all that proceedeth out of his mouth.

[1224] 1 Nephi 4:33–37 "And I spake unto him, even with an oath, that he need not fear; that he should be a free man like unto us if he would go down in the wilderness with us. And I also spake unto him, saying: Surely the Lord hath commanded us to do this thing; and shall we not be diligent in keeping the commandments of the Lord? Therefore, if thou wilt go down into the wilderness to my father thou shalt have place with us. And it came to pass that Zoram did take courage at the words which I spake. Now Zoram was the name of the servant; and he promised that he would go down into the wilderness unto our father. Yea, and he also made an oath unto us that he would tarry with us from that time forth. Now we were desirous that he should tarry with us for this cause, that the Jews might not know concerning our flight into the wilderness, lest they should pursue us and destroy us. And it came to pass that when Zoram had made an oath unto us, our fears did cease concerning him."

either. A man cannot even offer his own life, because it belongs to God who gave it. Indeed, there is nothing we own or can offer.[1225]

The comment regarding the inability to make a single hair "black or white" is emphasizing how little control we really have over things. Even our own bodies will take a course assigned it by God. They will age, and eventually die. We have our body as a stewardship. It is ours for a season, then we will lay it down. Until then, we serve a probation in which we are given power over these elements we occupy. But that stewardship is one designed to "prove" us, and show what we really are. When we gratify the body at the expense of others, or destroy our bodily temple housing our spirits by indulging uncontrolled appetites, we are unwise. We will lose these bodies before long and then, left with the same spiritual emptiness which caused the cravings in the first place, will find ourselves suffering. Whereas, if you discipline the body, keep it under control and subject to your spirit, then death can bring a release and freedom from suffering. It will be an odd reversal. One known only to those who go through it; at which point it is too late to change the outcome.

[1225] Mosiah 2:20–25 "I say unto you, my brethren, that if you should render all the thanks and praise which your whole soul has power to possess, to that God who has created you, and has kept and preserved you, and has caused that ye should rejoice, and has granted that ye should live in peace one with another—I say unto you that if ye should serve him who has created you from the beginning, and is preserving you from day to day, by lending you breath, that ye may live and move and do according to your own will, and even supporting you from one moment to another—I say, if ye should serve him with all your whole souls yet ye would be unprofitable servants. And behold, all that he requires of you is to keep his commandments; and he has promised you that if ye would keep his commandments ye should prosper in the land; and he never doth vary from that which he hath said; therefore, if ye do keep his commandments he doth bless you and prosper you. And now, in the first place, he hath created you, and granted unto you your lives, for which ye are indebted unto him. And secondly, he doth require that ye should do as he hath commanded you; for which if ye do, he doth immediately bless you; and therefore he hath paid you. And ye are still indebted unto him, and are, and will be, forever and ever; therefore, of what have ye to boast? And now I ask, can ye say aught of yourselves? I answer you, Nay. Ye cannot say that ye are even as much as the dust of the earth; yet ye were created of the dust of the earth; but behold, it belongeth to him who created you."

Additionally, Christ is suggesting that we speak in plain language, without the rhetoric of grand threats or promises. Speak simply. Speak out of an abundance of humility. Mean what you say, and do not obligate yourself to do what you cannot do.

Live simply, prepare to deal honestly with one another. And leave the heavens out of your promises if you cannot control them.

Do not commit yourself to do anything by swearing to God it shall be done. You have no control over when you will die, whether you will have another day of health to accomplish what you have vowed, or even if the thing about which you committed yourself will continue to be possible.

Be humble about what you are given. Be grateful.

These verses address a social standard that needed to be left behind. Coming out of that should be a replacement of plain speaking, humility about what we are able to do, and caution about the words we use.

In this reformation alone Christ proves Himself to be a sage. He was more than a wise teacher, He was the Great Teacher. This concept alone makes Him one of the greatest social reformers of the ancient world.

3 Nephi 12:38–39

"And behold, it is written, an eye for an eye, and a tooth for a tooth; But I say unto you, that ye shall not resist evil, but whosoever shall smite thee on thy right cheek, turn to him the other also;"

This is reforming the law of retaliation or *lex talionis*. When first adopted, the law of retaliation was designed to limit retribution. It was merciful in the context of the time. It prevented taking a life for an eye. The scope of the injury suffered put a limit on the scope of the retaliation permitted. I taught a class on this ancient law in the

BYU Education Week some years ago. It is too much to cover in this post in order to fully understand the ramifications of this law.

The popular understanding of that law is quite a distortion. The injury permitted was not actually exacted under the law. "An eye for an eye" meant that the victim was entitled to take the eye of the one causing the injury. In practice the eye was not taken. The value of the eye was agreed upon between victim and perpetrator. They sealed the agreement before two witnesses in the gate of the city. Then the debtor was obligated to pay the agreed sum (called "satisfaction"). If he defaulted the elders could take the eye as penalty for the default in payment, which stood as collateral for the debt.

Payment of "satisfaction" was permitted and given for offenses under the *lex talionis* except in the case of a limited class of offenses, including murder.[1226] In such cases it was considered too dangerous to allow satisfaction, and therefore the penalty needed to be carried out.

Here, Christ is replacing that entire body of law by substituting forgiveness and mercy for justice and recompense. The victim is being urged to seek nothing in return for his injury. Instead, the victim is to bear the injury and allow evil against themselves without retaliation for the offense.

This may seem odd, even wrong. However, there is an example of this in the Book of Mormon. Although many lives were lost in the process, it resulted in the salvation of many souls. The Anti-Lehi-Nephites were unwilling to take up arms to defend themselves, instead allowing their enemies to slay them. The result broke the hearts of those who were killing them, and many were converted by this

---

[1226] Numbers 35:31–32 "Moreover ye shall take no satisfaction for the life of a murderer, which *is* guilty of death: but he shall be surely put to death. And ye shall take no satisfaction for him that is fled to the city of his refuge, that he should come again to dwell in the land, until the death of the priest."

example.[1227] But the people of God were joined by more than the number who were slain.

The book by C. Terry Warner titled *The Bonds That Make Us Free: Healing Our Relationships, Coming to Ourselves* explains how the actions of those who forgive are able to affect the hearts of those who are forgiven. It is heartbreaking to hold onto anger when you have already been forgiven. He uses the principles of The Sermon on the Mount to affect the human heart. There is not merely freedom in forgiving others, there is power in it as well. Terry Warner's book is an examination of the principles of sin and forgiveness, and worth reading if you have not done so before.

We gain power by what things we suffer for the Lord's sake. Christ who loved the most, sacrificed the most. Those two things are linked together.

[1227] Alma 24:19–27 "And thus we see that, when these Lamanites were brought to believe and to know the truth, they were firm, and would suffer even unto death rather than commit sin; and thus we see that they buried their weapons of peace, or they buried the weapons of war, for peace. And it came to pass that their brethren, the Lamanites, made preparations for war, and came up to the land of Nephi for the purpose of destroying the king, and to place another in his stead, and also of destroying the people of Anti-Nephi-Lehi out of the land. Now when the people saw that they were coming against them they went out to meet them, and prostrated themselves before them to the earth, and began to call on the name of the Lord; and thus they were in this attitude when the Lamanites began to fall upon them, and began to slay them with the sword. And thus without meeting any resistance, they did slay a thousand and five of them; and we know that they are blessed, for they have gone to dwell with their God. Now when the Lamanites saw that their brethren would not flee from the sword, neither would they turn aside to the right hand or to the left, but that they would lie down and perish, and praised God even in the very act of perishing under the sword—Now when the Lamanites saw this they did forbear from slaying them; and there were many whose hearts had swollen in them for those of their brethren who had fallen under the sword, for they repented of the things which they had done. And it came to pass that they threw down their weapons of war, and they would not take them again, for they were stung for the murders which they had committed; and they came down even as their brethren, relying upon the mercies of those whose arms were lifted to slay them. And it came to pass that the people of God were joined that day by more than the number who had been slain; and those who had been slain were righteous people, therefore we have no reason to doubt but what they were saved. And there was not a wicked man slain among them; but there were more than a thousand brought to the knowledge of the truth; thus we see that the Lord worketh in many ways to the salvation of his people."

This teaching was not only given by Christ, but it was lived by Him also. In this statement, as in no other, He is defining who He is and revealing what His conduct invariably will be. This is the Lord's standard. This is the Lord's manner. The choice of turning the other cheek is taken from the Messianic standard described by Isaiah.[1228] We can also heal others by the things we willingly suffer. We can endure and forgive. As we do righteousness increases on the earth.

Saint Francis Assisi believed this, practiced it. In an age of darkness and apostasy, the Lord spoke with St. Francis, and sent angels to minister to him. He is appropriately referred to as a Saint. He lived the Sermon on the Mount. It is perhaps St. Francis, who above all others, proves a mortal may walk in the Lord's stePsalms Christ did it first and more completely than would any other. But St. Francis surely followed.

I have little doubt that the Lord's teachings are impractical in this world. But, then again, we are not called to live for this world, are we? The reason Zion always flees from this world is precisely because the Lord will not permit the world to overwhelm those who would surely be overthrown if not for His grace and protection. He will fight their battles to spare those in Zion from the necessity of becoming warlike.[1229]

I am amused by the martial inclinations of the Latter-day Saints. When the lamb and lion lie down together I suppose many of the Latter-day Saints expect to be able to hunt them both.

[1228] Isaiah 50:6 "I gave my back to the smiters, and my cheeks to them that plucked off the hair: I hid not my face from shame and spitting."
Isaiah 53:5 "But he *was* wounded for our transgressions, *he was* bruised for our iniquities: the chastisement of our peace *was* upon him; and with his stripes we are healed."

[1229] D&C 105:14 "For behold, I do not require at their hands to fight the battles of Zion; for, as I said in a former commandment, even so will I fulfil—I will fight your battles."

3 Nephi 12:40–42

"And if any man will sue thee at the law and take away thy coat, let him have thy cloak also; And whosoever shall compel thee to go a mile, go with him twain. Give to him that asketh thee, and from him that would borrow of thee turn thou not away."

This is the point Mark Twain quipped included him in the Bible. He suggested "Go with him Twain" is Divine notice given him.

The cloak covers the cloak. If someone wants one, give them both. Without conflict. Without retaliation. Give those who demand.

The law allowed a Roman soldier to compel a civilian to bear a load for a mile. Christ said submit, and go a second mile to demonstrate you have not been compelled at all. You have chosen to give the service.

When asked, give. When someone needs to borrow, let them.

What a markedly different world this would be.

The results of an entire society behaving in this manner would be Zion itself. There would be no poor. Those with the means would share, those in need would ask. The resulting cooperation and mutual assistance would solve many social ills. But such a society would necessarily be voluntary. To attempt to level the economic circumstances of society by force would be an imprisonment, not a liberation. Government cannot impose it, but men can voluntarily implement it.

In our early post-Nauvoo distress, there was a brief time when we flirted with notions like these. We did some voluntary collective work on providing a social system to benefit everyone. Those ended because of the bickering and turmoil. We went back to tithing, which still today allows us to retain our individual fortunes and limit sharing our individual misfortunes.

The question is what happens when a society continues to suffer from all the ills of our own, but a single individual chooses to live these principles. What then? Can a person really live like this when he or she alone is guided by these principles?

Common agreement is that this sermon's admonitions are impractical. They won't work. They can't be lived by a single person acting alone, or a small group acting together, because a larger corrupt society will overwhelm and exploit them. Therefore, Christ is teaching what cannot be done. At least cannot be done by anyone who is unwilling to try it. Occasionally we get a Mother Teresa or a Saint Francis, but they're Catholic. Surely it can't work with Latter-day Saints who are busy studying Steven Covey's books, polishing their resumes and looking to find a secure middle-management position from which to launch their successful careers. Maybe a handful of good, believing Catholics will found Zion. Then we can come in and help manage the results after it becomes well enough established. After all, we have the true franchise from which Zion will be built. We even own a bank already named for the venture.

It makes you wonder why Christ would preach something which only a handful of Catholics have successfully accomplished in an individual setting.

3 Nephi 12:43–45

"And behold it is written also, that thou shalt love thy neighbor and hate thine enemy; But behold I say unto you, love your enemies, bless them that curse you, do good to them that hate you, and pray for them who despitefully use you and persecute you; That ye may be the children of your Father who is in heaven; for he maketh his sun to rise on the evil and on the good."

Loving the ones you care for, associate with, and live nearby is sometimes easy. Hating those who show you disrespect or cause you injury is norMalachi Nevertheless, Christ teaches to love enemies,

bless those who are trying to do you harm, and pray for your persecutors.

This is the only way to become like Him. He is an intercessor. As
I've explained in *The Second Comforter*, becoming an intercessor for
others is part of development, through grace, to become as He is. It
is through this that charity becomes a part of your character.[1230] And
charity is a necessary attribute in character.[1231]

This treatment of enemies is how you prove your inner self. Only
by suffering, do we learn if we are converted. If you receive only
praise and adulation, authority and wealth, prestige and acceptance as
a result of following Christ, then you've never been proven. It is
through the sacrifice of your good name, reputation, position, wealth
and social standing that you learn if you truly trust in Christ.

When you actually do sacrifice all earthly things for Him, you will
have knowledge that the course of your life is pleasing to Him. Anything less than this will leave your mind in doubt. See Lectures on
Faith 6 discussion prior.

If you follow this teaching by Christ, you will convert yourself
first, then others. No-one can doubt the goodness of a life lived as
this teaching commends. Though such a life may not convert others
immediately, it will triumph.

Sometimes people die teaching the truth. They surrendered all
they were on the altar, thereby coming to know God. This teaching

---

[1230] Moroni 7:46 "Wherefore, my beloved brethren, if ye have not charity, ye are nothing, for charity never faileth. Wherefore, cleave unto charity, which is the greatest of all,
for all things must fail—"

[1231] 2 Nephi 26:30 "Behold, the Lord hath forbidden this thing; wherefore, the Lord
God hath given a commandment that all men should have charity, which charity is love.
And except they should have charity they were nothing. Wherefore, if they should have
charity they would not suffer the laborer in Zion to perish."
Moroni 7:47 "But charity is the pure love of Christ, and it endureth forever; and whoso
is found possessed of it at the last day, it shall be well with him."

would allow anyone to do the same. You would have to not only accept the idea, you would need to implement it.

Abinadi returned to bear witness of the truth, and then die. Alma was his only convert. But from the moment of Alma's conversion to the end of the Book of Mormon, every character who wrote in the plates descended from Abinadi's single convert.

Abinadi was a hinge character around whom the story of the Nephites would pivot from his life onward. But he had little success, and was killed by those to whom he ministered.

In some respects, dying for the cause of Christ is easier than living it. This teaching, however, shows how you can begin to live it.

It is not designed to be easy. As I discussed in *Beloved Enos*, sometimes it takes quite a bit of effort to come to terms with what the Lord requires of us. But that does not alter in the least the importance of doing it, or lessen the quality of the results obtained.

Keep in mind the Lord's admonition: "If ye love me, keep my commandments."[1232]

Remember also the Lord's statement that the things He is teaching "at this time" are necessary to enter into the kingdom of Heaven.[1233] These are not just sayings. They are meant to be acted on. It is in the doing of them you will meet Him. When you descend below where you are at the present, you will find the Lord. For He is condescending whenever He is seen.

Finally, Christ reminds us that the Lord blesses all with the sun, light, life and abundance. Both good and evil are blessed by Him. Therefore, the petty differences between the good and the bad are so insignificant when compared against an absolute standard of perfec-

---

[1232] John 14:15 "If ye love me, keep my commandments."

[1233] 3 Nephi 12:20 "Therefore come unto me and be ye saved; for verily I say unto you, that except ye shall keep my commandments, which I have commanded you at this time, ye shall in no case enter into the kingdom of heaven."

tion that the relative goodness and relative badness is inconsequential. So inconsequential that for any of us to be redeemed will require the atonement. Therefore, we all owe everything to Him. Only the redeemed come to realize and accept that while here. Everyone will eventually grasp that reality.

Accepting Him is the means for healing us. His open invitation to all can be seen in the sun shining on "both the evil and on the good." Everyone is bidden to come to the throne and receive healing, grace and forgiveness. To merit it, you must first give it. To obtain forgiveness you must give forgiveness. To have Him suffer for your sins, you must first suffer and forgive others of their sins committed against you.

Every balanced life surrenders claims for justice and shows mercy, thereby making a claim for themselves upon mercy.

3 Nephi 12:46–47

"Therefore those things which were of old time, which were under the law, in me are all fulfilled. Old things are done away, and all things have become new."

Christ will elaborate on this later as the audience puzzles over what is removed and what remains. But here Christ introduces the concept that the Law of Moses is now "fulfilled." Importantly, He says: "in me are all fulfilled."

When He walked on the Road to Emmaus on the day of His resurrection, He began with the Law of Moses and explained: "And beginning at Moses and all the prophets, he expounded unto them in all the scriptures the things concerning himself."[1234] I've spoken on this and then published the talk in the Appendix to *Eighteen Verses*. The talk shows how the rites and temple of the Dispensation of

---

[1234] Luke 24:27 "And beginning at Moses and all the prophets, he expounded unto them in all the scriptures the things concerning himself."

Moses testified to the details of His life. It ought to be noted that the thing "under the law, in [Christ were indeed] all fulfilled." His life was foreshadowed by the rites of Moses. His healing and His ministry, His history and His sacrifice, all were foreshadowed by the Law of Moses.

Since the Law pointed to Him, and He came to live His mortal life in conformity with that Law, it was now completed. The signpost was no longer necessary. The event had happened.

When He says, "Old things are done away" it is not because they are terminated. It is because they were fulfilled. He completed the circle. He lived and died under the Law, fulfilling every jot and tittle of its requirements.

Now it was time to push the meaning of the earlier Law deeper into the souls of His audience. "All things have become new." It is a new beginning, a new Dispensation, a new message. This message was delivered by the author of the Law of Moses not through an intermediary. This message comes from the Author in person.

Dispensations have their bounds. Beforehand, the prophets give, through prophecy, a limit on the things which are to come. When the prophesied events have unfolded and the measure has been met, then one Dispensation comes to an end while another opens. John the Baptist closed the Dispensation of Moses. Christ opened the Dispensation of the Meridian of Time. He recognizes the transition in this statement.

Whenever things are "become new" again, it is important to recognize the signs of the time.[1235] Those living contemporary with Christ who did not recognize the signs remained at Jerusalem and

---

[1235] Matthew 16:2–3 "He answered and said unto them, When it is evening, ye say, *It will be* fair weather: for the sky is red. And in the morning, *It will be* foul weather to day: for the sky is red and lowring, O *ye* hypocrites, ye can discern the face of the sky; but can ye not *discern* the signs of the times?"

were destroyed.[1236] It is important that you be on watch, for in the very hour you think it unlikely for Him to act He will act.[1237]

Everything was fulfilled by Christ, and everything prophesied will happen before He comes again. There is no more scrupulous a follower of the prophetic promises than the Lord. He inspired the prophecies, and intends that they all come to pass. In Him have all things been fulfilled, and in Him will all things yet remaining be fulfilled.

3 Nephi 12:48

"Therefore I would that ye should be perfect even as I, or your Father who is in heaven is perfect."

In the Matthew text Christ unequivocally limited this to His Father.[1238] Here "perfection" is achieved by both Christ and His Father.

Assuming the Matthew text is correct, the difference is significant. It is another confirmation that anyone who is mortal, including the Lord, stands in jeopardy every hour.[1239] He simply could not claim perfection while in mortality because mortality is a time of change, challenge and temptation. After all, He was tempted while

---

[1236] JS–Matthew 1:13–18 "Then let them who are in Judea flee into the mountains; Let him who is on the housetop flee, and not return to take anything out of his house; Neither let him who is in the field return back to take his clothes; And wo unto them that are with child, and unto them that give suck in those days; Therefore, pray ye the Lord that your flight be not in the winter, neither on the Sabbath day; For then, in those days, shall be great tribulation on the Jews, and upon the inhabitants of Jerusalem, such as was not before sent upon Israel, of God, since the beginning of their kingdom until this time; no, nor ever shall be sent again upon Israel."

[1237] JS–Matthew 1:48 "Therefore be ye also ready, for in such an hour as ye think not, the Son of Man cometh."

[1238] Matthew 5:48 "Be ye therefore perfect, even as your Father which is in heaven is perfect."

[1239] 1 Corinthians 15:30 "And why stand we in jeopardy every hour?"

mortal just as every human soul is tempted.[1240] Though He chose to give no heed to it, He was nevertheless tempted.[1241]

While mortal He looked to the Father in all things.[1242] After concluding His time in mortality, achieving the resurrection of the dead, He was given all power in heaven and on earth.[1243]

Therefore, if the Matthew text is correct, and the differences are accounted for in what we have just reviewed, then the admonition of Christ for our own perfection is not just an earthly endeavor. It is an invitation to follow Him and His Father into a loftier state, as well.[1244] One where the final realization will come only as we are able to endure greater glory than a mortal may possess.[1245]

It is good we know this commandment is possible to accomplish.[1246] It is hard to conceive of following the Son in this way. Yet it is He who pronounced it, and He who has promised to share the throne of His Father with all who will come to Him.[1247]

I am not perfect, nor anything like it. I have seen Perfection, know what it is, and can confirm I am nothing like it.

[1240] Hebrews 4:15 "For we have not an high priest which cannot be touched with the feeling of our infirmities; but was in all points tempted like as *we are, yet* without sin."

[1241] D&C 20:22 "He suffered temptations but gave no heed unto them."

[1242] John 5:30 "I can of mine own self do nothing: as I hear, I judge: and my judgment is just; because I seek not mine own will, but the will of the Father which hath sent me."

[1243] Matthew 28:18 "And Jesus came and spake unto them, saying, All power is given unto me in heaven and in earth."

[1244] Abraham 3.

[1245] Moses 1:5 "Wherefore, no man can behold all my works, except he behold all my glory; and no man can behold all my glory, and afterwards remain in the flesh on the earth."

[1246] 1 Nephi 3:7 "And it came to pass that I, Nephi, said unto my father: I will go and do the things which the Lord hath commanded, for I know that the Lord giveth no commandments unto the children of men, save he shall prepare a way for them that they may accomplish the thing which he commandeth them."

[1247] Revelation 3:21 "To him that overcometh will I grant to sit with me in my throne, even as I also overcame, and am set down with my Father in his throne."

A harmonious symmetry of light, majesty, holiness, glory and power are all around Him who is perfection. When I read the admonition to "be ye therefore perfect, even as I or your Father who is in Heaven is perfect" I can hardly grasp how that gulf between us could be bridged. I understand about the Lord's atonement. I have certainly been the beneficiary of it and will continue to be so. When I consider the infinite gulf between His and His Father's perfection, and my own imperfection, I am left completely stupefied at the idea it is even possible. Nevertheless, He gives no command which He does not provide means to obey. Therefore the means do exist.

When I hear from the casual observer of the LDS faith the stupidity about how we are going to "get exalted," I wonder at what the reaction will be when they finally realize how great the gulf separating us from that result is. I have some appreciation for what will be required, and know it will be eons before that end can be attained by any of us. It will not be magic. It will be through incremental improvement, being added upon, growing in light and truth, and perfectly natural in the process. Joseph Smith put it in these words in the King Follett Funeral Sermon:

> "When you climb up a ladder, you must begin at the bottom, and ascend step by step, until you arrive at the top; and so it is with the principles of the Gospel——you must begin with the first, and go on until you learn all the principles of exaltation. But it will be a great while after you have passed through the veil before you will have learned them. It is not all to be comprehended in this world; it will be a great work to learn our salvation and exaltation even beyond the grave."

We are not left without warning about how great the gulf is we are to cover in this bridge we are to cross. Even now it seems the best use of our time would be to meditate on the things of God day and night. The revelations inform us that "Whatever principle of intelligence we attain unto in this life, it will rise with us in the resurrection. And if a person gains more knowledge and intelligence in this life through his diligence and obedience than another, he will have so much the advantage in the world to come."[1248] Yet we seem collectively often pedestrians in a crowd milling aimlessly about presuming Christ will furnish us an easy time of it. His atonement removes from us all guilt and shame. But for perfection, we must acquire it bit by bit, grace for grace, line upon line, growing by accepting more until at last we have obtained what is needed. That will be our own doing. He provides the means, and His Father ordained the laws by which it can be done, and they provide us with free will and the capacity to choose, but we must choose. We must accept. We must press forward holding Their hands in order to arrive at last, after an infinitely long journey, in the courts of Heaven itself, fit to reside there.

Be ye therefore perfect.

And start on that this moment. For you haven't another moment to spare.

[1248] D&C 130:18–19 "Whatever principle of intelligence we attain unto in this life, it will rise with us in the resurrection. And if a person gains more knowledge and intelligence in this life through his diligence and obedience than another, he will have so much the advantage in the world to come."

3 NEPHI 13

3 Nephi 13:1–4

"Verily, verily, I say that I would that ye should do alms unto the poor; but take heed that ye do not your alms before men to be seen of them; otherwise ye have no reward of your Father who is in heaven. Therefore, when ye shall do your alms do not sound a trumpet before you, as will hypocrites do in the synagogues and in the streets, that they may have glory of men. Verily I say unto you, they have their reward. But when thou doest alms let not thy left hand know what thy right hand doeth; That thine alms may be in secret; and thy Father who seeth in secret, himself shall reward thee openly."

Giving should be done for its own sake, and not for a reward. Recognition for what a person has done is its own reward.

If this is a larger principle, and the reasoning underlying this applies throughout your service or good acts, then any recognition is your payment. In fact, the only way to reserve for yourself a blessing is to be either anonymous when you do it, or to be reviled, hated or persecuted for it. Otherwise you have your reward.

Applying this to like things it might be said that:

- When men name buildings after you for your achievements, you have your reward.

- When institutions heap awards upon you for your philanthropic acts, you have your reward.

- When they fill an auditorium up with people singing praises and paying tribute to you on your birthday, you have your reward.

- When honorary doctorate degrees are awarded to you for your life's work, you have your reward.

- When the Boy Scouts of America gives you a plaque, a title, and a commendation for your long support of their cause, you have your reward.

- When you sit at the head of a congregation, exciting envy from others wishing to hold your position, and are honored with praise, acknowledged as presiding and accepting deference for your status as local, area or regional leader, you may very well have your reward.

- If you minister to the downtrodden, the ill and infirm, then recount endlessly to others these acts, do you not "sound a trumpet before you" to be seen of men, and thereby collect your reward?

When Christ was called "good," He rebuked the one rendering praise with the retort: "Why callest thou me good? none is good, save one, that is, God."[1249] He would accept their persecution, derision and shame, but discouraged any praise. He accepted Peter's confession of His status as "the Christ, the Son of the Living God" but followed up that confession of faith with the admonition to not speak of it: "Then charged he his disciples that they should tell no man that he was Jesus the Christ."[1250]

[1249] Luke 18:18–19 "And a certain ruler asked him, saying, Good Master, what shall I do to inherit eternal life? And Jesus said unto him, Why callest thou me good? none *is* good, save one, *that is,* God."

[1250] Matthew 16:20 "Then charged he his disciples that they should tell no man that he was Jesus the Christ."

How can His servants exalt themselves to be more than He? How can the Servant's own servants make themselves greater than He? When the Master came and lived the most common of lives, how can His disciples build monuments named for themselves, tolerate no criticism, accept honor, praise and adulation and expect to be counted as His?

How can any man redeem or rescue another? Are not all in need of rescuing by Him who alone can provide deliverance? Acclaim and praise in this life preclude recognition from the Lord in the afterlife. Therefore, only a fool would welcome praise, adulation and recognition for good things done in mortality. Indeed, such recognized deeds are often a veneer covering a malignant character. As a result, the Lord offers a test to prove sincerity: Do it in secret. Do it without notice or praise. Do it not to be seen of men. Do it as an act in private between you and the Lord alone, without any earthly party becoming aware of the deed. Then the beneficiary will indeed give glory to your Father which is in heaven, and not to another man.[1251]

This new standard challenges not merely the acts of a person, but also the underlying reasons and intent for any acts that are done. Your conduct is not the measure. It is your heart. For that, it is best if men do not understand you. It is best if they misjudge you, attribute foul motive when motive is pure, ascribe evil to you when you are on the Lord's errand, and reject you though you are His. Only then can your heart remain true to Him and uncompromised by the praise of your fellow-man.

It is this teaching, if followed, that will result in the anonymous acts and unrecognized deeds that exalt a person. It will make you private in your devotions and obscure to your fellow man.

[1251] 3 Nephi 12:16 "Therefore let your light so shine before this people, that they may see your good works and glorify your Father who is in heaven."

3 Nephi 13:5–6

"And when thou prayest thou shalt not do as the hypocrites, for they love to pray, standing in the synagogues and in the corners of the streets, that they may be seen of men. Verily I say unto you, they have their reward. But thou, when thou prayest, enter into thy closet, and when thou hast shut thy door, pray to thy Father who is in secret; and thy Father, who seeth in secret, shall reward thee openly."

Like the previous verses, this verse is saying prayer ought to be private, not public. It should be between you and God. Others do not need to know of, see, or participate in your prayers. Most importantly, your prayers ought not be put on display for others to notice and admire.

There are public prayer occasions, of course. Those come every time a meeting opens and closes with a prayer. For such opportunities there will always be a prayer offered by one person, acting as the voice for those assembled. But the prayer is not the individual's. It is the prayer of all those assembled. This warning is about personal prayer, not group prayer.

These verses are confirming the principle that prayer should be kept private between you and God. It should not be put on public display to call attention to yourself. Those whose prayers are offered "for to be seen" are really not praying to God anyway. They are using the pretense of prayer to call attention to themselves. They want recognition. When they get recognition they have their reward. They got what they wanted: public notice.

As a result of this teaching I have some hesitation about praying at a public restaurant before a meal. If I do, it is private, unspoken, and only thought. I have always thought this teaching proscribed public prayer whenever it attracted notice.

This counsel, and the counsel immediately before, show just how solitary a journey it is back to the Lord's presence. It is not a group event. It is done in the privacy of your own heart, your own intent, and your own private conduct. It is your personal devotions which show the Lord who and what you are. By keeping these things secret between you and Him, you gain a power of familiarity with Him which will permit Him to comfort you.

I've tried to avoid ever speaking of personal matters, choosing instead to only focus on the Lord's teachings. Some people have expressed frustrations at the absence of personal details in what I've written or said. Those complaints reaffirm to me that I've weighed the matter correctly. It is not, and never has been about me or any man. It is about the Lord and His teachings. I have testified to His teachings and that they are both true and applicable to everyone. I've testified that high office and notoriety are not required, but the least are invited. When Zion finally comes, I doubt there will be many notable people there. It will be the man from Tennessee who is handy with mechanical repairs, whose calloused hands show dedication to labor for others It will be the patient Temple worker-couple who, despite the regimentation seen all around them, have pursued the Lord's will and found Him. It will be the patient and obscure people whose private devotion to the Lord is known to Him, acknowledged by His voice. The invitation to gather will come to them directly from Him.

It is in these teachings that I will be justified and required to end my public efforts. As they end, you will need to do as He has taught, and as I have endeavored to do. I will soon be ending this blog. I will be finishing up this phase of what I've been asked to do for the last several years, and hopefully be shown the courtesy of being allowed to return to my family and ward. The things I have written require a real person to stand behind them, to testify of them, and to take responsibility for what is said. I have allowed you to know who it is. But enough has been done. I look forward to returning to my own closet and laying down this more public effort.

Christ would have us all know the Father in the privacy of our individual lives. That is as true of Him as it is meant to be for us. How often He spent the night in private prayer. How often he separated Himself from His followers and prayed in secret to His Father. That is what we should accomplish more often. That is how we draw closest to Him.

You can as readily gratify your vain ambition by praying to be noticed as you can by aspiring and receiving a church position or rank. It is all vanity. There really is none who are good, except God alone.

3 Nephi 13:7–8

> "But when ye pray, use not vain repetitions, as the heathen, for they think that they shall be heard for their much speaking. Be not ye therefore like unto them, for your Father knoweth what things ye have need of before ye ask him."

Here is wisdom indeed. There is no magic formula for communicating with God. No list of what is to be said or repeated. No vain —meaning ineffective—repetitions. He "gets it" even before you speak. So the act of prayer is a formal way of showing

- Respect (by doing what He has asked)
- Devotion (by showing submission to Him)
- Obedience (by keeping a commandment to pray always), and
- Companionship (by taking the time alone with Him).

He knows what you need before you ask. Indeed, sometimes the needs we think we have are not what He knows we need even before we pray.

We think we need to get a solution to interior lighting for 8 barges. We come to Him in prayer expecting to receive help for that.

He knows what we really need is redemption from the Fall, instruction in the history of mankind, and knowledge of Him. He solves the lighting problem with a touch of His finger, but then goes on to reveal all things.

We think we need to know what church to join. So Joseph comes asking that one question in sincerity. He knows, however, the world needs a prophet to re-establish the long absent Church of Jesus Christ upon the earth.

We think we need to understand how to baptize. So Joseph and Oliver ask. He knows, however, the Aaronic Priesthood must be restored, and sends an angel to return it to the earth.

We think we need to know what our standing is before God. So Joseph asks, fully expecting to learn if his life has been acceptable. God knows, however, the time has come to send an angel having the everlasting Gospel to declare. So Moroni comes to declare the restoration of the book.

You take thought about what your cares are, but they are not what the Lord knows you need. Your cares are merely the tiniest of obstacles given you to remind you to pray. The Father operates on a much grander scale, dealing with the salvation of souls. He will use the man or woman of prayer as the means of accomplishing a great deal more then they imagined.

Pray. Ask simply. It is not necessary to be elaborate or long winded. State clearly what you believe you need. Accept what then comes in His answer. Trust He knows more than you. Trust He can give you what you need, even if you hadn't even thought about it as a need.

3 Nephi 13:9–13

"After this manner therefore pray ye: Our Father who art in heaven, hallowed be thy name. Thy will be done on earth as it is in heaven. And forgive us our debts, as we forgive our debtors. And lead us not into temptation, but deliver us from evil. For thine is the kingdom, and the power, and the glory, forever. Amen."

Simple. Direct. Plain.

Christ assures us that He is "Our Father" and not just His. We are all united in sharing that status with Christ. We are a family.

First He identifies the Father as "ours" and then, least we should presume too great a familiarity, He adds "hallowed be thy name." A name is important for many reasons. In the case of Deity, it was an ancient presumption that if you knew the name of an angel, demon, or god you could summon such a being by using that name. Here, however, Christ is applying sacred status to the Father's name. It is His Fatherhood that is emphasized, not His hallowed name.

The Father's will is not done on earth. Here, there is rebellion, rejection, chaos and despair. Here, order is imposed by the strong upon the weak. Men exploit, abuse and misrule. In heaven, however, the Father's rule establishes order, kindness and equity. Anyone who is aware of the fallen conditions here will ask for the Father's will to be done on earth, as it is in heaven.

That petition can also be read to mean: "Let me live on earth as if I were in heaven." Or, "let the Father's will come to earth by the life I live here." Or, "let me prove myself worthy of heaven's companion-ship, though I live here on earth."

The prayer links forgiving others to being forgiven. This is not merely a wise petition, it is also a statement of cause and effect. We merit forgiveness as we give it. It is by forgiving that we are forgiven.

We pay our debts by giving others forgiveness of their debts to us. I've written a chapter about this in *Come, Let Us Adore Him*. We merit what we give to others. We establish the criteria by which we will be judged as we decide how to treat others. He will return to this concept in 3 Nephi 14:2.

When the Father leads you, it will never be into temptation, but will always deliver you from evil. This is a petition which reminds us to be willing to be led. We are literally to ask the Father to help us be led by Him. Through Him we will obtain deliverance.

The Father owns the kingdom, the power, and glory. Mankind does not confer that upon Him. It is His. But mankind can acknowledge it. By making that acknowledgement we are able to have confidence in Him. We can trust His power to deliver, His ability to bring again His kingdom, and to bear and share in His glory as He has promised.

Many of these simple statements are confessions of our own desires and clarify we have understanding. God's kingdom, power and glory exist independent of our prayers. But when our prayers attest that we understand this, we are making our submission and meekness known to Him. We are stating our trust in Him.

We acknowledge His kingdom is His, to be restored in His time, with His power. It is His to control. We do not envy that control, nor attempt to force Him to do our bidding. We acknowledge that His right exists, independent of man's will or ambition. He will decide and we will accept. We can ask, but He will determine the events that will take place and when they will unfold.

This prayer is an acknowledgement that we are not trying to control God, but instead are willing to be subject to Him. He is the sovereign, we are the subjects.

We ask, He decides. If He determines to do a work we defer to Him. The greater the recognition of His kingdom, power and glory, the greater the confidence we have in His decisions. The less we are inclined to argue with Him or to substitute our desires for His.

When the Lord decides to bring again Zion, it will be because the Father has decided it is time to do so. It will not be because a group has volunteered to accomplish it. When He decides, and He is the author of it, no power under heaven will stand against it. When men have ambition to create what is in His power alone to do, then they will not just fail but will be swept away.

This petition to the Father instructs us in patience and faith.

3 Nephi 13:14–15

"For, if ye forgive men their trespasses your heavenly Father will also forgive you; But if ye forgive not men their trespasses neither will your Father forgive your trespasses."

This is an absolute condition. It is mandatory.

If you forgive not men their trespasses, neither will your Father forgive you your trespass.

You can't be forgiven by the Father if you do not forgive others.

It can't be done.

That grudge you harbor prevents the Father from forgiving you.

Those resentments you think are justified are keeping you from being forgiven by the Father.

Those injustices imposed upon you by others who are unthinking or cruel must be surrendered.

The early Saints were victimized by mobs in Missouri and Illinois. They wanted revenge. Brigham Young implemented a covenant to seek vengeance upon the murderers of Joseph Smith until the third and fourth generation. They did not build Zion.

The opposite of this is forgiveness. If you forgive, your Heavenly Father *will* forgive you. Offenses are opportunities for you to gain forgiveness. All you need to do is forgive them.

It is a simple, direct cause and effect. It was ordained before the world was founded, and applies universally in all ages and among all people.

The world is in Satan's grip largely because the world seeks vengeance and refuses to forgive.

Zion, on the other hand, will be filled with those who forgive. Of course that puts an absolute limit on those who can dwell there. . . . Very few indeed.

3 Nephi 13:16–18

"Moreover, when ye fast be not as the hypocrites, of a sad countenance, for they disfigure their faces that they may appear unto men to fast. Verily I say unto you, they have their reward. But thou, when thou fastest, anoint thy head, and wash thy face; That thou appear not unto men to fast, but unto thy Father, who is in secret; and thy Father, who seeth in secret, shall reward thee openly."

Again our devotion is to be entirely private. Your inner struggle to come into God's presence should be yours. Private. Personal. Individual. Secret.

The time may come after you have found Him that He will bring you into contact with others. The journey back to Him will be individual, and private.

After you find Him, you will be His. He can do with you as He chooses. When He appears to you in the flesh, He will give you commandments.[1252] He will teach you doctrine. He will direct what you should do. But that is later. Until then, the journey is private. There is nothing to announce. There should be no notice of your fasting, tithe paying, or praying. There are no notable deeds to be seen of men.

Men should see your washed face and never detect the fasting you are performing for Him alone.

[1252] 2 Nephi 32:6 "Behold, this is the doctrine of Christ, and there will be no more doctrine given until after he shall manifest himself unto you in the flesh. And when he shall manifest himself unto you in the flesh, the things which he shall say unto you shall ye observe to do."

Men should see your comfortable behavior and never appreciate what great things you have put on the altar in sacrifice to Him.

Men should never notice the mighty wrestle you are having with God.

When the wrestle has produced a covenant between you and God, even then the particulars of what you learn, what has been promised, what has been committed into your hands, and the things the Lord and you share should be kept between you and Him.

As I have said in *The Second Comforter*, some great things can be learned but not taught. Also, the Lord will never entrust truly sacred things to a person who is incapable of keeping them confidential. It is surprising how few people really believe in that principle. It is surprising how many people want that principle violated because they are curious, anxious and think it their right to receive what is purchased by someone else at a terrible personal price. It is surprising what things people will ask for and expect to be given, despite the fact that they haven't worked for them. It can't be shared by anyone other than you and the Lord. Whenever you disrespect that limitation by your questions, or demands you make to others, you postpone the time when you might have received greater things. You do not need a guru—You need the Lord. You do not need another John, Moses, Elias, Esaias, Isaiah, or Enoch.[1253] You need Him.

We see in scripture how easily and often messengers are made into idols. That is not what is to happen. It is even more of a perver-

---

[1253] D&C 76:100 "These are they who say they are some of one and some of another—some of Christ and some of John, and some of Moses, and some of Elias, and some of Esaias, and some of Isaiah, and some of Enoch;"

sion for men to set themselves up as idols, to be followed as if they were God. That is Satanic and evidence of a falling away.[1254]

The private devotions of a sincere Saint are more worthy, more ennobling, more developing than any public display has ever been, or will ever be. Small gatherings when He directs may be of aid from time to time. But almost all the sacred events involving Him will take place between you and Him alone. When a few have approached Him by themselves—alone, then at some point it may possible for Him to gather with them in small numbers.[1255]

Would you like to see Zion return? Then approach Him in private, keep your journey from the notice of others, gather to Him in secret. Then, when He has a few who can gather in His name, He will gather them. Ultimately there will need to be occupants for a city before a city will be founded by Him. But it all starts with these teachings we are presently reading.

This Sermon is first a description of Him.

It is also a description of His disciples.

It is a formula for returning to His presence.

It is the basis for the coming Zion.

[1254] 2 Thessalonians 2:3–4 "Let no man deceive you by any means: for *that day shall not come,* except there come a falling away first, and that man of sin be revealed, the son of perdition; Who opposeth and exalteth himself above all that is called God, or that is worshipped; so that he as God sitteth in the temple of God, shewing himself that he is God."

[1255] Matthew 18:22 "Jesus saith unto him, I say not unto thee, Until seven times: but, Until seventy times seven."

When the Father at last rewards you openly, it will be time for His arm to be revealed in terrible majesty.[1256] He will reward you openly indeed!

3 Nephi 13:19–21

"Lay not up for yourselves treasures upon earth, where moth and rust doth corrupt, and thieves break through and steal; But lay up for yourselves treasures in heaven, where neither moth nor rust doth corrupt, and where thieves do not break through nor steal. For where your treasure is, there will your heart be also."

Things here are in constant change. There are two great forces always at work. Entropy and decay are affect everything. All things grow distant, cold and less organized. The opposite is the force that creates and brings anew. Between decay and recreation, we find ourselves in a world where our hold will eventually slip away, and we will no longer be found among the living.

What will endure?

[1256] D&C 105:14 "For behold, I do not require at their hands to fight the battles of Zion; for, as I said in a former commandment, even so will I fulfil—I will fight your battles."

D&C 45:67–75 "And the glory of the Lord shall be there, and the terror of the Lord also shall be there, insomuch that the wicked will not come unto it, and it shall be called Zion. And it shall come to pass among the wicked, that every man that will not take his sword against his neighbor must needs flee unto Zion for safety. And there shall be gathered unto it out of every nation under heaven; and it shall be the only people that shall not be at war one with another. And it shall be said among the wicked: Let us not go up to battle against Zion, for the inhabitants of Zion are terrible; wherefore we cannot stand. And it shall come to pass that the righteous shall be gathered out from among all nations, and shall come to Zion, singing with songs of everlasting joy. And now I say unto you, keep these things from going abroad unto the world until it is expedient in me, that ye may accomplish this work in the eyes of the people, and in the eyes of your enemies, that they may not know your works until ye have accomplished the thing which I have commanded you; That when they shall know it, that they may consider these things. For when the Lord shall appear he shall be terrible unto them, that fear may seize upon them, and they shall stand afar off and tremble. And all nations shall be afraid because of the terror of the Lord, and the power of his might. Even so. Amen."

The monuments men build to themselves and their causes break down, decay, rust, erode and fade. They all pass away. The most enduring things are not what we build with our hands, but the truth that we teach. Truth will endure for eternity. It may be lost, fought or suppressed, but it will return. Truth will triumph.

The closest thing we have to eternal living is found in the great ideas and great revelations of the prophets and poets, philosophers and sages. The things made in our minds are what change humanity and elevate us to be more godlike. It is not the structures where men craving immortality engrave their names. It is not the statues in bronze and marble where because of vanity they enshrine their images. They will all pass away.

But an idea, a truth, a testimony from heaven—those will endure despite all hell raging. Send the moths, the rust and thieves against truth, and the truth will prevail despite this fallen world's conspiracy against it.

Where is your heart? What do you meditate on day and night? Do you dream of wealth and power, of fame and recognition? Do you ponder how you might acquire more and receive more? Do you meditate on the lusts of the body? What occupies the spare moments of your life?

Do you let virtue garnish your thoughts so that your confidence may be strong in the presence of the Lord?[1257] Do you meditate constantly on the things God has shown to you?[1258]

[1257] D&C 121:45 "Let thy bowels also be full of charity towards all men, and to the household of faith, and let virtue garnish thy thoughts unceasingly; then shall thy confidence wax strong in the presence of God; and the doctrine of the priesthood shall distil upon thy soul as the dews from heaven."

[1258] 2 Nephi 4:16 "Behold, my soul delighteth in the things of the Lord; and my heart pondereth continually upon the things which I have seen and heard."

Have you prayed and pondered so you may understand a great mystery?[1259] Have you prayed and fasted so as to be filled with the spirit of revelation?[1260]

Where your heart is, there is your treasure. Where your treasure is, there is your heart. They are linked. You can tell what is treasured and where the heart is by what things you meditate upon night and day with idle moments.

I've deliberately had a morning and afternoon post on this blog to assist in giving something to ponder twice during the day, at widely separated times. It is my view that there is nothing better to meditate on than the scriptures.

Here's a recent random reflection I had on one matter answered by scripture:

In a recent Gospel Doctrine discussion I was told about a teacher who was reluctant to admit David was a prophet, because David fell.[1261] The notion that a prophet could fall undermines the current false notion that a President of the LDS Church cannot fail. That is rubbish, of course. But it is well circulated and ardently defended rubbish.

- The need to preserve the idea means that the teacher needed to disqualify David from ever being accepted as a prophet.

[1259] D&C 138:11 "As I pondered over these things which are written, the eyes of my understanding were opened, and the Spirit of the Lord rested upon me, and I saw the hosts of the dead, both small and great."

[1260] Alma 17:3 "But this is not all; they had given themselves to much prayer, and fasting; therefore they had the spirit of prophecy, and the spirit of revelation, and when they taught, they taught with power and authority of God."

[1261] D&C 132:39 "David's wives and concubines were given unto him of me, by the hand of Nathan, my servant, and others of the prophets who had the keys of this power; and in none of these things did he sin against me save in the case of Uriah and his wife; and, therefore he hath fallen from his exaltation, and received his portion; and he shall not inherit them out of the world, for I gave them unto another, saith the Lord."

The reasoning goes that if David isn't a prophet then his fall
proves nothing.

- When Peter was preaching after Pentecost, he freely acknowledged David's status as a prophet.[1262] So even if the
Gospel Doctrine teacher won't admit David's status, the
scriptures do.

- I wonder how it is plausible to some folks to believe prophets cannot fall today, when they fell anciently? It seems to
me just a lazy way to shift responsibility for salvation away
from each individual and onto an institution. Clearly the
institution wants this idea to be accepted. No doubt someone will be damned for that notion.

- Anyone can fall. Seems to me that it is more important for
me to worry about my own fall than it is to foolishly trust in
some other person's success or failure. We are all accountable for our own sins.[1263]

- In the Topical Guide I read every entry under "Accountability" and could find nothing to support the notion that there
is accountability shifting from individual onto church president.

- Why do the gentiles always wind up having someone whom
they regard as their benefactor boss them around?[1264]

- When you make one mistake (prophet can't fall or lead astray),
then you compound it by needing another (David wasn't a

1262 Acts 2:29–30 "Men *and* brethren, let me freely speak unto you of the patriarch
David, that he is both dead and buried, and his sepulchre is with us unto this day.
Therefore being a prophet, and knowing that God had sworn with an oath to him, that
of the fruit of his loins, according to the flesh, he would raise up Christ to sit on his
throne;"

1263 Article of Faith 2 "We believe that men will be punished for their own sins, and not
for Adam's transgression."

1264 Luke 22:25 "And he said unto them, The kings of the Gentiles exercise lordship
over them; and they that exercise authority upon them are called benefactors."

prophet). Little wonder doctrine is not studied as much. Our foolishness would become exposed. Who was it that removed from a prophet his right to choose? When did moral agency to choose get taken away from a church president?

3 Nephi 13:22–23

"The light of the body is the eye; if, therefore, thine eye be single, thy whole body shall be full of light. But if thine eye be evil, thy whole body shall be full of darkness. If, therefore, the light that is in thee be darkness, how great is that darkness!"

The "eye" is better put "your mind's eye." It is what you meditate on, what fills you. You choose what you fill yourself with by what you give attention. What you notice is what you care to notice.

Christ's admonition is troubling because the cares of this world distract us all. They impose upon us all. But Christ advises us to search endlessly for light.

The difference between filling yourself with light and filling yourself with darkness is what thoughts you entertain.

Everything begins in the mind. Words and works flow from thoughts.[1265] While all three will be judged, it is in the mind where all else begins.

It is not enough to attempt to avoid evil by memorizing hymns. You can spend as many wasted hours humming hymns as singing rock songs. Neither one will particularly elevate you. Meditating on doctrine, pressing understanding, pondering deeply and engaging the mysteries of God are what will fill the mind with light.

[1265] Alma 12:14 "For our words will condemn us, yea, all our works will condemn us; we shall not be found spotless; and our thoughts will also condemn us; and in this awful state we shall not dare to look up to our God; and we would fain be glad if we could command the rocks and the mountains to fall upon us to hide us from his presence."

There is so much in our faith that distracts and substitutes for light and truth. Think about these verses and filling your mind with light and truth: "And that which doth not edify is not of God, and is darkness. That which is of God is light; and he that receiveth light, and continueth in God, receiveth more light; and that light groweth brighter and brighter until the perfect day. And again, verily I say unto you, and I say it that you may know the truth, that you may chase darkness from among you;"[1266]

The Psalms were quoted by Christ more than any other scripture. They are filled with truths worth meditation.

Having darkness within you does not require an effort to be deliberately vile. The cares of this world, and coping with Babylon is all that is needed to keep you from acquiring light. Finding light requires a deliberate effort to notice it and take it in.

When we are filled with light the heavens notice. In fact, it is the light within us that heaven notices even from afar.

3 Nephi 13:24

"No man can serve two masters; for either he will hate the one and love the other, or else he will hold to the one and despise the other. Ye cannot serve God and Mammon."

This is Christ's great division. We all have but one Master. Choose carefully.

[1266] D&C 50:23–25 "And that which doth not edify is not of God, and is darkness. That which is of God is light; and he that receiveth light, and continueth in God, receiveth more light; and that light groweth brighter and brighter until the perfect day. And again, verily I say unto you, and I say it that you may know the truth, that you may chase darkness from among you;"

This is another way to describe the "jealous God" of the Old Covenant.[1267] Since He requires everything of you, any holding back is infidelity to Him.

Christ is reaffirming God's primacy. Your affection for Him cannot be shared. It simply can't be done. When attempted, it shows you "hate" or "despise" Him, because when you share your fidelity, you reject His direction.

It is this principle that justified the earlier prophets in likening Israel to a "harlot" or a "whore" when she worshiped other gods.[1268] It is not possible to be converted to the Lord and not be devoted to Him.

All of what is "Mammon" is subordinate to God. The Lord's ways require the things you have in this life to be used for His purposes and according to His desire. His commandments cover all things, and you cannot divorce your temporal concerns from His teachings.[1269]

Devotion to Him requires that what you do, say, and think be aligned with Him. Conversion is a progressive process where you develop to be more like Him throughout life. You can't just "get a testimony" and then not be completely converted to Him. He expects to completely remake you. This sermon is the blueprint for the new creation you are to become.

[1267] Exodus 34:14 "For thou shalt worship no other god: for the Lord, whose name *is* Jealous, *is* a jealous God:"

[1268] Jeremiah 3:6 "The Lord said also unto me in the days of Josiah the king, Hast thou seen *that* which backsliding Israel hath done? she is gone up upon every high mountain and under every green tree, and there hath played the harlot."
Hosea 9:1 "Rejoice not, O Israel, for joy, as *other* people: for thou hast gone a whoring from thy God, thou hast loved a reward upon every cornfloor."
Judges 8:33 "And it came to pass, as soon as Gideon was dead, that the children of Israel turned again, and went a whoring after Baalim, and made Baal-berith their god."

[1269] D&C 29:35 "Behold, I gave unto him that he should be an agent unto himself; and I gave unto him commandment, but no temporal commandment gave I unto him, for my commandments are spiritual; they are not natural nor temporal, neither carnal nor sensual."

This statement deals in absolutes because the Lord's way is the way of absolutes. He can accept nothing less than all. The adversary knows this and is content with getting even a little from you. The adversary knows that a little compromise is everything when compromising your faithfulness to the Lord.

The world will accept anything half-hearted. The world knows you love it, if you will just give in a little to its persuasion. Contamination is contamination and will eventually poison you. So any degree of unrighteousness is enough to please the world. For the Lord, however, it is all or nothing. It is complete fidelity to Him which alone will satisfy. Keeping one foot in the world, while giving lip service to Him will never meet the requirements for loving Him.[1270]

Those who think the Lord is announcing a new, easier system to replace the earlier, more demanding Law of Moses do not understand His teachings. This is far more exact and moves the battleground into your heart. He is asking you to transform the soul. He is asking you to become like Him. This is not outward observances. However troubling and wearisome those may have been, they were at least something that could be done without battling in your heart with motive, intent and desires. Here Christ wants you to conform everything, even your desires, to be instruments of your salvation.

This is a call to a much higher way of life. It is a much deeper and more meaningful way to approach God. It is inside you.

3 Nephi 13:25

"And now it came to pass that when Jesus had spoken these words he looked upon the twelve whom he had chosen, and said unto them: Remember the words which I have spoken. For behold, ye are they whom I have chosen to minister unto this people. Therefore I say unto you, take no thought for

---

[1270] D&C 1:31 "For I the Lord cannot look upon sin with the least degree of allowance;"

your life, what ye shall eat, or what ye shall drink; nor yet for your body, what ye shall put on. Is not the life more than meat, and the body than raiment?"

The preceding teachings were given to all who were there. Christ changes the audience at this point, and addresses the twelve whom He had given power to baptize. To them He addresses the admonition: "Remember the words which I have spoken." These are two things: First, a Divine admonition to follow. Second, an empowerment to make it possible to do as He asks. Without both, they would have been unable to preserve the record of the teachings. As will become apparent from the text, they will later meet following His ascension and reduce the words taught to a transcript that all twelve will be able to present to the audience that assembles the next day.

The reason these same twelve who had power to baptize were given power to "remember the words [Christ] had spoken" was because they were "chosen to minister unto this people." When Christ chooses a minister to speak for Him, He enables them to accomplish the mission or ministry assigned to them.[1271] They receive His support. That makes them more than equal to the assignment given them.

It is the chosen twelve, and not the the multitude, who are told to "take no thought for your life, what ye shall eat, or what he shall drink." It is those who are to minister who are freed from the earthly cares of providing for their needs. Their lives are to be given over to ministering to others, and not to work for their support. The Lord intends to provide for them.

[1271] D&C 132:59 "Verily, if a man be called of my Father, as was Aaron, by mine own voice, and by the voice of him that sent me, and I have endowed him with the keys of the power of this priesthood, if he do anything in my name, and according to my law and by my word, he will not commit sin, and I will justify him."

This is a very narrow group to whom this promise is made. It does not include others in the audience. For the rest, we are required to provide for our families. If we fail to provide for them by laboring for their support, we have denied the faith.[1272] Wives are to be supported by their husband's labor.[1273] Children are to be supported by their parents.[1274] This requires all to labor.[1275] But as to these twelve, their labor is the ministry and their support will come from the Lord.

It is a small thing for the Lord to provide for His ministers. To Him property is nothing.[1276] He can provide for His ministers even if there is no apparent means to accomplish it.[1277] The Lord has pro-

---

[1272] 1 Timothy 5:8 "But if any provide not for his own, and specially for those of his own house, he hath denied the faith, and is worse than an infidel."

[1273] D&C 83:2 "Women have claim on their husbands for their maintenance, until their husbands are taken; and if they are not found transgressors they shall have fellowship in the church."

[1274] D&C 83:4 "All children have claim upon their parents for their maintenance until they are of age."

[1275] D&C 42:42 "Thou shalt not be idle; for he that is idle shall not eat the bread nor wear the garments of the laborer."

[1276] D&C 117:4 "Let them repent of all their sins, and of all their covetous desires, before me, saith the Lord; for what is property unto me? saith the Lord."

[1277] 1 Kings 17:8–16 "And the word of the Lord came unto him, saying, Arise, get thee to Zarephath, which *belongeth* to Zidon, and dwell there: behold, I have commanded a widow woman there to sustain thee. So he arose and went to Zarephath. And when he came to the gate of the city, behold, the widow woman *was* there gathering of sticks: and he called to her, and said, Fetch me, I pray thee, a little water in a vessel, that I may drink. And as she was going to fetch *it*, he called to her, and said, Bring me, I pray thee, a morsel of bread in thine hand. And she said, *As* the Lord thy God liveth, I have not a cake, but an handful of meal in a barrel, and a little oil in a cruse: and, behold, I *am* gathering two sticks, that I may go in and dress it for me and my son, that we may eat it, and die. And Elijah said unto her, Fear not; go *and* do as thou hast said: but make me thereof a little cake first, and bring *it* unto me, and after make for thee and for thy son. For thus saith the Lord God of Israel, The barrel of meal shall not waste, neither shall the cruse of oil fail, until the day *that* the Lord sendeth rain upon the earth. And she went and did according to the saying of Elijah: and she, and he, and her house, did eat *many* days. *And* the barrel of meal wasted not, neither did the cruse of oil fail, according to the word of the Lord, which he spake by Elijah."

vided food for thousands when necessary.[1278] Providing food for His people when needed is within His Divine power.[1279]

Why would the Lord give this commandment to the twelve? Why would He do it publicly? What responsibility does that impose upon the twelve? What responsibility does it impose upon the audience? If

---

[1278] Luke 9:13–17 "But he said unto them, Give ye them to eat. And they said, We have no more but five loaves and two fishes; except we should go and buy meat for all this people. For they were about five thousand men. And he said to his disciples, Make them sit down by fifties in a company. And they did so, and made them all sit down. Then he took the five loaves and the two fishes, and looking up to heaven, he blessed them, and brake, and gave to the disciples to set before the multitude. And they did eat, and were all filled: and there was taken up of fragments that remained to them twelve baskets."

[1279] Exodus 16:11–31 "And the Lord spake unto Moses, saying, I have heard the murmurings of the children of Israel: speak unto them, saying, At even ye shall eat flesh, and in the morning ye shall be filled with bread; and ye shall know that I *am* the Lord your God. And it came to pass, that at even the quails came up, and covered the camp: and in the morning the dew lay round about the host. And when the dew that lay was gone up, behold, upon the face of the wilderness *there lay* a small round thing, *as* small as the hoar frost on the ground. And when the children of Israel saw *it,* they said one to another, It *is* manna: for they wist not what it *was.* And Moses said unto them, This *is* the bread which the Lord hath given you to eat. This *is* the thing which the Lord hath commanded, Gather of it every man according to his eating, an omer for every man, *according to* the number of your persons; take ye every man for *them* which *are* in his tents. And the children of Israel did so, and gathered, some more, some less. And when they did mete *it* with an omer, he that gathered much had nothing over, and he that gathered little had no lack; they gathered every man according to his eating. And Moses said, Let no man leave of it till the morning. Notwithstanding they hearkened not unto Moses; but some of them left of it until the morning, and it bred worms, and stank: and Moses was wroth with them. And they gathered it every morning, every man according to his eating: and when the sun waxed hot, it melted. And it came to pass, *that* on the sixth day they gathered twice as much bread, two omers for one *man:* and all the rulers of the congregation came and told Moses. And he said unto them, This *is that* which the Lord hath said, To morrow *is* the rest of the holy sabbath unto the Lord: bake *that* which ye will bake *to day,* and seethe that ye will seethe; and that which remaineth over lay up for you to be kept until the morning. And they laid it up till the morning, as Moses bade: and it did not stink, neither was there any worm therein. And Moses said, Eat that to day; for to day *is* a sabbath unto the Lord: to day ye shall not find it in the field. Six days ye shall gather it; but on the seventh day, *which is* the sabbath, in it there shall be none. And it came to pass, *that* there went out *some* of the people on the seventh day for to gather, and they found none. And the Lord said unto Moses, How long refuse ye to keep my commandments and my laws? See, for that the Lord hath given you the sabbath, therefore he giveth you on the sixth day the bread of two days; abide ye every man in his place, let no man go out of his place on the seventh day. So the people rested on the seventh day. And the house of Israel called the name thereof Manna: and it *was* like coriander seed, white; and the taste of it *was* like wafers *made* with honey."

the twelve today were to be supported by only food given them by believers, clothes provided by followers, material given through donations from those to whom they ministered, would it be different than the system we have in place today? Would that be different from tithing money used for salaries paid them today? Would the supplemental income from book sales, service on boards of directors (which has been greatly reduced and was planned to be entirely eliminated) fit into the system Christ describes here? [President Monson's General Conference talk about his wife's surgery a while back included a reference to paying taxes. She was emerging from an eighteen day coma and her first words to him were about failing to pay the "fourth quarter income tax payment." (Abundantly Blessed, Ensign, May 2008.) These kinds of "quarterly income taxes" are self-employment taxes and would arise either from book royalties or service on boards of directors. His paycheck from the Church would have withholding and would not require quarterly deposits.]

Is the different, more simple and very direct connection between the disciples and those to whom they ministered of value today? Is our modern sophisticated society unable to provide similar support today? Is Christ's teaching on this point outdated? If it is, then can we disregard other portions also as outdated? How do we decide what to discard and what to keep?

3 Nephi 13:26–32

"Behold the fowls of the air, for they sow not, neither do they reap nor gather into barns; yet your heavenly Father feedeth them. Are ye not much better than they? Which of you by taking thought can add one cubit unto his stature? And why take ye thought for raiment? Consider the lilies of the field how they grow; they toil not, neither do they spin; And yet I say unto you, that even Solomon, in all his glory, was not arrayed like one of these. Wherefore, if God so clothe the grass of the field, which today is, and tomorrow is cast into the oven, even so will he clothe you, if ye are not of little faith. Therefore take no thought, saying, What shall we eat? or, What shall we drink? or, Wherewithal shall we be clothed? For your heavenly Father knoweth that ye have need of all these things."

Christ illustrates His teaching of how His disciples are to be supported by analogy after analogy. He likens the principle of how His disciple-ministers are to be supported to:

- Fowls of the air, provided for by God.
- Lilies of the field, whose glorious appearance comes from God.
- Grass of the field, which are adorned by natural beauty from God.

Inherent in these analogies is the message that so long as fowls shall fly, this principle ought to be followed. So long as lilies remain on the earth growing wild, this manner of supporting His disciples ought to be followed. So long as grass shall be here, this principle should be followed.

The hopelessness of man's presumed independence from God is stressed in His statement that by taking thought none of us "can add one cubit unto his stature." Our lives are not ours. They belong to Him. We have no independence from Him. We are *not* self-existent beings. We borrow all we are and have from Him. Even, as it turns out, the dust from which we are made belongs to Him.[1280]

If God gives us air to breathe, power to exist, the capacity to move, and sustains all of us from moment to moment, then how little faith is required to rely on Him to provide His disciples with food and raiment?

The analogy to Solomon is also telling. "Solomon, in all his glory" is a useful way to think of the greatest man can hope for himself. The glory of Solomon was legendary. The Queen of Sheba came

---

[1280] Mosiah 2:20–25 "I say unto you, my brethren, that if you should render all the thanks and praise which your whole soul has power to possess, to that God who has created you, and has kept and preserved you, and has caused that ye should rejoice, and has granted that ye should live in peace one with another—I say unto you that if ye should serve him who has created you from the beginning, and is preserving you from day to day, by lending you breath, that ye may live and move and do according to your own will, and even supporting you from one moment to another—I say, if ye should serve him with all your whole souls yet ye would be unprofitable servants. And behold, all that he requires of you is to keep his commandments; and he has promised you that if ye would keep his commandments ye should prosper in the land; and he never doth vary from that which he hath said; therefore, if ye do keep his commandments he doth bless you and prosper you. And now, in the first place, he hath created you, and granted unto you your lives, for which ye are indebted unto him. And secondly, he doth require that ye should do as he hath commanded you; for which if ye do, he doth immediately bless you; and therefore he hath paid you. And ye are still indebted unto him, and are, and will be, forever and ever; therefore, of what have ye to boast? And now I ask, can ye say aught of yourselves? I answer you, Nay. Ye cannot say that ye are even as much as the dust of the earth; yet ye were created of the dust of the earth; but behold, it belongeth to him who created you."

and marveled at what she saw in his court.[1281] This was splendor, wealth and power indeed! However, Christ reminds us that these man-made marvels are nothing compared with the beauty He can supply those who are "not of little faith." He can cover a man in glory indeed. Not as the world defines glory, but the real glory.[1282]

The purpose of putting a man in such a dependent state before God is not to find out whether God can take care of him. God already knows what a man needs before he should even ask. But the man will, by becoming so dependent upon God, acquire a broken heart and a contrite spirit, always quick to ask, quick to listen, quick to do. Vulnerability makes a man strong in spirit. Security and wealth make a man incorrectly believe in his independence from God.

[1281] 1 Kings 10:1–13 "And when the queen of Sheba heard of the fame of Solomon concerning the name of the Lord, she came to prove him with hard questions. And she came to Jerusalem with a very great train, with camels that bare spices, and very much gold, and precious stones: and when she was come to Solomon, she communed with him of all that was in her heart. And Solomon told her all her questions: there was not *any* thing hid from the king, which he told her not. And when the queen of Sheba had seen all Solomon's wisdom, and the house that he had built, And the meat of his table, and the sitting of his servants, and the attendance of his ministers, and their apparel, and his cupbearers, and his ascent by which he went up unto the house of the Lord; there was no more spirit in her. And she said to the king, It was a true report that I heard in mine own land of thy acts and of thy wisdom. Howbeit I believed not the words, until I came, and mine eyes had seen *it:* and, behold, the half was not told me: thy wisdom and prosperity exceedeth the fame which I heard. Happy *are* thy men, happy *are* these thy servants, which stand continually before thee, *and* that hear thy wisdom. Blessed be the Lord thy God, which delighted in thee, to set thee on the throne of Israel: because the Lord loved Israel for ever, therefore made he thee king, to do judgment and justice. And she gave the king an hundred and twenty talents of gold, and of spices very great store, and precious stones: there came no more such abundance of spices as these which the queen of Sheba gave to king Solomon. And the navy also of Hiram, that brought gold from Ophir, brought in from Ophir great plenty of almug trees, and precious stones. And the king made of the almug trees pillars for the house of the Lord, and for the king's house, harps also and psalteries for singers: there came no such almug trees, nor were seen unto this day. And king Solomon gave unto the queen of Sheba all her desire, whatsoever she asked, beside *that* which Solomon gave her of his royal bounty. So she turned and went to her own country, she and her servants."

[1282] D&C 93:28, 36 "He that keepeth his commandments receiveth truth and light, until he is glorified in truth and knoweth all things. . . . The glory of God is intelligence, or, in other words, light and truth."

He wants His disciples to be dependent upon Him. He wants them praying, and then grateful to Him for what He provides. He wants them, in a word, to become holy.

Such a system would be impractical in a post-industrial society like ours, wouldn't it?

3 Nephi 13:33

"But seek ye first the kingdom of God and his righteousness, and all these things shall be added unto you."

What comes first? Why?

How can "all these things" then "be added unto you?" What are "these things?" Is it the food, raiment, etc.?

Why would the Lord want the disciples to first seek the kingdom of God before promising that the things would be "added unto" them?

If they don't first seek the kingdom, then will things not be added to them?

What is "the kingdom of God?" Is there a difference between

- The Church of Jesus Christ

- The Kingdom of God

- Zion?

What is the "kingdom of God" if it is not the church? When is the "kingdom" to be found? What is necessary for it to exist? Joseph Smith taught: "What constitutes the Kingdom of God? an administrator who has the power of calling down the oracles of God, and subjects to receive those oracles no matter if there is but 3, 4, or 6 there is the kingdom of God." (William Clayton Journal entry January 22, 1843, capitalization as in original.) If we accept Joseph's definition, why would the disciples be encouraged to "seek the kingdom of God?"

What does the clarification that the "kingdom of God" should be sought first tell us about everything else?

Has the "kingdom of God" been here before now? Is it here now? What does it mean to call down the oracles of God?

Does man control this or does God?

What is man's role in establishing the "kingdom of God?" Is man's role confined to "seeking first" for it to come? How would man seek it?

If you want to "seek the kingdom of God" how would you go about doing so?

What does your "seeking" have to do with the return of the "kingdom of God?"

The Lord will not bring again Zion without there being a people who are prepared to receive what He intends to bring. How can you do that?

3 Nephi 13:34

"Take therefore no thought for the morrow, for the morrow shall take thought for the things of itself. Sufficient is the day unto the evil thereof."

This is the child's view of life. A child is perpetually in the "now" and does not regret yesterdays or plan tomorrows. It is all about what happens to you at the moment.

Each day's challenge is the end goal. In addition to severing the disciples from regular income, regular work for support, dependence on those to whom they minister for bread, drink, shelter and clothing, the Lord adds to their burden the heavy responsibility to "take no thought for the morrow." For them their ministry is to be moment to moment. No planning and rehearsals. No staging and frantic preparation. No three-year budgets. Only now. Forever only now.

It is an interesting position Christ wants to put His chief disciples into. It forces us to carefully consider why He would do so?

Is it to keep them humble?

Is it to prevent pride and arrogance?

Is it to require they remain in constant direct touch with at least some of those over whom they minister?

Is it to keep them keenly aware of the necessity of relying on Him?

If they cannot plan for more than the day's events, how can they plan a busy travel schedule to take them all over the world? Is that somehow built in already to the "sufficient is the day unto the evil thereof?"

What kind of life would this create for His disciples chosen to minister to others? Would they ever be able to minister to more than just a few at a time under this system? If they are limited to serving only a few at a time, then how would an entire church receive benefit from this kind of spontaneous ministry? What kind of changes would that make in how a church is run and organized?

Just how impractical do we think this manner of organizing would be in a multi-national, multi-lingual, 13 million member church? If it is impractical, should the Lord's teachings be revised or should we change our way of thinking about His church and system?

If this were to be implemented, how would you go about organizing it? Would you divide the world into twelfths? Within that division, would you expect the disciple assigned to "drop in" to stake conferences and ward meetings unannounced? Would that prevent central planning and budgeting by the chief disciples? Would it force the Presiding Bishop's office to take concerns for all temporal concerns and budgets? Why would letting an Aaronic Priesthood office be concerned with temporal affairs and freeing up Melchizedek Priesthood for spiritual concerns be an unwelcome change?

Would this fundamentally transform the role of leadership? How? Would it be chaos, or would it be an improvement? Why?

Just how dumb an idea is this that Christ is teaching to the chosen twelve? If not dumb, then it is at least of limited practicality when growth in numbers and locations makes it burdensome? Was Christ's teaching here short-sighted? Did He fail to make provisions for the modern church, with its global spread and cross-language needs and budgets?

When the Book of Mormon was restored, this sermon was restored to us. When restored, it clarified how this portion of the sermon was addressed to the presiding twelve disciples. Was there a Divine purpose or message behind it? Should it be considered as meaningful to us today? Christ lived an interesting life. He more or less followed this counsel, though in truth He understood and fulfilled the prophecies concerning Himself. Yet, throughout it all, He also seemed to surrender control to the Father in everything.[1283] He commented on how spontaneous a life He lived, and how unpredictable things were when following the Spirit.[1284]

[1283] Mark 13:32 "But of that day and *that* hour knoweth no man, no, not the angels which are in heaven, neither the Son, but the Father."

[1284] John 3:6–8 "That which is born of the flesh is flesh; and that which is born of the Spirit is spirit. Marvel not that I said unto thee, Ye must be born again. The wind bloweth where it listeth, and thou hearest the sound thereof, but canst not tell whence it cometh, and whither it goeth: so is every one that is born of the Spirit."

3 Nephi 14

3 Nephi 14:1–2

"And now it came to pass that when Jesus had spoken these words he turned again to the multitude, and did open his mouth unto them again, saying: Verily, verily, I say unto you, Judge not, that ye be not judged. For with what judgment ye judge, ye shall be judged; and with what measure ye mete, it shall be measured to you again."

This reiterates the doctrine in the Lord's instruction on prayer. Your judgment of others will become the basis for your own judgment by the Father. Apply mercy to receive mercy. Apply forgiveness to merit forgiveness. Act harshly to receive harsh treatment. Show strict judgment, and receive it in return. It is the perfect balance. What you send out returns to you. It is karma. The words are right out of Christ's own mouth.

More importantly, notice how He transitions from speaking to His twelve about their new, spontaneous ministry into the public judgment of what was to follow? In other words, if these thoughts are related, (and I think they are) then He is saying His twelve disciples may take a while to get to the needs of those assembled. Therefore, be patient. This new lifestyle for the disciples will be difficult on them. In order to receive a reward, those who are being ministered to need to bear patiently with the ensuing efforts of the twelve.

This was to be a new community formed among these people. In it, there will be servants called to minister (the twelve), who will be limited in what they are able to do. They will be needy, dependent, and vulnerable. They will have needs. Supply the needs without being put off by what they are not able to do. View them with compassion as they seek to do as they have been told. Don't withhold substance, food, raiment, or housing from them because you are unhappy with what little they have been able to do. Show them kindness.

The statement is broader than that, of course. It implies similar patience with everyone. But the point that this practice should begin with these twelve ministers ought not be lost.

The context of "judge not that ye be not judged" is framed by the statement that "with what judgment ye judge, ye shall be judged; and with what measure ye mete, it shall be measured to you again." We do "judge" one another because we must. But the judgment should err on the side of forgiving. It should err in favor of trusting motives to be pure, and intent to be good. We should be generous with our gratitude, evaluations and suppositions. When we know someone is misbehaving, we should make allowances for their shortcomings, forgive them before they ask, and impute no retribution because of their offensive conduct.

This does not make us better than another, it makes us whole. It allows the Lord to forgive us for our own, much greater offenses against Him. For when we are generous, we merit His Divine generosity. It is how we are healed. It is the means for our own salvation. Instead of thinking ourselves better than an offender, we should look upon them with gratitude for they provide the means to obtain salvation—provided we give them forgiveness from all their offenses.

This is why we should rejoice and be exceedingly glad.[1285] They enable us to obtain salvation by despitefully using us, as long as we measure them by the same standard that allows God to forgive us.

What perfect symmetry: You measure to others using instrument that will be used by God to measure back to you. So your ready forgiveness is how God will treat you. All those grudges can be replaced with petitions to God to forgive those who abused you. As you lay aside all those sins against you, committed by others, it will purge from you all your own sins.

Straight and narrow indeed . . . But oddly appropriate and altogether within your control.

3 Nephi 14:3–5

> "And why beholdest thou the mote that is in thy brother's eye, but considerest not the beam that is in thine own eye? Or how wilt thou say to thy brother: Let me pull the mote out of thine eye—and behold, a beam is in thine own eye? Thou hypocrite, first cast the beam out of thine own eye; and then shalt thou see clearly to cast the mote out of thy brother's eye."

The defect in judging is the position from which we proceed. We are blind. We have too many subjective problems in our background. Our training, education, culture, presumptions, prejudices, "things we just know to be true", ignorance, preoccupations and impatience interfere with our perceptions. We act on errors and reach wrong conclusions. We measure with defective tools, then decide the matter from the wrong measure.

[1285] 3 Nephi 12:10–12 "And blessed are all they who are persecuted for my name's sake, for theirs is the kingdom of heaven. And blessed are ye when men shall revile you and persecute, and shall say all manner of evil against you falsely, for my sake; For ye shall have great joy and be exceedingly glad, for great shall be your reward in heaven; for so persecuted they the prophets who were before you."

Christ is reminding us that whenever we are inclined to correct another person, more often than not, we suffer from whatever defect we see in others. This is why we notice it. We see it because it is really us. We are sensitive to the problem because we own the problem.

First, whenever we see something amiss in another, start with the realization that we are seeing ourselves. Start inside. Ask, "why does this bother me?" "Am I really seeing myself in a mirror?" Then be grateful you saw another person display your problem. You now know what is wrong with you. Forgive them, fix you.

The tendency to withhold patience is more often than not because their "mote" excites your notice through your own "beam." A "mote" is a speck, a bit of sawdust. A "beam" is a board. Yours is the greater defect. For in you is not only the defect, but the tendency to judge others harshly. Both are wrong.

When you have at last purged the defect, struggled to overcome and conquer the temptation or tendency, perhaps the price you pay to do so will make you humble enough to assist another. Not from the position as judge and condemner, but from the position of one who can help. When you "see clearly," then you may be able to "cast the mote out of thy brother's eye." For now you see him as your "brother." And in a kindly and affectionate manner you may act to reclaim him. Not as a judge, but as a brother.

This is a continuing petition to make things better. But the only way you make them better by starting inside. It is not for you to work on others, nor move outside your own range of defects, until you have first fixed what you lack. When you can proceed with charity to assist others to overcome what you have overcome yourself, then it is appropriate to approach your "brother" in kindness to help. Until then, stop judging and start removing "beams" from yourself.

Brilliant and peaceful. Revolutionary and kind. Christ is the ultimate True Teacher. He could teach such things because He was such things. His disciples will, in turn, take His teachings and His example and do likewise.

3 Nephi 14:6

"Give not that which is holy unto the dogs, neither cast ye your pearls before swine, lest they trample them under their feet, and turn again and rend you."

This is a preamble to what immediately follows. It is a caution about how to weigh what can be said, and what is to be kept private between a person and the Lord.

Almost without exception, people who are unable to keep sacred things which are most sacred will never receive exposure to the most sacred. The Temple ordinances are an elaborate test of ones trustworthiness. There are a variety of things designated as "most sacred" which are then "guarded by covenants and obligations" that require they not be revealed "except in a certain place" which will always be limited. The material then revealed is to be kept as "most sacred," though in truth, it is a test where symbolic information is imparted to allow the spiritually mature to learn by symbol some hidden meaning and mystery about God. To the immature, the material is worthless and meaningless. Nothing of value is gained. It is a symbol without an interpretation. It can only be an idol to them as they mistake the symbol for underlying meaning.

When a person treats the information in an appropriate way, they "prove" themselves[1286] worthy of weightier information to be

---

[1286] Abraham 3:25 "And we will prove them herewith, to see if they will do all things whatsoever the Lord their God shall command them;"

given them.[1287] Then they are laid under a strict command that they shall not impart, only according to the heed and diligence which another should give to the word.[1288]

What is holy belongs to those who make themselves holy through their repentance. It does not belong to the unclean, who are "dogs" and unrepentant.

When the price is paid, the person trusted, and the mysteries shown them, they possess pearls of great price. Such things do not belong to "swine" who are unclean and unrepentant, unwilling to do what is needed to qualify for the Lord's presence, unthankful and unholy.

Entrusting the things that are in truth "most sacred" to those who are not qualified will arouse their anger. They will "turn and rend you" because you have shown them something which excites their envy, jealousy, hatred and fear. They know you have something they lack. They resent you because of what they cannot easily obtain. Therefore, you must measure carefully what you give to others. The final arbiter of the decision to impart is not made by you, it is made by the Lord.

Those who are eager to share with others any tidbit of information they learn about the sacred are not helping anyone, and may forfeit things themselves. Why would they do such a thing? Is it to make themselves look good; therefore vanity? Is it to try to help others? If it is to help, then the information should not be shared; the

---

[1287] D&C 132:20–21 "Then shall they be gods, because they have no end; therefore shall they be from everlasting to everlasting, because they continue; then shall they be above all, because all things are subject unto them. Then shall they be gods, because they have all power, and the angels are subject unto them. Verily, verily, I say unto you, except ye abide my law ye cannot attain to this glory."

[1288] Alma 12:9 "And now Alma began to expound these things unto him, saying: It is given unto many to know the mysteries of God; nevertheless they are laid under a strict command that they shall not impart only according to the portion of his word which he doth grant unto the children of men, according to the heed and diligence which they give unto him."

manner in which the information is gained should be shared. Teaching another the way to receive sacred information for themselves is charitable. Showing off sacred information is worse than foolish, it will bless no one, and destroy both the unprepared audience and the unwise speaker.

I have tried to be an example of this principle. First I learned something, then I began to teach it. When teaching, I have carefully measured anything I have taught against the Lord's cautions and limitations. I have affirmed in the fewest words that the promises made by the Lord are true, and that I am a witness of their truth. But I have not shared anything beyond the process, which I have taught so others may learn how to proceed. It has not been about me, or about anything I may know. It has been about the Lord and the process to know Him. It is clear that some people are completely uninterested in anything other than some new disclosure, some new mystery unfolded. They are not interested in anything other than to be titillated. I cannot help them. I have nothing to offer. But if someone wants to approach God, then I may be able to teach something of value in what I've written. But not if they are unwilling to start at the first and proceed through everything I've written in the order they were written. Jumping to the end of the process is worthless. Gathering tidbits is unwise as it gives you only enough information to be dangerous. It is the path to follow Christ that matters.

Getting to know the Lord is the definition of salvation.[1289] Getting to know me will save no one. It is foolish to consider anything or anyone more important than learning the means to come back to the Lord.

[1289] John 17:3 "And this is life eternal, that they might know thee the only true God, and Jesus Christ, whom thou hast sent."

3 Nephi 14:7–8

"Ask, and it shall be given unto you; seek, and ye shall find; knock, and it shall be opened unto you. For every one that asketh, receiveth; and he that seeketh, findeth; and to him that knocketh, it shall be opened."

Just after the caution to not give holy things to the unworthy, Christ reminds all of their obligation to ask, seek and knock. If you will ask it will be given to you. If you seek, you will find it. If you knock, things will be opened to you. But be careful not to give what is holy to the unworthy.

These ideas are related in two ways:

First, if you want what is holy, then stop being a "dog" or a "swine." Ask, seek and knock.

Second, if you are one who is qualified and will receive holy things by your willingness to be repentant, then press forward by asking, seeking and knocking. If you do, the things which are most holy will be given.

"For every one that asketh, receiveth." Really? Everyone? Even you? That is what Christ is saying. However, the manner in which you will receive is illustrated by "The Missing Virtue" in *Ten Parables*. Meaning that the effort to receive what you have asked the Lord could take nearly two decades, and a great deal of internal changing before you acquire what you lack. Receiving may include not only what you've asked to receive, but also everything you do not have in order to finally qualify to receive what you seek.

What do you associate with "findeth?" Does it suggest to you active effort, or passive receipt? To "find" something you are missing (even a small thing) what must you do? If searching is required to locate, then what do you suppose the Lord is implying by the word "findeth?"

What does it mean that "it shall be opened?" Does "opening" imply merely a view? Does it suggest also 'entering in?' If it opens to view, and you then fail to 'enter in' has "opening" been worthwhile? Has anything been accomplished? Does it suggest that there is activity required of someone who has something "opened" unto them?

It is my view that the words chosen all imply a burden upon the one who asks, seeks and knocks. They are not entitled to anything just by speaking the words. They must make the effort to search into and contemplate the things they seek. Then they must change and repent of everything amiss in their lives that is revealed to them. This is to be done before they can see what is to be shown to them. If, for example, a person wants to see the other side of the mountain, they can ask daily for a view to be opened to them without ever seeing the other side. But if the Lord prompts them to take the path to the top, the Lord has given them the means to "find" and "have opened" to them the very thing they seek. Provided, of course, they are willing to walk in the path to the top of the mountain. When they remain on the valley floor, asking or demanding more, they are not really asking, seeking and knocking. They are irritating and ungrateful. The Lord's small means are capable of taking the one who seeks to the very thing they desire.[1290] But without cooperation with Him they can receive nothing.

The Lord's small means are how great things are brought to pass.[1291] But for some people the Lord's answers are never enough. However, when the humble who ask, seek and knock follow Him in

---

[1290] Alma 37:7 "And the Lord God doth work by means to bring about his great and eternal purposes; and by very small means the Lord doth confound the wise and bringeth about the salvation of many souls."

[1291] 1 Nephi 16:29 "And there was also written upon them a new writing, which was plain to be read, which did give us understanding concerning the ways of the Lord; and it was written and changed from time to time, according to the faith and diligence which we gave unto it. And thus we see that by small means the Lord can bring about great things."

these small means, they will eventually stand in His presence and partake of eternal life. But not until they have done as all others have done before them. Faith is only replaced by knowledge when the faith is strong enough to rend the veil. At that point, there is no great advantage to the person who has already attained to this understanding by their faith. I've written about this in *The Second Comforter*. It is a true principle and remains true even today.

3 Nephi 14:9–11

"Or what man is there of you, who, if his son ask bread, will give him a stone? Or if he ask a fish, will he give him a serpent? If ye then, being evil, know how to give good gifts unto your children, how much more shall your Father who is in heaven give good things to them that ask him?"

This is not self-evident. If it were, then there would be more people with faith. The truth revealed here is that God is always going to bestow a worthy gift upon the person requesting it.

He will not give you a "stone" if you request "bread." He will give you "bread." He knows the difference. He will not disappoint you.

He knows better than any kind and caring earthly father what the needs of His children are. He intends to meet them.

However, when His children ask for something ("bread") and they do not yet qualify to receive, He sets about preparing them to receive it. He is willing to give. We are not always prepared to receive. Therefore, when He intends to bestow the gift upon the person requesting it, He first prepares the vessel.

We are impatient. We want quickly what can sometimes only be obtained in patience. We are in a rush, but our development requires patience. Some things require time and persistence to prepare us for the blessing we seek. Joseph remarked: "The things of God are of deep import, and time, experience, and careful and ponderous, and solemn thoughts, can only find them out." This is the way of God. It is adapted to give us what we lack, even if we are unaware of what we lack.

The Father always intends to give to those who ask, seek and knock just as Christ has explained. However, the Father knows "much more" than do we as to how to "give good things to them that ask." He will not merely give the thing requested. He will add to it such things as are needed to prepare you to receive them.

This, then, is the process: We ask. Without a request, the laws governing things prevent bestowal. We can't be given until first we ask.

When we have asked, the Father will give. He will give "every good gift" needed, and not just what has been asked. If there is, (as is almost always the case) a gulf between what you have asked of Him, and your capacity to receive it, then He will set about giving you every needful thing to enable you to receive.

If you ask for strength, He will provide you with that experience necessary to develop the strength you seek. If you seek for patience you will be given Divinely ordained experiences by Him that are calculated to develop in you what you have sought. He knows you and knows what you need. Whatever is asked of Him, He will set about to ordain.

It will come in a perfectly natural progression. It will occur in accordance with both natural and eternal law. If you fight against it, you prolong the time when you will receive what you have asked of Him. If you cooperate, it will flow unto you without compulsory means in a natural progression.[1292]

[1292] D&C 121:46 "The Holy Ghost shall be thy constant companion, and thy scepter an unchanging scepter of righteousness and truth; and thy dominion shall be an everlasting dominion, and without compulsory means it shall flow unto thee forever and ever."

If you do not ask, it will not be given. If you do not seek, you cannot possibly find. If you are unwilling to knock, the door will remain shut to you. But if you do these things, then you must cooperate with Him as He prepares you to receive what He will bestow.

After asking, seeking and knocking, then a process is invoked in which the Father prepares you to receive. You will receive as soon as He can prepare you by experience, by careful, thoughtful, ponderous thought through time and experiences adapted to give you what is asked. When, at last, you have been adequately prepared, you will have gone through exactly what every other soul before you has experienced to prepare them. There are no shortcuts. There are no exceptions. It is in accordance with laws ordained before the foundation of the world. Everyone who has obtained what you seek will have done so in conformity with the very same laws. The Father will work with you to prepare you to receive what you seek.

This is a reaffirmation by Christ of the process and the Father's role in bringing it to pass. If you trust Him, trust also His Father's deliverance of you. You will be delivered. You will receive from Him who knows how to bestow every good gift what you have asked of Him.

3 Nephi 14:12

"Therefore, all things whatsoever ye would that men should do to you, do ye even so to them, for this is the law and the prophets."

This thought has been taken from the talk and made a law unto itself. Perhaps it belongs there. But it also integrates into the sermon as well.

Remember what preceded this comment. The Father is the giver of "good gifts" and will give you "bread" when you ask it. He will never give you a "stone" when you ask of Him bread.

This follows. You must also become the giver of good gifts. You must also provide to others what they need from you. How you give, unlocks the Father's ability to give to you. Every principle is eternal. Every life requires the balance.

When you seek, you must free the Father's hand to give to you by what you give to others. Without equitable treatment of others, the Father cannot give you.

Your relationship with your fellow man defines your relationship with the Father. Your kindness towards others establishes the conditions of His ability to give kindness to you.

Be careful how you treat others. It affects how the Father is permitted to treat you. It is an eternal principle.[1293]

The law and all the prophets were attempting to teach us to deal equitably with one another. What Christ is summarizing is the intent of all that has been given to us in the law and prophets.

Give what you want. Be fair, even generous. It will return to you. No matter how this life disappoints, discourages or frustrates you, keep pressing forward with good cheer. It will be for your good and, as it all concludes, will return to you glory.

This is how the world can be redeemed. This is how Zion will be brought again. It will be the Lord's doing, because it will be through following His commandments that people can be prepared. Those who will participate will necessarily need to heed His commandments. If they do, there will be no poor among them. They will be of one mind and one heart, because they will share the same vision of how to live. They will give one another what they would like to receive, and the result will be the return of a society that has rarely existed on

---

[1293] Alma 41:15 "For that which ye do send out shall return unto you again, and be restored; therefore, the word restoration more fully condemneth the sinner, and justifieth him not at all."

this earth. Heaven can guide and teach us how it is to be done. But we must do it.

Even if no one else will live this principle, you can. If you do, the Lord is able to "take up His abode with you" and even bring you to the Father.[1294] Not in some distant time, nor merely "in your heart." It is literal.[1295]

The way to prove these teachings is to live them. If you do, you will know the doctrine's truth.[1296]

In this brief statement Christ has captured the underlying message of all the prophets from Moses to Christ. It is the reason for God working with Israel. It is the way for any person to find their way back to God.

This message is succinct, profound, and able to transform life. Christ was the Master Teacher. In this brief statement He has proven His standing as the greatest source of truth of all those who have instructed others. It is because of this ringing truth that Christ's message has endured through millennia of apostasy and darkness. Words such as these will outlast empires, shine in darkness and subdue critics. He was and is indeed the way, the truth and the life.[1297]

3 Nephi 14:13–14

"Enter ye in at the strait gate; for wide is the gate, and broad is the way, which leadeth to destruction, and many there be who

---

[1294] John 14:23 "Jesus answered and said unto him, If a man love me, he will keep my words: and my Father will love him, and we will come unto him, and make our abode with him."

[1295] D&C 130:3 "John 14:23—The appearing of the Father and the Son, in that verse, is a personal appearance; and the idea that the Father and the Son dwell in a man's heart is an old sectarian notion, and is false."

[1296] John 7:17 "If any man will do his will, he shall know of the doctrine, whether it be of God, or *whether* I speak of myself."

[1297] John 14:6 "Jesus saith unto him, I am the way, the truth, and the life: no man cometh unto the Father, but by me."

go in thereat; Because strait is the gate, and narrow is the way, which leadeth unto life, and few there be that find it."

This is re-affirmation of man's tendency to reject the right way. The narrowness of it requires surrender of the selfish, parting with pride and sacrifice of self-will.

Many prefer their ignorance to light. Therefore, they will not draw toward the light when it is revealed to them. Without drawing closer to the light they cannot comprehend what the Lord is teaching. It makes no sense to them. For it requires light to comprehend light. Therefore unless a person is willing to increase in light they are left in darkness and unable to apprehend any of what saves them. It remains a mystery to them.

The way to darkness is broad and easy. It requires no effort. It welcomes you. It tempts you with its ease. Because there are "many who go in thereat" it is also popular. When, therefore, you take opinion polling and focus group testing as the measure of a proposition you are only joining to the wide, broad way which will be popular.

Truth challenges. It requires change. It informs you of your faults and mistakes. It is difficult because you are called to rise above what the world is doing, what the world is saying and what the world accepts as good and true. This tendency to want to be popular can twist you away from truth quicker than any other corrupting influence here. This is why Nephi cautioned about the latter-day churches which crave popularity and acceptance.[1298]

[1298] 1 Nephi 22:23 "For the time speedily shall come that all churches which are built up to get gain, and all those who are built up to get power over the flesh, and those who are built up to become popular in the eyes of the world, and those who seek the lusts of the flesh and the things of the world, and to do all manner of iniquity; yea, in fine, all those who belong to the kingdom of the devil are they who need fear, and tremble, and quake; they are those who must be brought low in the dust; they are those who must be consumed as stubble; and this is according to the words of the prophet."

There will only be a "few who find it." Even in the day in which we live, the measure will always be "few." Not in a relative sense, but in an absolute sense. Few. Period. Only a small number.

Looking down through the ages, speaking with the vision of a prophet, the number of those who, living in the last days would have the Father's name upon their forehead, were only 144,000.[1299] Though from all ages the number would be in the millions.[1300] Still, we live in the time when a living number who are prepared for the return of Christ will be but few in an absolute sense.[1301] Even if they have wives and children, yet the number will remain but few.

It is foolish to believe the conditions for salvation are any different for you than they were for Enoch, Moses, Abraham, Isaiah, Elijah, Peter or Joseph. This Gospel is the same. Always and in every generation it is the same. The odds are that but few of those who are living will go in thereat. All the opinion polling to test for popular acceptance of a message cannot deliver a message from God to mankind. It can only entice you to the broad, wide gate "which leadeth to destruction."

[1299] Revelation 7:3–4 "Saying, Hurt not the earth, neither the sea, nor the trees, till we have sealed the servants of our God in their foreheads. And I heard the number of them which were sealed: *and there were* sealed an hundred *and* forty *and* four thousand of all the tribes of the children of Israel."

[1300] Revelation 7:9, 13–14 "After this I beheld, and, lo, a great multitude, which no man could number, of all nations, and kindreds, and people, and tongues, stood before the throne, and before the Lamb, clothed with white robes, and palms in their hands; . . . And one of the elders answered, saying unto me, What are these which are arrayed in white robes? and whence came they? And I said unto him, Sir, thou knowest. And he said to me, These are they which came out of great tribulation, and have washed their robes, and made them white in the blood of the Lamb."

[1301] D&C 77:11 "Q. What are we to understand by sealing the one hundred and forty-four thousand, out of all the tribes of Israel—twelve thousand out of every tribe?
A. We are to understand that those who are sealed are high priests, ordained unto the holy order of God, to administer the everlasting gospel; for they are they who are ordained out of every nation, kindred, tongue, and people, by the angels to whom is given power over the nations of the earth, to bring as many as will come to the church of the Firstborn."

The Lord could not be more plain. The teachings which preceded this statement are His invitation. Here He gives His prophetic description of the audience's response. From all those who will read or hear His words, every soul will be accountable. From among those, like you, who are accountable, there will be but "few who find it."

Why is that so? What is so important about the world's acceptance that a fool will treasure it before their own salvation? What can the world offer in exchange that you tempt you to give your soul?[1302] How many will lament when the summer is passed, the harvest has come, that their soul has not been saved.[1303]

This is a sobering remark by the forgiving Lord. He invites all to come to Him. But He is realistic about how few will respond. It requires repentance, baptism, receiving the Holy Ghost and living by every word which comes from Him. It is strait and therefore narrow. But it lies in a straight path before you. You can know you are on it when you encounter the gate-keeper, for He has no servant there. He alone maintains that gate through which entry to salvation is gained.[1304]

Study, therefore, to show yourself approved.[1305]

[1302] Matthew 16:26 "For what is a man profited, if he shall gain the whole world, and lose his own soul? or what shall a man give in exchange for his soul?"

[1303] D&C 45:2 "And again I say, hearken unto my voice, lest death shall overtake you; in an hour when ye think not the summer shall be past, and the harvest ended, and your souls not saved."

[1304] 2 Nephi 9:41 "O then, my beloved brethren, come unto the Lord, the Holy One. Remember that his paths are righteous. Behold, the way for man is narrow, but it lieth in a straight course before him, and the keeper of the gate is the Holy One of Israel; and he employeth no servant there; and there is none other way save it be by the gate; for he cannot be deceived, for the Lord God is his name."

[1305] 2 Timothy 2:15 "Study to shew thyself approved unto God, a workman that needeth not to be ashamed, rightly dividing the word of truth."

3 Nephi 14:15–20

"Beware of false prophets, who come to you in sheep's clothing, but inwardly they are ravening wolves. Ye shall know
them by their fruits. Do men gather grapes of thorns, or figs
of thistles? Even so every good tree bringeth forth good fruit;
but a corrupt tree bringeth forth evil fruit. A good tree cannot
bring forth evil fruit, neither a corrupt tree bring forth good
fruit. Every tree that bringeth not forth good fruit is hewn
down, and cast into the fire. Wherefore, by their fruits ye shall
know them."

This test is only necessary if He intends to send prophets. The
test is given so you may identify both true and false prophets. Implicit in this, is the obligation to personally account for your response
to those He sends, and those who claim to be sent by Him. You
must choose. Your choice will count for and against you. You must
grow to apply the test correctly.

The concept of "sheep's clothing" is worth pondering. Why is it
even possible for such a thing as "sheep's clothing?" Think about it.
The attire or mantle they pretend to possess is necessarily "sheep-
like" to the casual observer. That is, the "office" or the position or
conduct or credentials of the false prophet must be misleading. They
should appear bona fide. They need to seem authentic.

Now, lest you be confused about the "wolves" who occupy these
positions, it does not mean an utterly corrupt, completely perverse
man. It only requires the "wolves" to be unable to deliver a true message from the Lord. It only requires that they not be sent with an
authentic message from Him. They must pretend to be His, but He
has nothing to do with their message.

So, how are we to distinguish between the "sheep" and the "wolves"
who come as "prophets" from the Lord? In a word, it is the "fruit."
What does the message produce?

A false prophet's message will produce as its fruit vanity, corruption, evil, foolishness, arrogance, self-assuredness, error, distance from the Lord, poor understanding, popularity, wealth, success, ease, false hopes, ingratitude, pride, displays of popularity, worldliness, hard hearts and ten thousand other meaningless or deceptive fruits.

A true prophet's message will produce repentance.

The only good fruit which can be offered in this world is repentance. When mankind lays down their sins because of a message, that message comes from Him. All others are distractions and invite you to err. The fruit which gives eternal life is repentance and a return to Christ.

When the message comes from a false prophet, you can know the messengers, along with those who listen to it, and the message itself will be "hewn down, and cast into the fire." It will be purged.

When the message comes from a true prophet, you can know the message, along with those who heed it, and the messenger will survive the burning which is to come, because they are purged by repentance and can abide the day of wrath.

Few there be that find it, indeed . . . It needn't be so. But as Joseph Smith commented:

> "The world always mistook false prophets for true ones, and those that were sent of God, they considered to be false prophets, and hence they killed, stoned, punished and imprisoned the true prophets, and these had to hide themselves 'in deserts and dens, and caves of the earth', and though the most honorable men of the earth, they banished them from their society as vagabonds, whilst they cherished, honored and supported knaves, vagabonds, hypocrites, impostors, and the basest of men." (DHC 4:574.)

I suppose that will always be the case. However, we have a guarantee the President of The Church of Jesus Christ of Latter-day

Saints is unable (and will always be unable) to lead us astray. It is little wonder we cherish, honor and support that office as we do; preferring it even above scripture. (See "Fourteen Fundamentals for Following the Prophet," Ezra Taft Benson, BYU Address, February 26, 1980, the second fundamental; recently spoken of in our last General Conference.)

3 Nephi 14:21

"Not every one that saith unto me, Lord, Lord, shall enter into the kingdom of heaven; but he that doeth the will of my Father who is in heaven."

This was a favorite quote from President Kimball. It really puts Christ's followers on notice that confessing with the lips with no accompanying action to obey Him will not allow anyone into the kingdom of heaven.

Christ could not be more clear in this statement. The evangelical crowd quotes Paul's statement, "For with the heart man believeth unto righteousness; and with the mouth confession is made unto salvation," as proof to contradict the Lord.[1306] Paul does not explain salvation in that brief aside. Confession requires the confessor to go forward and present their entire life as a living sacrifice, continually obedient unto God (as he explains later in the very same letter).[1307] This foolish error is creeping into Mormonism with each passing day. From Professor Steven Robinson's rapprochement in How Wide the Divide? to Alonzo Gaskill's awful mistake called *Odds Are You're*

[1306] Romans 10:10 "For with the heart man believeth unto righteousness; and with the mouth confession is made unto salvation."

[1307] Romans 12:1–2 "I beseech you therefore, brethren, by the mercies of God, that ye present your bodies a living sacrifice, holy, acceptable unto God, *which is* your reasonable service. And be not conformed to this world: but be ye transformed by the renewing of your mind, that ye may prove what *is* that good, and acceptable, and perfect, will of God."

Going to Be Exalted, the erosion of doctrine to conform to the evangelical "market" continues apace.

They teach for doctrines the commandments of men. Their creeds are an abomination. The professors of these creeds are all corrupt. (I'm only quoting Christ.)[1308] We would be better informed to draw the starkest, widest and clearest distinctions between ourselves and them, rather than seeking to be regarded as another brand of mainstream Christianity.

Calling Christ "Lord, Lord" will accomplish nothing. There will be those who claim they are "of Christ" but who are no better than the liars, thieves and whoremongers.[1309] It is not a "brand name" to associate with. It is a Teacher to follow.

Christ teaches the will of the Father. Conforming to the will of the Father is required to "enter into the kingdom of heaven." Confession without conformity to His will is worse than meaningless. It is evidence that you are superstitious and foolish. You want Christ as a magic talisman, to be invoked to control the outcome of your life. But you do not want to honor Him by doing as He teaches. You do not want to live as He would want you to live. You do not want to surrender your sins and seek after truth and light.

The simple life which Christ describes in this sermon is how we are to conform to His will. We have taken it bit by bit to examine

---

[1308] JS–H 1:19 "I was answered that I must join none of them, for they were all wrong; and the Personage who addressed me said that all their creeds were an abomination in his sight; that those professors were all corrupt; that: 'they draw near to me with their lips, but their hearts are far from me, they teach for doctrines the commandments of men, having a form of godliness, but they deny the power thereof'."

[1309] D&C 76:99–104 "For these are they who are of Paul, and of Apollos, and of Cephas. These are they who say they are some of one and some of another—some of Christ and some of John, and some of Moses, and some of Elias, and some of Esaias, and some of Isaiah, and some of Enoch; But received not the gospel, neither the testimony of Jesus, neither the prophets, neither the everlasting covenant. Last of all, these all are they who will not be gathered with the saints, to be caught up unto the church of the Firstborn, and received into the cloud. These are they who are liars, and sorcerers, and adulterers, and whoremongers, and whosoever loves and makes a lie. These are they who suffer the wrath of God on earth."

how living that life should be accomplished. This is the blueprint for understanding the Lord and meeting Him. It is not intended to cause pride, but to provoke repentance. It is the means by which we can know Him.

As the sermon is ending, He reminds those present that calling out to Him and honoring Him with the title of "Lord" will never be enough. You must do as He taught.

There is no other way.

The path is identical for everyone.

You are as capable of doing this as any person who ever lived here. The difference between you and those who have succeeded only exists so long as you refuse to repent. Repentance will cure your lack of faith. Your confidence will increase in the Lord as you lay aside the sins which beset you.

The symmetry of Christ's sermon is astonishing. The closing call to follow Him is unmistakably sobering. It is not enough to sit in an audience honoring Him by showing brief attention to His talk. The talk must become alive in you.

3 Nephi 14:22–23

"Many will say to me in that day: Lord, Lord, have we not prophesied in thy name, and in thy name have cast out devils, and in thy name done many wonderful works? And then will I profess unto them: I never knew you; depart from me, ye that work iniquity."

Another group will call out to Him in the Day of Judgment saying, "Lord, Lord" showing respect and honor by their lips. It is not the lips which honor Him. The heart must follow His path.[1310]

Who will claim to have "prophesied in [His] name?"

Who will claim to have "cast out devils in [His] name?"

Who will claim to have done "many wonderful works" in His name?

What will their conduct in mortality have been in order to justify this claim in the Day of Judgment?

Despite claims to have "prophesied," and to have "cast out devils," and to have performed "many wonderful works," these people are unknown to Him. He will respond: "I never knew you; depart from me, ye that work iniquity."

How can "prophesying in Christ's name" be a work of "iniquity?"

How can "casting out devils" in Christ's name be a work of "iniquity?"

How can a person do "many wonderful works" in Christ's name yet still be doing "iniquity?"

How can people use the Lord's name with apparent success in claiming to have "prophesied," and to have "cast out devils," and done "many wonderful works" yet still be someone He does not know.

How would you determine if you were known to Him?

What would He (not you) need to do in order for you to be known to Him? How would you come to know Him and He to know you?

Do you now see why I have written what I've written? The message is an invitation to come to have Him know you. To have Him

---

[1310] JS–H 1:19: "I was answered that I must join none of them, for they were all wrong; and the Personage who addressed me said that all their creeds were an abomination in his sight; that those professors were all corrupt; that: 'they draw near to me with their lips, but their hearts are far from me, they teach for doctrines the commandments of men, having a form of godliness, but they deny the power thereof'."

take up His abode with you. To affirm to you what your true standing is before Him. Joseph Smith could not know what his standing was before God until he asked the Lord, and received a manifestation from Him.[1311] How can you know if you do not similarly ask.

This teaching by Christ does not challenge the reasons men claim to be justified. He does not say they "falsely claim" to have prophesied in His name. He merely accepts the claim without criticism. These people will genuinely believe they were prophesying, casting out devils, and doing what they believe to be many marvelous works in His name. Yet their hearts are far from Him.

Therefore, take care that you do not mislead yourself by presuming the things which are done by you in His name are accepted by Him. It is a terrible thing to take His name in vain. To claim He has sent you when He has not, is not only wrong, it is inviting the Lord to say to you in the last day: "Depart from me, ye that work iniquity."

The commandment at the front end is to not take the Lord's name in vain.[1312] The result at the back end is revealed here. Take care in how you presume your acts are in harmony with Him. Until He speaks to you, and affirms that you have a work to do for Him, you may only be working iniquity.

3 Nephi 14:24–25

"Therefore, whoso heareth these sayings of mine and doeth them, I will liken him unto a wise man, who built his house upon a rock—And the rain descended, and the floods came,

---

[1311] JS–H 1:29 "In consequence of these things, I often felt condemned for my weakness and imperfections; when, on the evening of the above-mentioned twenty-first of September, after I had retired to my bed for the night, I betook myself to prayer and supplication to Almighty God for forgiveness of all my sins and follies, and also for a manifestation to me, that I might know of my state and standing before him; for I had full confidence in obtaining a divine manifestation, as I previously had one."

[1312] Exodus 20:7 "Thou shalt not take the name of the Lord thy God in vain; for the Lord will not hold him guiltless that taketh his name in vain."

and the winds blew, and beat upon that house; and it fell not, for it was founded upon a rock."

The "wise man" is the one who is saved.

The "house" is an eternal family, continuation of seed, or eternal life.

The "rock" is Christ.

The descending storm represents the waters of chaos that destroyed the lives of the rebellious at the time of Noah. The rain, winds, floods are descriptive of God's judgment of mankind at that moment. Any soul must build their character, the light they possess, and their choices on Christ to withstand the day of judgment. If they do not, they construct their life on the unstable sand of this broken world, and nothing will endure.

Stability into eternity is built upon Christ's teachings. He came to us to show by example and to teach by word the things which all who are saved must become.

Few are interested in becoming what He was.

This summation is brief, cutting to the heart of the matter. But it is powerful in its plain language.

Christ was the Master Teacher. He said, with great clarity, in a few direct words what He wanted us to understand.

If we fail to heed this warning, then our eternal weakness is because of our choice. If we heed it, then He has provided both the teaching and the example to let us follow.

It is interesting how history has been affected by Christ's teachings. Wars and empires have claimed Christ as their sponsor. He has been a shield for every excess and wickedness imagined by man.

These comments are not about how to build a country, empire or corporation. It is about how to build your life. You cannot control anything other than your choices. But you can choose to follow Him, build your life on the teachings we have been looking at in this sermon. If you do, you build upon the Rock of Heaven.[1313]

[1313] Moses 7:53 "And the Lord said: Blessed is he through whose seed Messiah shall come; for he saith—I am Messiah, the King of Zion, the Rock of Heaven, which is broad as eternity; whoso cometh in at the gate and climbeth up by me shall never fall; wherefore, blessed are they of whom I have spoken, for they shall come forth with songs of everlasting joy."

3 NEPHI 15

3 Nephi 15:1

"And now it came to pass that when Jesus had ended these sayings he cast his eyes round about on the multitude, and said unto them: Behold, ye have heard the things which I taught before I ascended to my Father; therefore, whoso remembereth these sayings of mine and doeth them, him will I raise up at the last day."

Christ affirms that the sermon He just delivered was His sermon and teachings "before [He] ascended to [His] Father." This sermon was likely delivered at many gatherings by Him during His mortal life. For example, when, Mark mentions Him teaching without any discussion of the content (Mark 2:13), this sermon was likely being repeated by Him. There are other occasions when His message was not preserved, but where He was clearly teaching. The remark here suggests the sermon was not a one-time event. Rather it constituted His mortal ministry's primary message.

Why do you suppose He "cast His eyes round about on the multitude?" Was that mentioned because it was important to your understanding? What should you understand by this act?

Why does He mention "ascending to the Father?" Why is it important for these people to know of that event? What does that event tell you about Him?

What is the difference between "remembering these sayings," and "remembering and doing these sayings?" Do you both remember and do them?

What does the promise to be "raised up at the last day" mean? Unto what would the Lord raise one up? Can you rise from the dead and be "raised up at the last day?" Would there be more to His "raising up at the last day" for someone who had done as He taught?

The way Christ lived His life gives Him the right to teach us all what we need to do in order to be saved. He understood because He lived these principles.

He "looks upon" each of us because we can all live these teachings. Adding a little at a time, bit by bit, precept by precept, we can all live them. Not in a rush, but deliberately and with appropriately measuring each of life's events against His teachings as they come to us.

We are capable of much more than we think.

In fact, we are capable doing and being everything He has been teaching us. He hasn't given this talk to govern the lives of some special, small group of distant icons. They were meant to be the means for healthy living. They are how we are supposed to deal with one another.

Remember them. Then live them. He will "raise you up" not only in the last day, but each day as you have His Spirit to be with you.

3 Nephi 15:2

"And it came to pass that when Jesus had said these words he perceived that there were some among them who marveled, and wondered what he would concerning the law of Moses; for they understood not the saying that old things had passed away, and that all things had become new."

In the preceding verse I asked why Christ was looking at the group. Now we see the answer. He looked about at those who listened to Him because He was taking in their presence. He was listening to them. Not with the ears, but with His eyes and His heart. He "perceived" what concerned them.

These people derived their security from the Law of Moses. It was the tradition they were raised with; it was what they understood. The Lord's declaration that it had "passed away" was disorienting.

It is troubling to find your religious tradition has run its course, and will be replaced. People crave certainty and order. This desire is so strong in people that they will endure almost anything in order to keep what is familiar to them.

Once the Lord declared that the law of Moses was fulfilled it raised concerns about how, if at all, the Sabbath was to be kept. How were disputes to be managed? What were the laws respecting interest or usury? Servitude for debt? Punishment for certain crimes? What were the rules to govern society as life went forward?

What does it mean that "all things had become new?" Were the things He just said to take effect now? What of animal sacrifice? What of the other offerings? How were religious festivities to be kept, if they were to be kept at all? Which? When?

The Lord recognized these people did not understand what the old things passing away meant. He realized there was fear and confusion because of the statement. They needed more teaching. They needed further explanation.

Moments of transition in religious epochs are troubling. Most people simply do not want to accept the new acts performed by the Lord, and those He sends. They want to wait. They want to see if the new change prospers; let others decide first, and then join after there is proof of success. They want the security of following along with others. When there are 20 million followers of a new movement, then they can accept the new movement. Not before. The problem is that by the time a movement has acquired 20 million followers, the world has required such compromises to have been made that the original movement has been diluted, altered, compromised and weakened. It may be moving forward claiming to have authority, but it will likely have lost much of its power along the way.

Followers of the Lord who were there on the day of this sermon were being told how the new movement was to proceed. He perceives the insecurities of those who are listening. He will take time to explain what is coming next.

The Lord is patient. He will instruct those who follow Him sufficiently that they can go forward with His new dispensation. However, He will expect them to perform exactly as He has taught before they can receive exactly what He has promised.

It is perfect. It is ever the way of the Lord. When He makes an offer, anyone can accept it. But it must be accepted on the terms He established. If you cannot understand, it is not because He did not make it clear enough. Rather, it is because you will not obey in order to gain the light necessary to comprehend what He is teaching. It is your choice to draw away rather than toward Him. As a result, you cannot understand.

3 Nephi 15:3–5

"And he said unto them: Marvel not that I said unto you that old things had passed away, and that all things had become new. Behold, I say unto you that the law is fulfilled that was given unto Moses. Behold, I am he that gave the law, and I am he who covenanted with my people Israel; therefore, the law in me is fulfilled, for I have come to fulfil the law; therefore it hath an end."

Here is the Lord's announcement that He who gave the law to Moses. He was on the mount. He was the great I AM of the earlier covenant. He is Jehovah. He covenanted with "[His] people Israel." Indeed, it was He who both made the covenant, and then fulfilled it. He is the one who went before and the one who came after. He was the beginning and the end of the law of Moses. In Him it was fulfilled.

All the sacrifices offered in the Mosaic system of worship were designed to point to, and testify of Christ's ministry. He established the system beforehand to point to His mortal life. They testified of Him as the great and final sacrifice. From the Passover sacrifice of an unblemished lamb, to the altar of incense before the Holy of Holies, the entire Mosaic covenant was made to symbolize His life.

This was the reason He spent most of the day of His resurrection on a seven mile walk explaining to two of His followers that the entire system of worship they followed pointed to Him. His sacrifice was necessary because Moses and the prophets all pointed to Him.[1314] I've explained this further in the Appendix to *Eighteen Verses*

[1314] Luke 24:13–27 "And, behold, two of them went that same day to a village called Emmaus, which was from Jerusalem *about* threescore furlongs. And they talked together of all these things which had happened. And it came to pass, that, while they communed *together* and reasoned, Jesus himself drew near, and went with them. But their eyes were holden that they should not know him. And he said unto them, What manner of communications *are* these that ye have one to another, as ye walk, and are sad? And the one of them, whose name was Cleopas, answering said unto him, Art thou only a stranger in Jerusalem, and hast not known the things which are come to pass there in these days? And he said unto them, What things? And they said unto him, Concerning Jesus of Nazareth, which was a prophet mighty in deed and word before God and all the people: And how the chief priests and our rulers delivered him to be condemned to death, and have crucified him. But we trusted that it had been he which should have redeemed Israel: and beside all this, to day is the third day since these things were done. Yea, and certain women also of our company made us astonished, which were early at the sepulchre; And when they found not his body, they came, saying, that they had also seen a vision of angels, which said that he was alive. And certain of them which were with us went to the sepulchre, and found *it* even so as the women had said: but him they saw not. Then he said unto them, O fools, and slow of heart to believe all that the prophets have spoken: Ought not Christ to have suffered these things, and to enter into his glory? And beginning at Moses and all the prophets, he expounded unto them in all the scriptures the things concerning himself."

and won't repeat it here. He is affirming to the Nephites what He had earlier affirmed to Luke and Cleopas the day He was resurrected. (I've explained why I believe Luke to be one of these two in *Come, Let Us Adore Him*, and won't repeat it.)

When the original revelation was given to Moses, it pointed to His great mortal ministry. This is His way. He will tell us beforehand so that when the events occur we can recognize His hand.[1315]

These Nephites are not unlike us. They wondered at the transition from one era or dispensation to another. So also in our day there is to be a transition from the original message and promise into the fulfillment of the revelation and promise. The revelation given to us in 1830 when the Book of Mormon was published to the world was intended to inform us about the coming changes we will see through the Lord's hand. We have yet to see the larger fulfillment of the promised events contained in the Book of Mormon. Gentiles are in the spotlight. But as they fade economically, militarily, socially and politically from center stage, they will fade in significance from the Lord's final great work, as well. We spent months covering those promises and prophecies. They will all certainly come to pass. As they do, false traditions will not be able to keep pace with the rapid changes to come. The law given to Moses served to point to a greater work. The Book of Mormon prepares and points to another greater work soon to come, as well.

Do not think the Lord changes. He is ever the same. As a result, the tests, trials and experiences of believers in any generation will mirror one another. Some wondered at the Lord's fulfillment of the earlier law. There will also be those who are struck with wonder as the Book of Mormon prophecies unfold. If there was ever a time when the caution to be careful about false prophets pretending to be

---

[1315] Amos 3:7 "Surely the Lord God will do nothing, but he revealeth his secret unto his servants the prophets."

sheep, it is certainly in our generation. Keeping your eye on the Lord, and His promises is more important now than ever before. He is reliable, even if governments, others and institutions fail you.

The fulfillment of the Lord's covenants is a wonderful thing. When it happens it proves He cares[1316], He keeps covenants[1317], and He is in control.[1318] It is not something to fear, but instead to welcome. As things change, and the pace of change itself accelerates, take heart. Though there will be perplexities of nations with distress[1319], there is still the promise Abinadi reminded us of that the Lord will bring again Zion.[1320]

We ought to identify with the message Christ gave these Nephites. We are going to see similar fulfillment of covenant promises made by Him in the not so distant future.

[1316] D&C 133:52 "And now the year of my redeemed is come; and they shall mention the loving kindness of their Lord, and all that he has bestowed upon them according to his goodness, and according to his loving kindness, forever and ever."

[1317] Deuteronomy 7:9 "Know therefore that the Lord thy God, he *is* God, the faithful God, which keepeth covenant and mercy with them that love him and keep his commandments to a thousand generations;"

[1318] Psalms 93:1–5 "The Lord reigneth, he is clothed with majesty; the Lord is clothed with strength, *wherewith* he hath girded himself: the world also is stablished, that it cannot be moved. Thy throne *is* established of old: thou *art* from everlasting. The floods have lifted up, O Lord, the floods have lifted up their voice; the floods lift up their waves. The Lord on high *is* mightier than the noise of many waters, *yea, than* the mighty waves of the sea. Thy testimonies are very sure: holiness becometh thine house, O Lord, for ever."

[1319] Luke 21:25 "And there shall be signs in the sun, and in the moon, and in the stars; and upon the earth distress of nations, with perplexity; the sea and the waves roaring;"

[1320] Mosiah 15:29–31 "Yea, Lord, thy watchmen shall lift up their voice; with the voice together shall they sing; for they shall see eye to eye, when the Lord shall bring again Zion. Break forth into joy, sing together, ye waste places of Jerusalem; for the Lord hath comforted his people, he hath redeemed Jerusalem. The Lord hath made bare his holy arm in the eyes of all the nations; and all the ends of the earth shall see the salvation of our God."

3 Nephi 15:6–8

"Behold, I do not destroy the prophets, for as many as have not been fulfilled in me, verily I say unto you, shall all be fulfilled. And because I said unto you that old things have passed away, I do not destroy that which hath been spoken concerning things which are to come. For behold, the covenant which I have made with my people is not all fulfilled; but the law which was given unto Moses hath an end in me."

The Lord does not make a promise and fail to fulfill it.[1321] Therefore, when a promise has been made by Him, it will come to pass. But the promise must be His. No agent or spokesman can speak in His name and obligate Him to perform unless the words spoken are His. Even if a man should qualify to hold sealing power, that power will only bind what is in conformity with His word.[1322] There is no obligation on Him to perform what is not sealed by the Holy Spirit of Promise.[1323] So it is not every person who speaks, even if in a position of leading others, claiming "Lord, Lord" as they do, whose

---

[1321] D&C 1:38 "What I the Lord have spoken, I have spoken, and I excuse not myself; and though the heavens and the earth pass away, my word shall not pass away, but shall all be fulfilled, whether by mine own voice or by the voice of my servants, it is the same."

[1322] Helaman 10:5 "And now, because thou hast done this with such unwearyingness, behold, I will bless thee forever; and I will make thee mighty in word and in deed, in faith and in works; yea, even that all things shall be done unto thee according to thy word, for thou shalt not ask that which is contrary to my will."

[1323] D&C 132:18 "And again, verily I say unto you, if a man marry a wife, and make a covenant with her for time and for all eternity, if that covenant is not by me or by my word, which is my law, and is not sealed by the Holy Spirit of promise, through him whom I have anointed and appointed unto this power, then it is not valid neither of force when they are out of the world, because they are not joined by me, saith the Lord, neither by my word; when they are out of the world it cannot be received there, because the angels and the gods are appointed there, by whom they cannot pass; they cannot, therefore, inherit my glory; for my house is a house of order, saith the Lord God."
D&C 88:3 "Wherefore, I now send upon you another Comforter, even upon you my friends, that it may abide in your hearts, even the Holy Spirit of promise; which other Comforter is the same that I promised unto my disciples, as is recorded in the testimony of John."

words obligate the Lord to fulfill. But the opposite is also true. If the person is clothed with nothing other than the Lord's private commission to speak, if he speaks the Lord's words they will "all be fulfilled." Abinadi was so obscure a character that we don't know if he was Lamanite or Nephite. He is the only person in the entire Book of Mormon record with the name Abinadi. He came from nowhere, was imprisoned by the leading authorities of the church, and was killed by those who presumed to exercise judgment over him. Yet it was he who bore the Lord's words. The entire society he preached to were held to account for both his words and how they reacted to them (and him).

When the Lord speaks of fulfilling the things to come, He is both ratifying the past prophets whose words have not come to pass, and He is establishing an eternal principal. It is as true today as it was anciently. When a message comes from Him, it is binding. The message is His. The power to make His message binding upon mankind is His. The right to govern all mankind is His.

The first clarification the Lord wants the people to understand is that His words are, and will remain sovereign. They will not be rescinded. It is not the prophets, nor the promises of His great unfolding work foretold by prophetic messages that will end. It is only the law of observances given through Moses that has now been fulfilled. It is not abandoned, but rather it is fulfilled. It pointed to Him. He lived it. He fulfilled every foreshadow, every type, every promise under that law. It was His to give, and it was His life that fulfilled it.

The intergenerational work of saving mankind is always the same. The promise to save through the chosen lineage all of mankind is still in effect. It existed before Moses, and will continue after the fulfillment of the law of Moses. The great prophecies and promises pointing to His second coming remain in effect. His first coming only fulfilled Moses' law. His second will fulfill the rest of the promises concerning Him as the great Deliverer, the world's judge, and the one whose right it is to rule as "King of kings and Lord of lords."

The crowd entertained apprehensions that the prophets were now "destroyed" by Him. He made it clear that was not the case. This is why Isaiah and Zenock remain relevant to our day. This is why He will even quote from Isaiah and add Malachi to the Nephite scriptures. This is why the Lord continues to entrust men with messages which bind Him to do His final, strange work. He intends to both fulfill and inform us so we may prepare against the day of judgment. His mission is to redeem, not to surprise or confuse the worthy. If a person will but listen to Him and those He sends, they will be prepared for the coming calamities.

The consistency of this message is so profound that it reconfirms that Joseph Smith is not the source of the Book of Mormon. This is a record of the Lord's doings among an ancient and fallen people. It is not an invention of a New England farm boy. The idea Joseph Smith wrote this account is beyond incredible. It simply isn't true. This is from the Lord, not a man. A person can get closer to God by abiding its precepts than from any other book. It is the lifeline given to us for our day. We ignore it and dismiss it at our peril.

3 Nephi 15:9–10

"Behold, I am the law, and the light. Look unto me, and endure to the end, and ye shall live; for unto him that endureth to the end will I give eternal life. Behold, I have given unto you the commandments; therefore keep my commandments. And this is the law and the prophets, for they truly testified of me."

It is Christ who is "the law." Not a man or men. Nor even those sent by Him. They are relevant only to the extent they point to Him. When they attract notice for themselves, they interfere with His great work. He alone is the "law." He alone is the "light."

He answers the concerns these listeners have about the source they are now to look to for life and salvation. "Look unto me" He proclaims. He, not the law, is their future. They are to seek for and establish a more direct line of communication between themselves and Him.

He is the "law"—meaning that His words (both in the preceding sermon and in the revelations He will grant them) is to govern. Not a prior set of performances and ordinances.

He is the "light"—meaning, understanding will increase as they choose to follow Him. They will understand with increasing clarity as they move closer to Him. He will illuminate their understanding, because some things can only be apprehended when you draw close enough to Him for them to emerge from darkness and confusion.

"Look unto [Him]"—meaning, it is not a rule-book, ordinances or traditions which are to guide them. He will. Personally. By His involvement in their lives, through revelation, and with the comforter or Holy Ghost which He has promised to send.

"Endure to the end"—meaning, both here and in the hereafter. It will be a great while beyond this life before you have reached the "end" He desires you to attain. Therefore, enduring requires you to fight against all that opposes truth for so long as you are allowed to participate in the battle. Not passively, taking in what is wrong and showing tolerance for it, but instead actively standing for truth as long as you exist, here and hereafter.

"Ye shall live"—meaning, the kind of life which Christ gives. That life is not mortal, though you will begin it as a mortal. That is life eternal, which is to know Him and His Father. It was designed to begin here.

"To him that endureth to the end I will give eternal life"—meaning, such people will come to live as Christ and His Father live. Or, in other words, to know truth and be filled with light.[1324]

"Keep my commandments"—meaning, listen and respond to what He directs. Take what He offers. Do not decline to go and do as He bids you to do; not what you presume will please Him, but what He has counseled you to do. If you do not know what that is, then you do not read the scriptures and ask. You are deliberately without knowledge of what He would ask of you.

"This is the law and the prophets"—meaning, the culmination of all that has been given by Him is for man to come to know Him. This was the purpose behind all the symbols, all the rites, all the ordinances. It is still the purpose underlying it all. Come to Him. Not to a building and think yourself redeemed because you are part of a select group welcomed there. Come to Him. Not to a man who will promise you heaven itself, but to Him who will open to you the heavens.

"For they truly testify of [Him]"—meaning they have and do testify of Him. Not of themselves. Not of a program. Not of an organization. Not of men. They testify of Him. Continually. Not intermittently, occasionally and without knowledge of Him. They do not borrow light from others, but they testify of the things which they know from Him. They will always do so. This is one of the ways you can detect "wolves" from "sheep" as they come professing religion. The true sheep will testify of Him whom they know. The wolves will ask you to follow men, and they interfere with knowing Him. Though you do all the wolves bid you to do, yet you will grow more distant from Him.

[1324] D&C 93:28, 36 "He that keepeth his commandments receiveth truth and light, until he is glorified in truth and knoweth all things. . . . The glory of God is intelligence, or, in other words, light and truth."

Our Lord is indeed a consuming fire, and is unwilling to share adoration with mere men claiming themselves to be worthy of adoration.[1325]

3 Nephi 15:11–14

"And now it came to pass that when Jesus had spoken these words, he said unto those twelve whom he had chosen: Ye are my disciples; and ye are a light unto this people, who are a remnant of the house of Joseph. And behold, this is the land of your inheritance; and the Father hath given it unto you. And not at any time hath the Father given me commandment that I should tell it unto your brethren at Jerusalem."

Christ has identified Himself as the "light. " Now refers to His chosen twelve disciples as His "disciples," and a "light unto this people." Why? How can He be the "light" and also make disciples who follow Him a "light" to others as well? What would a disciple need to be in order for them to also reflect His light to others? How would that be accomplished? What happens if the disciples no longer reflect His light, but instead seek to be a light unto themselves?[1326]

Notice He identifies them as a "remnant of the house of Joseph." This would be Joseph of Egypt. Why is "this . . . the land of your inheritance" if it is the tribe of Joseph? How was Joseph given the Americas as his promised land? Was that foreseen? If so, how long has the Lord had in mind the establishment of Joseph in the promised land of the Americas?

Why is the "Father" the one who has given the land of inheritance to Joseph? Why not Jesus Christ? Why does the Father keep in His authority to divide the land for inheritance?

[1325] Deuteronomy 4:24 "For the Lord thy God *is* a consuming fire, *even* a jealous God."

[1326] 2 Nephi 26:29 "He commandeth that there shall be no priestcrafts; for, behold, priestcrafts are that men preach and set themselves up for a light unto the world, that they may get gain and praise of the world; but they seek not the welfare of Zion."

What does it mean that the Father did not give Christ "commandment that I should tell it unto your brethren at Jerusalem?" If Christ knew it, why wouldn't He tell it to the "brethren at Jerusalem?" Why would Christ know something of this significance and keep it to Himself?

I've explained in *The Second Comforter* the subject of the failure of the Nephites to ask about the "other sheep" which will occupy some of this phase of the sermon. I'm not going to repeat it here, but would refer you to that discussion on the topic.

Why do you suppose the Lord would point out this monumental failure of the disciples at Jerusalem to ask about the "other sheep?"[1327] What is it about the failure to seek knowledge from the Lord that makes people both stiffnecked and filled with unbelief?[1328]

When the Lord will tell those who ask of Him, why is it offensive to Him that people fail to ask?

Is the admonition to "ask, seek, knock" more than an admonition? Is it in fact a commandment? Are you required to search into the mysteries of God, and know more day by day as a result of inquiring of Him? Can you substitute for that by asking others about mysteries? Why not? Why is it essential to gain your knowledge from Him?

Does the Lord's phrasing tell you something important? ('not at any time hath the Father given me commandment that I should tell it

---

[1327] 3 Nephi 16:4 "And I command you that ye shall write these sayings after I am gone, that if it so be that my people at Jerusalem, they who have seen me and been with me in my ministry, do not ask the Father in my name, that they may receive a knowledge of you by the Holy Ghost, and also of the other tribes whom they know not of, that these sayings which ye shall write shall be kept and shall be manifested unto the Gentiles, that through the fulness of the Gentiles, the remnant of their seed, who shall be scattered forth upon the face of the earth because of their unbelief, may be brought in, or may be brought to a knowledge of me, their Redeemer."

[1328] 3 Nephi 15:18 "And now, because of stiffneckedness and unbelief they understood not my word; therefore I was commanded to say no more of the Father concerning this thing unto them."

unto your brethren at Jerusalem")? Is Christ constrained to not disclose until those at Jerusalem ask of Him?[1329] What does that say about how this area of revelation is governed? Must the inquiry precede the revelation? What does it mean about the duty to inquire? Again, I've explained this in *The Second Comforter*, and would refer you to that discussion.

There must be a "living relationship" between you and the Living God. If it is not alive, then God must be dead to you. And you dead to Him. Ask, for He has promised to answer. Seek, for He has just promised you will find. Knock, for He has just assured you it will open to you. Now He is walking through a subject where much could have been revealed had the inquiry been made. It will be followed in turn by the Nephite failure to ask about the "other sheep" just as those at Jerusalem failed to ask. Again, see the discussion in *The Second Comforter* for more on this.

The next portion of this sermon is dealt with in *The Second Comforter,* or in an earlier series of posts on this blog. I'm going to skip forward at this point to cover portions I have not discussed before.

[1329] 3 Nephi 16:4 "And I command you that ye shall write these sayings after I am gone, that if it so be that my people at Jerusalem, they who have seen me and been with me in my ministry, do not ask the Father in my name, that they may receive a knowledge of you by the Holy Ghost, and also of the other tribes whom they know not of, that these sayings which ye shall write shall be kept and shall be manifested unto the Gentiles, that through the fulness of the Gentiles, the remnant of their seed, who shall be scattered forth upon the face of the earth because of their unbelief, may be brought in, or may be brought to a knowledge of me, their Redeemer."

3 NEPHI 18

3 Nephi 18:1–2

"And it came to pass that Jesus commanded his Disciples that they should bring forth some bread and wine unto him. And while they were gone for bread and wine, he commanded the multitude that they should sit themselves down upon the earth."

The Lord requires His disciples to bring some bread and wine to Him. It suggests that all 12 of these disciples were asked to retrieve the items. "While they were gone for bread and wine" suggests that all 12 were involved. Perhaps there were others, as well. What is to take place next would likely require the effort of more than 12, for it will involve all 2,500 of those present.[1330]

We know what is coming. But taking this from the perspective of the Nephite audience, what would gathering "bread" foreshadow? Would they associate it with the Table of Shewbread? Would they expect a wave offering? What might their anticipation be as they awaited the arrival of the bread? How might their expectations have

---

[1330] 3 Nephi 17:25 "And the multitude did see and hear and bear record; and they know that their record is true for they all of them did see and hear, every man for himself; and they were in number about two thousand and five hundred souls; and they did consist of men, women, and children."

prepared them to receive a new ordinance? Would what follows have reaffirmed Christ fulfilled the law of Moses?

Why did the Lord ask for "wine?" What is there in the symbol of "wine" that testifies of Him? We know that in exigencies we can substitute water for wine.[1331] But the Lord requested "wine" to be brought for the ordinance He was about to introduce.

Section 27:2 was given because the Prophet Joseph was on his way to procure wine from an enemy who wished him harm. The possibility of the wine being adulterated was significant. Since an angel met Joseph on his way and revealed that a substitute could be used, it is likely if wine had been procured it would have been poisoned. The revelation gives precautions to be taken in preparing wine for the sacrament.[1332] The Saints were to prepare their own wine, and know it is safe for use in the sacrament.

To conform to this revelation, when the Saints moved west there was a "Wine Mission" established in Southern Utah. The Mormon Wine Mission did not have a formal separate existence, but was within the boundaries of the Cotton Mission of 1861. The Saints made their own wine because of D&C 27:3–4. If the Saints did not make the wine themselves, they were to use water. Therefore, to conform to the pattern of the Lord, and the revelation to guard against the mischief of enemies, the wine mission was established to produce wine for the sacrament.

Master vintner John C. Naegle was called by Brigham Young to establish and operate a winery in Toquerville and to instruct people

---

[1331] D&C 27:2 "For, behold, I say unto you, that it mattereth not what ye shall eat or what ye shall drink when ye partake of the sacrament, if it so be that ye do it with an eye single to my glory—remembering unto the Father my body which was laid down for you, and my blood which was shed for the remission of your sins."

[1332] D&C 27:3–4 "Wherefore, a commandment I give unto you, that you shall not purchase wine neither strong drink of your enemies; Wherefore, you shall partake of none except it is made new among you; yea, in this my Father's kingdom which shall be built up on the earth."

in the wine making process. The operation that Naegle presided over built a rock house for production which included a wine cellar underneath large enough to accommodate a wagon and a team of horses and allow them to turn around. In the production house were located the vats, presses, and other production equipment to produce and ferment the wine. They produced 500–gallon casks. The wine was shipped in smaller 40–gallon casks. It was distributed through ZCMI. Wine making became an important Southern Utah industry.

As President Grant elevated the Word of Wisdom from wise advice to a strict commandment, the practice of using wine in the sacrament came to an end. Since that time Latter-day Saints have taken a dim view of using wine in the sacrament.

Ask yourself, however, which is a more appropriate symbol of the Lord's supper: water or wine? If water were more so, then why did the Lord not institute use of water among the Nephites in the ceremony He is about to introduce in the verses which follow? Why is the sacrament prayer in both Moroni 5 and D&C 20:78–79 spoken for "wine" rather than water?

Are we morally superior because we use water instead of wine? Have we replaced a powerful symbol with a fanatical rule? Is there such a risk of adulterated or poisoned wine by anti-Mormon suppliers that we are justified in not using wine in the sacrament?

Well, the stage is being set by the Lord for the Nephites in this verse. He is gathering attention for an ordinance to be instituted. For His purposes, our Lord asks for bread and wine. We should not impose a false cultural assessment on these words. We should not rewrite them because of our prejudice and bigotry into something other than what they say.

From the symbol of the crushed grape, its blood spilled and then allowed to ferment, comes a symbol of the great work of the Lord. The grape juice changes through fermentation from something which affects the senses. As the Psalmist puts it wine gladdens the heart.[1333] His blood was spilled and then grew into a new power intended to gladden the heart of all those who will receive it.

The Prophet was overshadowed with foreboding on the day of his death. The reason Stephen Markham was not with them in the jail at the time the final assault took place was because he had been sent to purchase wine by the Prophet. The jailer allowed the wine to return to Joseph, Hyrum, John and Willard, but Steven Markham was excluded. There were only four in the jail when the killings occurred. The reason they sent for wine was to gladden their hearts and lift their spirits from the oppression which hung over them. It was a day of triumph for evil and the spirit of that day was heavy. The wine and John Taylor's singing were to console them in the terrible moments preceding the attack by 200 conspirators intent on killing Joseph and his brother.

We have become so fanatical about being teetotalers that the story of Joseph's use of wine on the day of his martyrdom is largely unknown today. Instead the tale of him refusing to drink whiskey as a sedative for the bone operation in his youth is retold. This is used to reinforce President Grant's harsh view of the Word of Wisdom.

Now, I am advocating nothing. I abstain from all forms of alcohol, possess a temple recommend, and accept the current view of absolute abstinence from any form of alcoholic consumption. But I do not believe it is a virtue. Nor do I believe substitution of water for wine increases the sanctity of the sacrament. It may do just the opposite.

It is often the case that when men attempt to "improve" on the Lord's teachings they go backward.

[1333] Psalms 104:15 "And wine *that* maketh glad the heart of man, *and* oil to make *his* face to shine, and bread *which* strengtheneth man's heart."

3 Nephi 18:3–4

"And when the Disciples had come with bread and wine, he took of the bread and brake and blessed it; and he gave unto the Disciples and commanded that they should eat. And when they had eaten and were filled, he commanded that they should give unto the multitude."

It is interesting these 12 are consistently referred to as "disciples" and not as "Apostles." There isn't a single "Apostle" in the Book of Mormon record. Only "disciples." There are 12 of them, and they are treated exactly as were the Apostles in Jerusalem. This was a distinction David Whitmer believed to be significant. He disliked the claim to restore Apostles.

Well, the disciples are described as "twelve" or "the twelve" in the first references. Then they are called "disciples." In the printing we have the "D" capitalized. This is an attempt by typesetting to distinguish and make more important these "big-D" disciples from other run-of-the-mill "small-d" disciples. But printers should not trick your mind into accepting the distinction. The Lord leveled these twelve. He made them merely disciples, which is a term applied with equal meaning to any of those who were present on that day.

The twelve are taught, then asked to teach. The twelve overhear the Lord break and then bless the bread. The record at this point does not include the words Christ used to bless the bread. Moroni corrects that by adding it in at a later time in the account. Here is what Christ taught when He blessed the bread:

"The manner of their elders and priests administering the flesh and blood of Christ unto the church; and they administered it according to the commandments of Christ; wherefore we know the manner to be true; and the elder or priest did minister it—And they did kneel down with the church, and pray to the Father in the name of Christ, saying: O God, the Eternal Father, we ask thee in the name of thy Son, Jesus Christ, to bless and sanctify this bread to the souls of all those who partake of it; that they may eat in remembrance of the body of thy Son, and witness unto thee, O God, the Eternal Father, that they are willing to take upon them the name of thy Son, and always remember him, and keep his commandments which he hath given them, that they may always have his Spirit to be with them. Amen." (Moroni 4:1–3.)

Notice in the narrative the Lord "commanded that they should eat." This is an interesting phrasing. It is more than an invitation. It is more than an offering. It is a commandment. Why? What is it about partaking of His sacrament, eating in remembrance of the body of Christ, that **must** be done? Why is it a commandment?

Notice, also, the disciples ate until they were "filled?" Does this mean their stomachs were sated? Does it mean their souls were affected? Does it mean both? How were they "filled" by partaking of the bread?

Did they need to be "filled" themselves before they would be permitted to minister to others? Was that why the Lord required them to first partake then be filled before they were commanded to minister to the others?

When they ministered to the multitude, what was it they "gave" to the multitude? Was it the bread alone? Was it also something that had "filled" them? What was going on in this ceremony?

Why would people who had seen, touched, knelt at the feet of the risen Lord, need to partake of the bread as a "witness" and "remembrance" of Him? How can this add to what they had already received? Why is the sacrament sacred enough to be celebrated by the Lord with people who are in His very presence?

Does this change in any respect how you view the sacrament? If so, how?

3 Nephi 18:5

"And when the multitude had eaten and were filled, he said unto the Disciples: Behold there shall one be ordained among you, and to him will I give power that he shall break bread and bless it and give it unto the people of my church, unto all those who shall believe and be baptized in my name."

Notice now the "multitude" takes part in eating the bread and "were filled." This raises the question of how they were filled. Were their stomachs filled because of the amount they ate? Did they eat until they were filled, or did they get filled on just a small amount of bread? Or was this a spiritual filling where each heart was touched and each person's countenance before the Lord filled with light?

This is a group which has just a few hours before engaged in a "hosanna shout" before the Lord.[1334]   Now, however, they are "filled." It is a profound moment with deep significance.

The Lord then tells the disciples that "there shall be one ordained among you" to break the bread. Notice it is "one." All twelve have been asked to pass the sacrament to the multitude, but from among them "shall one be ordained" to receive "power that he shall break bread and bless it." Why would only "one" be chosen to do this? All twelve had been given the power to baptize.[1335] Only one of them is to bless the sacrament. What does that suggest about the sanctity of the sacrament, if it is performed in the correct manner? Should it be viewed as a "higher ordinance" because of the more exclusive reservation of the "power" conferred by the Lord? What does that tell us

---

[1334] 3 Nephi 11:17 "Hosanna! Blessed be the name of the Most High God! And they did fall down at the feet of Jesus, and did worship him."

[1335] 3 Nephi 11:21–22 "And the Lord said unto him: I give unto you power that ye shall baptize this people when I am again ascended into heaven. And again the Lord called others, and said unto them likewise; and he gave unto them power to baptize. And he said unto them: On this wise shall ye baptize; and there shall be no disputations among you."

about the manner we ought to proceed? Have we missed something in our reading of these verses?

Now the record is written by Nephi.[1336] He is the first one called by the Lord.[1337] He is the first one given power to baptize by the Lord.[1338] But the identity of the person given "power that he shall break bread and bless it" is not recorded. We can know it is Nephi because he was always the one given the other power first. More to the point, however, we can know it was him because he kept the record. Had it been another, he would have told us. But since it was him, he declined to draw further attention to himself. Identifying himself previously was necessary for the narrative to be complete. Here, however, identifying himself would call undue attention. As a humble follower of Christ, it was not appropriate for him to do so, therefore the disciple is unnamed in our account.

Why is "power [to] break bread and bless it" conferred separately from the power to baptize? In our Section 20, the authority is coextensive.[1339] Why does the Lord separate it among the Nephites? Since we have this account, does it add any instruction for us about the significance of the sacrament?

[1336] 3 Nephi 1:2 "And Nephi, the son of Helaman, had departed out of the land of Zarahemla, giving charge unto his son Nephi, who was his eldest son, concerning the plates of brass, and all the records which had been kept, and all those things which had been kept sacred from the departure of Lehi out of Jerusalem."

[1337] 3 Nephi 11:18 "And it came to pass that he spake unto Nephi (for Nephi was among the multitude) and he commanded him that he should come forth."

[1338] 3 Nephi 11:18–21 "And it came to pass that he spake unto Nephi (for Nephi was among the multitude) and he commanded him that he should come forth. And Nephi arose and went forth, and bowed himself before the Lord and did kiss his feet. And the Lord commanded him that he should arise. And he arose and stood before him. And the Lord said unto him: I give unto you power that ye shall baptize this people when I am again ascended into heaven."

[1339] D&C 20:38–39, 46 "38 *The duty of the elders, priests, teachers, deacons, and members of the church of Christ*—An apostle is an elder, and it is his calling to baptize; And to ordain other elders, priests, teachers, and deacons; . . . The priest's duty is to preach, teach, expound, exhort, and baptize, and administer the sacrament,"

Sometimes we neglect things because of our familiarity with them. We presume wrongly that we understand them because of their frequent repetition. Here, however, the sacrament seems to take on greater significance. It achieves a pinnacle that exceeds even touching the risen Lord.

When we share food with one another, we become part of the same material. We share substance. When a meal is shared, life is shared. We become one of the same substance.

The substance which binds us is the "body of Christ" in symbol. Christ "broke" the bread before it was blessed. What does breaking the bread symbolize about Christ? How is His broken body intended to unite us with one another, and with Him?

Why is the broken bread distributed to those who "shall believe and be baptized in my name?" Does the order matter? Can a person be baptized before they believe, later come to believe, and then receive the sacrament correctly? Or must they come to believe first, then receive baptism second, before it is proper to partake of the sacrament? We've been working our way through the Lord's commandments deliberately trying to unlock their specific requirements. They are simple. They can be done by anyone. But they are specific and should be followed in the same manner the Lord instituted them. This is the "straight path" which He says is narrow and few will find. Perhaps it is not found because we proceed with inexactitude to do what He has laid out before us with exactness.

The Lord occupies the role as Master and as Example. He bids us to follow Him. And He tells us His way is plain. If we confuse it, muddle it, and fail to do it as He has asked us to do, then it is not His failure, but ours. He has made it clear that He respects no one, but is open to all. But it is open on the exact terms. And some times the terms are exacting.

3 Nephi 18:6–7

"And this shall ye always observe to do, even as I have done, even as I have broken bread and blessed it and given it unto you. And this shall ye do in remembrance of my body, which I have shown unto you. And it shall be a testimony unto the Father that ye do always remember me. And if ye do always remember me ye shall have my Spirit to be with you."

If the last post did not make the matter clear enough, the Lord emphasizes here the formula He has provided in this ordinance:

- "Always observe to do." It is to be done, and when it is done it is to be done in an "observant" way.
- "Even as I have done." His example is intended to clarify and define the manner the ordinance is to be observed. He regulates it by what He has done.
- "Even as I have broken bread and blessed it." The manner, the process, the gestures of breaking it first and then blessing it second, are to be followed exactly.
- "And given it unto you." When it is broken, then blessed, those who qualify by having repented and been baptized receive it as a gift or token from Christ. It is His body.

Now the Lord clarifies in explanation what He has earlier clarified in the blessing: This is to be done "in remembrance of [His] body." It is through His body that He, the living sacrifice, shows us the way. A loving God has died for us. His body is a testimony of life, obedience, sacrifice, cruelty, forgiveness, death, resurrection, immortality, power and glory. When you remember His life you should remember all that is associated with it.

Here the Lord reminds the Nephites they are to remember the body "which [He] has shown unto [them]." The sacred embrace and ceremony of recognition (a term I coined in *The Second Comforter*), should return to the mind of those present whenever they received the bread again. The Lord could give no greater testimony of what He had done, who He was, and how He served them than by showing to them His risen body still bearing the marks of crucifixion.

The act is intended to be a "testimony unto the Father that ye do always remember [Him]." The act of testifying is not composed merely of the act of eating the bread. To actually testify to the Father you must (1) repent, (2) be baptized, (3) receive the bread after it has been properly blessed with power, and (4) remember His body and the ten things symbolized through it.

This is the acceptable sacrifice the Father will receive as a "testimony" of Christ.

Should you perform this, then you will receive power to "have [His] Spirit to be with you."

These are simple steps. They are possible to be performed. When they are, the Father receives the act as a testimony before Him of the truth that you do always remember His Son. It will be recorded in heaven, and will be a witness for your salvation in the Day of Judgment.

These are solemn things. It is clear enough that we accomplish these things. But it is not clear how often they are performed, even in a church, which at one time, conducted a ceremony twice each Sunday, and today conducts it once each Sunday.

It is interesting the Lord should give us language that makes "observing to do" and "as He has done" a required part of the process. Those words are probably best when viewed in their clearest meaning, and accomplished with exactitude. Though He measures our hearts, when instructions are given in simplicity, one fair measure of the heart is how closely we follow the instruction.

Since the result is to have His Spirit to be with you, it should be a simple matter to determine by reflection if you have His Spirit as your companion. If you can feel that He is always with you, then you have an acceptable testimony to the Father. If you do not, then perhaps you should revisit the steps He has provided to see what you might improve. There is a law irrevocably decreed before the foundation of the world upon which all blessings are predicated. And when we receive any blessing from the Lord, it is by obedience to the law upon which the blessing is provided. Therefore, it makes sense that you can determine the extent to which you have followed the formula by the result promised. Having Christ's Spirit to be with you is significant enough proof that you should know the truth of the matter. Since you know the means by which to judge, see that you judge the matter correctly.[1340]

3 Nephi 18:8

"And it came to pass that when he said these words, he commanded his Disciples that they should take of the wine of the cup and drink of it, and that they should also give unto the multitude that they might drink of it."

In this description we do not have mention of the blessing pronounced upon the wine. Moroni will later clarify that it was blessed and provide us the words of His blessing:

"The manner of administering the wine—Behold, they took the cup, and said: O God, the Eternal Father, we ask thee, in the name of thy Son, Jesus Christ, to bless and sanctify this wine to the souls of all those who drink of it, that they may do it in remembrance of the blood of thy Son, which was shed for them; that they may witness unto thee, O God, the Eternal Father, that they do always remember him, that they may have his Spirit to be with them. Amen." (Moroni 5:1–2)

[1340] Moroni 7:18 "And now, my brethren, seeing that ye know the light by which ye may judge, which light is the light of Christ, see that ye do not judge wrongfully; for with that same judgment which ye judge ye shall also be judged."

Once again it is a "command" to partake. The Lord, knowing how critical this act is for salvation and a testimony before the Father, makes it a command that the disciples drink of it.

Wine was generally either purple or red. Our blood is purple when deprived of oxygen in our veins, and red when filled with oxygen in our arteries. These two colors of blood inside our bodies are akin to the predominate colors of wine.

Once again it is the disciples who partake first. Then, after having partaken, they pass it to the multitude. This illustrates the practice of receiving it before being able to pass it to others. It is not possible to pass along what has not first been received. This is true of all the Lord's ordinances. It is one of the reasons Alma re-baptized himself the instant he first began to baptize others.[1341] Those who bless are to be sanctified by partaking, then they pass the sacrament as sanctified ministers. Those who are passing are not more important, but rather they are first purified. Then those to whom they minister may receive the ordinance from those who are already clean.

Our modern practice is to pass the sacrament first to the "presiding authority" who is present. The presiding authority (who is always mentioned at the beginning of the meeting) is identified, and then the priests who pass the sacrament bring it to that person first. After he partakes, the sacrament is passed to others. We show great deference to authority in our system. In the 3 Nephi events presided over by the Lord, He shows great deference to purity.

The Lord's commandment to the disciples is followed by the instruction to provide the wine to the multitude "that they might drink." The ones officiating are "commanded," whereas the multitude is provided the opportunity to follow by example. Instead of a

---

[1341] Mosiah 18:14 "And after Alma had said these words, both Alma and Helam were buried in the water; and they arose and came forth out of the water rejoicing, being filled with the Spirit."

"commandment" to the multitude, there is an invitation. Clearly the Lord understands the importance of example and respects free will. Those who want to follow Him closest will be told what they must do. Then others are invited to follow of their own free will, and not by compulsion.

This systematic progression begins with knowledge of the Lord. They met Him. They felt the prints in His side, hands and feet. They had no veil separating them from Him. Yet, despite this knowledge, He walks them through ordinances where they qualify to return permanently to His presence. The ordinances are important enough for the Risen Lord to personally conduct and instruct on how to perform them. It is not merely what we believe, nor what we understand, but it is also what we do that matters. We must follow Him and His Divinely ordained ordinances. But to do so we need to perform them as He has instructed.

We require a priest to repeat the entire sacrament prayer if he gets a word wrong or adds a word while pronouncing the blessing. In this we show how exact we believe the ordinance is to be followed. That is a proposition with which I wholly agree. We should perform it in every particular as the Lord has instructed. When we do, then the promise of having His Spirit to always be with us is realized.

3 Nephi 18:9

"And it came to pass that they did so, and did drink of it and were filled; and they gave unto the multitude, and they did drink, and they were filled."

Partaking of the broken bread filled the disciples, and then the multitude, so again drinking the wine filled both.

What were they filled with?

Since this is an ordinance where the promised result is to "have His Spirit to be with them,"[1342] is any meaning of "filled" adequate apart from being filled with His Spirit? Clearly this ceremony is not performed to merely fill the belly. It hearkens back to His promise to those who hunger and thirst for righteousness, that they are to be filled. What the Lord presents in ceremony is the fulfillment of the earlier promise in His sermon. There is a beautiful symmetry to His sermon, His promise, the catalyst ordinance, and the reality of being "filled" which is missing from the New Testament record. In this respect, as in so many others, the Book of Mormon is the preferred, and more revealing account of the Lord's ministry.

The Lord's work is to bring about redemption for mankind. He redeems. In ceremony, and now in reality, He is working with a multitude to bring about their preparation and redemption. It is a Master Teacher, proving by His words and deeds, that He knows how to lead souls to salvation.

It is of interest that the record prepared by Mormon in such a painstaking effort takes the time to include these details for our instruction. They are intended not merely as history, but also as a guide. The plan of salvation is to be shared, so that others may follow it and themselves be "filled" with His Spirit.

Now note the prayers all refer to Christ's Spirit. This is something apart from the Holy Ghost. It is Christ's Spirit which is to "always be with them."

What does it mean to have Christ's Spirit to be with you? To guide you?

This is an important point, and worthy of some discussion by Joseph in *The Lectures on Faith*. If you haven't revisited that little book

---

[1342] 3 Nephi 18:7 "And this shall ye do in remembrance of my body, which I have shown unto you. And it shall be a testimony unto the Father that ye do always remember me. And if ye do always remember me ye shall have my Spirit to be with you."

and that discussion for a while, you may want to do that. I've recommended that it be read once a year. The Lectures on Faith was added to the scriptures as part of the Doctrine and Covenants. It was subsequently removed without a Church vote to agree to its removal. However, the new publications adding sections were sustained, and the tradition we have is that by sustaining the new versions with additions, it implies we also sustained the deletions. Therefore, they stand removed. Despite that, it is worth another read through, much like reading any scripture, it should happen at least annually.

The Spirit of Christ is also referred to in D&C 84.[1343] It is also described using the word "light" instead of His Spirit[1344]. If you read those carefully you realize that connecting with His Spirit or His light will also put you in contact with everything else governed by Him. He is the light which "enlighteneth your eyes, which is the same light that quickeneth your understandings".

This is why Joseph commented that the closer a man draws to God the clearer his understanding will be on all subjects. Greater light means clearer perception. It involves discerning between truth and error. It allows you to see what is dark, and who is dark, and

---

[1343] D&C 84:45–47 "For the word of the Lord is truth, and whatsoever is truth is light, and whatsoever is light is Spirit, even the Spirit of Jesus Christ. And the Spirit giveth light to every man that cometh into the world; and the Spirit enlighteneth every man through the world, that hearkeneth to the voice of the Spirit. And every one that hearkeneth to the voice of the Spirit cometh unto God, even the Father."

[1344] D&C 88:5–13 "Which glory is that of the church of the Firstborn, even of God, the holiest of all, through Jesus Christ his Son— He that ascended up on high, as also he descended below all things, in that he comprehended all things, that he might be in all and through all things, the light of truth; Which truth shineth. This is the light of Christ. As also he is in the sun, and the light of the sun, and the power thereof by which it was made. As also he is in the moon, and is the light of the moon, and the power thereof by which it was made; As also the light of the stars, and the power thereof by which they were made; And the earth also, and the power thereof, even the earth upon which you stand. And the light which shineth, which giveth you light, is through him who enlighteneth your eyes, which is the same light that quickeneth your understandings; Which light proceedeth forth from the presence of God to fill the immensity of space— The light which is in all things, which giveth life to all things, which is the law by which all things are governed, even the power of God who sitteth upon his throne, who is in the bosom of eternity, who is in the midst of all things."

what is light and who is filled with light. The light of a person's countenance is upon them, and if the Lord's Spirit fills you then you can see others just as He sees them.

It was His Spirit that enabled the Nephites to become one. With it, Zion becomes possible. Without it, Zion is only a theory to be abused and misunderstood. Without it, Zion is a vain ambition of conspiring men. It will not come to pass. With His Spirit, Zion is inevitable, because He will bring again Zion. If you would like to see the course of this doomed people changed at least as to your part, then these teachings and following these ordinances are the means by which the Lord's Spirit becomes available to you.

3 Nephi 18:10

"And when the Disciples had done this, Jesus said unto them: Blessed are ye for this thing which ye have done, for this is fulfilling my commandments, and this doth witness unto the Father that ye are willing to do that which I have commanded you."

The phrasing is ambiguous but becomes clear from context. The reference to "big-D" disciples actually introduces the ambiguity. If the printer had left it "little-d" disciples then the meaning would be clear. The "thing which ye have done" is a reference to partaking of the wine. By introducing the "big-D" disciple term it can change the entire thing to be "the thing which ye have done" is to pass the sacrament, rather than to partake of it.

Well, the "thing which ye have done" that prompts the Lord to proclaim "Blessed are ye" is to have symbolically partaken of His blood. They have a part of Him by having eaten of His flesh and drank of His blood. They are now among those who demonstrate they hunger and thirst after righteousness. They are disciples indeed.

Followers of the Master. Obedient to Him and willing to take His name upon them.

This is again identified as a "witness unto the Father" rather than a witness unto anyone else. It is not even a witness unto Christ. Nor is it a witness unto one another. It is a witness unto the Father.

This sacred event marks the testimony of faith by those who follow the Lord as a witness to the Father. These people prove they have faith in, and will obey His Son. The Father provided the Son as the Redeemer of all mankind. The only way back into the exalted state of the Father is through the saving sacrifice of the Son. It was the Son who opened the door for that return by the burdens He assumed while in His mortal body. He came under the same circumstances we did. He was separated from the Father by the veil. He suffered weaknesses of the body. He suffered the temptations of mankind, and He gave them no heed.[1345] This made it possible for Him to bring many others to glory.[1346]

To have part in His glory, we must partake of His flesh and blood. Both symbolically by our own bodies being made a living sacrifice,[1347] and through ordinance by partaking of the symbols of His life, death, resurrection. For the body of Christ rose from the dead, and we have that same hope. If we are to follow Him, we must be like Him. Taking upon ourselves His flesh and blood is not optional. It must be done to testify to the Father, who alone accepts us into His family. If we think to take upon us the name of Christ, but fail

---

[1345] D&C 20:22 "He suffered temptations but gave no heed unto them."

[1346] Hebrews 2:10 "For it became him, for whom *are* all things, and by whom *are* all things, in bringing many sons unto glory, to make the captain of their salvation perfect through sufferings."

[1347] Romans 12:1 "I beseech you therefore, brethren, by the mercies of God, that ye present your bodies a living sacrifice, holy, acceptable unto God, *which is* your reasonable service."

to have this witness before the Father, then we have failed to secure the required testimony before the Father.

This is a required process for those who are His.

3 Nephi 18:11

> "And this shall ye always do to those who repent and are baptized in my name; and ye shall do it in remembrance of my blood, which I have shed for you, that ye may witness unto the Father that ye do always remember me. And if ye do always remember me ye shall have my Spirit to be with you."

The prayer pronounced upon the sacrament reflects these same aspirations. However, this is not a petition in prayer, but a promise from the Lord. He affirms that for those who have "repented" of their sins, and "are baptized" in His name, He promises a result.

When, having done as He has asked, a person remembers His blood through this ordinance, bearing in mind that it was shed "for you" then you can properly "witness unto the Father." The witness you make to the Father by this remembrance is that "ye do always remember Christ."

This memorial before the Father, when done right, results in the promise of Christ that "ye shall always have His spirit to be with you."

This is a covenant. This is the Lord promising. His word cannot fail. He is establishing for you the means by which you can have as your guide and companion His Spirit. His light. His presence in your life.

This is more intimate than touching His side, hands and feet. This is to have His Spirit within your touch at all times. You become an extension of Him, properly taking His name upon you. For you are then, indeed, a Christian.

He will christen or anoint you, not with the symbol of oil, but with the reality of His Spirit. This anointing is the real thing, of which the oil was meant only to testify.

The Holy Ghost was intended to become a companion at the time of baptism. The Spirit of Christ is intended to become a companion in your very person as well. When there are two members of the Godhead represented in your living person, then it is the Father who receives this testimony of you, about you, by you and for you. You become His, for these three are one.

There is more going on here than an ordinance and a testimony. This is the means by which a link is formed that can and will result in the Father taking that which is corruptible and changing it into that which is incorruptible. Though, like Christ, a man or woman may be required to lay down their life, they shall have power given them to take it up again. For that which has been touched by the incorruptible power of His Spirit cannot be left without hope in the grave. All such people die firm in the knowledge they are promised a glorious resurrection.[1348]

This, then, is eternal life.

3 Nephi 18:12–13

"And I give unto you a commandment that ye shall do these things. And if ye shall always do these things blessed are ye, for ye are built upon my rock. But whoso among you shall do more or less than these are not built upon my rock, but are built upon a sandy foundation; and when the rain descends, and the floods come, and the winds blow, and beat upon them, they shall fall, and the gates of hell are ready open to receive them."

[1348] D&C 138:14 "All these had departed the mortal life, firm in the hope of a glorious resurrection, through the grace of God the Father and his Only Begotten Son, Jesus Christ."

The Lord again returns to the earlier sermon's language and meaning. He reiterates how building upon the rock belonging to Him is done by observing the ordinances established by Him.

You should not do "more" than He has commanded.

You must not do "less" than He has instructed.

You must do as He has commanded, instructed, and shown. He does it to provide by His example, the way it is to be done.

If we err it is not because He failed to teach. He has made it plain to us that we may know the way to follow.

When we do more or less, we find ourselves in the sand, and no longer standing upon Him, the Rock of Heaven.[1349]

Those finding themselves in the tempest of this life, tossed about by the turbulence of the sins and errors found at every turn, will fall if they are not built upon Him, the Rock of Heaven. They cannot withstand the storm because they are not anchored in Him who has the power to endure, to preserve and to save. They may cry out "Lord, Lord" but they did not do what He said. He will respond He never knew them. To be known by Him in that day will require the testimony before the Father to have been made. For the means by which He can recognize and protect them from the gates of hell is found in that testimony before the Father, given as a result of this ordinance.

The way is plain, simple, even easy. It is marked by Him at every turn. There is no great elusive mountain to climb. If we fail, it is because we are unwilling to look to Him and be saved. It is because we

---

[1349] Moses 7:53 "And the Lord said: Blessed is he through whose seed Messiah shall come; for he saith—I am Messiah, the King of Zion, the Rock of Heaven, which is broad as eternity; whoso cometh in at the gate and climbeth up by me shall never fall; wherefore, blessed are they of whom I have spoken, for they shall come forth with songs of everlasting joy."

despise the simplicity of it all, and look for something more. We refuse to look upon Him who alone can save.[1350]

It is always amusing to see those who wrongly conclude that the Lord has abandoned His people because they fail to experience any power from Him. They do not do what the Lord commands, then they fail to receive the blessing He promised. When it is not received, they blame Him. When all along it was their own failure to do as He commanded that caused their problems.[1351]

Those who claim to be His, calling out "Lord, Lord," but who do not do what He has instructed cannot blame the Lord. They have only themselves to blame.

3 Nephi 18:14

"Therefore blessed are ye if ye shall keep my commandments, which the Father hath commanded me that I should give unto you."

The Lord's whole purpose is to bless us. He offers blessings freely. But we will not accept them. We refuse to offer an acceptable sacrifice before the Lord. It will be a long time yet before the sons of

---

[1350] 1 Nephi 17:41 "And he did straiten them in the wilderness with his rod; for they hardened their hearts, even as ye have; and the Lord straitened them because of their iniquity. He sent fiery flying serpents among them; and after they were bitten he prepared a way that they might be healed; and the labor which they had to perform was to look; and because of the simpleness of the way, or the easiness of it, there were many who perished."

[1351] D&C 58:31–33 "Who am I, saith the Lord, that have promised and have not fulfilled? I command and men obey not; I revoke and they receive not the blessing. Then they say in their hearts: This is not the work of the Lord, for his promises are not fulfilled. But wo unto such, for their reward lurketh beneath, and not from above."

Levi offer an offering in righteousness to the Lord.[1352] The sacramental offering is a type of the earlier Levitical offerings.

However, when an acceptable offering has been made, the Lord will always bless those who keep the commandments respecting His ordinances.

Changing these things in the least robs the ordinances of the very power they were intended to confer.[1353]

If you keep His commandments, the inevitable result is a blessing from Him. The greatest of these blessings is, of course, to be remembered by Him in the day of judgment. The next greatest is to always have His Spirit to be with you.

It is of note that Christ points to the Father in all things, and therefore points to the Father in this teaching, as well. The commandments He teaches are those "which the Father hath commanded [Him] that [He] should give unto you." In every respect the Son points to the Father. It is always the Father's will and the Father's glory Christ seeks to uphold.[1354]

The Son seeks our glory and exaltation, while giving credit to the Father for all He does. Though the Savior occupies the central role in the process, He serves others. Selflessly He instructs us on how we may be blessed and glorified. Selflessly He points to the Father as the

---

[1352] D&C 13:1 "Upon you my fellow servants, in the name of Messiah I confer the Priesthood of Aaron, which holds the keys of the ministering of angels, and of the gospel of repentance, and of baptism by immersion for the remission of sins; and this shall never be taken again from the earth, until the sons of Levi do offer again an offering unto the Lord in righteousness."
JS–H 1:69 "Upon you my fellow servants, in the name of Messiah, I confer the Priesthood of Aaron, which holds the keys of the ministering of angels, and of the gospel of repentance, and of baptism by immersion for the remission of sins; and this shall never be taken again from the earth until the sons of Levi do offer again an offering unto the Lord in righteousness."

[1353] Isaiah 24:5 "The earth also is defiled under the inhabitants thereof; because they have transgressed the laws, changed the ordinance, broken the everlasting covenant."

[1354] Moses 4:2 "But, behold, my Beloved Son, which was my Beloved and Chosen from the beginning, said unto me—Father, thy will be done, and the glory be thine forever."

one to receive your testimony by obedience. Selflessly He explains the Father is the one who has commanded these things. But through it all, it is Christ who has been the messenger of salvation. He is the one whose sacrifice made possible our redemption. It is Christ whose body and blood we must partake for redemption. It is Christ of whom the Father testifies.[1355] Christ bears testimony of the Father. The Father bears record of the Son. In one eternal round, they form a circle. It is Christ's work and the Father's commandment which invites us to join in that circle and become one with Them.

How simple the ways provided for us in this condescension of God. How plain the way has been given. Yet we find reasons to do "more or less" than what is asked. For that we forfeit blessings which might otherwise have been ours.

This is powerful material. Assuming we decide to "do" rather than to "say."

3 Nephi 18:15

"Verily, verily, I say unto you, ye must watch and pray always, lest ye be tempted by the devil, and ye be led away captive by him."

The caution is always added to "watch and pray always." It is not enough to fall into the correct way. You must prevent, at every turn, a misstep taking you off that path.

The devil always tempts to "do more or less" than we are instructed. To accomplish his desired results, the devil only needs to persuade you to do a little more, or do a little less, and he will have

---

[1355] 3 Nephi 11:7 "Behold my Beloved Son, in whom I am well pleased, in whom I have glorified my name—hear ye him."
Matthew 17:5 "While he yet spake, behold, a bright cloud overshadowed them: and behold a voice out of the cloud, which said, This is my beloved Son, in whom I am well pleased; hear ye him."
Luke 9:35 "And there came a voice out of the cloud, saying, This is my beloved Son: hear him."

succeeded. He does not need to cut you off by a great big sin when a small one will work just as well.

Lately, we've been looking carefully at the details of the account of the sacrament among the Nephites. As with anything, varying this by "more or less" is a temptation. That temptation comes from the devil. He knows better than any of us that changing ordinances is intended to rob them of their efficacy.

When good intentions lead to the conclusion that you can or ought to change an ordinance in any particular, it does not matter how well intended the underlying reason is for the change. The purpose is to defile. As Isaiah put it: "The earth also is defiled under the inhabitants thereof; because they have transgressed the laws, changed the ordinance, broken the everlasting covenant."[1356] For what reason would you change the Lord's ordinances:

- People are not interested in them?
- People are offended by them?
- They seem to include unimportant details?
- They seem to conflict with your understanding of another scripture?
- The performance is uninspiring to the skeptical mind?
- The performance can be improved by a change?
- They seem to hold no real meaning?
- They can have better acceptance if altered?
- People no longer know or understand them?
- People just don't care enough to observe the details?

Perhaps there are ten-thousand reasons for making a change. Maybe you are not tempted by all, but just one of those reasons. But so long as there is one reason which persuades you, that is enough. The devil knows he must only persuade you on one point, one time

---

[1356] Isaiah 24:5 "The earth also is defiled under the inhabitants thereof; because they have transgressed the laws, changed the ordinance, broken the everlasting covenant."

to get you to change the ordinance. Once he has managed that, he has robbed the ordinance of power, defiled the earth because of its inhabitants, persuaded you to transgress the law, and destroyed the everlasting covenant.

This is a wonderful teaching from Christ. He would like us to be ever watchful precisely because the devil intends to interrupt the Gospel every time it appears on the earth. In general, it takes less than 200 years for an apostasy to set in among the people chosen by God to receive a dispensation of the Gospel. Only in a few isolated instances, among a few people, have there been occasions where the ordinances remained unchanged. Those people successfully resisted every argument presented in favor of changing the ordinances and breaking the covenant with God.

The goal of our adversary is to lead us into captivity. When we lose the key to knowledge because we forfeit the light given by ordinance to us, then we struggle about in the dark. Left to your own reasoning, it is possible to establish all kinds of aberrations, calling bad good, and the light darkness. Then only isolated voices remain to challenge the overwhelming majority who believe they have improved things by their tampering.

This pattern is warned against by the Lord. He lays bare the source of such things. It is all of the devil. He is the architect of that ruin.

So it is with the entire sermon the Lord has delivered, along with the new ordinance He has just introduced. The whole is meant to be understood and followed. It is the path back to truth and light. It was meant to become our guide, our way of life. For the most part, we have very good reasons why we do not follow it.

3 Nephi 18:16

"And as I have prayed among you even so shall ye pray in my church, among my people who do repent and are baptized in my name. Behold I am the light; I have set an example for you."

The "prayer" referred to here is the sacrament prayer. There is one among the twelve disciples who is given power to dedicate the emblems of the sacrament. But all of them are to do likewise in the Church in the future.

He has provided the example for them to follow. He has taught them how, and then demonstrated how. He has explained why. Now He tells them to do "even so" in His church.

But notice once again the Lord defines His church. It is those who "do repent and are baptized in [His] name." This ordinance is not for those who are casual investigators of His doctrine. It is not for those who, though baptized, have not repented. It is reserved for those having the proper qualifications. Without having done these things first, the sacrament of the Lord's body and blood are eaten and drank to their condemnation. Instead of it being a testimony before the Father of their faithfulness, it becomes a testimony of their unfaithfulness.

Notice the Lord explains His role as "light." He "set an example for you" and therefore is "the light." The "light" is the guide. It is the pattern. It shows you the way to go. He has done that in word and in action, so that He can claim to be the "light" for those to follow.

In turn, He has told these disciples they must also become "a light unto the people."[1357] To accomplish that it is essential they must "set an example for" them; meaning that they follow as the Lord has led them. Not an example of vainglory or superiority. Instead to

---

[1357] 3 Nephi 15:12 "Ye are my disciples; and ye are a light unto this people, who are a remnant of the house of Joseph."

meekly do as He has bidden them to do. Adding nothing, leaving nothing undone. Honing in on the things He would have done, and going about to do them.

The "light" must reflect the Lord's teachings and the Father's will. Otherwise it is darkness. A light cannot shine as His if it is distorted to reflect credit upon the man rather than the True Light, our Lord. When an erring soul entertains mistaken admiration for a man, they are damned.[1358] Therefore, if a person is called upon to be a light, they cannot seek to attract notice for themselves.

The Lord saves. Messengers sent by Him point to Him. They mirror His acts, teachings and practices. They do not seek their own will, but only the will of Him who sends them.

Throughout this visit between the Lord and the Nephites, we are given an extended view of how the Lord establishes His church and doctrine. So long as it is followed, it has the power to allow mankind to always have His Spirit to be with the followers. However, when they depart from the practices and keep merely a form of godliness, they lose the power He sends to us.

These teachings are important enough for the Lord to dwell on, and Mormon to etch them into metal plates. They should be carefully studied, explicitly followed, and greatly appreciated.

[1358] D&C 76:99–101 "For these are they who are of Paul, and of Apollos, and of Cephas. These are they who say they are some of one and some of another—some of Christ and some of John, and some of Moses, and some of Elias, and some of Esaias, and some of Isaiah, and some of Enoch; But received not the gospel, neither the testimony of Jesus, neither the prophets, neither the everlasting covenant."

3 Nephi 18:17–18

> "And it came to pass that when Jesus had spoken these words unto his Disciples, he turned again unto the multitude and said unto them: Behold, verily, verily, I say unto you, ye must watch and pray always lest ye enter into temptation; for Satan desireth to have you, that he may sift you as wheat."

The image of Satan "sifting as wheat" is interesting for several reasons. One involves the early claim, now discredited, that the ancient Nephite civilization did not cultivate wheat. Under that argument they would not have understood the analogy. However, once stores of ancient wheat and barley were discovered, the criticism was debunked. There's a BYU article on this by Robert R. Bennett titled "Barley and Wheat in the Book of Mormon."

Satan "desires to have you." You are wanted. Not because he has your best interest in mind, but because he wants control. He wants to gain power over others, limit their choices, and make them his slaves.

The manner wheat was sifted was to use a sieve to separate grain from husks, tares, stones and other chaff. The wheat would be kept, the refuse tossed into a pile to be discarded. Sifting was vigorous and tossed the grain about to separate it. This suggests being completely under Satan's control, being tossed about, and being discarded. It is a horrifying image, because the result would be domination by the adversary of your soul.

Satan's great desire has always been to separate men from their agency. He seeks to enslave those who fall under his power. Using wickedness, appetites of the flesh, drug dependence or other addictions, the end goal is always the same. He seeks control. He craves the god-like power to have dominion over others. Since he forfeited any right to gain power in a godly way, he seeks now ungodly power through coercion and compulsion.

Whenever you find compulsion, dominion, control, or force being employed, you have found Satan.[1359] He wants to cut you off from
heaven, and uses control to limit access to the heavens. When people
voluntarily surrender their responsibility to follow the Lord, Satan
has acquired by persuasion what he craves to acquire through force.

The antidote for falling under Satan's control is to "watch and
pray always." Why watch? Why "pray always?"

To watch is to be observant and detect elements of control, dominion and compulsion. It is to become vigilant in separating the will
of men from the will of God. It is to keep the Lord's teachings in
mind, and to measure any person's teachings, actions and persuasions
against the standard the Lord has explained.

To "pray always" is to retain a personal connection with heaven.
Particularly, to retain that connection through the Holy Ghost, and
through Christ's Spirit, you seek to always have with you. If this is a
lively connection, you are able to avoid being "sifted." If it lapses
into darkness, you are vulnerable to being taken captive.

These are simple expressions anyone can understand. It is not the
difficulty of the teaching, but the difficulty of the implementation
which keeps people bound in darkness. Traditions, widespread acceptance of false ideas, excuses for failure, and rationalizations for
why things are as they are, all prevent us from reading these teachings
with the eyes of a child. The Lord's teachings are distorted even as

---

[1359] D&C 121:37–41 "That they may be conferred upon us, it is true; but when we
undertake to cover our sins, or to gratify our pride, our vain ambition, or to exercise
control or dominion or compulsion upon the souls of the children of men, in any
degree of unrighteousness, behold, the heavens withdraw themselves; the Spirit of the
Lord is grieved; and when it is withdrawn, Amen to the priesthood or the authority of
that man. Behold, ere he is aware, he is left unto himself, to kick against the pricks, to
persecute the saints, and to fight against God. We have learned by sad experience that it
is the nature and disposition of almost all men, as soon as they get a little authority, as
they suppose, they will immediately begin to exercise unrighteous dominion. Hence
many are called, but few are chosen. No power or influence can or ought to be maintained by virtue of the priesthood, only by persuasion, by long-suffering, by gentleness
and meekness, and by love unfeigned;"

they are being read by the blinders we wear. When the eye is filled with darkness, how great is the darkness within. Christ spoke about that in the previous sermon.

3 Nephi 18:19–20

"Therefore ye must always pray unto the Father in my name; And whatsoever ye shall ask the Father in my name, which is right, believing that ye shall receive, behold it shall be given unto you."

When you "always pray unto the Father" in Christ's name, there will be an inevitable closeness between you and Him. You draw closer to those with whom you associate. Praying always triggers that association. As with everything else, it is dynamic, not static. You move closer or you move farther apart, but you do not remain static.

What does "whatsoever ye shall ask" include? If you think Christ is inviting you to turn the Father into a short-order cook, jumping to your will, you do not understand this process. However, this is how some people view prayer. It is a list of wants, desires and aspirations to be imposed on the Father.

What does the limitation "which is right" do to modify "whatsoever ye shall ask?"

What does "whatsoever ye shall ask, which is right" mean?

Who determines whether a request you make "is right?" What about those occasions when the Lord invites someone to "ask anything of Him"?[1360] Is there any limit to what might be asked at that

---

[1360] 1 Kings 3:5 "In Gibeon the Lord appeared to Solomon in a dream by night: and God said, Ask what I shall give thee."
3 Nephi 28:1 "And it came to pass when Jesus had said these words, he spake unto his disciples, one by one, saying unto them: What is it that ye desire of me, after that I am gone to the Father?" (If you do not understand this concept it is explained in *Beloved Enos*. It occurs in a very specific setting.)

moment? What does that suggest about those persons this offer is extended?

The purpose of this teaching by the Lord is to invite harmony between those who ask, and the Father, who gives. Inspired requests to Him are intended to come to you by revelation, so you may understand what you should ask. Then, when you have conformed your will to His, what you receive is according to His will, and not your own.

Throughout, the Lord is leading those who will follow into a condition of unity with the Father and the Son. The goal has always been the same. The teachings have always been the same. The Lord's great Intercessory Prayer taught the same concept.[1361] The ability to be "one" with them is not accomplished by men persuading God to follow man's will. It is accomplished in the same manner as Christ

---

[1361] John 17:1–26 "These words spake Jesus, and lifted up his eyes to heaven, and said, Father, the hour is come; glorify thy Son, that thy Son also may glorify thee: As thou hast given him power over all flesh, that he should give eternal life to as many as thou hast given him. And this is life eternal, that they might know thee the only true God, and Jesus Christ, whom thou hast sent. I have glorified thee on the earth: I have finished the work which thou gavest me to do. And now, O Father, glorify thou me with thine own self with the glory which I had with thee before the world was. I have manifested thy name unto the men which thou gavest me out of the world: thine they were, and thou gavest them me; and they have kept thy word. Now they have known that all things whatsoever thou hast given me are of thee. For I have given unto them the words which thou gavest me; and they have received *them,* and have known surely that I came out from thee, and they have believed that thou didst send me. I pray for them: I pray not for the world, but for them which thou hast given me; for they are thine. And all mine are thine, and thine are mine; and I am glorified in them. And now I am no more in the world, but these are in the world, and I come to thee. Holy Father, keep through thine own name those whom thou hast given me, that they may be one, as we *are.* While I was with them in the world, I kept them in thy name: those that thou gavest me I have kept, and none of them is lost, but the son of perdition; that the scripture might be fulfilled. And now come I to thee; and these things I speak in the world, that they might have my joy fulfilled in themselves. I have given them thy word; and the world hath hated them, because they are not of the world, even as I am not of the world. I pray not that thou shouldest take them out of the world, but that thou shouldest keep them from the evil. They are not of the world, even as I am not of the world. Sanctify them through thy truth: thy word is truth. As thou hast sent me into the world, even so have I also sent them into the world. And for their sakes I sanctify myself, that they also might be sanctified through the truth. Neither pray I for these alone, but for them also which shall believe on me through their word; That they all may be one; as thou, accomplished it. That is, by conforming to the will of the Father even when it is painful, or terribly burdensome.[1362]

The whole meaning of this promise is captured in the qualification that it must be that "which is right." If you acquire an understanding of what "is right" then by asking for it, you submit to the Father's will. Even if you would shrink from it, beg that it may pass from you, and cower at the thing required of you. When you "ask of the Father in Christ's name" for whatsoever "is right" despite your desire for things to be otherwise, you are going to become one with Them. Then you will be like Them. At this time you will learn the great truth that the will of the Father IS indeed "whatsoever is right."

Joseph Smith explained it:

> "When the Lord has thoroughly proved him, and finds that the man is determined to serve Him at all hazards, then the man will find his calling and his election made sure, then it will be his privilege to receive the other Comforter, which the Lord hath promised the Saints."

Father, *art* in me, and I in thee, that they also may be one in us: that the world may believe that thou hast sent me. And the glory which thou gavest me I have given them; that they may be one, even as we are one: I in them, and thou in me, that they may be made perfect in one; and that the world may know that thou hast sent me, and hast loved them, as thou hast loved me. Father, I will that they also, whom thou hast given me, be with me where I am; that they may behold my glory, which thou hast given me: for thou lovedst me before the foundation of the world. O righteous Father, the world hath not known thee: but I have known thee, and these have known that thou hast sent me. And I have declared unto them thy name, and will declare *it*: that the love wherewith thou hast loved me may be in them, and I in them."

[1362] D&C 19:18–19 "Which suffering caused myself, even God, the greatest of all, to tremble because of pain, and to bleed at every pore, and to suffer both body and spirit—and would that I might not drink the bitter cup, and shrink— Nevertheless, glory be to the Father, and I partook and finished my preparations unto the children of men."

3 Nephi 11:11 "And behold, I am the light and the life of the world; and I have drunk out of that bitter cup which the Father hath given me, and have glorified the Father in taking upon me the sins of the world, in the which I have suffered the will of the Father in all things from the beginning."

The way heaven knows a man has arrived at that point is by the offered prayers. When they seek to do the will of the Father, and the requests are "what is right," then the heavens cannot withhold anything from that man. Indeed, the Lord will prompt the right questions by what the Lord says to that man, so that the knowledge of that man will reach into the heavens.[1363]

Therefore, you must not only "pray always unto the Father in Christ's name," but you must also grow in understanding, humility and meekness so you may "ask the Father" for that "which is right." This is a process. Christ is explaining it in His sermon.

[1363] Ether 3:9–20 "And the Lord said unto him: Because of thy faith thou hast seen that I shall take upon me flesh and blood; and never has man come before me with such exceeding faith as thou hast; for were it not so ye could not have seen my finger. Sawest thou more than this? And he answered: Nay; Lord, show thyself unto me. And the Lord said unto him: Believest thou the words which I shall speak? And he answered: Yea, Lord, I know that thou speakest the truth, for thou art a God of truth, and canst not lie. And when he had said these words, behold, the Lord showed himself unto him, and said: Because thou knowest these things ye are redeemed from the fall; therefore ye are brought back into my presence; therefore I show myself unto you. Behold, I am he who was prepared from the foundation of the world to redeem my people. Behold, I am Jesus Christ. I am the Father and the Son. In me shall all mankind have life, and that eternally, even they who shall believe on my name; and they shall become my sons and my daughters. And never have I showed myself unto man whom I have created, for never has man believed in me as thou hast. Seest thou that ye are created after mine own image? Yea, even all men were created in the beginning after mine own image. Behold, this body, which ye now behold, is the body of my spirit; and man have I created after the body of my spirit; and even as I appear unto thee to be in the spirit will I appear unto my people in the flesh. And now, as I, Moroni, said I could not make a full account of these things which are written, therefore it sufficeth me to say that Jesus showed himself unto this man in the spirit, even after the manner and in the likeness of the same body even as he showed himself unto the Nephites. And he ministered unto him even as he ministered unto the Nephites; and all this, that this man might know that he was God, because of the many great works which the Lord had showed unto him. And because of the knowledge of this man he could not be kept from beholding within the veil; and he saw the finger of Jesus, which, when he saw, he fell with fear; for he knew that it was the finger of the Lord; and he had faith no longer, for he knew, nothing doubting. Wherefore, having this perfect knowledge of God, he could not be kept from within the veil; therefore he saw Jesus; and he did minister unto him."

3 Nephi 18:24–25

"Therefore, hold up your light that it may shine unto the world. Behold I am the light which ye shall hold up—that which ye have seen me do. Behold ye see that I have prayed unto the Father, and ye all have witnessed. And ye see that I have commanded that none of you should go away, but rather have commanded that ye should come unto me, that ye might feel and see; even so shall ye do unto the world; and whosoever breaketh this commandment suffereth himself to be led into temptation."

Here is another clarification for the earlier sermon. When admonished to "let your light so shine before this people that they may see your good works and glorify your Father which is in heaven"[1364] what the Lord meant is that it is He who should be held up. He alone. Not you, or your good intentions, your conspicuous acts or philanthropy. Not you at all. Him.

The obligation to hold up a light is circumscribed by His direction that He "is the light which ye shall hold up." Nothing and no one else. He is the lifeline. Therefore, when you offer, preach, teach, exhort and expound, He must be at the center of this prophesying, or you are engaging in priestcraft.[1365]

The Lord has "prayed unto the Father" in their presence. Therefore, His example points to how prayer is to occur, and to whom it is addressed. They "all have witnessed" this, and know for themselves how it is to be done.

He has not told any of those who were present to go away. He has brought the same message to all. He gives them His example of

---

[1364] 3 Nephi 12:16 "Therefore let your light so shine before this people, that they may see your good works and glorify your Father who is in heaven."

[1365] 2 Nephi 26:29 "He commandeth that there shall be no priestcrafts; for, behold, priestcrafts are that men preach and set themselves up for a light unto the world, that they may get gain and praise of the world; but they seek not the welfare of Zion."

liberality: "Ye see that I have commanded that none of you should go away, but rather have commanded that ye should come unto me." No one is refused. All are welcomed. Whether those in the multitude thought someone was unworthy, or whether there were some with conflicts, it did not matter. All were invited. None were refused. They are all "commanded that they should come unto Him."

What is the reason we are commanded to come to Him? It is so "ye might feel and see." So that you might know Him. So that you can also be a witness of His physical evidence of suffering, crucifixion and death. The wounds He bears could not be received without death. His body testifies that He died. His body also testifies of His resurrection. Despite the wounds which memorialize His suffering and death, He lives! He stands before you in life! He has risen!

As you testify of Him, you must invite others to likewise come "that they might feel and see" Him. This is how witnesses of Him are commanded to "do unto the world." This is their ministry, their burden, their witness, and their command from Him. When they fail to testify, teach and proclaim, they "break this commandment and suffer themselves to be led into temptation." This is why the Lord required at my hands the book *The Second Comforter*. That is how He directs all those who are "commanded to come unto Him, that they might feel and see." It will not be in vague innuendo or veiled language. It may not be in a published book, and may well be in private. But they will all be required to invite others to likewise "come unto Him" that everyone "might feel and see" our Risen Lord.

He is accessible. He invites. More than that, He commands. All are commanded and "none of you should go away." We think it a great thing when someone testifies of Him. Yet He wants all to "come" so that everyone "might feel and see" Him.

If we have the same Gospel, we have the same commandments.

The Book of Mormon is, as I have testified in everything I have written, not merely a book of scripture. It is the preeminent volume of scripture for our day. All other volumes of scripture are not just inferior to it, but vastly so. It is the covenant we are condemned for neglecting. It is the reason I have found Him. For above all else, I have used the Book of Mormon to direct my thoughts, actions, teachings and understanding. Here in these verses we see again—He is inviting us, using the text of the Book of Mormon to find Him, individually, for ourselves.

This Book is the restoration of the Gospel. Unfortunately, most people have missed that. Nevertheless, it is true.

3 Nephi 18:26–27

> "And now it came to pass that when Jesus had spoken these words, he turned his eyes again upon the Disciples whom he had chosen, and said unto them: Behold verily, verily, I say unto you, I give unto you another commandment, and then I must go unto my Father that I may fulfil other commandments which he hath given me."

Christ first introduced Himself by reference to the Father in 3 Nephi 11.[1366] He reiterates the connection between Him and the Father again in this scripture. He does not only testify of the Father. He makes it clear that everything done is by the will or command of the Father.

If Christ is the example in all things (and He is). Then in this He serves once again to clarify things for us.

Christ did not come to do His own will, but submitted to the will of the Father. Just like Christ submitted to the will of the Father, we

---

[1366] 3 Nephi 11:11 "And behold, I am the light and the life of the world; and I have drunk out of that bitter cup which the Father hath given me, and have glorified the Father in taking upon me the sins of the world, in the which I have suffered the will of the Father in all things from the beginning."

too are invited to submit to the example and teachings of Christ. We ought to put away our own agendas. We ought to give credit to Him. We follow Him, we trust Him, we seek His will.

This is not just a passing point. It is the central point. Studying to know, and then working to do the will of Christ is our responsibility.

As Christ served the Father, we are to serve Him.

Christ becomes our Father when we are born again. He is the one who liberates us from sin, and will liberate us from death. Our resurrected bodies come to us as a gift from Him. Therefore, He is literally the Father of our bodies, because they return to us as a gift from Him.

As Christ has set an example in following the Father, He has thereby become our Father. We follow Him if we are hoping to go where He is.

Notice also the Lord has "other commandments" which He knows He is obligated to fulfill. The Lord has a continuing ministry under the direction of the Father. His ministry is not confined to the appearances we have in current scripture, but comprehends visits to those who have faith in Him throughout the world. He continues that ministry today, as promised in John 14:18.[1367]

Part of the "commandments which [the Father] hath given" to Christ include the ministry to save, redeem and teach those who abide the conditions to be taught. Today as in times past.

3 Nephi 18:28–29

"And now behold, this is the commandment which I give unto you, that ye shall not suffer any one knowingly to partake of my flesh and blood unworthily, when ye shall minister it; For whoso eateth and drinketh my flesh and blood unworthily eateth and drinketh damnation to his soul; therefore

---

[1367] John 14:18 "I will not leave you comfortless: I will come to you."

if ye know that a man is unworthy to eat and drink of my flesh and blood ye shall forbid him."

This commandment about partaking of the bread and wine is the one He needed them to understand. They should take precautions to prevent those who they know to be unworthy from partaking. The reason is merciful. When they partake of His flesh and blood unworthily, they establish a testimony before the Father of their unworthiness.

Remember the bread and wine become a testimony to the Father.[1368] The observance comes to the attention of the Father. It is a witness before Him. Therefore, when the flesh and blood are taken by those who are unworthy, the witness which comes to the Father is of their unworthiness. The Father cannot look upon sin with the least degree of allowance.[1369] When a person comes before the Father in a witness of their unworthiness, such a person "eateth and drinketh damnation to his soul." This person has asked the Father to take notice of their unworthiness.

It is the responsibility of those who minister these things to "forbid him" in such circumstances. They are their brother's keeper. Though it may be difficult for the person to be warned, it is merciful to do so. The sacrament is to be offered to the worthy, never offered to the unworthy. The worthy should "forbid" the unworthy from taking.

This is not an unkind teaching. It is not exclusionary or discriminatory. It is based on the doctrine Christ teaches, and the import of the act which witnesses to the Father. That witness occurs whenever

---

[1368] 3 Nephi 18:10 "And when the Disciples had done this, Jesus said unto them: Blessed are ye for this thing which ye have done, for this is fulfilling my commandments, and this doth witness unto the Father that ye are willing to do that which I have commanded you."

[1369] D&C 1:31 "For I the Lord cannot look upon sin with the least degree of allowance;"

the sacrament is properly administered, with appropriate power to bless, in a setting the Lord has authorized, by those who have repented and are properly baptized. Among such people the bread and wine should be given only to those who are worthy.

Now, the responsibility is on the ones administering the bread and wine. But the duty only extends to those who are "knowingly . . . unworthy." That is, the ones who administer are not obligated to police others. They are not required to interview and determine worthiness. They are only to take note of such things as come to their attention and require the conclusion that the recipient is "unworthy." Obvious misdeeds are important, private matters and individual failings are not consequential to the ones administering the rite.

"Therefore, if ye know that a man is unworthy to eat and drink [Christ's] flesh and blood ye shall forbid him." But only if you "know" such is the case. Then, you should "forbid" him from doing so. Not by force, but by refusing to minister the sacrament to him. This becomes impractical, however, when it is a tray passed down a row of people, who cannot be forbidden to partake. In that kind of ceremony, the individual cannot be forbidden except through general teaching and warning. Then the individual is free to choose for themselves whether to heed the caution or to ignore it. The question remains, however, if that relieves the persons ministering the sacrament from their obligation to "forbid him" if he is known to be unworthy.

These are interesting points. All the more so because the Lord has taken the time to teach us these principles. And for Him to teach them, and provide them to us as part of restoring the Gospel to our day, I presume that informs us these points are to be followed.

Whether we choose to follow His teachings or not becomes, for most of us, a matter of convention and acceptance of popular behavior. If these teachings are found in the Book of Mormon, but not observed by us in how we proceed each Sabbath, then we tend to feel comfortable that what we do is right and the text has been corrected by modern practice. It is an interesting conclusion to draw. One which, upon careful examination, does not always leave us with the same feeling of comfort.

Well, the Lord had this to say about us in 1832: "your minds in times past have been darkened because of unbelief, and because you have treated lightly the things you have received—Which vanity and unbelief have brought the whole church under condemnation. And this condemnation resteth upon the children of Zion, even all. And they shall remain under this condemnation until they repent and remember the new covenant, even the Book of Mormon and the former commandments which I have given them, not only to say, but to do according to that which I have written—".[1370]

I am glad others are responsible for enacting the Church Handbook of Instructions, and not me. I was glad to attend the leadership meeting and be again informed about this newly revised handbook for use today. It was just a few short years ago President Hinckley's administration reduced it by a third. Now it has been further reduced by 12%. That is, in my view, a very healthy trend. If this keeps up we may eventually wind up with nothing but the scriptures to guide us.

3 Nephi 18:31–32

"Nevertheless, ye shall not cast him out from among you, but ye shall minister unto him and shall pray for him unto the Father, in my name; and if it so be that he repenteth and is baptized in my name, then shall ye receive him, and shall minister unto him of my flesh and blood. But if he repent not he

---

[1370] D&C 84:54–57 "And your minds in times past have been darkened because of unbelief, and because you have treated lightly the things you have received— Which vanity and unbelief have brought the whole church under condemnation. And this condemnation resteth upon the children of Zion, even all. And they shall remain under this condemnation until they repent and remember the new covenant, even the Book of Mormon and the former commandments which I have given them, not only to say, but to do according to that which I have written—"

shall not be numbered among my people, that he may not destroy my people, for behold I know my sheep, and they are numbered. Nevertheless, ye shall not cast him out of your synagogues, or your places of worship, for unto such shall ye continue to minister; for ye know not but what they will return and repent, and come unto me with full purpose of heart, and I shall heal them; and ye shall be the means of bringing salvation unto them."

Even if you know someone has violated the commandment, has partaken unworthily after you have forbidden them to do so, *even then* you are "not to cast him out from among you." Instead the Lord puts on His disciples the burden of making intercession for him, praying "unto the Father, in [Christ's] name" for such a man. For the Lord reminds us that, "if it so be that he repenteth and is baptized in [His] name" then the man's repentance will take care of his failure.

Notice the burden on His disciples. What does it mean to "minister unto him" who has transgressed? What does it mean to "pray for him unto the Father" when you know he has eaten and drank "damnation unto his soul?" Why would the Lord have His followers first forbid, then, when the forbidding fails, to follow it up with patience and prayer for the offender? Is this another extension of the teachings the Lord gave in the sermon previously? Does this again testify to you of how serious the Lord is about how kind and patient we are with others?

How long are you to bear with the offender, hoping for his repentance? When do you decide that he is determined to "repent not?" What does it mean, after you have determined the man will not repent that "he shall not be numbered among my people?" What does that suggest about further fellowship with that man? Why would that be coupled with "that he may not destroy my people?" What would such an unrepentant man need to do before you could decide he was attempting to "destroy my people?" How would you decide that?

Now, even if you think you have a basis for deciding all this against the man, "nevertheless, ye shall not cast him out of your synagogues, or your places of worship." Did you see that? We are not to forbid even the man who is intent upon destroying the Lord's people from our places of worship. What selfless behavior is this? Enduring persecution! It is as if the Lord expects His followers to bless those who curse them, to do good to them who despitefully use them.

Why such patience? Because "ye know not but what they will return and repent, and come unto me with full purpose of heart, and I shall heal them; and ye shall be the means of bringing salvation unto them." If there is a chance for repentance, the Lord wants us to bear with, succor and uplift the non-repentant soul who drinks damnation. How often we would do otherwise. Christ instructs us to be more like Him in all we do. It is only by this patience, kindness, gentleness and meekness that He has been able to save my soul. Can a grateful person do anything less for another? Can we expect to forebear any less with the unrepentant than the Lord has with us?

How godlike the Master is in all His teachings. How much higher are His ways than are ours.

The Lord affirms that He knows His sheep. Not only knows them, but "they are numbered" to Him. He cares for each of them.

If we can add another to His fold by our own patient ministrations, then we ought to readily do so. If we do, then He will give us the credit for what we have done: "ye shall be the means of bringing salvation unto them." Did you catch that? He gives us the credit for the success! We merely follow what He instructs us to do, and if there is any benefit realized He gives us the credit for doing so. Our Savior is more than a good example. He is perfect in all His doings.

It is little wonder that in the end every knee will bow before Him. Gratitude will bring some to their knees. Shame will bring the rest. No one will expect to stand or sit in His presence. For in Him we find a soul of such greatness that kneeling alone can give vent to the feelings He inspires.

SUMMARY

The foregoing was taken from a blog on which I posted thoughts daily, once early in the morning and once mid-afternoon, over the better part of 2010. The purpose was to give those who came to the blog an opportunity to be reminded twice a day of teachings from the Book of Mormon. This is the primary text of scripture for our day. It, above all other volumes of scripture, was intended to become the basis for the last day covenant between God and man. It has been neglected, and as a result we have fallen under condemnation. The only way to remove that condemnation is to repent, and remember this book, not merely to say but to do what it teaches. A revelation given in 1832 told the Latter-day Saints the following: "And your minds in times past have been darkened because of unbelief, and because you have treated lightly the things you have received—Which vanity and unbelief have brought the whole church under condemnation. And this condemnation resteth upon the children of Zion, even all. And they shall remain under this condemnation until they repent and remember the new covenant, even the Book of Mormon and the former commandments, which I have given them, not only to say, but to do according to that which I have written." (D&C 84:54–57.)

I have written previous books, and now added the blog which is preserved in this book, intending to do what little I am able to remove the condemnation under which we have labored since 1832. I have tried to provide a twice-daily reminder to keep the Book of Mormon on top of our thoughts. This book is not merely a collection of expressed ideas, but also has the unexpressed idea that the approach given here may give you a system of thought through which you can approach the Book of Mormon in your individual study.

My thoughts are far less important that learning to meditate upon the Book of Mormon yourself. It is a deep well, from which we have failed as yet to draw except in the most shallow of takes. We need to do more. We need fewer superficial expositions, fewer scholarly attempts to show its antiquity, and far more done to understand its doctrine. More importantly, we need to do more to live its teachings. It was designed to be a covenant. The revelation condemning us speaks of it as the "new covenant, even the Book of Mormon." A covenant is more than merely a collection of stories about an ancient people. It is intended to animate how we act. It is intended to control how we approach God.

God is approachable. He is accessible. It was always intended for man to live in a covenant relationship with Him. He was supposed to be a familiar personage to mankind. When I wrote my first book, *The Second Comforter: Conversing With the Lord Through the Veil*, it was the Book of Mormon which became the primary source for scriptural teachings about returning to God's presence. That book demonstrates the Book of Mormon contains the most holy, most lofty, most edifying doctrines of the restored Gospel of Jesus Christ. It was intended to be a covenant. Until we recognize it as that, we will remain under condemnation.

I have avoided giving details of my own return to God's presence. I have instead taught the process by which you may do so. My own experiences are not important, other than to me. I cannot save you, nor can my experiences benefit you. You must have your own. You also must return to His presence. He was always intended to be your Teacher. Any other teacher can only benefit you by pointing to Him.

In account after account, the Book of Mormon is filled with Second Comforter experiences. It is the great manual on the return to God. Witness after witness testifies to God's accessibility. I add my voice to that chorus. I also believe to my core the only reason I have been able to find Him is because I took the Book of Mormon seriously; not only to say but to do what it teaches.

Come remove your own condemnation. Take this volume of scripture as a guide. Not merely as a series of stories with some virtue to teach, but as a manual for returning to God's presence. Follow its teachings and you will find it is the most correct book. You will discover that you are able to draw closer to God by abiding its precepts than you can from any other book. It is the primary scripture for our day.

Made in the USA
San Bernardino, CA
11 December 2016